Cultural Materialism

CULTURAL ⤳ POLITICS

A series from the Social Text Collective

Aimed at a broad interdisciplinary audience, these volumes seek to intervene in debates about the political direction of current theory and practice by combining contemporary analysis with a more traditional sense of historical and socioeconomic evaluation.

Cultural Materialism

On Raymond Williams

Edited by

Christopher

Prendergast

for the Social Text Collective

**Cultural
Politics,
Volume 9**

University of Minnesota Press
Minneapolis
London

The following essays first appeared in *Social Text* 10, no. 30 (1992) and are reprinted by permission: Cornel West, "In Memoriam: The Legacy of Raymond Williams"; Christopher Prendergast, "Introduction: Groundings and Emergings"; David Simpson, "Raymond Williams: Feeling for Structures, Voicing 'History'"; Morag Shiach, "A Gendered History of Cultural Categories"; Michael Moriarty, "'The Longest Cultural Journey': Raymond Williams and French Theory"; David Lloyd and Paul Thomas, "*Culture and Society* or 'Culture and the State'"; and Catherine Gallagher, "Raymond Williams and Cultural Studies."

Grateful acknowledgment is made for permission to reprint the following: Stephen Heath and Gillian Skirrow, "Interview with Raymond Williams," first published *in Studies in Entertainment: Critical Approaches to Mass Culture*, ed. Tania Modleski (Bloomington: Indiana University Press, 1986), copyright Stephen Heath, by permission; Gauri Viswanathan, "Raymond Williams and British Colonialism," first published *in Yale Journal of Criticism*, 4, no. 2 (1991): 47-66, by permission.

Published by the University of Minnesota Press
111 Third Avenue South, Suite 290, Minneapolis, MN 55401-2520
Printed in the United States of America on acid-free paper

Library of Congress Cataloging-in-Publication Data

Cultural materialism : on Raymond Williams / edited by Christopher
Prendergast.
     p. cm. — (Cultural politics ; v. 9)
     Includes index.
     ISBN 0-8166-2280-9 — ISBN 0-8166-2281-7 (alk. pbk.)
     1. Williams, Raymond—Political and social views. 2. Social evolution.
3. Culture. I. Prendergast, Christopher. II. Series: Cultural politics
(Minneapolis, Minn.) ; v. 9.
GN360.C85 1995
306—dc20   94-36190

In memory
of
Jim Prendergast

Contents

In Memoriam
The Legacy of Raymond Williams
Cornel West

Raymond Williams was the last of the great European male revolutionary socialist intellectuals born before the end of the age of Europe (1492-1945). I use this long string of adjectives not to pigeonhole the complex and multiple identities of Williams, but rather to examine and evaluate his grand achievements and incomplete efforts in light of the social crises and political travails of his time. And to keep this legacy alive is, in part, to keep in view how he made and remade himself—cast and recast his ways of life and ways of struggle—under circumstances (usually adverse circumstances) not of his choosing.

In my brief comments, I shall suggest that Williams's major contribution to our present-day challenges is not simply that he taught us how to think historically about cultural practices or how to approach political matters with a subtle cultural materialist orientation in a manner that stands head and shoulders above any of his generation. Rather, Williams speaks to us today primarily because he best exemplifies what it means for a contemporary intellectual leftist to carve out and sustain, with quiet strength and relentless reflection, a sense of prophetic vocation in a period of pervasive demoralization and marginalization of progressive thinkers and activists. His career can be seen as a dynamic series of critical self-inventories in which he attempts to come to terms with the traditions and communities that permit him to exercise his agency and lay bare the structural and personal constraints that limit the growth of those traditions and communities.

These critical self-inventories take the form of powerful cultural histories and fictions and often persuasive cultural critiques of the European past and present, in order to create new possibilities for left thinkers and activities. In this sense, Williams's deep historical sensibilities were grounded in a *prospective* outlook that never loses sight of human struggle against transient yet formidable limits. Whatever the intellectual fashion of the day—from F. R. Leavis to Louis Althusser, Jacques Lacan to Michel Foucault—Williams remained wedded to subtle humanist notions of struggle and hope found in traditions and communities. In fact, one of his distinctive contributions to Marxist theory was to revise the understanding of class conflict—inseparable from but not identical with class struggle—by highlighting how, in relatively cold moments in human societies, class conflict is mediated through social, cultural, or educational changes that ensure the muting of class struggle. Like Gramsci, Williams injects notions of contestation and incorporation into the understanding of class conflict while reserving class struggle for that hot moment in societies in which structural change becomes a conscious and overt engagement of forces. Again his aim is to tease out the concrete and credible lines of action for progressive thinkers and activists.

Williams's creative attempts to make and remake himself by means of critical self-inventories occurred on three major terrains. On the *ideological* terrain he had to navigate between the deformation of communism in the name of Stalinism and the degeneration of socialism in the name of Fabianism. The former was a vicious autocratic statism that repressed civil society and regimented its citizens—an undeniable affront to Williams's socialist democratic values; the latter—a naive gradualism that assumed that the enemy was a mere party rather than a "hostile and organized social formation"— was an unacceptable conclusion given Williams's historical materialist analysis.

On the *academic* terrain, Williams sought to counter conservative traditions of thinking about culture represented by T. S. Eliot and F. R. Leavis by refining crude left reflections about the relation of culture and democracy, art and socialism. And on the *political* terrain, Williams sought to reconceive the notion of revolution such that cultural practices were neither overlooked nor viewed in a simplistic manner. The point was not only that culture—including popular culture—was to be viewed as a crucial site of struggle, but also that the very ways in which culture was understood in capitalist societies had to be demystified and transformed. In reading Williams's masterpieces, *Culture and Society* (1958), *The Long Revolution* (1961), *The Country and the City* (1973), and *Marxism and Literature* (1977), we get a sense of the evolution of his own democratic socialism, cultural materialism, and revolutionary activism.

Yet, in all honesty, what also attracted me to Williams's work was his refusal to sidestep the *existential* issues of what it means to be a left intellectual and activist—issues like death, despair, disillusionment, and disempowerment in the face of defeats and setbacks. He understood on a deep level that revolutionary activity was as much a matter of feelings as facts, of imagination as organization, of agency as analysis. Therefore he highlighted what most left thinkers tend to ignore: *the need for vision and the necessity of linking vision to visceral forms of human connectedness.* His preoccupation with vital traditions and vibrant communities, sustaining neighborhoods and supportive networks, reflected his sensitivity to how ordinary people in their everyday lives are empowered and equipped to deal with defeats and setbacks. In his six novels as well as his often overlooked gem *Modern Tragedy* (1966), Williams explores the highly mediated links between human struggle, bonding, and place. This exploration is neither an extraneous affair of nostalgic yearning for the Welsh *Gemeinschaft* of his youth nor an escapist inclination to displace the political for the personal. Rather, he is grappling with one of the central problematics of our moment: how to articulate visions, analyses, and forms of praxis that anchor socialist politics to the contingent constructions of identities of degraded and downtrodden peoples. These new identities—often associated with the "new" social movements of women, people of color, formerly colonized persons, gays, lesbians, and Greens—emerge from various cultural politics of difference that put a premium on bonding and place, common experiences in time and similar situations in space. In the late sixties, Williams began to struggle visibly with his Welsh European identity—as is manifested in his novel *The Fight for Manhood* (1979). Yet it is precisely at this point that Williams's grand example falls short; that is, where he appears more a creature of his time than a creator who links us to the coming epoch. Edward Said has made this point in terms of Williams's "relative neglect of the affiliation between imperialism and English culture" (*Nation*, March 5, 1988). I would add that though Williams provides indispensable analytical tools and historical sensibilities for reflections on empire, race, color, gender, and sexual orientation, the relative silences in his work on these issues bear the stamp of his own intellectual and existential formation, and his later attempts to accent a Welsh nationalist identity within his socialist project bear this out.

Those of us born and shaped after the end of the age of Europe must begin with the legacies of the European empire—legacies of deeply inscribed white supremacist and male capitalist metropoles—as well as with the declining U.S. and Soviet empires. And as expanding cultures of consumption slowly erode traditions, communities, neighborhoods, and networks, new cultural configurations must be created if any substantive sources of struggle and hope for fundamental societal change can be preserved and sustained. In this regard, the last problematic Williams gallantly yet inadequately confronted becomes our major challenge. And if we plan to meet it, we must do so by, in part, standing on his shoulders, and hope we meet it as well as he did others.

Acknowledgments

The present volume comes out of what was initially a special issue of the journal *Social Text* devoted to the work of Raymond Williams, which some of my colleagues on the journal's collective encouraged me to put together. Without that encouragement, the present volume would not exist, at least not with me as its editor. I am grateful to them for opening a window of opportunity that enabled me to return to a body of work I had not been engaged with in quite the same way before. I should also like to thank the students in my comparative literature seminar at the Graduate School of the City University of New York, from whose active commitment to reading and discussing Williams's writings I benefited greatly. More personal thanks go to Bruce Robbins, who gave me every support and encouragement right from the beginning of the project; to John Brenkman and Michael Moriarty, who commented usefully on a draft of my introduction; and to Biodun Iginla of the University of Minnesota Press, who was unfailingly helpful in seeing the project through to publication.

Finally, for reasons too numerous to mention, I dedicate this book to the memory of my father.

Introduction:
Groundings and Emergings
Christopher Prendergast

Raymond Williams's death, in January 1988, has naturally occasioned many retrospective assessments, but, for a combination of brevity, sweep, and finality, perhaps none quite matches the opening remark of the memorial address delivered by Cornel West at the National Film Institute in 1988: "Raymond Williams was the last of the great European male revolutionary socialist intellectuals born before the end of the age of Europe (1492-1945)." This remarkable sentence—subsequently elaborated by West in a deeply sympathetic engagement with the spirit of Williams's work—arguably veers between the bold and the rash. At one end of the spectrum, it stands as a magnificent tribute (implicitly ranking Williams with, amomg others, Gramsci, unquestionably for Williams the most important of twentieth-century left theoretical and strategic thinkers), while, at the other end, in the emphasis on endings and closures, it implies a perspective of completion that many might wish to contest. But, either way, as a form of remembering, it has the great merit of giving both the life and the death over to *history*, to the terms of historical formation as a horizon of both possibilities and limits, or—to put the point according to one of Williams's most enduring contributions to historical analysis—as a nexus of the residual, the dominant, and the emergent. At the very least, this takes the business of memorializing in the direction Williams himself undoubtedly would have wanted, and certainly beyond the tedious Oedipal scenarios of succession and confession to which we have been treated elsewhere.

Nevertheless, if in certain respects it is appropriate to start here,

1

with West's first sentence, the idiom of memorial is not the primary concern of this volume. Paying homage in a statement that, however politically and humanly generous it is, includes the words *end* and *last* comes close to an act of burial (though the rest of West's address shows just how far he actually is from burying Williams). It is not a question of remembering in order to forget, of mourning—in the psychoanalytical sense evoked here by John Higgins in connection with the paltry burial rites performed by the journal *New Formations*—in the name of a certain "postmodernism" whereby Williams again is seen as belonging to a previous age: not, as in the grand sweep of West's piece, to the "age of Europe," but more parochially to (the phrase itself indicates the preposterousness of the view) the pre-"poststructuralist" age, in relation to which Williams is posed as a thinker "reluctant to question the integrity of identity." This is of course nonsense, at many levels and from many points of view, not only because, as Higgins argues, "poststructuralist" deconstruction of the "integrated" subject not only leaves entirely unaddressed pressing and difficult questions of personal identity (arguably much of the ambiguity of the guru Lacan is that, on these latter questions, his views can plausibly be seen as at once disconcertingly radical and entirely useless). Even on its own terms and assumptions, it traduces one of the major tendencies of Williams's own work. Indeed, even West, who, for strong political reasons, wishes to place Williams in the closure of a historical epoch, also affirms that keeping the legacy alive is, within the limits of its historical moment and formation, very precisely "to keep in view how he made and remade himself, cast and recast his ways of life and ways of struggle."

The principal intention behind the essays gathered here is thus quite the opposite of a burial: it is to keep alive a body of work (while in some instances querying what Williams himself meant by the "living" and the "lived") by reading out from it, by at once extending and problematizing it. With respect to the latter, for example, West's inclusion of the adjective *male* is a case in point, not only definitionally but also provocatively correct: on questions of gender and feminism Williams made right-sounding noises (as in the concluding moments of the interview with Stephen Heath and Gillian Skirrow), but if the noises were honorably well-meant, they were also for the most part so generalized as to be virtually useless. While it would be absurd to turn against him in the relevantly predictable way of one of his favorite expressions ("real men," as against dead abstraction), it is nevertheless true that the expression did not stretch often enough to become "real men and women." As Morag Shiach observes, in another opening sentence that truly sets the cat among the pigeons, "Feminists can find much of use to them in the work of Raymond Williams; they cannot, however, find many women."

In any case, whether as exploration, redirection, or critique (the mix varies according to the interests and commitments of the contributors), the principal focus I have sought to maintain through the proliferation of views and arguments is on the space of the "emergent" in Williams's work and thus on the work as instantiation of one of its own major categories. How we "place" the work is essentially the question of where we go with it from here, in the knowledge that, as with all genuinely emergent forms, the routes are not traced out in advance. David Simpson speaks of the quietly authoritative "voice" we so often hear in Williams's writings (indeed making of the partial assimilation of writing into speech the focus of a theoretical inquiry into the very sources and grounds of Williams's thought). But alongside the directness and confidence of address, we should also remember the many hesitancies and uncertainties as well as the constant reaching for "complexity"; they are crucially connected to any account of the work in terms of the energies of the emergent. Robert Miklitsch suggests that "complexity" is not just a feature of Williams's thought, but that the latter is actually constituted by the category of complexity as such and that it is at its weakest when it reduces to the simple. Certainly, the endlessly backtracking and self-qualifying style (what Robin Blackburn has called his "characteristic mode of piling qualification upon complexity") tells of a strategy not merely of ordinary intellectual scrupulousness but also of active unsettlement of terms and positions (from a man who had many existential and political preferences for settled forms of life over the huge disruptions of modernity). We need only look again at the opening paragraph of *Marxism and Literature* and follow the self-destabilizing movements of its vocabulary: the typical movement away from "concept" back to "problem," the acceptance of the "awkwardness," the "gaucherie" of "radical doubt," the openness to "the moment of crisis," "the jolt in experience" and the corresponding refusal of "ready insertions," notably into the very concept to which most of a working life had already been devoted. This opening paragraph both reapproaches and reproblematizes this concept—namely, the concept of "culture."

For "culture," its meanings, formations, and politics, is of course what the work is famously about, from the early soundings in *Culture and Society* through to the later development of the notion of cultural materialism and the accompanying run of definitions: culture as the creation of "meanings and values," as a "whole way of life," and, in the formulations of cultural materialism, as "constitutive human process" inseparable from the totality of "social material activity." The essays in this volume work at the contours, borders, and fault lines of the terrain designated by these well-known definitions, indeed now so well known that they can trip all too easily off the tongue as the ready-made formulas by which "Raymond Williams" circulates in contemporary intellectual life. From its own particular angle of interest, each of the essays brings a question or confronts an issue across the wide range of agendas and references appropriate to a discussion of Williams's work today. Here, in order of appearance of the essays, is a brief summary of their contents (it should, I hope, be clear that their arrangement in three sections—"theory," "history, politics, literature," and "cultural studies"—is a mere convenience that should not be allowed to blur the manifold relations of overlap between the three in both Williams's writings and the essays themselves).

David Simpson tracks across nearly the entire corpus one of its anchoring concepts—the notorious "structure of feeling"—and more generally (in an emphasis I shall want to pick up on myself shortly) the whole question of grounds and foundations in Williams's thought. Morag Shiach considers the deeply complex and uncertain status of the categories of cultural materialism for feminist critique as categories at once powerfully available for feminist appropriation yet appropriable only against the silences, absences, or, more damagingly, the immersion of the writings (including the novels) in male narratives of socialist solidarity and bonding. Robert Miklitsch situates the encounter with Marxism (and a number of related matters) in a particular history of debate about Williams's own work. Also from within the terms of Williams's encounters with Marxism, Michael Moriarty traces potential alignments with "French theory"—

often against the grain of Williams's own professed hostility to it—in the specific areas of structural linguistics and semiology. John Higgins similarly broaches Williams's thinking about language, and from there rehearses at length what is briefly touched on also by Moriarty: the curious saga of salutary skepticism, missed opportunity, and possible affinity with regard to psychoanalysis, particularly—in that last connection—psychoanalytical theories of the construction of the subject, though any proposed affinity here comes up rapidly against a limit defined by resistance to the Lacanian view of the constitutively divided nature of desiring subjectivity. As we shall see, "division" is Williams's bête noire, associated almost exclusively with the social division of labor under capitalism. This has important consequences for the theory of "culture" as a theory that takes little account of the Lévi-Straussian view of culture as separation from nature, a theory that not only is important for the psychoanalytical notion of culture as the "symbolic order," but also, from the emphasis on severance from the natural order, has corresponding implications for the whole question of "history" (to leave nature for culture is to enter into consciousness of irreversible linear time).

The question of history indeed recurs in a number of the essays, often in relation to questions of literature and politics. It is very much part of Simpson's engagement with the theoretical issues of Williams's work and—with a strong empirical focus on actual historical material as well—of the contributions of Kenneth Surin, Peter de Bolla, Gauri Viswanathan, Cora Kaplan, John Brenkman, and David Lloyd and Paul Thomas. A recurring preoccupation is the applications and implications of Williams's notion of the "structure of feeling." Kenneth Surin picks it up in connection with Williams's important, though often neglected, work on tragedy, notably of course in the book *Modern Tragedy*, exploring both the possibilities and the problems of Williams's attempt to give new content and relevance to the category of the "tragic" in terms of the alignment of the structure of feeling with twentieth-century political experience, centrally the experience of revolution. Peter de Bolla examines the notion of structure of feeling in connection with the arguments and methods of *The Country and the City* around the topoi of landscape and the country house in eighteenth-century England, suggesting that while Williams remains exemplary for thinking the relation between

aesthetic artifact and historical formation, there are still many epistemological and methodological problems bound up with the use of
structure of feeling as a means of getting from representations to the
real ("lived experience"). *The Country and the City* is also the main
point of departure for Gauri Viswanathan's examination of the historical articulations of William's theory of culture around questions
of empire and colonialism. Viswanathan identifies a limiting condition here, not in terms of the occasionally touted but palpably false
claim that Williams was insensitive to these questions (the concluding chapters of *The Country and the City* give the lie to this claim),
but by way of the more searching, and for that reason necessarily
controversial, argument that William's account of culture in terms of
the crosssing of class formation and national formation entailed a
methodological blockage such that the discussion was ill-equipped
to engage fully with the dimension of empire.

The dispatch to empire was of course one of the forms of what
Williams in *The Long Revolution* called the "magic" resolutions
adopted by some of the English novels of the 1840s, and it is with
the English novel of the 1840s, specifically Charlotte Brontë's *Jane
Eyre*, that Cora Kaplan revisits the relevant arguments of both *The
Long Revolution* and *The English Novel from Dickens to Lawrence*.
She too, from a perspective combining feminist concerns, psychoanalytical theory, and social history, takes up the concept of the structure of feeling at once to emphasize its value as a way of grasping
the mutual imbrication of the social and the personal in fictional
structures while also arguing that, within the proffered terms of
Williams's account of this relation in the work of Charlotte Brontë,
one can go only so far with it because the gendered origins and
character of the "feeling," of the relation between the personal voice
and the lived history of marginalization and solitude, are inadequately articulated. The example of the novel, though this time by
way of Williams's own fictional practice in *Border Country*, also
serves to frame John Brenkman's essay, specifically posing the historical and personal memory of the 1926 General Strike that plays
such a crucial role in that novel as itself the historical ground for un-
raveling the tangled story of Williams's evolving negotiation of the
relations between Marxism, socialism, and democracy. The long
piece by David Lloyd and Paul Thomas that closes this section is also
concerned with Williams's work on class, politics, and culture in

nineteenth-century England; as an inquiry into the ideas and demands articulated by the radical press, Chartism, and working-class discourse in the 1830s and 1840s, it undertakes the kind of detailed historical research required by some of the arguments of *Culture and Society* but, precisely in its discovered detail, demands a rethinking of those same arguments, notably around the problematic place in Williams's cultural theory of the powerfully metonymic figure of Matthew Arnold.

Matthew Arnold, of course, is also an important reference point for any debate about the value of Williams's ideas for that splendidly emergent but hotly controversial formation, cultural studies, the principal theme of Part III. In their own divergences of view and contributions to that debate, Catherine Gallagher and Stanley Aronowitz reflect what Stuart Hall has said of cultural studies: that it is "not a thing" or any "one thing" (Gallagher muses that it may not be anything determinate at all). This indeterminacy is variously and polemically focused by Gallagher and Aronowitz (and, to some extent, by Miklitsch) around four principal aspects of the contemporary situation of cultural studies: as uncertain disciplinary object in the academy; as theoretical problem turning on the difficult relation between materiality and abstraction bound up with any definition of culture as "signifying practices"; as historical development in relation to a wider social and institutional crisis; and as engaging a politics of everyday life outside the essential but often self-sealing enterprise of academic definition and inquiry. It will be clear from these multiple considerations that, however massively Williams's presence inflects the relevant debates, the debates have a great deal further to run.

Finally, and relatedly, there is the move from cultural theory into the analysis of popular culture and so-called (for Williams, often miscalled) mass culture. Peter Hitchcock reviews William's work on television in terms of an account of the making of news programs (with particular reference to the coverage of China at the time of Tiananmen Square). This in turn is accompanied by an interview with Williams, on the subject of television and mass media generally, conducted by Stephen Heath and Gillian Skirrow some years ago. There are several reasons for reprinting it here. One is that it confirms the view of Williams's work described by Skirrow in the interview as "a model of how intellectuals can work on popular culture and mass culture without being above it or outside it, or de-

featist or pessimistic about it" (while at the same time remaining resolutely opposed to easy populist reductions laying claim to progres-
sivist credentials; it is crucial to Williams's view that certain *forms* of
mass culture are, precisely by virtue of their formal properties, along
with the economic and social conditions of their production, absolutely irredeemable at the level of their content). Another reason
for including the interview is that it is not simply a question-and-
answer session, but a genuine exchange, an inter-view as a play of
different views from different substantive positions. Finally, it is included because the interview form is the closest we can get to hearing the famous "voice" (though "hearing" the voice via the tape re-
corder and transcription to written and printed form rejoins one of
the major theoretical issues raised by Simpson about the interpretation of Williams's work as a whole: namely, the speech/writing distinction as a framework for reexamining what in Williams's own
writings is the relatively underexamined category of the "living" and
the "lived").

It will be clear, from this schematic summary alone, that the range of
interlacing topics and problems the essays address is formidable.
This in turn raises the question of how the essays might be suitably
framed in a set of introductory remarks. I am assuming that it is not
necessary to describe the main outlines of Williams's work. Although to go forward with the work one must of course go back
over the ground it covers, we already have at our disposal many exegetical maps with which to chart the terrain, and there seems little
point in adding to the list yet another synopsis. In any case, though
none of the pieces here is purely exegetical, some furnish, as part of
the arguments they develop, much of the context and history that
are relevant to situating and understanding Williams's work in its
wider background. Particular note should be taken here of the essays by Simpson and Miklitsch. For readers relatively unfamiliar
with Williams's writings, Simpson's contribution could serve as,
among other things, an introduction to some of its main lines and
developments through time, while Miklitsch provides some sense of
the detailed exchanges and reviews that have taken place, principally though not exclusively in Britain, around Williams's ideas,
both during his lifetime and since his death.

As a framework for the essays, therefore, it would perhaps be more useful in these introductory observations to refocus both the work and the commentary on it less as a summary of contents than as a statement of a number of problematics. I shall concentrate on two general areas of both possibility and difficulty around the question of "culture." First, we need to remind ourselves that Williams's theoretical reflection on culture, however flexible and self-revising, is also tied to a set of anchoring positions. One point of departure would then be to consider some of its founding moves and assumptions, thus indeed going back over the ground but in order to reach down into its groundings. Second, I shall consider ways in which the theoretical work on the idea of culture both entails and is developed as a cultural politics, with particular reference to the troubled question of Williams's relation to "modernity" (and, beyond that, the spaces of the so-called postmodern).

A concern with grounds and foundations is an important structural feature of Williams's work as a whole (*ground*, interestingly, is also a recurring term in the opening pages of Arnold's *Culture and Anarchy*). In one of the interviews published in the collection *Politics and Letters*, for example, Williams speaks of "an absolutely founding presumption of materialism." The context is a relatively uninteresting, even unnecessary, argument about ontology versus epistemology in which, characterizing the moment of structuralism and semiology as a time of "rabid idealism," Williams claims that "the natural world exists whether anyone signifies it or not." The substantive argument is not for the moment the issue (its target—as Michael Moriarty's essay shows—is in fact a straw man, confirming that, in its major negative forms, the relation with "structuralism" constituted one of the few intellectual disaster areas of Williams's work). My present point, however, bears less on substance and more on rhetoric, the extent to which Williams's claim illustrates the presence in his writings of what Simpson rightly calls a "foundational rhetoric." It is often a strong rhetoric, as instanced here by the adverb *absolutely* (we will find the words *absolutely* and *absolute* in a similar connection elsewhere). In our antifoundationalist times, this sort of thing strikes an oddly disconcerting note. We must, however, attend to it; it will take us to many of the questions currently relevant to the interpretation and reception of Williams's work, above all in connection with the category of "culture."

The characterization of culture in Williams's writings recurringly attracts three adjectives from his own lexicon of favored keywords, all of which work together in the theoretical enterprise of generalizing the notion of production out from its classical restriction to economy into the manifold domains of social life: *primary, active,* and *whole.* To these three adjectives correspond three negative emphases (on what culture is not), which together generate the terms of Williams's pathbreaking critique of entrenched ways of thinking about culture. First, culture is not secondary, a delayed effect of a prior determining instance, but is itself prior or primary. Second, it is not passive, a mere superstructural reflection, but is itself an active force in the social construction of reality (or, more accurately, it is to be grasped as at once producing and produced within the complex and mobile totality of social process). Third, and above all, it is not separated from the rest of social life (as in the standard specialization of culture as the arts), but has to be seen in terms of a principle of wholeness. Much of Williams's work must be understood as an abiding, in some circumstances even obstinate, resistance to the categories of separation and specialization, which (like system and abstraction)[1] are commonly posed as the categories of an instrumental capitalist rationality, consecrating an entire new order of the division of labor and hence of social relations.

The general argument spread out across these diverse sources is shaped more or less consistently from the three major negative emphases in the account of culture I have mentioned. Of the three, it is especially the third that calls for close inspection. The first two of course have their own problems, in particular the theoretical implications of the generalized extension of the category of production for the question of causality (which, as Williams's interlocutors in the *Politics and Letters* interviews stressed, would seem to require some conceptually differentiated hierarchy of relations or "levels" of determination). Second, there are the related implications and political consequences for the notion of class, since if—to take the famous example from "Base and Superstructure in Marxist Cultural Theory"—the notion of production applies equally to the maker of the piano and the player of the piano, the logic of such a view, taken to an extreme, could seriously compromise the theory of the class "basis" of social formation to which Williams elsewhere in his work is strongly committed. Whatever these difficulties, it is nevertheless unlikely that one would wish nowadays to quarrel with a conception of culture that emphasizes its significance as both primary and active, at least where such an emphasis is designed essentially to highlight the role of cultural production in the general process of the social construction of reality.

The major problems, however, arise with the various meanings that attach to the third founding term, *whole*. We need to remember here that this is more than an emphasis; it is also an unbending insistence—against a reified, systems-analysis language of separable "levels" or a postmodern vocabulary of plural fragmentation—on wholeness or connectedness (*connection* is another highly valorized keyword; both the fiction and the nonfiction could be interestingly charted in terms of the vicissitudes of this one word). Culture accordingly is understood within the notions of "indissoluble totality," "whole indissoluble practice," "the wholeness of history," and so on.[2] The phrasing resonates in multiple directions, back to and across many sources: the tradition of English cultural critique described in *Culture and Society*, the varying forms of Marxist theory, including the form, associated in particular with Althusser, that we call structuralist Marxism, and from there, principally in terms of the question of language, to the ideas of Saussure and Vološinov. Thus, despite the rapprochement with semiotics in the later definition of culture as "signifying practices" and the related association of cultural materialism with "historical semiotics," semiotics and structuralism (at least of the kind that come out of Saussure) fail the test of wholeness; in the language of system, function, and so forth that is used to talk about language, they divide speaker from medium ("the connected aspects of a single process" are "divided and dissociated") and so, like all formalisms, fall into the trap of "objectivism" and end by offering a "reified account" of human communication (these are the terms of the chapter on language in *Marxism and Literature*). Similarly, Marxism, in its classical association with base-superstructure models of explanation, not only gets culture wrong (by failing to see it as primary, active, and so on). Worse, by violating the principle of wholeness, by separating and specializing culture as a category apart from the "base" of economic activity—in turn seen as "the most important sphere of 'production'"—it is also "at some important points a prisoner of the social order which it is offering to analyze" (*Towards 2000*), paradoxically complicit in the techno-rationality of modern capitalist modes of human socialization that propose as normal and "basic"—foundational—the model of performance-oriented, nature-mastering *homo economicus*.

My concern here is not with the detail of these arguments (though it is very much the concern of some of the essays) but with their general form, in particular the way they rest on some appeal to a "ground." The relevant model or figure is not, however, spatial (as in the hierarchical figure of "a fixed and definite spatial relationship" that Williams says governs the base-superstructure model). The location of the ground is less spatial than temporal, a site in a story of *beginnings*, of how it is at the start, prior to the distorting effects of specialization and separation. Here, for example—to stay with *Marxism and Literature*—is the idiom of grounds and foundations in particularly active guise. The general thrust of his approach, Williams tells us, is to reject "the two-stage model . . . in which there is *first* material social life and *then*, at some temporal or spatial distance, consciousness and 'its' products" (Williams's emphasis); again, "consciousness is seen *from the beginning* as part of the human material social process" (emphasis added); language "is involved *from the beginning* in all other human social and material activity" (emphasis added). Finally, consider this sentence from "Base and Superstructure in Marxist Cultural Theory":

> If we have the broad sense of productive forces, we look at the whole question of the base differently, and we are then less tempted to dismiss as superstructural, and in that sense as merely secondary, certain vital productive social forces, which are in the broad sense, *from the beginning*, basic. (emphasis added)

The italicized terms tell the story—and it *is* a story, the foundational gesture as a whole fable of beginnings, origins, and priorities. More accurately, there are two stories, complementary but not fully compatible. The first has it that there is no single beginning (as in the rejection of a certain Marxist insistence on labor, or a particular concept of labor, as "the single effective origin"). Origins rather are multiple, and in that multiplicity phenomena and practices are coextensive. This, however, is not the originary multiplicity of deconstruction, the paradoxically antiontological ontology of being-as-*différance*, dispersed, heterogeneous, and nonidentical from the word go; in Williams's account, it is not that at the beginning things are aboriginally divided, but that they are simultaneously coextensive and interacting. The argument is not just that culture is there at the beginning (as itself "primary") but also that at the beginning, before separation and specialization, culture is whole or part of a whole process, once again "connected"; instead of the notion of a "single effective origin," writes Williams, "the real emphasis should be on connected practice."

On the other hand, cutting across this story of the originally multiple and coextensive there is another story that speaks more of priorities, indeed even of "absolute" priorities. In the *Politics and Letters* interviews Williams repeats both the view of the interconnected wholeness of social process and the buttressing adverb *absolutely*: "I am absolutely unwilling to concede to any predetermined class of objects an unworked priority." Yet when it is a question of contrasting the allegedly reified formalist notion of system with the more active notion of process, Williams can also write unhesitatingly that "here [in the idea of 'social process'], as a matter of *absolute priority*, men relate and continue to relate *before* any system which is their product can as a matter of practical rather than abstract consciousness be grasped or exercise its determination" (emphasis added). The quarrel with the language of system and abstraction thus yields another fable of origins, in which there is an ultimate grounding or "absolute priority," reaching back beyond abstraction into the lived, the primordial domain of experience and feeling. "System" is thus not only a category of a (contested) mode of thought that thinks in terms of first and second; insofar as it corresponds to something in reality, it is itself what comes second, after some kind of primary "relating," which would then carry the weight of the loaded vocabulary of experience, feeling, and emotion. Interestingly, the term *absolute*, along with *primary*, turns up again, in *Towards 2000*, in an account of emotion as that which "has an absolute and primary significance." It also translates importantly into Williams's account of the novel, specifically Emily Brontë's *Wuthering Heights*, where the significance of the Cathy-Heathcliff relationship—significant for the terms in which Williams will theorize the "structure of feeling"—lies in the fact that it is the "kind of relationship" that is "there and absolute before anything else can be said." In short, if everything is there at the beginning, it would seem that some things are more at the beginning than others.

This double narrative of beginnings is thus shadowed by a degree of internal contradiction, and a good deal else besides. As such it furnishes a useful, because intrinsically unstable and hence potentially fertile, point of departure for an enterprise concerned as much with prospects for as with retrospects on Williams's work. For it would be fair to say that many of the fundamental intellectual questions surrounding Williams's account of culture, and especially its elaboration as cultural materialism, turn on the status of his fables of beginning and priority. What then is their status? Is their purpose to support claims of an empirically historical kind, to do with what actually came "first"? Are they instead logical fictions, like Rousseau's "state of nature," an analytical presupposition or a heuristic device without which we cannot make sense of the actual social order? Does "beginning" therefore refer less to "real history" than to the procedures involved in how we set about *thinking* the social? (On one page of *Marxism and Literature*, where the vocabulary of beginnings is particularly dense, the text shifts from what appear to be statements about actual beginnings in social processes to beginning moves in how we think about those processes, statements about "what begins as a mode of analysis.") Or, finally, are they fables constructed simply to reflect moral and emotional preferences, what Williams wants to believe because of the consequences of not so believing? "Wholeness," for instance, in a great deal of the writing is clearly not just a theoretical postulate or descriptive term, and it is significant that, in the relevant pool of collocationary terms, Williams generally preferred the word *wholeness* to the more analytically freighted *totality*. The reason seems to have been that the former also had certain affective and ethical resonances, thus knotting Williams's text in ways that make it extremely difficult to disentangle analysis and values (through precisely that gesture of separation to which Williams was so strongly opposed).

This mixing of descriptions and judgments ("judgment is inevitable," says Williams in *Politics and Letters*), of the logicoanalytical and the appraisive, around the idea of a primary and grounding wholeness of process tells of a more general way of looking at the world, whereby culture is not just the area of the production of "meanings and values" within the total social formation, but is itself privileged *as* a meaning and a value; culture is a "good" with which to oppose the antihuman values of economism and productionism and a social order based on a radical division of function and faculty. In this context, the emphasis on wholeness, continuous connected practice, and so forth reveals—as Lloyd and Thomas trenchantly (though in my own view one-sidedly) argue[3]—the continuing and probably unexpungeable traces in Williams's own thought of the tradition explored in *Culture and Society,* in particular the paradoxical Arnoldian-Leavisite view of culture as distinct (from "society") but whose distinctness consists in making whole what has been divided and atomized. It is therefore not surprising that, as with all such fables, the validity of this view is presumed rather than demonstrated. Or if grounds are given for the assertion of a ground, it is usually based on the self-validating authority of "experience": the proof that things are connected is that people, in their ordinary lives, know them to be so. But then not all people know this; indeed, it is precisely a feature of experience in modern times ("my own time," says Williams) that it is constituted by and within a divided social order in such a way as "to block any awareness of the unity of this process [the indissolubility of the whole social-material process]." Williams ruefully concludes, in the *Politics and Letters* interviews: "I can see that my appeals to experience [in those earlier definitions] to *found* this unity was problematic" (emphasis added). Once again we have the language of foundations, but this time as openly confessed problem.

Yet if Williams concedes that there is no "absolutely" reliable court of appeal for the assertion of foundation, the assertion itself nevertheless still stands. Indeed, "standing," simply standing there, is probably what in the final analysis Williams's foundationalist rhetoric adds up to. Certainly it could not *with*stand for very long the corrosive skeptical examinations of contemporary antifoundationalism. But then scarcely anything could withstand that, including—in a wonderfully circular paradox—itself (it is worth recalling here what Fredric Jameson said in *Postmodernism* regarding "the tendency of 'foundations' to return via some extreme form of the return of the repressed within the most anti-foundational outlooks"). This presumably is why Williams does not so much argue the grounding move as simply make and assume that move (and perhaps also why, in the *Politics and Letters* interviews, while making various concessions to his interlocutors on this and other matters, he nevertheless led them such a song and dance). In the final analysis, we are tacitly invited to take it or leave it, to stand there with him or to walk away (for, after all, if we are to place our trust in anything, experience would seem to be the best bet). The difficulty is that if we accept the invitation to stand there with him, it is still unclear whether where we stand, in the arguments about culture, is more a place of the residual than of the emergent, a place that, despite all the resistances and qualifications, remains demarcated and informed by the old Leavisite notions of the "organic community."

This aspect of Williams's thinking has been much discussed in the past, indeed has always been at the forefront of debate about his work; and it naturally resurfaces in many of the essays here. The truth of the matter is that the place in question (the "legacy," in West's term) is probably best seen as a combination of the residual and the emergent, at once disabling and enabling, boxing us in but nevertheless allowing us to move on. It is not therefore a question of posing and deciding the issue as an either/or choice, either one thing or the other. The challenge of the work is that it is both, though, as both and as challenge, it does not as a consequence offer a comfortable do-nothing aporia. Ken Hirschkop has rightly said that the most enabling thing about Williams for us is that "he literally taught many of us how to think about culture and politics together." We cannot, however, disentangle this from what on certain assumptions must also appear disabling. Or to put this in a more upbeat way, Williams puts us on the spot, in various senses of the term, challenging us to move on but without the illusion that we can do so effortlessly, in a free-floating euphoria of emancipation. At the level of general theory, one possibility might be to retain the indispensable emphasis on connection while detaching it from the more holistic and value-laden notion of wholeness, thus permitting a way of thinking the social that is more compatible with a sense of the fluid, heterogeneous, and fragmentary character of social formations. The later work, notably the book *Culture* (published in the United States under the title *The Sociology of Culture*), moves toward just this view; by consistently approaching "totality" ("the whole social order") from the notion of "complex real processes," the argument both demands and engenders as crucial to the actual analytical programe of a "sociology of culture" a strongly maintained attention, alongside the continuing stress on the connected, to the concrete and differential specificity of cultural practices.

The general point, however, is that to go forward with Williams we have to carry a lot of baggage, even as we jettison some of it; the question then is how we carry it and what we do with it. Thus, if we move away from purely theoretical questions about what is entailed by Hirschkop's claim, what, for example, in terms of a cultural politics, do we do with the extremely weighty matter of Williams's attitude to the famous "project of modernity" (an attitude that for some is entirely incompatible with any plausible commitment to the emergent)? Insofar as, following Weber, modernity is to be understood as the rationalized order of the systematic "differentiation of the spheres" producing, again in Weber's terms, "specialists without spirit and sensualists without heart," Williams mobilized what remained of his Leavisite-Lawrentian sympathies in support of a position of resolute opposition. This, however, comes through in a variety of not necessarily equivalent guises, and perhaps nowhere at once more strongly and more problematically than in the late inquiries into the related concept of modernism (as a series of essays published posthumously under the title *The Politics of Modernism: Against the New Conformists*).

This is a vexing area for all of us. The new conformists initiate and complete the process whereby the phenomenon of the twentieth-century diasporic, deracinated, cosmopolitan writer, characteristically migrating or exiled to the great metropolitan centers of the capitalist and imperialist West, is packaged as a selective and marketable ideology of modern*ism*. It is significant that "modernity" gets addressed here primarily via the question of "literature," as another point of resistance in Williams's thought to the pressure to specialize generated by and within the modern itself. This in turn gives a context for Williams's long engagement with literature as both critic and writer. Just as Williams refuses the specializing movement that restricts culture to the arts, so he is root-and-branch opposed to the specialization of literature as a separable and autonomous function (as distinct, radically distinct, from posing literature as a set of *specific* practices). From *The Long Revolution* through *Keywords* and other works, Williams returns again and again to the fact, and demonstration of the fact, that the concept of literature is not a given or a constant, but that it has a history—precisely a history of increasing specialization from writing in general to printed texts to fiction and works of imagination (the latter definition being essentially a nineteenth-century invention).

What I want to take here from this alignment of modernity, modernism, and literature is a convergence of historical separations, the late separation of the concept of "literature" from a wider formation, and the separation of the (avant-garde) writer from rooted location and community. Against those late specializations and separations, Williams's argument is again an argument for seeing or making things whole, and again, in the conduct of the argument, an embedding of analysis in a value language; what seems to count most for Williams is, relatedly, an aesthetic of integration and a culture of (relative) settlement, as modes of life and practice in which connections are to be found or can be made. This is one reason why Williams returns time and again in his writings on literature to the idea of realism and a certain tradition of the novel. Here he is very close (especially in *The English Novel from Dickens to Lawrence*) to Lukács, preferring to the art of dispersal and fragmentation promoted by the sanctioned versions of modernism an art that connects, especially—as Simpson and Kaplan note—forms that join, as mutually necessary for intelligibility, individual experience and social formation. His own novels are themselves—sometimes perhaps in an excessively demonstrative mode—geared to just this aesthetic, in their very plots and structures always relating consciousness and experience back to origins ("beginnings") in community and change in collectively lived history.

Yet in the case of his own novels it is now impossible for us to overlook the limitations and blind spots of the insistence on connection as both social and aesthetic category. Consider, for example, the obvious patriarchal sense of the formula in the novel *Volunteers*: "changed but connecting, father to son." We might find ourselves correspondingly suspicious of any attack on cosmopolitan modernism in the name of rootedness against the rootless, especially when the former starts to attract disturbing appeals to the category of the "natural" (the ratified version of the avant-garde, writes Williams, derives from the loss of a "naturalized continuity with a persistent social settlement" and, in an extremely puzzling formulation, works "to naturalize the thesis of the *non*-natural status of language"). To my mind (again the matter is controversial; Higgins, for instance, brings a more sanguine view to Williams on modernism), there is an uncomfortably strained quality in much of the writing of *The Politics of Modernism*, above all in the closing pages of the essay "When Was Modernism?" Here we see Williams deep in the characteristic effort of making difficult discriminations, but the difficulty often shifts from tension to tenseness, a barely concealed hostility, informed by what, at its worst, we have to call prejudice. Thus when modern literary cosmopolitanism is represented in terms of the experience of "endless border-crossing," we suddenly feel the sharp edge of scarcely contained aggression surface in the writing: "The whole commotion is finally and crucially interpreted and ratified by the City of Emigrés and Exiles itself, New York" (this from the man who wrote the novel *Border Country* and described his own life as an endles renegotiation of borders).[4]

Here, frankly, alarm bells start to ring, and we are perforce obliged to think of other, deeply uncongenial forms of the attack on the "cosmopolitan." Nevertheless, it would of course be fatuous to see Williams as an antitechnological pastoralist or agrarian antimodernist, a kind of Heidegger of the left. In the critique of a certain modernism, we have to remember the guiding political perspective, above all the argued claim that the marketed selective tradition of modernism Williams is anxious to contest rests on the centrality of Western metropolitan culture to the consolidation of empire and the globalization of capital (in this connection it would be important to emphasize again, the fundamental caveats entered by Viswanathan notwithstanding, the last chapters of *The Country and the City*). It is above all in these terms, with their reach, however incomplete, into the history of empire and modern capitalism, that the negative picture of the project of modernity is sketched, rather than as a recipe for taking refuge in fantasy constructions of the premodern. As the demolition job on the sentimental fictions of "knowable community" in *The Country and the City* shows, whatever Williams meant by "settlement," it had nothing to do with the imaginary social orders discussed in relation to some of the novels of George Eliot or with the connoted class narrative behind the denotative opening sentence of Jane Austen's *Sense and Sensibility* ("The family of Dashwood had been long settled in Sussex"), and still less of course with what Arnold called, in pages expressly written to denounce working-class militancy (the "Hyde Park rough"), "that profound sense of settled order and security, without which a society like ours cannot grow and live at all."

On "modernity" Williams is probably close in spirit to Habermas, at least in full recognition of the damage done to the life world by the instrumental rationalities coming out of the Enlightenment, but this in no way makes Williams an enemy of the Enlightenment *tout court.* On the contrary, we need only remind ourselves here of Williams's very strong stance on the importance and value of the natural sciences, notably in the essay on Timpanaro in *Problems in Materialism and Culture* (indeed, such is Williams's enthusiasm for natural science, once freed from its fantasies of technomastery, that in *Politics and Letters* he even confessed to the dream of a form of *literary* study linked to the procedures of natural science: "If I had one single ambition in literary studies it would be to rejoin them with experimental science").

If, then, Williams gives short shrift—indeed, even in somewhat surprising guises—to reactionary forms of premodern nostalgia, could we usefully situate him in relation to any of the recognized terms of the postmodern? Given that the latter is quite radically and determinedly antifoundationalist, this would seem most implausible, though, as Higgins notes, to whose disadvantage, intellectual and political, is by no means obvious. Williams himself hardly uses the word *postmodern,* and when he does it is not with any evident enthusiasm (he does not appear to have shared Jameson's view that "for good or ill, we cannot *not* use it"), and would probably have felt about many of its manifestations what Cornel West once said in response to a question about the future of rap—that it would end up "where most American postmodern products end up: highly packaged, regulated, distributed, circulated and consumed." Where, in its left versions, postmodernism means the politics of new social movements, Williams gave his strong support, on the tacit assumption, however, that postmodern also meant postcapitalist. In *Towards 2000,* he wrote of the need for "a new kind of socialist movement" based on "a wide range of needs and interests." But he was also quick to add, as part of that account, a claim for the gathering of these diverse needs and interests in "a new definition of the general interest." The idea of the general interest, like its neighbor, the idea of a common culture, is the political correlative of the analytico-ethical stress on the virtues of "wholeness"; it engages principles of solidarity and community and seeks, in the formulation from *Resources of Hope*, the "creation of a condition in which the people as a whole participate in the articulation of meanings and values."

Reference to the general interest has tended to disappear from left discourse, partly from the pressure of the multiculturalist case, partly, and relatedly, because of the hijacking of the idea by the political right, especially in the United States. Yet if it is true that the left has ceded the terrain in question in part because the right has been so adept at commandeering it, this could well be a mistake. Williams almost certainly thought it was a mistake, and much of his lesson is that, beyond short-term considerations of tactical moves and positions, in the long range it is essential to reclaim it. Similarly, he had little interest in a pluralized postmodernity that comes out as multicultural consumer spectacle. The argument in Williams is always that a cultural politics cannot be just a politics of cultural difference and cultural rights (though the latter are, of course, for Williams crucial in contexts of social inequality, discrimination, blockage of access to resources, and all the other impediments to the creation of a truly democratic culture). There still remains, however, the difficult question of cultural clash (as notoriously in the Rushdie affair). Here there are not many plausible choices. We can opt for fashionable adaptations of Lyotard's incommensurability thesis as one version of the postmodern (but this idea is ultimately a "liberal" idea in the sense of posing the social order on the model of the agon, akin to the competitive relations of the marketplace). Or, as Williams encourages us to do, we can try to think the politics of culture in terms of the idea of the fully human culture, where the emergent in cultural theory would be the attempt to think the conditions, the "grounds," of the emergence of a common culture, but without—as Williams always stressed—losing sight of the relations of power and subordination that at once block, and so imperatively require, that very project.

How these notions of the general interest, the common culture, and community might be reclaimed, and what might be counted as genuinely new in a new definition, are issues that Williams's work, understood as a cultural politics, compels us to address. In particular it asks us to think about where we "stand" once we have disembarrassed ourselves of the older, universalist and metaphysical view of the common good built on a shared human essence (for example,

Arnold's "best self," which it is the task of culture to form in order that the subject recognize the "higher reason" of the state). Williams's principal point here is that a consequence of abandoning the universal in this sense should not then be a simple frittering away in a certain language of the postmodern of the notions of social solidarity and collective project.

"Community" is a prime example. Other than as sentimental flourish in the direction of lost *Gemeinschaft* or as synonym for special interest group, "community" does not in fact get a very good press these days, or indeed any press at all (it has no entry, for example, in the index of one of this book's companion volumes, *Universal Abandon? The Politics of Postmodernism*). Taking Williams seriously is among other things squirming uncomfortably in that silence, though there is of course the difficulty that Williams's own writings can also occasionally leave us squirming, especially when the word *natural* reappears, in talk of something called "natural communities"; it is surely right to see here a disabling movement in Williams's thought from the complex to the simple. On the other hand, we should also remember here Williams's warning against the "projection of simple communities,"[5] and above all perhaps the severance of the valued senses of community from certain versions of the "national," as, for example, in the observations in the Heath-Skirrow interview on the uses of television to create via its audience the sense of "false nation."

In this connection, we should also note the rejection, in the same interview, of the idea of national community on the grounds of its exclusiveness ("this idea of the nation, . . . of people whom we 'recognize,' excludes the majority of the people of the world whom we don't recognize and watch on television"). This not only counters a familiar view of Williams's thought as beset by a "nativist" view of the national, it also rejoins an important general emphasis in contemporary critique of the idea of "community." The interesting feature of Williams's thinking on these matters is that it absorbs this emphasis while insisting on moving beyond it, in one of many enactments of the category of necessary complexity. There is, for example, the important point—more or less lost these days for the reasons plausibly stated by Viswanathan, but important nevertheless—that, while a narrow view of the "national" is entirely alien to the spirit of Williams's work, his thinking about popular culture, especially in the early texts, derives a great deal of its force and continuing relevance from what he found in Gramsci's reflection on the progressive resources within the national tradition.

For it is not at all clear that, once we have passed the idea of single community through the filter of rigorous skeptical analysis, we are left with anything particularly useful beyond the moment of critical negativity itself. What we are typically left with—in, say, the work of deconstruction on the category of the "political" (for example, Jean-Luc Nancy's *La communauté désoeuvrée*), or in certain versions of the theory of radical democracy—is little more than an account of community understood as resting on an exclusionary act, whereby a "we" is constituted by reference to a "them." Community, on this account, is thus critically dissolved into communitarian fantasies (often around some metaphor of a "body") of bonding and binding that both menace difference within the group and constitute it as alien "other" outside the group. But this sort of account also entails a reduction from the complex to the simple, starting out as necessary critique of a certain model of "imagining" community (in Benedict Anderson's term), but then, in its own generalization as model *tout court*, becoming a polemical straw man; the positive (but complexified and non-nostalgic) senses of community are entirely lost or severely curtailed. They either disappear from the argument or they are retained in a form that leaves them stranded on an imposssible horizon of utopian desire—a view that, beyond a self-evident truism or two, is just about useless for anything resembling a practical cultural politics that would involve both the affirmation of solidarities and the negotiation of priorities within those solidarities. In addition, it also effectively leaves the way open for colonization of the term *community*, along with its neighbor *culture*, by practices of everyday language that, especially in the United States, empty it entirely of meaningful content (prize specimens include "the defense community," "the culture of poverty," "the money culture").

Once again, turning to Williams in connection with these losses and perversions can seem to be going backward rather than forward, back into the terms of an old-fashioned humanism. But then what precisely does this now mean? Williams himself speaks of the "humanist error." In Williams's text the phrase is not in quotation marks, but it is ambiguous whether the word *error* is implicitly in or not in quotation marks, cited in an irony with a nice imprecision as to what is actually being ironized. Naturally, Williams repudiated humanist-voluntarist notions of agency that abstracted an atomized "individual" from the social. On the other hand, he completely shared E. P. Thompson's rejection of the reduction of active subjectivity to the notion of passive interpellation sponsored by a certain reading (misreading, some would claim) of Althusser. It is in this respect that we can speak of Williams's "humanism," as, in the words of Cornel West, a "subtle humanism," constantly attentive to historical contextualization and determination while unmovably grounded in an ethics of agency. One reason Williams found Gramsci's notion of hegemony so attractive is that it appeared to allow for that particular combination of historical boundedness and active agency. West's implicit point about Williams's humanism is that Williams is ultimately unthinkable without the ethical, not in the sense of a prescriptive moralism, but as the ethical grounding of political and social action in a set of relations between community, democracy, and socialism. This presumably is also one of the things Hirschkop means when he says that Williams taught us how "to think about culture and politics together," as terms of potential empowerment.

These, of course, are no longer (never were, other than in strange sectarian dreams) fixed relations. Williams's particular brand of humanism can, however, now be read as representing a tonically unfixing endeavor, especially with regard to what are currently establishing themselves as the new orthodoxies. Today socialism has to justify itself before the court of the concept of democracy. In the light of recent experience, that is as it should be. Williams's example nevertheless suggests that this can be a two-way transaction. Democracy today revolves around two great ideas, the idea that society consists of freely competing individuals and the idea that society consists of freely cooperating individuals. That last phrase ("freely cooperating individuals") is Williams's, from all the way back in the discussion of democracy in *The Long Revolution*. It can, of course, come out sounding like a bankrupt platitude. But at a time when the idea of democracy as competition is all the rage, this is exactly the moment to attend to its full force. Similarly, at a time when the idea of socialism seems to be on the run and the intellectual smart money is going elsewhere, Williams gives us some terms for holding on to, as well as rethinking, that idea, for building again, precisely from "ground" level (for example, thinking the relation of "production" to "need" beyond the terms of the "bureaucratic-command" economy, at a time when the smart players, some of them laying claim to left credentials, insist that, both generally and in the writings of Williams himself, the former is inseparable from the latter).

Moriarty, alluding no doubt to Williams's fine review essay ("Beyond Actually Existing Socialism," later published in *Problems in Materialism and Culture*) on Rudolf Bahro's *The Alternative in Eastern Europe*, muses on what Williams might have said to us with respect to the events in Eastern Europe and their implications for the future of the idea of socialism. There are certainly profound, deeply grounded continuities here (Williams interestingly remarks of the Bahro book that reading it in 1980 took him back to the late 1950s of *The Long Revolution*, that "it was for me a remarkable experience, in that it came through, quite personally, as another version of the project of *The Long Revolution*"). We cannot of course know what he would have said, had he lived to see the beginning of the nineties, but he would doubtless have tried to keep alive, amid the ruins of a certain edifice, what he called "tenses of the imagination." While nothing would seem further from the exhaustingly self-nuancing Williams style than the genre of the slogan, it might not be far from the spirit of a legacy attuned to the possibilities of the emergent to conclude by recalling the striking poster carried by some East German students at the time of the collapse of the Berlin Wall: "Socialism is dead. Long live socialism!"

NOTES

1. Catherine Gallagher in her essay raises the important theoretical issue of abstraction, questioning the relation, even implied identity, of terms in the expression "cultural materialism." Gallagher queries, even breaks, the relation between the "cultural" and the "material" by arguing, roughly, the following: if culture belongs to the domain of signification ("signifying practices," as Williams says), then it necessarily partakes of abstraction; abstraction, however, is exactly what, from *Culture and Society* through *Marxism and Literature*, aroused Williams's hostility, perhaps because of the Leavisite residues of "organicist" thinking subsequently glossed as a Marxist "materialism." Hence the choice of the example of *money* around which to organize her critical observations regarding the idea of cultural materialism. According to Gallagher, it is not just that Williams got money wrong, but that getting money wrong—in particular paradoxically describing as "material" money in its most abstract guise as a sign in the process of exchange—points to a basic flaw in Williams's whole approach to culture. In other words, in the case of money, it is a question not just of overcoding but of a movement from the physical to the abstract as the place where culture happens, but then in ways that complicate any alleged material-

ity of cultural production. It is certainly true—as Moriarty's essay also intimates—that the whole place of abstraction in Williams's thinking requires a lot of sorting out.

2. While the meaning of *indissoluble* is fairly clear here, it does sit somewhat uneasily with the image of "solution," being "in solution" (in the sense of liquid), that Williams deploys in both *The Long Revolution* and *Culture* to represent the idea of lived social process.

3. The neglected introduction to *Problems in Materialism and Culture* ("A Hundred Years of Culture and Anarchy") is a devastatingly severe *political* placing of Arnold's argument about culture in the context of the 1866 Hyde Park demonstrations that so disturbed Arnold in the first of the lectures that became *Culture and Anarchy*. Lloyd and Thomas claim, also in a footnote, that, in their view, this later Williams text does not, however, break the hold on Williams of the general logic of Arnold's way of thinking about culture. This is clearly a point for debate.

4. Against what is arguably parochial, one must emphasize Williams's committed internationalism, not just as political solidarities but also in his own intellectual life, especially from the period of *Marxism and Literature* onward. In the introduction to the latter, Williams situates and defines his own sense of intellectual "at-homeness" in terms of the crossing of boundaries on a grand scale: "I had opportunities to extend my discussions in Italy, in Scandinavia, in France, in North America, and in Germany, and with visitors from Hungary, Yugoslavia, and the Soviet Union. This book is the result of that period of discussion, in an international context in which I have had the sense, for the first time in my life, of belonging to a sphere and dimension of work in which I could feel at home."

5. Given the persistence of the generalized (and underinformed) image of Williams as caught up in regressive nostalgias for earlier social forms, we should note that the refusal of the "projection of simple communities" is a constant emphasis from *Culture and Society* onward. It is thus important to remind ourselves that the "reach for complexity" is there from the beginning and that, among other things, the attempted imagining of an alternative social order involves acceptance of specialization, division of labor, and technology. Consider, for example, the passages in the chapter on T. S. Eliot in *Culture and Society* (portions of which are discussed by Lloyd and Thomas) that reject "merely a form of the regressive longing for a simpler non-industrial society" and advance the claim that "in any form of society towards which we are likely to move, it now seems clear that there must be . . . a very complex system of specialized developments. . . . A culture in common, in our own day, will not be the simple all-in-all society of old dream. It will be a very complex organisation, requiring continual adjustment and redrawing. At root, the feeling of solidarity is the only conceivable element of stabilization in so difficult an organisation. But in its issue it will have to be continually redefined, and there will be many attempts to enlist old feelings in the service of an emerging sectional interest. The emphasis that I wish to place here is that this first difficulty—the compatibility of increasing specialization with a genuinely common culture—is only soluble in a context of material community and by the full democratic process." What such "compatibility" might look like in more precisely specified terms remains of course one of the great open questions, in both Williams's work and elsewhere. The merit of Williams's contribution is at least to have kept the question in play, as distinct from submitting to prevailing forms of "complexity" as inevitable, natural, and permanent. For a very useful discussion of the relation of community and complexity in Williams's thinking, see Ken Hirschkop, "A Complex Populism: The Political Thought of Raymond Williams," *News from Nowhere*, no. 6 (February 1989): pp. 12–22.

Part I

Theory

Raymond Williams: Feeling for Structures, Voicing "History"
David Simpson

How else could we entitle that word "history," now, except in speech marks, under the sign of vocative instability, outside any assumed consensus? As perhaps the most overemployed item in the vocabulary of literary-critical and cultural analysis, "history" may well also be the least decisive. We return to history, work toward history, and espouse a historical method, but few of us can say exactly what we mean by history, except in the most gestural way. Those of us who worry about it at all find ourselves necessarily mired in complex theoretical retractions and modifications, bewildering enough to sponsor some fairly radical insecurities. Others, sensing a probable dead end street, run for the cover of the kind of "new historicism" that looks to history as to a safe and approved harbor, a place where one may sleep peacefully, lulled by anecdotal stories, after tossing on the stormy seas of deconstructive and theoretical Marxist uncertainty.

In *Keywords*, Raymond Williams had a go at saying not what history is but what it has been taken to mean, and he offered a compromise, if not quite a solution, in the particularities of showing and telling, ostension and invocation: "*History* itself retains its whole range, and still, in different hands, *teaches* or *shows* us most kinds of knowable past and almost every kind of imaginable future."[1] The urgency of history is not, then, in its wholeness or totality but in its immediate applicability to a range of options for reading the past and projecting the future. It instructs and points out; it is part of the present.

In the saddest and most untimely sense of the word, Raymond

Williams himself is now history, and in the aftermath of his death one feels a temptation to believe in the possibility of saying something final about him, about his place in history, his understanding of history, even, perhaps, about Raymond Williams *and* history, in the grandest of senses. This is of course an illusion. Even the most minimally sophisticated and merely textual hermeneutics suffices to warn us that the object will shift accordingly as various kinds of attention are focused upon it. And Williams's texts are unusually polyphonous both in their genres (novels, criticism, political journalism, etc.) and in the flexibility of their subject positions and discursive attitudes (inside and outside Marxism, Leavisism, the Labour Party, literary theory, and so on). There will be a lot to say, and for a long while, about his texts and about the practical interventions they record or recommend. But there is another dimension to consider, one ironically sympathetic to the original hermeneutic ambition that sought to recover authenticity rather than (or as well as) to record chronologically cumulative indeterminacies. With Raymond Williams, more than with most, one hears a voice. It is a voice that death has not undone, a voice that suggests that metaphors of passing, of a wake, or waking, are more opportune than those of finality for describing the legacy we now have to consider.

Let me be briefly autobiographical in order to situate what I am about to say. I knew Raymond Williams hardly at all, but listened to him a lot, in lectures and meetings. I did not, then, have a particularly intimate relation to him of the sort that might have made his voice immediate and memorable, as are those of our loved ones. But I do hear his voice every time I try to read or think about his writings. I would not propose my own impressions as worth pondering were it not for their being shared by others (for instance, the editor of this volume), to the extent that this voice might be supposed to be *written into* the text of Williams's work. We may suggest that this voice has been worked upon, cultivated, and in some way intended. If the vocalic does indeed function in our culture as the signifier of subjective integrity, then Williams had an intuitive ability to make this work for him against what he saw as the inhumanities of "writing"— of theory, abstraction, schematization, the techniques he often identified with the cruel facilitation of global rationalization, and, sometimes, with the sparse theoretical paradigms of European Marxists.

The voice, of course, commonly functions in writing as an image of presence. We write "what I mean to say" rather than "what I mean to write." There is a long tradition in British culture of a preference for the language of ordinary persons in a state of vivid sensation—the iconography of sincerity and authenticity. In Williams's case, this has been noticed. John Higgins has put it well:

> His voice was remarkable; the voice of an authority. It was conversational, almost to the point of dullness, but sustained throughout by that curiously academic power, the intellectually cautious assertion of the radical.[2]

And, before him, Terry Eagleton wrote at length about this "unmistakably individual voice," sensing a meaning in all of its intonations:

> What appears at first glance the inert language of academicism is in fact the stage of a personal drama, the discourse of a complex, guarded self-display. A closed private idiom is cast into public oratory: the speaking voice slowly weaves its authoritative abstractions at the same time as it shocks by its sheer idiosyncrasy, its mannered yet candid trust in its own authenticity. It is a style which in the very act of assuming an unruffled, almost Olympian impersonality, displays itself (not least in its spiralling modifications) as edgily defensive, private, and self-absorbed. It is a mode of self-confession which is simultaneously a self-concealment—the style of a thinker intellectually isolated to the point of eccentricity, driven consequently to certain sophisticated gambits of self-defence and self-justification, but none the less resolutely offering his own experience as historically representative.[3]

Eagleton's remarks argue convincingly for the worked-upon quality of this casualness, and for the anxious personal motivations behind the cultivation of the purportedly general mode of writing-speaking (I want, just once, to call it "speakwrite"). Williams's books are notorious for their repeated reliance upon such categories as "lived experience," "real people," and "actual events." Whatever the text, his mode was always dramatic. As Eagleton has written elsewhere:

> Words for him were condensed social practices, sites of political struggle. . . . He himself spoke pretty much as he wrote, weightily, rhetorically, constructing and composing his speech rather than slinging it provisionally together.[4]

Historical semantics carried great weight for Williams as an analytical tool, from *Culture and Society* onward: he believed that whole social and historical tendencies could be tracked through the changing meanings of words. But, in speaking "pretty much as he wrote," he further worked to collapse the distinction between speaking and writing. Many of his books were the texts of lectures, unapologetically reproduced without footnotes, those conventional academic signatures of premeditation and after-recollection, and of a dispersed rather than an immediate community. It is hard not to see this tactic as some kind of intuitive response to the problematization of the writing-speech relation that became, for so many, obligatory after the work of Derrida in the 1960s. The new self-consciousness about metaphors of presence certainly proved very threatening to that other cult of immediacy so popular in Williams's Cambridge: Leavisism, which was not so much an incarnation as an expiring simplification of Leavis's own critique, soon domesticated from its angry beginnings into a lazier form of assumed common sense.

Williams never avowed such simple solutions, even as his connections with the Leavisite methodology were clear enough in his predilection for the language of vitality and immediacy. But he did gamble, I am suggesting, on the credibility of the voice as a persuasive counterattack upon the antisubjectivists who came to be a majority among left academics after 1968. Some of his critics have denounced this vocalic emphasis (perhaps, more recently, in response to the somewhat unfortunate example of Mr. Kinnock). In attributing to Williams a "Celtic feel" for words, Eagleton himself opened something of a door for such detractors as Peter Cadogan who, in the predictable calling to accounts that followed Williams's death, situated his "brilliant rhetoric" along with that of Bevan, Lloyd George, and Kinnock as an example of "how well the Welsh beguile the English."5 I would not have said that "brilliant rhetoric" fits the Williams whose voice I still hear, which functions indeed by the deliberate eschewal of brilliance and the almost complete denial of anything resembling wit. Even those sympathetic to Williams have sometimes felt that he got the balance wrong, as when, in the high-intensity context of speech-action that marked the "Cambridge debate" in the early 1980s, Williams's patiently and relentlessly delivered histories of faculty confrontation sounded all too much like writing. He could, then, have things both ways. In the heat of a polemical moment, Williams's spoken interventions had the effect (not always achieved) of drawing us into a long perspective that at once explained and complicated the desire to make an immediate difference. Meanwhile, in the written work, we were constantly reminded of the necessity of preserving the integrity of the actual, the living, the felt. It is a strange middle ground, and one that may have excused Williams from the extreme demands of either medium, writing or speaking, as it excused him also from the obligation to meditate explicitly ("theoretically") on the relation between them that was, as I have said, such an urgent question for so many after Derrida and 1968.

Admirers and detractors share, then, a recognition of Williams's heavy reliance upon the voice. To list all the instances of scripted vocalization would be tedious. Williams's Cobbett has ideas that "jump at us from his pages. It is as if we can hear him speaking them, in his usual plain and simple and decided way."[6] Here it is Williams who can tell us what is "usual," as if he talks with Cobbett all the time. But he failed to hear the uglier voices in Cobbett, for instance the sadosexual sensationalism of *The Bloody Buoy* and other anti-French Revolution tracts. The pressures of the Industrial Revolution worked, for some, to cause Cobbett's "great voice" to fade into an "antique mumble," but not for Williams:

> There is a sense of history as connecting rather than separating his time and ours. Not then this period and that, but a common country, in an actual succession, inheritance, of lives. And not then writing as style: the critical or textual study; but writing as a practice, within this country and inheritance: the giving and taking of energy, in this durable form, to attempt or actually to make new kinds of relationship. William Cobbett as a contributor, in this continuing life.[7]

The potential for evasiveness in the invention of voice out of writing is clear enough. It appears in a different form in Williams's own responses to the interlocutors of *Politics and Letters*, whose weighty and complex objections to and qualifications of his work are mostly met with a benign "well, of course, you have a point there," or words to that effect. Only later, and often in a different place, can we see if and how the point has taken, and by then the question has been removed from the sphere of interactive disagreement and made part of a seamless personal meditation.

These tactics and tendencies go largely unnoticed, or at least undiscussed, by Williams himself. But there is at least one remarkable exception to that habit, prompted by his reflections on the implications of Lucien Goldmann's visit to Cambridge. Here, and in a rare moment, Williams is led to reflect on the ordinary-language obsessions of British intellectuals (himself included) and on their (his) tendency to take for granted an extant community of speech:

> In humane studies, at least, and with mixed results, British thinkers and writers are continually pulled back towards ordinary language: not only in certain rhythms and in choices of words, but also in a manner of exposition which can be called unsystematic but which also represents an unusual consciousness of an immediate audience: a sharing and equal-standing community, to which it is equally possible to defer and to reach out. I believe that there are many positive aspects of this habitual manner, but I am just as sure that the negative aspects are serious: a willingness to share, or at least not too explicitly to challenge, the consciousness of the group of which the thinker and writer—his description as intellectual raises the precise point—is willingly or unwillingly but still practically a member. . . . This pull towards ordinary language was often, is often, a pull towards current consciousness: a framing of ideas within certain polite but definite limits.[8]

The barely spoken question Williams asks himself is why, given the potential complementarities of their work, it had taken so long for him to come to grips with Goldmann and with the tradition for which he stood. By way of explanation, he refers to the "mobility and impersonality" of Goldmann's project, which thus has all the negative features of what we may call *writing.* So that it is then the living voice and presence of Goldmann himself that comes as such a surprise:

> But it was then interesting to me, having read his work presented in those familiar ways, to hear the voice of a different mind: mobility in that other sense—the quick emotional flexibility, the varying stares at his audience, the pacing up and down of this smiling man in his open-necked shirt, more concerned with a cigarette than with notes but concerned above all with the challenge of his argument, a challenge that evidently included himself. There was a sense of paradox: of amused but absolute seriousness, of provisional but passionate conviction; a kind of self-deprecating and self-asserting boldness. Perhaps the paradox was Goldmann in Cambridge, but it may be more.[9]

More indeed. Williams here finds that theory has a human face, a pedagogic form divine, and wonders why he had imagined otherwise. In this somewhat shabby-bohemian figure of the compulsive intellectual he sees a fellow worker he could never find in the high-academic prose of the Marxist theoretician. He has found, in other words, Goldmann's voice.

Williams's emphasis on and faith in the voice obviously had much to do with the experiential bias to which many have attributed the shortcomings of his method, in general and in particular. We know, after Terry Eagleton, that Williams's writings do tend toward a "left-Leavisism" or "socialist humanism," and depend upon a distinct "romantic populism." There has indeed been, as Eagleton put it, a "muted strain of anti-intellectualism" in Williams's attitudes to Marxism—though it is muted indeed in comparison to the position taken by his distinguished compatriot E. P. Thompson on the question of Althusser.[10] Williams's nativist streak prevented him from paying more than lip service to the critique and understanding of colonialism, and he barely acknowledged the implications of the feminist movement. He often participated uncritically in the Englishman's distrust of theory (even as a Welshman), and he arguably created a spectacular red herring in his sustained attack on a base-superstructure model that was never quite the orthodoxy he claimed it to be.[11] Jan Gorak reasonably notes that for all the talk of communities, Williams himself was a compulsive loner, claiming "independence from even the most elementary source" and able to reconcile so many oppositions only because he failed to "identify them precisely."[12]

These things, and others like them, have been said, and should be said. We will continue to have a Williams for falsification as well as one for reconstruction; presumably we could not expect to have the one without the other. As Stuart Hall has wryly noted, "finding out what *Culture and Society* left out has become, over the years, something of an intellectual game."[13]

Here I would like to set out a preliminary account of a specific element of Williams's legacy, one that details the relationship between the personal and the historical as implicit in the various definitions of the "structure of feeling." This relationship still seems to me one of the major debates in Marxist cultural theory; Williams's work offers, I think, an example of how to approach it that is largely cautionary but still in many ways exemplary. If much of what follows reads as a continuing critique of the vocalic method, I would still maintain that we have something important to learn from Williams's formulations, and that we definitely cannot afford to ignore the motivations behind those formulations. For if Williams sets out, at some level, to captivate us by the spell of the voice, his own and others, then he also, in the range of his reflections on the dialectic of self and society, encourages us to think about the gestation or possibility of the very subjective integrity he so often takes for granted, and of which his composite writing-speech is intended as the primary signifier.

And so to that famous and distinctly personal item of methodological vocabulary, the "structure of feeling." This is a key formulation that occurs throughout Williams's career, functioning at times quite loosely and on other occasions subjected to attempts at more exact definition. It figures in what has been called the "left-Leavisite" phase, and it remains central in Williams's later efforts to confront Marxist theory on something of its own terms. And yet, for all its obvious importance to the life's work of a major intellectual, it has not proved to be an exportable concept. To the best of my knowledge, no one has much picked it up, used it, or refined it. This being so, it seems useful here to try to decide what exactly Williams meant by it, and thus to find out what we can learn from his meanings. For the apparent nontransferability of this concept is not, I think, simply a function of a generational preference for other models. It is partly that, to be sure: Althusserian state apparatuses have been more popular, along with other analogous antisubjectivist paradigms (Foucauldian discourse, for example), than special-case rhetorics of the sort that Williams invokes in describing the structure of feeling. But there are also some fundamental problems and unsolved ambiguities in the exposition of the structure of feeling that must remain evident even to those who incline toward a subjectivist emphasis within the dialectic of personal and general. Factoring these out may help us to plot the possible futures that Williams's work has for materialist and Marxist theory.

The phrase "structure of feeling" occurs somewhat casually in Williams's foundational *Culture and Society* (1958). It first appears as a symptom of Carlyle's favorably interpreted "direct response" to the condition of England: Carlyle captured "that structure of contemporary feeling which is only ever apprehended directly," and which is not to be identified with formal systems or doctrines. It is further proposed as an attribute of the novels of the 1840s. And, in an apparently different evaluation, the same structure of feeling is offered as the equivalent of a negative definition of ideology: when George Eliot, in *Felix Holt*, describes the lives of working people, Williams finds that her personal intelligence surrenders "virtually without a fight, to the general structure of feeling about these matters which was the common property of her generation." It is this "general structure of feeling" that characterizes the reformist fiction of the mid-nineteenth century: it sees that things are wrong, but it cannot become involved.[14]

So far, then, the structure of feeling seems to define something very like ideology in its classic and negative sense—the false consciousness emanating from a (ruling or emergent) class interest. But we also have here an endorsement of some degree of direct apprehension, of felt conviction (in Carlyle), along with the implication that it is the gift of great literature to perform this apprehension. The doctrinal content of the structure of feeling seems to be found wanting (in Eliot), while the writer is commended for a committed and lively embodying of it. The structure is unsatisfactory but the feeling is valued, both as it originated in composition and as it conveys us back from the present to an intuition of what things felt like. We seem here to have an unholy alliance between Williams's literary vitalism and his critical distance from nineteenth-century reformist ideology.

In *The Long Revolution* (1961), "an attempt to reach new ground"[15] and to integrate a general theory of human creativity into an account of the interrelation of cultural and political revolution, Williams offers his first sustained account of the structure of feeling. Significantly, he here presents as one of the basic problems in cultural history the task of recovering from the past a "felt sense of the quality of life at a particular place and time." It is art, he opines, that can best give us this sense, for art records something "actually lived through" and able to produce "an actual living change." The structure of feeling is now glossed as something at once "firm and definite" yet operative in "the most delicate and least tangible parts of our activity"; it is in one sense "the culture of a period," but it is culture conceived as an aesthetic-individual experience, as "the particular living result of all the elements in the general organization." It is especially evident in the arts, and it is at the heart of communication itself, and thus is a "very deep and very wide possession." It changes with the generations and is never simply learned but always created.[16]

Williams does not seem to sense the need to address the very difficult question of how we decide that what we receive from the past is truly of the past. He admits that we can never completely relive it, but wants to sustain a privileged role for art (and, in at least this instance, documentary culture) in affording us access to it, and precisely by way of art's capturing the structure of feeling. His awareness of what he calls the "selective tradition" does not interfere with his assumption of a relatively direct transmission of the structure of feeling; as if we may indeed choose between different ones, but what we get is real enough when we do get it. These images of "actual life" are posited as immune to or significantly unaffected by the processes of refiguration that affect every other supposed object of knowledge in the past. One could say, as Williams does, that the whole process of interpretation is "active," in the sense that the past is always read as pertaining to a present. But this would incline the structure of feeling toward a strictly "presentist" application, one concerned with history only as it affects us now, with no objectivist epistemological assumptions left standing. But Williams does not intend such a reading, for the "actual analysis" of the 1840s that follows is quite objectivist in its rhetoric. Not only does an in-depth reading of the documentary tradition take us behind and beyond the selective tradition, which privileges only a very small group of texts (a reasonable hypothesis), but the structure of feeling accessible through the art of the period takes us behind the various fixed formations of the "social character" (another term that is here introduced as equivalent to ideology, in that it is class-specific).[17]

But here again there is a confusion of focus. On the one hand the structure of feeling is said to "correspond" to the "dominant social character" and to be primarily evident in the "dominant social group." This makes it, once again, look very like what others have called ideology. On the other hand, it carries the signatures of an interaction between all the extant social characters, and thus records, so to speak, ideology in ferment or in transition, and with an emphasis on a notion of agency emanating from the consciousness of the artist. Williams seems to want to offer art and literature as the most complex barometer of movement at the ideological level, and to propose the structure of feeling as a kind of supersensitive indicator of such movement. (One could say that it is made up of different ideologies, in ferment, or that it is in itself a particular kind of mixed ideology.) Thus, in the 1840s, authors do remain "bound" by a negative ideology, but the best literature goes beyond this, straining it to breaking point by projecting a "radical human dissent." It does this by humanization rather than by theory or argument, as it transcribes the "deepest feelings in the real experience of the time," and it is this that defines a novel like *Wuthering Heights* as the record of an emergent "new feeling."[18]

Literature thus both reproduces and reformulates ideology, and in its reformulations it becomes, implicitly, a vanguard element. This privileged evaluation of the literary is, however, a dubious benefit. On the one hand it presumably customized, for British literary critics, a set of concerns that they could otherwise encounter only in a vocabulary that must have seemed alien and technocratic, as it did to Williams himself. On the other hand, it reproduced the hypothesis of art as world historical in a way that desperately calls out for interaction with exactly those more skeptical, technocratic vocabularies employed by the most subtle of the European Marxists. When historical change is pending, Williams wants to show us that art gets in first; or, at least, some art does. Because he chooses to discuss mainly the most prescient literature, no even tentatively complete analysis of historical determination can be attempted.

In *Modern Tragedy* (1966) the innovatory, ahead-of-the-game aspect of the structure of feeling is oddly underemployed. Instead, the phrase is used to describe something as general as the Greek worldview, now forever lost. There is a "mediaeval structure of feeling," a bourgeois structure of feeling (apparent in Lessing's work), and a liberal structure of feeling.[19] But in *Drama from Ibsen to Brecht* (1968) there is another sustained attempt to specify a definition, one that takes over verbatim some of the phrasing of *The Long Revolution* and adapts it to the analysis of modern drama. Here, structures of feeling are placed in dialectical relation to "conventions." The exposition is somewhat obscure, but there seems to be implied a temporal metamorphosis; conventions begin as inherited forms that are challenged by structures of feeling, which then themselves become the new conventions to be challenged in their turn. In dwelling upon the structure of feeling, Williams claims to intend a move toward totalities: "What I am seeking to describe is the continuity of experience from a particular work, through its particular form, to its recognition as a general form, and then the relation of this general form to a period." The structure of feeling is first apparent as a strictly personal formation, even to the point of signaling isolation or alienation. The artist will at first find himself rejecting and being rejected by the "established formations," but gradually he will be seen to be speaking for others, and eventually for "a new way of seeing ourselves and our world." The emphatic small-scale innovation of the structure of feeling, together with its location in the work of literature, gives Williams permission to reproduce the disciplinary preference of literary criticism for beginning "quite locally, in what is still called practical criticism, with direct analysis," with a "first study" that is "local, particular, unique."[20] But what is never tested or proven is the relation of any of these literary particulars to any more general social-historical formation. Formal novelties may evolve, indeed, into new artistic conventions, and as such they have a teleological component. But Williams gives us no tools for understanding such conventions in precise relation to nonliterary and hence "total" history. The historical prescience of art then comes to be judged largely as it develops forms that other artists replicate.

The literary-critical definition of the structure of feeling has the effect of distracting Williams from any detailed engagement with nonliterary historical data. Literature is assumed to be the barometer of a general culture, but no exact interactions are specified. This literary-critical priority allows Williams to float the structure of feeling as a prototheoretical concept that never quite takes on a sharp outline, and it is thus quite comfortable in the arguments of some of his most "antitheoretical" work. It functions thus in *The English Novel from Dickens to Lawrence*, published in 1970, at a time when the threats to the special status of literary criticism in the academy were becoming more and more unignorable, and when the appeal of French theory was winning numerous converts among the disciples of English common sense. The book is full of oblique references to these developments, and emphatic in its defense of the unique quality of literature as "a whole way of seeing that is communicable to others, and a dramatisation of values that becomes an action." Again, art records "the pressure and structure of active experience, creating forms, creating life," and at its heart is the structure of feeling, something that is "lived and experienced but not yet quite arranged as institutions and ideas."[21]

The argument, familiarly, seeks to preempt the priority of institutions and ideas. Additionally, the book is significantly, if quietly, proud of the national literature, and perhaps verges upon nationalistic sentiments as it celebrates even while qualifying "a creative confidence, a creative centre, that is there and impressive, continuously impressive: the English, specifically English, novel." Williams pronounces this the product of a "self-confident insulated middle-class," but he responds positively to its aesthetic achievements. One might assume that by "specifically English" he means not Welsh, or Scots, or Irish. But, in time and place, one takes the message to be, also, not French, not abstract, not deceived by the appeal of ideas that are merely clear and distinct, rather than vital and complex.[22]

But, just a year later, in "Literature and Sociology" (1971), Williams approaches the structure of feeling in a more theoretically strenuous mood, after hearing Goldmann's voice and recognizing his own affiliations with the genetic structuralism from which he also begged to differ. The structure of feeling is now declared apparent "above all, in fundamental choices of form," along the lines suggested in *Drama from Ibsen to Brecht*. It retains its identity with the "real" and to the "specific literary phenomenon" but it now finds that specificity not just in a vitalist immediacy of human response but also in formal decisions. Structure, as it were, gains a little ground at the expense of feeling. But again Williams insists that he is not referring to the "changes of formal idea and belief which make up the history of consciousness," or to the "changes of formal institution and relationship" that compose the material of "the more accessible, indeed the more normal, history." He wants, that is, to be able to continue to deny something that may be called "formal," here fobbed off onto the generalist methods of other disciplines. He continues to want the literary structure of feeling to "precede" these more general forms. And the literary form, in its microcosmic incarnation in the structure of feeling, is so little removed from an original experience that it may be respected as such.[23]

No new definitional work is done in *The Country and the City* (1973), which continues to use the structure of feeling as a self-evident category, somewhat akin to but always more complex and un-stable than what he occasionally, here, calls "ideology."[24] And *Key-words*, despite its long entry on "structural," is hardly the place for a discussion of such a famously personal concept. It is in *Marxism and Literature* (1977) that the question is again focused, as it per-haps had to be in Willliams's fullest, albeit defensive, engagement with the now unignorable "theory."[25] Here, the obsession with mak-ing sure that the structure of feeling gets first into the patent book causes Williams to identify it not just with emergence—already too fixed a category—but with "*pre-emergence*, active and pressing but not yet fully articulated, rather than the more evident emergence which could be more confidently named." For all its appearance in a modernized and theoretical format, the spirit and most of the letter of the structure of feeling has not much changed since its critical ar-ticulation in *The Long Revolution*. It remains the signature of a "liv-ing presence," now explicitly a corrective to "the reduction of the so-cial to fixed forms that remains the basic error" of much Marxist theory. Williams is still preoccupied with "something" about subjec-tive experience that he imagines the mainline theorists to be missing out: "the experiences to which the fixed forms do not speak at all, which indeed they do not recognize" because they are beyond the "available meaning," being "actively lived and felt." The formal em-phasis learned from Goldmann and Lukács remains, but within a doggedly miniaturist rhetoric: "We are talking about characteristic el-ements of impulse, restraint, and tone; specifically effective ele-ments of consciousness and relationship." The minuscule items of complex literary language—"an unease, a stress, a displacement, a la-tency"—are the heralds of a future, "social experiences *in solution*," not yet "*precipitated*." But Williams nowhere proves that the com-plex uses of "ideology" evident in the European Marxist tradition are inadequate for a description of these literary phenomena. Moreover, his one example, the Victorian novelists who intuited a general analysis for the condition of poverty that the "official" ideology could only imagine as the result of individual failings, seems dis-tinctly weak, and not at all incompatible with a complex model of ideology. Furthermore, it is really not about literary forms at all.[26]

Inevitably, the interlocutors of *Politics and Letters* (1979) engage with the definition of the structure of feeling. And Williams genially admits that he has himself "never been happy" with the term, even as he defends it for its suitability to the "actual conventions of literary or dramatic writing" rather than for its "theoretical satisfaction."[27] Again, there is a fine line between a reasonable emphasis on the generic features of literary writing, those that are "quite internal to the work," and a less defensible literary exceptionalism, in the traditional literary-critical manner. Nor is the case assisted by the blurring between the formal-literary and general ideological data that constitute "examples" of the structure of feeling. Under pressure from his interviewers Williams concedes the descriptive ambiguity of his various uses of the phrase, but his attempt to address it only resurrects one of the fundamental problems. He proposes that "the peculiar location of a structure of feeling is the endless comparison that must occur in the process of consciousness between the articulated and the lived." What we might choose to call ideology—the articulated— is constantly under pressure from discordant elements in exemplary personal experience. Here Williams not only sidesteps any response to the critical commonplace that specifies the articulated nature of *all* descriptions of what is lived, but also fails to make clear how we are to establish that such contradictions are in fact "pre-emergent," indications of a social formation about to take form, rather than simply idiosyncratic or arbitrary. It would seem that the only way to make the concept work would be to insist that the structure of feeling define *only* something in the past, something that we know, with the wisdom of hindsight, to have been pre-emergent. But yet, because the conditions for judging pre-emergence are so dominantly literary, we still have to worry about the danger of disciplinary tautology, whereby certain forms are read as historically significant just because later writers used them, without any testing assessment at any point in the process of what a general history might be.[28]

The degree to which the structure of feeling is *not* articulated to the point of "theoretical satisfaction," despite its deployment throughout twenty years of major critical work, suggests a strong resistance to such theorization. It is at once central and vague, an insistence on "something beyond" the extant debate, without any exact address to the terms of that debate, or any allusion to its arguable cognates—for instance, to Macherey's important emphasis on contradiction as the normative literary embodiment of ideology. Eagleton is right to pronounce that much of the time the structure of feeling is just another name for ideology.[29] By avoiding the obvious association, Williams avoids also the debate about it, and thus permits himself an untroubled foundational rhetoric that either cannot be theoretically factored out, or can be so factored only by adding in missing links and crucial limitations. All in all, the structure of feeling is a symptom of Williams's vocalic idealism, or faith in the resonance of the voice, so that it fails to embody itself fully in literary *forms* (as it occasionally promised to do), and always remains content to appeal for verification to what is supposedly "lived and felt."

The emphasis on the personal and the particular that informs Williams's investment in the voice, and in structures of feeling, is of course itself a familiar professional (de)formation peculiar to literary critics: show us the rule, and we will show you the exception. Chris Baldick has remarked on the compulsiveness of Williams's insistence "on the need for specificity, in the most unspecific manner."[30] It is as if Williams played out a ritual of self-inscription into the society of hypervigilant literary-critical intelligences, those who seemingly have to keep on proving that they see more finely, more sensitively, and more humanely than others. This professional disposition favoring the individual against the system, if such it be, could only have been enhanced by Williams's (very reasonable) disillusionment with the Labour Party, and with all prospects of achieving worthwhile change by working through orthodox political channels. The commitment to "unique individuals, in real relationships,"[31] is at once the power and the paucity of Williams's work. As a corrective to any tendency toward theoreticism, toward a forgetting of the practical implications and applications of any formally systematic paradigm, Williams's work, his *voice*, can function as an urgent blast of the trumpet, the louder for being so softly "spoken." But because such reminders are dependent upon the very evolution of events in historical time and place, because they have to remain occasional, they cannot themselves be theorized. His voice is thus the voice of a conscience, of our conscience. The degree to which Williams's invocations of actual men and women in "lived experience" remain unspecified and beyond prediction is also the degree to which they are available for incarnation within the minds of latter-day readers, who must ask themselves constantly when reading Williams, "Am I missing something, someone, somewhere?" and "What would this mean to person A, or for person B?" Williams's

legacy becomes in this way a distinctly moral, ethical one, an attention to the problems of any passage from the theoretical cup to the
practical lip, even as he does not himself predict the outcome of that
problem.

The Country and the City is very moving in its invocation of personal memories, and in its deliberate naming of the otherwise mute
and inglorious agricultural workers whose labor made possible the
literary modalities of the pastoral. Though these persons, so deliberately designated *as* persons, can never be known to us, they are
voiced by Williams as incantations bidding us to think upon the persons we do know and have known, and they can be powerfully effective in that way. If we look to Williams's argument for a worked-
out incorporation of these personal signifiers into a *theorized* or
unperformative syndrome relating the personal and the historical,
we will, however, mostly be disappointed. All too often these affirmations and identifications work to head off any reflection of the
sort that is now widely held to be obligatory for a fuller historical argument conducted at the level of theory. And the appetite for immediacy seems to have led Williams himself into sympathies that he
might otherwise not have defended. He confessed to a strong personal empathy even for Edmund Burke,[32] and the two figures he
chose to report on at length were Cobbett and Orwell, both outsiders, both enemies of "the system" (a usage that Cobbett, indeed,
may well have invented). Orwell's compulsive exceptionalism is indeed critiqued, but Cobbett's is not demystified: he remains, for
Williams, "the last authentic English radical."[33] In the case of Carlyle
also, in *Culture and Society,* idiosyncrasy becomes for Williams almost a virtue in itself, so powerful is his desire to register the value
of the individual voice.

Uniqueness and individuality, the integrity of the single voice, are
as important to Williams's political agenda as they are to his literary
and cultural criticism. As early as *The Long Revolution* he announced "individual uniqueness" as the rationale for a politics, "the
permanent basis of the case for democracy as a system of government." The indifference of the political parties to this permanent
basis led him to note acerbically, in *The Year 2000,* that "all significant social movements of the last thirty years have started outside
the organised class interests and institutions," a fact that brought
him, visibly, to a postparty politics: in "the making of many so-

cialisms" there would be "an absolute refusal of overriding national and international bodies which do not derive their specified powers directly from the participation and negotiation of actual self-governing societies."[34] There is a linkage, as one would expect, between the literary criticism and the general political agenda. As, in the structure of feeling, the barely perceptible tremor of original sensibility emerges, finally, into an achieved social formation, from self to others, so, in the political arena, the initiatives of different interest groups ("communities") should emerge, uncoerced, into a society of mutual tolerance and cooperation. If the problems of the structure of feeling are largely epistemological, those of the political ideal are practical: how to convert this admirable ethics (how things should be) to a recognition of how they are, and of how (without terrible violence) they might be made otherwise.

The linkage of the literary and the political is incipient, though never specified, in an interesting moment in *Politics and Letters*, where Williams remarks that any long revolution must require a short revolution to put it in place. Here he emphasizes the importance of a training period, a "considerable process of preparation" necessary to ensure that the short revolution does not produce merely ephemeral results. Here one might imagine that art and literature, with their capacity for sensing the pre-emergent and for representing it in structures of feeling, might have an important role to play in bringing to consciousness the about-to-be movements of history. Williams does not say this, here, but he implied something like it in *The Long Revolution*, where he declared that "dramatic forms have a real social history, in prospect as well as in retrospect," as a "major and practical index of change and creator of consciousness."[35]

The emphasis on the voice, and on the feeling that redesigns the structure, does not in my view produce methodologically precise paradigms for literary or cultural analysis, for the reasons I have already suggested. The primary appeal is to the conscience, and to the possibility for a future method, always to be rendered within specific place and time. Even the promising association between literary form and pre-emergent social formations is too hortatory, too reliant upon an assumed relation between art and general history, and too marked by literary exceptionalism to stand as a way of solving problems about the description of past literatures in relation to culture and history. This was, finally and despite appearances, not really Williams's vocation and perhaps not even his task. The value of his lifelong and deeply serious warnings against the dangers of abstraction and unlocalized theory is a strongly presentist one, and one can respond to it without necessarily endorsing the particular remedies he himself proposed for the contemporary condition. He seems to have felt these abstractionist tendencies around him all the time, in both political and academic life, and that feeling of alienation from the theoretical mainstream surely had the effect of inhibiting him from taking account of those creative initiatives in the European tradition—one thinks of Benjamin, of Adorno, of Sartre, of Macherey, among others—that were also concerned with the investigation of his own major *theoretical* question: that concerning the relation of the personal and the historical.

In the elaboration of this question, he maintained a commitment to what is usually called totality: "I would then define the theory of culture as the study of relationships between elements in a whole way of life." But the wholeness, as I have said, is almost always deduced from a few parts, and literary parts at that. His critics have trenchantly pronounced that "it is not possible to work back from texts to structures of feeling to experiences to social structures."[36] But, with totality as much under attack as it is at the present time, it continues to be important to look at Williams's attempts to approach it, which we may characterize as the vitalist-empathic alternative to the more familiar theoretical-analytical paradigms of the European tradition. Throughout Williams's work there is a sustained effort to describe a relation between the individual and the general, which he seems to feel as the major problem of both theory and politics. It is there in *The Long Revolution*, in the extended discussion "Individuals and Societies," and it is the topic of some of the most interesting of his later reflections.[37] In one of his last reviews he wrote of the need for "a model of self-accounting" that would show the general in the particular, effecting a conjunction of the "true generalities of class formation" with the range of specificities indicated by family, community, occupation, gender, education, and sheer idiosyncrasy.[38] If the task be one of working as many particular details as possible into a (generative and residual) model of historical determination, with an aspiration toward the recognition of totalities on non-a priori principles, then Williams's work will remain important for the roads both taken and not taken. Voices must always remain unheard until they speak, and disrupt what can otherwise only be an imagining. If the voice be indeed the vital component in Williams's message for us now, then it by definition must function as the reminder of an incompletion, a something outside whatever theoretical closure we sense we are about to achieve. As such, it is the element of *ongoing* history in all history, the admission of which must always take us forward to an unpredictable future. For me, this explains the odd effect of Williams's lifework, which remains unignorable even as it cannot be held within a closed theoretical framework that we can attribute to him. If we still hear him, then it may be because saying itself was a large part of what he came to say. That very insight, positive as it sounds, must still itself be held open to critique. For is not the appeal of the voice itself a symptom of a reaction against modernity, against the unignorable conditions of what we call *writing*; that is, the conditions of dispersal and complexity, temporal and spatial, within which we live so much of our lives? Or is this so principally in theory, and pondered principally in theory, thus causing us to forget the unremembered acts, kind and unkind, of the daily life in which we all significantly subsist? Because *this* is an urgent question, Williams's voice remains resonant. And we will still hear it, even as we cannot resist calling for a history that is, among other things, a history of voices.

NOTES

1. Raymond Williams, *Keywords: A Vocabulary of Culture and Society*, rev. ed. (New York: Oxford University Press, 1983), p. 148.

2. John Higgins, "Raymond Williams and the Problem of Ideology," in *Postmodernism and Politics*, ed. Jonathan Arac (Minneapolis: University of Minnesota Press, 1986), p. 112.

3. Terry Eagleton, *Criticism and Ideology: A Study in Marxist Literary Theory* (1976; reprint, London: Verso, 1980), p. 23.

4. Terry Eagleton, "Resources for a Journey of Hope," *New Left Review*, no. 168 (1988): 10.

5. Eagleton, "Resources," p. 10; Peter Cadogan, letter to the *London Review of Books*, April 5, 1990, p. 4.

6. Raymond Williams, *Cobbett* (Oxford and New York: Oxford University Press, 1983), p. 44.

7. Williams, *Cobbett*, pp. 69, 55.

8. Raymond Williams, "Literature and Sociology: In Memory of Lucien Goldmann" (1971), in *Problems in Materialism and Culture: Selected Essays* (1980; reprint, London: Verso, 1982), pp. 11-12.

9. Williams, *Problems in Materialism and Culture*, pp. 13-14.

10. Eagleton, *Criticism and Ideology*, pp. 22, 25, 27, 32. I refer of course to Thompson's essay "The Poverty of Theory or an Orrery of Errors," first published in 1978; see *The Poverty of Theory and Other Essays* (New York and London: Monthly Review Press, 1978), pp. 1–210. Williams at this time endorsed the need for theoretical work, but without much specifying the debate in terms of proper names. *Marxism and Literature* may be read as his response.

11. See, convincingly, Terry Eagleton, "Base and Superstructure in Raymond Williams," in *Raymond Williams: Critical Perspectives*, ed. Terry Eagleton (Boston: Northeastern University Press, 1989), pp. 165–75; and Eagleton, *Criticism and Ideology*, p. 42.

12. Jan Gorak, *The Alien Mind of Raymond Williams* (Columbia: University of Missouri Press, 1988), pp. 12, 44.

13. Stuart Hall, "Politics and Letters," in Eagleton, ed., *Raymond Williams: Critical Perspectives*, p. 60.

14. Raymond Williams, *Culture and Society, 1780-1950* (1958; reprint, Harmondsworth: Penguin, 1971), pp. 85–86, 99, 119.

15. Raymond Williams, *The Long Revolution* (1961; reprint, Harmondsworth: Penguin, 1965), p. 8.

16. Ibid., pp. 63–64, 51–52, 64, 65.

17. Ibid., pp. 66, 70, 80.

18. Ibid., pp. 80, 84, 85.

19. Raymond Williams, *Modern Tragedy* (Stanford, Calif.: Stanford University Press, 1966), pp. 18, 21, 28, 87.

20. Raymond Williams, *Drama from Ibsen to Brecht* (London: Chatto and Windus, 1968), pp. 17, 19.

21. Raymond Williams, *The English Novel from Dickens to Lawrence* (New York: Oxford University Press, 1970), pp. 59, 138, 192.

22. Ibid., p. 122.

23. Williams, *Problems in Materialism and Culture*, pp. 24–25, 26.

24. See, for example, Raymond Williams, *The Country and the City* (1973; reprint, St. Albans: Paladin, 1975), pp. 80, 89, 114.

25. Raymond Williams, *Marxism and Literature* (1977; reprint, New York: Oxford University Press, 1978). See, for example, p. 6: "This book is not a separated work of theory. . . . Every position in it was developed from the detailed practical work that I have previously undertaken." Williams's fetishization of the vocabulary of "practical work" is a reproduction of British-Baconian methodological inductivism as well as an obvious fantasy identification with the artisan or working class.

26. Ibid., pp. 126, 24, 25, 130–34. The images of solution and precipitation are taken on from *Drama from Ibsen to Brecht*, p. 18.

27. *Politics and Letters: Interviews with New Left Review* (1979; reprint, London: Verso, 1981), p. 159.

28. Ibid., pp. 164, 168.

29. Eagleton, *Criticism and Ideology*, p. 33

30. Chris Baldick, "An Extending Humanism," *Times Literary Supplement*, November 3-9, 1989, p. 1205.

31. Williams, *Long Revolution*, p. 48.

32. Williams, *Politics and Letters*, pp. 121–22.

33. Raymond Williams, *The Year 2000* (New York: Pantheon, 1983), p. 185.

34. Williams, *Long Revolution*, p. 117; *Year 2000*, pp. 172, 198.

35. Williams, *Politics and Letters*, p. 421; *Long Revolution*, p. 299.

36. Williams, *Long Revolution*, p. 63; *Politics and Letters*, p. 170.

37. Williams, *Long Revolution*, pp. 89-119. See also, among others, *Problems in Materialism and Culture*, pp. 103, 114-16; and *Marxism and Literature*, pp. 192-98.

38. Raymond Williams, "Desire," in *What I Came to Say* (London: Hutchinson, 1989), p. 31.

A Gendered History of Cultural Categories
Morag Shiach

We can overcome division only by refusing to be divided.[1]

Feminists can find much of use to them in the work of Raymond Williams; they cannot, however, find many women. Williams's methodology of historical semantics, his insistence on complexity in the analysis of social forces and developments, his refusal to be placed by the texts and definitions of the dominant culture all speak to women who are trying to reformulate historical categories and to resist the obviousness of textual meanings, but they do not speak *about* women. This sort of division leaves feminist critics in an uncomfortable, although familiar, position: terms and arguments that have been blind to gender and to the sexual division of labor nonetheless seem inescapable elements for our own critique. Julia Swindells and Lisa Jardine have described the same division, analyzing

> what has allowed the Left . . . to continue to address a constituency
> exclusively made up of labouring men, in spite of insistent demands
> from other groups (notably women) who recognize *themselves* as be-
> longing with the Left.[2]

In relation to Williams's work, however, the demands have been far from insistent. Instead, his work mostly has been greeted with silence by feminist critics and historians. Even where the theoretical influence seems most undeniable, as in Juliet Mitchell's "Women: The Longest Revolution," there is no detailed discussion of his work. None of the key texts of socialist-feminist analysis of the seventies and eighties has anything to say about Williams, although his work lay behind many of the concepts and techniques of left historical and cultural critique in this period. Looking through a series of texts from this period, the silence is eerie, though whether it is polite or angry is hard to tell.

The lack of sustained feminist critique leaves its mark on Williams's own writing. When he is challenged about the neglect of "problems of women and the family" (a problematic formulation to which I will return) in his work, Williams expresses only a sense of confusion:

> The women's liberation movement has been entirely right to raise the transitional demand of payment for housework, or—something I feel very strongly about—for mothers of young children who are incredibly hard worked and who are really neglected today because there is no profit to the social order from them. . . . These are the kinds of contradiction within the very real process of liberation that I would have tried to analyse. I wish I had done so in *The Long Revolution*, and I also wish I understood what prevented me from doing so, because it wasn't that I was not thinking about the question.[3]

His response to the late-eighties question "What about the women?" is significantly more defensive, but offers little more substance. He refers his readers to his novels, which do indeed deal with historical developments and conflicts within the family, and to his brief analysis of the work of women novelists such as Elizabeth Gaskell and Emily Brontë in relation to the construction of gender:

> I know this was the moment in admitted social life and in fiction when men stopped weeping and it is exactly the same moment as the emergence of that remarkable generation of women novelists.[4]

As Williams's own work shows us, such absence, confusion, and defensiveness points not to oversight, or to accidental neglect, but to real structural problems. This was certainly the conclusion arrived at by Juliet Mitchell in 1966 when she wrote about the ways in which left thought seemed to have given up on engagement with the social and economic history of women. Mitchell insisted that this phenomenon was not explicable in psychological or moralistic terms but had, rather, to be referred to deeper structural causes.[5] Her attempt to do this led her to a recognition of the recalcitrance of the concepts of "production" and "economic base" with respect to the history and the structural role of women. Production and economic base were also two of the key concepts to which Williams turned his theoretical attention in the seventies, but his analysis did not engage with the significance of these terms for a theorization of the structural role of women in the social formation.

The evidence of noncommunication at this point becomes unsettling and leads us to ponder the parallel theoretical projects demonstrated by Carol Watts in her article "Reclaiming the Border Country: Feminism and the Work of Raymond Williams."[6] This article was the first to break the uneasy silence of feminist critics about the details and implications of Williams's political and cultural project. Watts sets out to examine some of the major theoretical and methodological innovations of Williams's work and argues that they overlap at many points with questions being posed from within feminism. Thus Watts stresses Williams's recognition of the importance of "the new social movements" to the building of a socialist politics; his critique of the adequacy of an abstract concept of production (as opposed to the recognition of the complex relations between forces of production and reproduction within any social formation); his cultural materialism as a mode for the analysis of economic and ideological structures; and, finally, his remarks on the reifications of contemporary culture represented by the massive increase in pornography. Watts argues that these initiatives mirror, but can also illuminate, key areas of socialist feminism, in particular the analysis of the structural role of domestic labor within a capitalist economy and the competing claims of the economic and the ideological as the founding bases of the oppression of women.

Having begun with the rumored absence of women in Williams's work, Watts goes on to argue that much of the material necessary for a feminist critique of contemporary social relations is "in fact *already* there" (89). If this is true, however, it is so only in a very provisional way. At many levels the absences remain both more striking and more compelling. These at least seem to be what lie behind Jane Miller's sense of frustration when she asks:

> Why should a thinker who was throughout his life prepared to revisit and rethink absolutely central tenets of Marxism be so unwilling to countenance even the questions which feminists have addressed to Marxism?[7]

Miller is struck by the absence in Williams's writing of women as active agents, as producers or transmitters of culture. She also writes about the ways in which marriage as an institution seems to escape Williams's more general recognition of the profound links between economic and emotional structures and argues that Williams fails to recognize the ways in which gender can complicate class identities. Finally, in a fascinating reading of Williams's fiction, she demonstrates how its narratives of social change, of modernism, and of the development of politicized identities find their roots in D. H. Lawrence's gendered imaginary of authenticity, exile, and the threats of fragmentation. For Miller, these recognitions produce a kind of impasse, which is registered in terms of an intense emotional response: "the simultaneous admiration, rebelliousness, affection, rage, regret and resentment Williams and his work provoke in me" (63).

Thus Watts and Miller offer two very different responses to Williams: one claiming that his importance for feminism is "already there" in the texts, the other expressing anger and disappointment about the absence of women as active historical agents in the work of such an important and innovative Marxist critic. Clearly, different questions are being asked. One set of questions tends to underestimate the difficulty of moving from parallel theoretical projects to sustained synthesis, while the other creates an impasse of frustration and anger. We need to understand both the aspirations and the disappointments that lie behind these responses before it will be possible to look again at the legacy of his work for the project of socialist feminism.

The theorization of this double response lies behind much of Swindells and Jardine's *What's Left?*, which probes the terms in which the British left constructed its metaphorical and historical understanding of class in the sixties and seventies. For Swindells and Jardine, the difficulty for any feminist appropriation of the terms of these debates and analyses lies in the ways in which they place women resolutely within the family. Looking at key texts by George Orwell or William Morris, and at critiques of them in the work of E. P. Thompson or Raymond Williams, Swindells and Jardine argue that women are placed consistently within the sphere of the domestic, providing a kind of moral grounding for the narratives of male working-class identity, and are thus removed from "the landscape of class, poverty, and struggle" (13). Certainly, the domestic is the space of women in Williams's fiction, and any movement away from this space is seen as a move away from authenticity and class identity.[8] Also, his recognition of the legitimacy of feminist rewritings of key historical narratives is shaped by his identification of the feminist project as a kind of moralism.

Thus, Williams's 1983 review of Barbara Taylor's *Eve and the New Jerusalem,* entitled "The New Morality," equates the complex history of nineteenth-century feminism discussed by Taylor with "certain moral ideas of socialism."[9] The importance of Taylor's project is acknowledged, and the inadequacy of the earlier accounts of labor history, "so oriented to the organisations of male workers and male voters," is recognized. Yet Williams's account here still leaves women outside "labor" and suggests that their history is to be found instead in the complexity of thinking and of practice around "the family." The same location of women outside the space of the working class can be found in "Towards Many Socialisms" (1985), where Williams discusses the need for pluralism within the socialist project, saying:

> Significant numbers of people are outside this class, in its ordinary residual terms, without in any predetermined way being its enemies. This is evident in the sexual division of labour, now being so widely challenged.[10]

Thus, the sexual division of labor is placed outside the "ordinary residual terms" of the working class. The problems this raises become clearer in Williams's 1986 review of Carolyn Steedman's autobiographical exploration of her own history and that of her working-class mother, *Landscape for a Good Woman.*[11] Here Williams once more recognizes the force of Steedman's critique of available versions of working-class consciousness and describes her writing as a challenge to "a masculine mode" (32). He cannot, however, recognize the book as a necessary and gendered development of available mythologies or narratives of class identity, but sees it rather as a threat to the integrity of a socialist project. He warns of its possible association with

> the now rampant politics of the Right, which seeks to substitute such individually-shaped desires for the difficult practices of common and sharing provision. (34)

This feels like a double bind: women can reenter history only through the family, but exploration of the politcal consequences of such a constricted space threatens to take women away from a recognizable narrative of class and toward the fetishism of "desire" (33).

For Swindells and Jardine, the placing of women within the space of the domestic, within reproduction rather than production, represents a problem for feminist theory and practice—a problem not just of exclusion but of a wide range of concepts that are blind to their own gendered history. This analysis may provide us with some clearer understanding of why the parallel theoretical projects identified by Watts, with Williams's work appearing to shadow so closely many of the concerns of feminism, have not so far produced any sustained synthesis of his work within the context of a feminist critique.

Watts begins her reading of Williams by drawing attention to his emphasis on "the centrality of human reproduction and nurture in relation to production" (89). Here she is alluding to a number of articles in which Williams challenges the adequacy of the abstract category of production, which he argues has been conflated with the determining "base" of the social formation within Marxist theory.[12] The difficulty is to connect this critique in a nonreductive way with the project of feminism. The point is that a move to "nurture" or to "reproduction" cannot deliver a feminist politics if these concepts simply become a metaphor for the historical identities of women. The move to nurture is not a move to where women are, but a move to where people are; the notion of a production that excluded such dimensions and practices was always, as Williams himself recognizes, profoundly false, an "abstraction." Of course, as an important qualification, women have been placed within the space of reproduction and nurture in much greater numbers than men, but that historical fact should not overdetermine the categories of our social analyses.

So a socialist feminism cannot consist simply in the addition of the domestic, of reproduction, or of nurture to an already existing set of theoretical concepts and legitimizing narratives. If women are to enter into the complexity of historical relations, the understandings of class, and of production need to be transformed. Williams certainly does offer resources for such a project since he recognizes the inadequacy of the existing concepts: *Marxism and Literature* is an extended and sustained critique of the existing terms of Marxist social and cultural analysis. Yet this is never connected in his work to a recognition of women as part of a class identity and history. The conceptual broadening that Williams advocates starts with the male worker within production and opens out:

> From castles and palaces and churches to prisons and workhouses and schools; from weapons of war to a controlled press; any ruling class, in variable ways though always materially, produces a social and political order.[13]

In other words, the understanding of production is extended to include the material production of cultural forms, but the gendered history of the concept remains unchallenged. As we have seen, even such a broadening out leaves the spatial metaphor of class identity relatively intact, with women "outside" the working class. Thus Williams cannot respond, except by offering generalized support, to the articulations of Marxist feminism. He can recognize the objective importance of new social movements but cannot see them as in any sense internal to his own class project.

Thus the division in the responses of feminist critics to his work: some respond to what they feel ought to be its implications, others respond with frustration and anger to what it does not say. If we are to move beyond these two responses, each in its own way potentially paralyzing, we need to recognize that, whatever the importance and the potential of Williams's work for feminism, feminist critique is not already there. Nor is his work rendered irrelevant to feminism by the absence of women in so many of his narratives and analyses. Instead, we need to place his theoretical and methodological insights in relation to particular questions and problems that have emerged from within the sphere of feminist critique. Williams's work will not simply deliver a feminist politics, but it may help in the difficult political and theoretical task of developing a feminist analysis of the role of gender in the construction and maintenance of the contemporary social formation.

> *The analytic categories, as so often in idealist thought, have, almost unnoticed, become substantive descriptions.*[14]

One of the most characteristic and most theoretically productive elements of Williams's writing is his use of "keywords" as a means to investigate the relations between changing historical structures and changing critical and cultural vocabularies. Williams insists that "no generation speaks quite the same language as its predecessors."[15] Each historical period can be associated with a certain "structure of feeling," a concept that has much in common with the Foucaldian "episteme" but seeks to historicize emotional as well as cognitive frameworks. The structure of feeling of a particular period refers to the terms in which it is possible to understand social reality, or to posit the possibility of change; it describes the characteristic fears, desires, and blindnesses of the period. This is not a static or mono-lithic concept, since there are competing structures of feeling in any period. It does, however, allow Williams to connect cultural vocabu-lary and literary form with the pressures of developing historical forces. The most condensed version of Williams's attempt to iden-tify changing structures of feeling in the changing vocabulary of so-cial and cultural criticism can be found in his *Keywords: A Vocabu-lary of Culture and Society* (1976), but the technique is widespread throughout his writing.

Williams's attention to historical semantics serves as a means to open up the changing meanings of a given term, and thus to chal-lenge the obviousness of contemporary meanings or associations.[16] As such, it is a technique that seems to have much to offer feminism, since feminism often has to begin by confronting the limitations or presuppositions of existing theoretical or critical vocabularies. I would like to explore in the rest of this essay the ways in which Williams's historical semantics might be read in the context of femi-nist debates about a couple of key terms in cultural analysis—"mass culture" and "literature"—and also the terms that might need to be added to Williams's keywords to produce a "vocabulary of culture and society" that could address the significance of gender in the shaping of social and individual identities.

Williams identified the problematic nature of the concept of mass culture first of all in *Culture and Society* (1958). The conclusion is a critique of theories that see in modernization and democratization, in increased literacy and expanded education, the inevitable terms of a cultural decline. The main enemy here seems to be T. S. Eliot, whose *Notes Towards the Definition of Culture* (1948) insisted that the preservation of significant culture depended on social hierarchy and on minority access to an extended education. Williams lays out the history of the concept of culture throughout *Culture and Society*, showing how this term with its complex set of potentially oppositional meanings has come to be associated with a very specific and narrow set of social practices. His aim here is political: "The working out of the idea of culture is a slow reach again for control."[17] He then moves more explicitly toward the social attitudes and assumptions embedded in the concept of mass culture, arguing that "there are in fact no masses; there are only ways of seeing people as masses" (289).

Williams argues that the category of mass culture is the result of an abstraction that always places this assumed space of manipulation and inauthenticity "out there": "the masses are always the others, whom we don't know and can't know" (289). He is, of course, aware that the development of the concept is a response to real social change: to the growth of urban populations; to the employment of large numbers of workers in factories; and to the development of cheap and widely accessible forms of mass-produced entertainment.[18] What he aims to challenge is the automatic assumption that such changes imply a cultural decline.

The point, as ever, is complex. Mass culture is a response to major social changes and dislocations, but it is also a misrecognition. It proposes the reduction of significant numbers within the social formation to a level of passivity and manipulation that renders them politically irrelevant, if not positively dangerous. Williams captures the difficulty of the concept as follows:

> The version of the ordinary people as masses is not only the conscious creation of the élites (who work very hard at it, by the way). It is also a conclusion from actual experience within the forms of a society which requires the existence of masses.[19]

The point is that the concept of "the masses" corresponds to a need within developed capitalism for an alienated and fragmented workforce. Thus its apparent "obviousness" as a description of contemporary social and cultural experience. In *The Politics of Modernism*, Williams returns to the concept of mass culture, seeing it as the product of a dislocated and uprooted intelligentsia:

> The early Frankfurt School in Germany . . . had genuinely found . . . new and penetrating methods of formal-historical analysis. . . . The work of Benjamin, early Adorno, Löwenthal and others was a striking

advance, which cannot be cancelled by—though it has to be separated from—the eventual and enclosing, even self-cancelling theorization of its survivors, in radically changed and dislocating social and historical situations: their strange reinstatement of the autonomy of art in what was in effect the ending of significant history by the development of what they called 'mass society.'[20]

In both instances, then, Williams recognizes the social forces that produce this abstraction of social relations and cultural forms into the category "mass." What he seeks to do is to challenge the overdetermined obviousness of the concept, and to argue that mass culture is only one way of seeing, or of theorizing, the cultural relations of the modern capitalist state.

Mass culture emerges in *Culture and Society* as "a central and very difficult issue which more than any other needs revision" (287). His aim is to replace the "bad fiction of our second-rate social analysts" with a detailed account of changes in the material production of culture and their relation to developments in other forms of material production and of social organization.[21] He aims to unsettle the category, to reveal the assumptions about social relations that govern its use.

In this critique of the concept of mass culture, Williams prefigures more recent feminist analyses of its significance as part of a negative imaginary of femininity as debased and corrupting. He also offers a historically grounded, detailed account of the connections between such discursive categories and social relations of power and domination, which could perhaps provide the means to move feminist critique beyond the recognition of the metaphorical association of mass culture and the feminine, and toward a more extended analysis of the importance of gender in the constitution of institutions and practices of cultural production.

The metaphorical association of mass culture with the feminine was recognized by Andreas Huyssen in *After the Great Divide*.[22] Huyssen set out in this book to explore the links between the self-constitution of modernism, with its commitment to autonomy, linguistic experimentation, and self-referentiality, and the simultaneous demarcation and exclusion of texts and practices deemed to be corrupting in their banality. In this context, it is perhaps not surprising that T. S. Eliot should emerge as such a crucial figure in the constitution of a critical consensus that sets the terms for anxieties about the addictive and destructive properties of mass culture. Huyssen goes on to argue that this "great divide" between the aesthetic and mass culture was articulated in terms of a metaphorical association of the devalued term with the feminine.

Such a claim can be supported by attention to a broad range of writers and cultural critics. Thus, Henry James, when he seeks to represent the corrupting and aesthetically demeaning effects of an expanded readership for the novel, creates the character of Mrs. Highmore, a popular novelist who is comfortable with her recognition that it is "the age of trash triumphant."[23] She is contrasted throughout James's story with the character of Ralph Limbert, the artist who is incapable of shaping his ideas and his style according to the demands of a popular audience. The absolute disjunction between these two types is reinforced by the voice of the narrator, an unsuccessful critic who endorses the power of the aesthetic and charts with apparent fascination the constant threat to artistic integrity represented by women and domesticity. Mrs. Highmore does not simply write bad fiction for mercenary reasons, but rather writes in a popular and debased style as a result of "intuition." She thus comes to be identified with the social meanings of mass culture, unable to escape despite her desire to write at least one "serious" book that would not make money. Ralph, on the other hand, proves constitutionally incapable of being anything other than an artist, and when the economic and emotional pressures of domesticity, of a wife with "her babies and her headaches," threaten this pure state he is rather unceremoniously killed off.

If James's concern here is with the threat to the (male) individual subject represented by a rampant and feminized mass culture, subsequent critics have stressed the social meanings and implications of such a threat. The dangers of totalitarianism represented by the erosion of a critical aesthetic sphere certainly motivated Adorno's prolonged critique of the politically damaging effects of the development of what he called "the culture industry," or mass culture. Adorno's analysis of the cultural and social significance of the development of technologies of mass communication has been profoundly influential in the development of media studies, and the adequacy of his analyses of particular cultural forms has been much debated. What has received much less attention, however, is the sexual politics of his metaphorical invocation of the qualities of mass culture.

Thus, in "The Schema of Mass Culture," for example, Adorno says: "In its [own] mirror mass culture is always the fairest in the land."[24] This is surely a debased form of the self-referentiality of the aesthetic, with mass culture preening itself with all the blindness, egotism, and violence of a fairy-tale witch. Adorno goes on to ascribe to mass culture "the sense of order characteristic of a dominant housewife" (59) and to suggest that in its falsity and its deceptiveness "mass culture is unadorned make-up" (67). In each of these terms we find the mobilization of a cliché of femininity and its association with deception, threat, and superficiality, which serves to add a psychic charge to the terms of Adorno's analysis of social and cultural change. If we add to this T. S. Eliot's remark that "totalitarianism appeals to the desire to return to the womb," we can begin to see the outlines of a sexualized theory of social and cultural forms that equates femininity with the political dangers of mass culture.[25]

The recognition of such sexualized metaphors certainly suggests that feminists have a stake in challenging the obviousness of the category of mass culture and its associated meanings. It does not, however, tell us very much about why mass culture came to be associated with femininity in this negative sort of way. It may be that any significant discursive hierarchy tends to gender the devalued or lower term *feminine.* It may also be that within a patriarchal culture, all social developments that are perceived as a threat to the integrity of the individual (male) subject are associated with the feminine. This would certainly help to make sense of Christine Buci-Glucksmann's argument the feminine emerges as an allegory of the modern in the late nineteenth century.[26] If we want to claim any more significant connection between mass culture and the feminine, however, we need to move beyond the recognition of metaphorical ascription and toward a historical reading of the role of women and the importance of gender in the cultural transformations of the late nineteenth and early twentieth centuries.

Such a move is certainly facilitated by Williams's methodologies of cultural materialism. Williams offers models for the reading of historical change and its cultural meanings, which acknowledge structures of power (through the concept of hegemony) without denying their social and subjective complexity.[27] This kind of move can also be found in the work of Patrice Petro, whose analysis of the history of cinema in Weimar Germany sets out to connect metaphorical ascriptions of femininity with the "high percentage of women in early film audiences [which] was in fact perceived as an alarming social phenomenon."[28] In other words, she tries to understand the development of analytic categories in a way that acknowledges the importance of gender, but does not allow it to be reduced to metaphor. Her aim is "to explore the ways in which modernity was experienced differently by women" (71).

It is important to acknowledge once more, however, that such a project cannot be derived from Williams's work without a modification of his historical narratives in the light of feminist theoretical and historical work. This is perhaps particularly necessary in connection with the concept of modernity, which became the focus of much of Williams's work in the 1980s. The politics of modernism was, arguably, central to Williams's writing from the 1950s, when his engagement with Eliot and Leavis amounted to a contestation of their equation of industrialization and democratization with cultural decline. In the eighties, however, Williams turned his attention to aesthetic modernism, assessing its claims for radicalism.[29] This project was apparently shaped by his conviction that there was a continuity between the abstract forms of aesthetic modernism and what he saw as the damaging abstractions of much contemporary literary theory. In both cases he detected a kind of accommodation, a critique that remained internal to the bourgeoisie and accepted too many of the terms and pratices of the dominant culture.

What is striking about Williams's version of modernism, however, is that it consists almost entirely of male-authored texts. Criticizing the received canon of modernism—Proust, Kafka, Joyce—Williams suggests instead "Mayakovsky, Picasso, Silone, Brecht, . . . D'Annunzio, Marinetti, Wyndham Lewis, Ezra Pound."[30] The modification is aimed at foregrounding the political ambiguity of the modernist project, but it offers no insight into "the ways in which modernity was experienced differently by women." This is important because the historical period Williams is analyzing here is crucial to an understanding of the role and meaning of gender in the twentieth century. The emergence of the concept of feminism in the 1890s, the development of psychoanalysis, the growth of the suffrage movement, and the opening up of higher education to women are all part of the

phenomenon of modernity, and part of the meanings that are nego-
tiated within "modernism." Recognition of this might serve to connect Williams's analysis of critiques of the family with his observation that

> at the same time the claims of human liberation, against forms of prop-
> erty and other economic controls, are being more widely made, and in-
> creasingly—for that is the irony of even the first phase—by women.[31]

The political demands of women at this period need to be articulated in terms other than ironical juxtaposition to a male-authored
critique: they need to be seen as part of the project and practices of
modernism. Similarly, Williams's analysis of "The Bloomsbury Fraction," in many ways an exemplary account of the social roots and
meanings of a particular cultural moment, identifies the limitations
of the Bloomsbury project in terms of "social conscience" and the
centrality of the "civilized individual."[32] This analysis is based very
largely on the career and writings of Leonard Woolf, and it has very
little to say about the women members of the Bloomsbury group.
Again, more attention to the experiences and writings of these
women might have served to modify Williams's account. For example, Williams does not mention Virginia Woolf's advocacy, in *Three
Guineas*, of a Society of Outsiders: an organization of women in opposition to fascism that seems to recognize very clearly the limits of
individualism and of social conscience.

   That the historical and theoretical analysis of the concept of mass
culture takes us to the center of questions of power, political change,
and cultural authority is a measure of Williams's insight in his identification of the "keywords" of contemporary social discourse. The
same centrality and importance for feminist critique can be identified in other terms with which Williams engages, such as *nature, the
family, public/private, equality, sensibility*, and *man*. I would, however, like briefly to discuss one more term that seems to raise central
issues for feminist cultural critique: the category of "literature."

   Williams identifies the contemporary meanings of literature as
the result of a long history of exclusion and of separation. He shows
how the term shifts from an association with classicism and learning
to an identification of texts that are deemed to express or to contain
an "imaginative truth" and a "national tradition."[33] At this point,
Williams argues, literature begins to function in a way that is "ac-

tively ideological" in its self-confirming versions of significant social experience and its reduction of history to a series of fictional texts.

Examples of such a specialization of meaning can certainly be found in the texts of F. R. Leavis, whose "great tradition" sought to construct a moral and historical narrative from "the field of fiction belonging to Literature."[34] For Leavis, this meant the identification and privileging of texts that were "significant in terms of the human awareness they promote" (10). "Literature" thus became a very particular set of texts whose specificity could only be recognized in relation to a critical vocabulary of "maturity," "refinement," "civilization," and "moral seriousness" (25). The legacy of such specialization of meaning is clear in the methodology and scope of the many "histories of English literature" that have been published in the last twenty years. Alastair Fowler's *History of English Literature*, published in 1987, for example, takes for granted the narrowing of meaning Williams describes, and places this much-reduced canon within a clearly formalistic grid of interpretation. Thus Fowler describes the organizing principle of his history as the "history of literary forms" and stresses that his interest lies in the transformations and developments that are "internal to literature," rather than in the possible relations between cultural change and a broader social history.[35]

Williams becomes increasingly aware of the sorts of texts, and the sorts of cultural and historical questions, that are exluded from this version of "the literary," which he sees finally as a "closing off" of important elements of cultural experience. He is consequently worried by the extent to which Marxist critics have accepted literature as a self-evident category and set of values. Williams accuses Marxist critics of accepting a narrowed definition of literature even while arguing that literature must be won over to a new interpretation or read in relation to a different understanding of history, rather than considering the "complicated facts which ['literature'] partially reveals and partially obscures" (46).

The same acceptance of the "literary" as an intact and identifiable sphere characterized early feminist literary studies that set out either to contest readings of male-authored texts or to add women writers to the canon on the basis of their aesthetic achievements. Neither of these activities explicitly challenged the constitution of the literary or the critical vocabulary in terms of which it could apparently be recognized.

Returning to F. R. Leavis, we can perhaps see why his versions of the literary seemed to feminist critics at first to pose no particular methodological problems. After all, his "great tradition" contained both George Eliot and Jane Austen and so seemed to guarantee the presence of women writers, provided they possessed the appropriate qualities of seriousness and maturity. The unhappy fate of Emily Brontë and Christina Rossetti in Leavis's canon, however, points toward a set of problems that might be seen as symptomatic of the dilemma feminist critics faced when they tried to find available critical terms for the assessment of women writers who wrote not with seriousness but with passion, not with maturity but with anger, and not organically but rather in fragments of dialogue and parody. Leavis acknowledged the problem: he wanted to stress the importance of *Wuthering Heights*, but he could only do so in a footnote where he admits Emily Brontë's brilliance and regrets that she does not quite "fit" in his tradition. Similarly, even though he describes Christina Rossetti as the author of one of the finest poems of the nineteenth century, Leavis excludes her from his "revaluation" of the tradition of English poetry, simply mentioning in passing "her own thin and limited but very notable distinction."[36]

Given the centrality of *Wuthering Heights* as a text for feminist critics interested in exploring the links between psychic, social, and textual structures, the incapacity of Leavis's critical discourse of moral seriousness to deal with it led to a broad questioning of the adequacy of such a critical discourse and of its supporting history of literature.[37] The overwhelming absence of works by women in published histories of English literature began to seem structural rather than contingent. Finally, the development of important work on the politics of representation, on pleasure, and on sexuality in the broader fields of cultural and film studies produced an increasing unease about the forms of analysis and debate that were being cut off by the insistence on the specificity of the literary.

What we find in feminist criticism in the eighties, then, is a more general questioning of the procedures of canon formation, a recognition that the texts that form a "literary history" reflect and embody a series of social developments and judgments:

Feminist scholarship has also pushed back the boundaries of literature in other directions, considering a wide range of forms and styles in which women's writing—especially that of women who did not perceive themselves as writers—appears.[38]

The point is stressed again by the editors of *The Feminist Companion to Literature in English* (1990), who argue that in order to constitute an archive of women's literary and cultural history it is necessary first to challenge "the tight grip of a narrowly defined tradition of writing" and to give attention not only to canonized genres but also to "diaries, letters, writing for children and popular forms."[39]

Williams's work could make very significant contributions to such a project, offering a model of cultural analysis that identifies the social interests and forces that construct the category of literature without giving up on the importance of detailed readings of particular literary texts and genres. His texts offer important historical models and analytic strategies for dealing with this necessarily double emphasis that otherwise threatens to fragment feminist criticism into a series of nonproductive conflicts between the rival claims of history, theory, and literature.

Cultural materialism and historical semantics thus have much to contribute to the theorization of key problems within contemporary feminism. Williams's work offers us a methodology and a series of crucial theoretical insights into the relations between social and cultural change: the nature of "determination," the social meanings of analytic categories, and the ways in which social power constructs and articulates itself across cultural texts. His project of uncovering the historical determinations of "keywords" within social discourse offers a particularly fruitful area for feminist research, especially where it intersects with already-constituted debates about the historical experience of women or the social construction of gender. In closing, however, I would like to suggest a modification to Williams's "keywords of culture and society" that might serve to foreground the terms in which women have had to negotiate their histories and their identities.

Many of the histories and analyses in Williams's *Keywords* could, as I have indicated, be transformed by a recognition of the importance of gender. As well as those I have mentioned, I would certainly want to include *class, community, democracy, history, labor, modern, romantic,* and *work* in such a category. I would also suggest, however, that a feminist version would need to add quite a number of terms to Williams's list if it were really to constitute a gendered history of cultural categories and of social change. I list my terms, as Williams does his, in alphabetical order:

the body	madness
child care	misogyny
consciousness	motherhood
consumerism	pin money
family wage	race
femininity	rape
feminism	representation
gender	reproduction
homosexuality	sexism
hysteria	sexuality
kinship	wife

I intend no completeness, but wish simply to draw attention to areas that were marginal to Williams's "vocabulary of culture and society" but seem crucial to the social experience and identities of women. The work of historical and linguistic analysis, of course, remains to be done.

NOTES

1. Raymond Williams, *The Country and the City* (London: Hogarth, 1985), p. 306.

2. Julia Swindells and Lisa Jardine, *What's Left? Women in Culture and the Labour Movement* (London: Routledge, 1990), p. vii.

3. Raymond Williams, *Politics and Letters* (London: NLB, 1979), p. 149.

4. "Media, Margins and Modernity: Raymond Williams and Edward Said," in *The Politics of Modernism*, ed. Tony Pinkney (London: Verso, 1989), p. 195. This article is a transcript of a talk given in 1986; Williams uses the same example, in answer to the same question, in an interview in 1987: "The Politics of Hope: An Interview" in *Raymond Williams: Critical Perspectives*, ed. Terry Eagleton (Cambridge: Polity Press, 1989), pp. 180–81.

5. Juliet Mitchell, "Women: The Longest Revolution," in *Women: The Longest Revolution* (London: Virago, 1984), p. 21.

6. Carol Watts, "Reclaiming the Border Country: Feminism and the Work of Raymond Williams, *News from Nowhere*, no. 6 (1989): 89–108.

7. Jane Miller, "The One Great Silent Area" in *Seductions: Studies in Reading and Culture* (London: Virago, 1990), pp. 38–69 (p. 48).

8. In *The Second Generation*, Kate, the wife of a trade union activist, has an affair with an academic. This is represented as a search for a freedom that is illusory and as a move toward an identity that is fundamentally compromised.

9. Raymond Williams, "The New Morality," *Guardian*, March 17, 1983, p. 16.

10. Raymond Williams, "Towards Many Socialisms" in *Resources of Hope*, ed. Robin Gable (London: Verso, 1989), pp. 295–313 (p. 304).

11. "Desire," reprinted in Raymond Williams, *What I Came to Say* (London: Hutchinson Radius, 1989), pp. 30–35.

12. Raymond Williams, "Base and Superstructure in Marxist Cultural Theory," in *Problems in Materialism and Culture* (London: Verso, 1980), pp. 31–49, and "Base and Superstructure," in *Marxism and Literature* (Oxford: Oxford University Press, 1977), pp. 75–82.

13. Raymond Williams, "Productive Forces," in *Marxism and Literature*, pp. 90–94 (p. 93).

14. Williams, "Base and Superstructure," *Marxism and Literature*, p. 80.

15. Raymond Williams, "Structures of Feeling," *Marxism and Literature*, pp. 128–35 (p. 131).

16. In fact, Quentin Skinner has argued very convincingly that to see the problem simply as one of meanings is to underestimate the complexity of possible relations between language and social change. Skinner argues that a historical semantics would have to address not only changes in the meaning of a particular word but also changes in the criteria governing its applicability in specific contexts as well as changes in the range of attitudes it can be used to express. See Quentin Skinner, "Language and Social Change" in *Meaning and Context: Quentin Skinner and His Critics*, ed. James Tully (Cambridge: Polity Press, 1988), pp. 119–32.

17. Raymond Williams, *Culture and Society* (Harmondsworth: Penguin, 1963), p. 285.

18. This history has also been explored by Asa Briggs in "The Language of 'Mass' and 'Masses' in Nineteenth-Century England," in *The Collected Essays of Asa Briggs*, vol. 1 (Brighton: Harvester, 1985), pp. 34–54.

19. Raymond Williams, *The Long Revolution* (Harmondsworth: Penguin, 1965), p. 379.

20. Raymond Williams, "The Uses of Cultural Theory," in *Politics of Modernism*, pp. 163–76 (p. 169).

21. Williams, *Long Revolution*, p. 361.

22. Andreas Huyssen, *After the Great Divide: Modernism, Mass Culture, Postmodernism* (Basingstoke: Macmillan, 1988).

23. Henry James, "The Next Time," in *The Figure in the Carpet and Other Stories*, ed. F. Kermode (Harmondsworth: Penguin, 1986), pp. 305–53 (p. 309).

24. Theodor W. Adorno, "The Schema of Mass Culture," in *The Culture Industry: Selected Essays on Mass Culture*, ed. J. M. Bernstein (London: Routledge, 1991), pp. 53–84 (p. 58).

25. T. S. Eliot, *Notes Towards the Definition of Culture* (London: Faber & Faber, 1948), p. 68.

26. Christine Buci-Glucksmann, "Catastrophic Utopia: The Feminine as Allegory of the Modern," *Representations*, no. 14 (1986): 220–29.

27. Relevant examples would include *The Country and the City*, where Williams explores the relations between the changing social relations of urban and rural life and the development of particular literary genres, and *Problems in Materialism and Culture*, where he seeks to connect communication and production in nonreductive ways.

28. Patrice Petro, *Joyless Streets: Women and Melodramatic Representation in Weimar Germany* (Princeton, N.J.: Princeton University Press, 1989), p. 8.

29. See *Politics of Modernism*.

30. Raymond Williams, "When Was Modernism?" in *Politics of Modernism*, pp. 31–35 (p. 34).

31. Raymond Williams, "The Politics of the Avant-Garde," in *Politics of Modernism*, pp. 49-63 (p. 57).

32. Raymond Williams, "The Bloomsbury Fraction," in *Problems in Materialism and Culture*, pp. 148-69.

33. Raymond Williams, "Literature," in *Marxism and Literature*, pp. 45-54.

34. F. R. Leavis, *The Great Tradition* (Harmondsworth: Penguin, 1983), p. 9.

35. Alastair Fowler, preface to *A History of English Literature* (Oxford: Basil Blackwell, 1987).

36. F. R. Leavis, *Revaluation: Tradition and Development in English Poetry* (Harmondsworth: Penguin, 1978), p. 13.

37. For consideration of the importance of *Wuthering Heights* for feminist criticism, see Juliet Mitchell, *Women: The Longest Revolution*.

38. Lillian S. Robinson, "Treason Our Text: Feminist Challenges to the Literary Canon," in *The New Feminist Criticism*, ed. E. Showalter (London: Virago, 1986), pp. 105-21 (p. 116).

39. Virginia Blain, Patricia Clements, and Isobel Grundy, eds., introduction to *Feminist Companion to Literature in English* (London: Batsford, 1991).

News from Somewhere: Reading
Williams's Readers
Robert Miklitsch

"If I could but see a day of it," he said to himself; "if I could but see it!"
—William Morris, *News from Nowhere* (1890)

Orwell's 1984 is no more plausible than Morris' 2003. . . . but . . . there is also Morris' 1952 (the date of the revolution), and the years following it: years in which the subjunctive is a true subjunctive, rather than a displaced indicative, because its energy flows both ways, forward and back, and because in its issue, in the struggle, it can go either way.
—Raymond Williams, "Utopia and Science Fiction" (1978)

The Thatcher government installed itself in December 1979, and if "the crisis of socialism in Britain did not come in one day,"[1] 1979 still seems, in retrospect, a watershed in the postwar political history of the United Kingdom. The force of this proposition is even more apparent when one considers that thirty years before, to the month, *New Left Review* was launched and, with it, the journal of a generation—not, however, the first but the second generation (not, in other words, the Old Left but the New Left).

In Williams's second novel, *Second Generation* (1964), Peter Owen typifies this new movement, "a whole younger generation of British cultural theorists" who were emerging in their own right even as Williams wrote his novel, though, ironically enough, it is Peter's mother, Kate, whose Francophilia "anticipates the structuralist 'turn'" and "heady blend of Louis Althusser and Jean-Luc Godard" that would characterize the second generation.[2] Yet if the

71

generation of 1968 is, as Williams said, "almost as historical as those of 1956 or 1936" (*NN* 9), then perhaps it is time—with the death of Williams and the demise of the New Left—to turn to the next, emergent generation. This in fact is the subject of the "new," timely *News from Nowhere* ("Raymond Williams: The Third Generation") which—together with *Raymond Williams: Critical Perspectives*[3]—represents not only a belated reappraisal of Williams's work but also an instance of the second and third generations' debt to the first.

The Origin and "Economy" of Cultural Studies

> *The* Four Quartets *completely dominated reading and discussion in Cambridge at the time. . . . I recall coming out of one of these discussions, not with enemies but with friends who considered themselves socialists and yet were endorsing Eliot's work. . . . I said to myself—a ridiculous expression that must have been some echo of an Eliot rhythm—"here also the struggle occurs." Looking across at the university church and doing nothing about it. But my perception was itself a perfectly correct one. There was class struggle occurring around those poems and that criticism.*
>
> —Raymond Williams, *Politics and Letters* (1979)

Thesis: If Cambridge English is the specific institutional precondition of "cultural materialism," cultural studies bears a determinate relation to English studies.

Specifically, the crisis of English studies—and the origin, therefore, of cultural studies—is a function of two "intellectual" formations: Marxism and Leavisism.[4] While Leavisism installed the "study of literature as *the* object of knowledge of English Studies" (*NN* 62), British Marxism in the 1930s turned its eyes to the East—to the Soviet Union and the "economic miracle" that the revolution had supposedly wrought. Thus, when Williams returned from Normandy and the Guards Armoured Division, English Marxism, 1930s-style, offered him next to nothing, "compounded as it was of vulgar Marxism, bourgeois empiricism and Romantic idealism."[5]

But if English Marxism was, according to Terry Eagleton, an "intellectual irrelevance" (*CI* 23), Leavisism was culturally *and* politically relevant, profoundly so. Its "immense attraction" lay, for Williams, in its "stress on education" (a legacy of Matthew Arnold), its "discovery of practical criticism" (a legacy of I. A. Richards), and its "cultural radicalism" (a legacy of the "culture and society" tradition). In fact, with respect to cultural radicalism, it should be remembered that Leavisism was always something of an "outlaw's enterprise," both Cambridge and not Cambridge, and that its influence is inconceivable outside of not only the context of Cambridge (e.g., the English Tripos) but also the force field of its primary ideological antagonist, Marxism, an ideological "whetstone" against which it was obliged to define and focus its positions.[6]

Admittedly, the Marxism against which Leavisism defined itself was, as I have indicated, something of a dead horse in 1945: while "domestic" British Marxism was at an "impasse," its "answers" unable to "meet the questions," "foreign" Marxism in the form of Zhdanovism was, according to Williams, "telling people to stop minding their little souls" in order to begin the "tough job of communist construction" (the latter a screen of sorts "for the actual repudiation of writers in Russia" [*PL* 73]). Williams's self-defined attempt, then, to "unite radical left politics with Leavisite literary criticism" appears, in retrospect, positively quixotic. And yet, with the demise of *Scrutiny* (1932-53) and the Soviet suppression of the East German uprising (the death of Stalin was less significant for Williams since he was no longer a member of the Communist Party),[7] it was clear—at least to Williams—that something was needed, something that was party neither to Cambridge nor to the Party, neither to Leavisism nor to communism. That something was cultural politics, the critique of civil society announced in *Culture and Society* (1958).

Published a decade after Eliot's *Notes toward the Definition of Culture* (1948) and Leavis's *Great Tradition* (1948)—and almost twenty-five years after Richards's seminal *Principles of Literary Criticism* (1924)—*Culture and Society* signals a turn to cultural studies that would eventually transform the "landscape" of English studies, a cultivated, carefully weeded estate that had already been dramatically remapped by the founding fathers of what, after John Crowe Ransom, would come to be known as the New Criticism.[8] But if *Culture and Society* can now be seen as a complex, dialectical response to certain Leavisite assumptions about the text and tradition, for Williams it was designed to contest the ruling ideas of its time, especially the "use of the concept of culture against democ-

racy, socialism, the working class [and] popular education" (*PL* 98).
Unlike the "selective vision of culture" formulated and codified in
Scrutiny, it sought—in Williams's words—"to recover the true complexity of the tradition" confiscated by "Eliot, Leavis and the whole
of the cultural conservatism that had formed around them—the people who had preempted the culture and literature of [England]" (*PL*
112). From this seemingly counterhegemonic perspective, Williams's
early culture criticism—his elaboration of what Eagleton calls the
"space constituted by the interaction of social relations, cultural institutions and forms of subjectivity"[9]—represents a strong rereading
and rewriting of Leavis(ism).[10]

   Though Williams has maintained that the "very success of [*Culture and Society*] created the conditions for its critique" (*PL* 100), it
nonetheless remains a very real question whether and to what extent his "oppositional" project was able to escape the dominant ideology of its day. Is *Culture and Society* merely an instance—as Eagleton, for example, has claimed—of left Leavisite literary criticism?
Or, less simply, if Williams's work is in some sense discontinuous
with the New Criticism, its "scientistic objectivism" and "positivist
empiricism,"[11] is there a way in which that work is continuous, even
complicitous, with it?

   In a reading of *Politics and Letters* that comprises a reading of
Culture and Society, Stuart Hall has argued that the problem with
the latter text is "methodological": since Williams's method frequently merges with the idiom it is analyzing—what Hall calls a "*lit-
erary-moral* mode of discourse" (*RW* 59)—the book offers "no rallying point" outside this discourse from which its strengths as well as
limitations might be identified. Despite its "oppositional" intent, then,
Culture and Society is ineluctably part of that "Leavisite inheritance"
of which it is ostensibly a critique. For Hall, the text that marks
Williams's "heroic" if not always successful "attempt to break finally
with the idiom and method" of the "culture and society" tradition is
not *Culture and Society* but *The Long Revolution* (1961). Recollecting Marx and Engels on Hegel (as well as Althusser on all three), Hall
opines that the latter is not just a "settling of accounts"—and therefore a "text of the break"—but *the* text where Williams begins to
"construct a cultural theory" (*RW* 61). Williams himself seconded
this opinion in "Writing and Society," where he notes that *The Long
Revolution* signals a "shift of emphasis," one that would later result

in a rejection of the "dominant paradigm" (*WS* 209). That paradigm was—and perhaps still is—English studies.

Still, if for Hall as well as for Williams, *The Long Revolution* breaks with an "inadvertent conservatism," Williams's break with the *institution* of English studies is only explicitly played out in the three late Cambridge lectures collected in *Writing and Society* (1983): "Crisis in English Studies," "Cambridge English Past and Present," and "Beyond Cambridge English." Appropriately enough, the Cambridge English faculty was the audience to whom Williams addressed the following "hard question," a question that is becoming increasingly hard to ignore:

> Can radically different work still be carried on under a single heading or department when there is not just diversity of approach but more serious and fundamental differences about the object of knowledge? . . . Or must there be wider reorganization of the received division of the humanities, the human sciences, into newly defined and newly collaborative arguments? (*WS* 211)

In retrospect, it is clear that along with, inter alia, Richard Hoggart's *Uses of Literacy* (1957) and E. P. Thompson's *Making of the English Working Class* (1963),[12] Williams's Cambridge lectures remain the "signs of a discursive break" (Bowen [*NN* 83]).

To claim as much is not, however, to insinuate that cultural studies should become the next "master discipline" (since such a devoutly wished state of affairs would merely displace the problem of disciplinarity) nor that such a counterhegemony would mean the extinction of English studies (since cultural studies is historically predicated, as a project, on the academic division of knowledge).[13] To canonize cultural studies as *the* institutional solution to the crisis of English studies is not only to ignore that literary-cultural history of which it is in part a product (one thinks immediately of modernism), it is also to ignore the historical development of capitalism and *its* forces and effects.[14]

In other words, if it is impossible to talk about cultural studies without talking about the history of English studies, it is equally impossible—or at least theoretically irresponsible—to talk about institutions without talking about political economy. Thus, in "The Determinations of Cultural Materialism," Terry Murphy breaks with a strictly "literary" critique of the origins of cultural studies, analyzing the formation and development of English studies as an institutional response to the demands of early-twentieth-century capitalism. Those demands are linked for Murphy to periodic crises, so much so that one might say capitalism is always already in crisis, and that English studies, as one among many "ideological state apparatuses,"[15] is inescapably implicated in the play of this political economy, especially in the "contradiction between the technological demands of the productive forces for a more literate society and the conservative demands induced by the maintenance of capitalist relations to 'police' this literacy" (*NN* 58).

As the titles of some influential texts testify—I am thinking of D. A. Miller's *The Novel and the Police* (1987), Frank Lentricchia's *Ariel and the Police* (1987), and Simon Watney's *Policing Desire: Pornography, AIDS, and the Media* (1987)—this contradiction between the "cultural literacy" imperative and capital's concomitant need for "discipline and punishment" has not gone unnoticed in the academy. Still, if one understands this contradiction in terms of capital knowledge as well as power knowledge—if, in other words, one takes a less monolithically Foucauldian view of the picture—one can remark the scare in the "scare quotes" ("police") and accent, at the same time, the consensual nature of capitalist crisis management (i.e., the interimplication of "democratic liberal capitalism" and the postwar "age of consensus").[16]

With its stress on consent rather than coercion (or, in Gramsci's terms, "direction" rather than "domination"), this reaccentuation allows one to introduce the notion of hegemony, which I insert here in order to anticipate what I see as a potential problem in Murphy's reading of the "rise of English." According to this reading—which relies heavily on Ernest Mandel's "overarching theory" of capitalogic as it is developed in *Late Capitalism* (1975)—English studies is to the second technological revolution what cultural studies is, or will be, to the third technological revolution. More specifically (and imperatively), at the "level of dominant institutional discourse," Marxists should—according to Murphy—"welcome a mutation from Leavisism (general theory of English Studies) to cultural materialism (general theory of cultural and media studies)" (*NN* 59).

Ironically enough, given his passing critique of Jameson, Murphy recollects here Jameson's own Mandel-derived account of a "new radical cultural politics" in "Postmodernism; or, The Cultural Logic of

Late Capitalism.''[17] Indeed, Murphy implicitly invokes Jameson's "culturalist" appropriation of Mandel when he argues that Jameson's sense of the postmodern as the "end of subversion" is a defensive and revolutionarily defeatist misreading. Of course, having invoked 1968 and the *May Day Manifesto,* "one of the high points of the critique of civil society," Murphy is defending certain "first generation" fathers—in this case, Stuart Hall, Edward Thompson, and Williams himself—against certain "second generation" sons, especially seemingly less engaged and militant ones such as Jameson (who, as Murphy notes, "owes much to the work of Williams" [*NN* 70-71]).

Though Jameson's understanding of postmodernism is rather more sophisticated than Murphy's comments suggest, the real problem with Murphy's "Determinations of Cultural Materialism" is that his reading of the "cultural logic of capitalism" betrays an economic reflectionism that is a "direct" result, like Jameson's, of an uncritical reliance on Mandel. Simply put, it is not at all self-evident that Mandel's exposition of late capitalism—"systematic and powerful as it is," as Jameson says—is in any sense definitive. Put another, stronger way: to use *Late Capitalism* to write the history of cultural politics is to reproduce Mandel's history of political *economy,* a productivist history that has some dubious, not to say dire, political implications. These implications are, I want to argue, almost completely contrary to the spirit *and* letter of Williams's "whole" project.

For example, with respect to *Late Capitalism* itself, one might argue that Mandel's own reliance on classical Marxist categories—on, in particular, the *grand récit* or master narrative of the modes of production—"legislates against a thorough analysis of the ways, not only in which the mode of production has changed, but also in which it is newly and complexly articulated in (and from) contemporary modes of representation and ideological formations."[18] The net effect of such conceptual legislation is that it reinforces the "hegemony" of the economic within Marxist discourse and thereby structurally subordinates, all too classically, other overdetermined/determining instances. More tersely, the result is yet another objectivist crisis theory.

One can see the same reductive process at work on a less "molar," more "molecular" level by considering the difference between the titles of two parallel works: Williams's *Problems in Materialism and*

Culture and Murphy's "Determinations of Cultural Materialism." What for Williams is a "problem in" is, for Murphy, a "determination of." To be fair to Murphy, his attempt to theoretically reformulate cultural materialism explicitly takes into account determination as determinism. Thus, drawing on Mandel, he explains that the ideology of technological determinism is to late capitalism as linguistic determinism is to English studies. Yet even as one concedes the general force of this proposition (structuralism certainly was, in retrospect, an especially extreme example of language as system, as *langue*), one wonders about the use value of such homologies. If for Williams the relation between culture and materialism is a problem, and one *within* which we as subjects are situated, for Murphy—and even more so for Jameson—the determinations of, respectively, cultural materialism and postmodernism are rather unproblematically economic and periodic. In fact, one might argue that the genitive approach is itself a reflexive, albeit perverse, "expression" of a severely restricted understanding of *political* economy. Read this way (admittedly, against the grain), Murphy's capitalogistic reformulation of cultural materialism constitutes a kind of theoretical reformism that is considerably more Jamesonian, or cultural-*economic*, than he would care to admit.

From (Political) Economy to Hegemony: History, the Base-Superstructure Model, and the Crisis of Marxism

> *I think of Marxism . . . as a way of helping you sleep at night; it offers the guarantee that, although things don't look simple at the moment, they really are simple in the end. You can't see how the economy determines, but just have faith, it does determine in the last instance! The first clause wakes you up and the second puts you to sleep. It's okay, I can nod off tonight, because in the last instance, though not just yesterday or today or tomorrow or as far as I can see forward in history, in the last instance, just before the last trumpet, as St. Peter comes to the door, he'll say, "The economy works."*
>
> —Stuart Hall, "Discussion" (1988)

The ultimately orthodox reinscription of the economic in the last instance at work in Murphy's "Determinations of Cultural Materialism" could not be further from Williams's own insistent, even relentless interrogation of the classical Marxist valorization of the "base."

Indeed, for those toiling in the sometimes withered vineyards of what Laclau and Mouffe call the "Marxist Vulgate," one of the most tonic, exhilarating aspects of Williams's work is its Marx-like skepticism about the received wisdom of Marxism. So, in that "classic" revision of the base-superstructure model in *Problems in Materialism and Culture*, Williams asserts that if we "look at the whole question of the base differently," we are "less tempted to dismiss as superstructural, and in that sense as merely secondary, certain vital productive social forces, which are in the broad sense, from the beginning, basic" (*PM* 35). The key word here is *basic*, a graphic touch that signals that Williams's emphasis on re-production represents a *transformation*, not a reversal, of this once classical-Marxist, now cultural-theoretical problem.

But perhaps I am being "premature" here.

In a footnote to the introduction to *Raymond Williams: Critical Perspectives*, Eagleton maintains that although some of his formulations about Williams's work in *Criticism and Ideology* (1976) were "unacceptably acerbic and ungenerous," he "would still defend many of [them]" (*RW* 11). It comes as no surprise, then, that in "Base and Superstructure in Raymond Williams" (1989), his contribution to *Critical Perspectives*, Eagleton returns to the critical terrain of "Mutations of Critical Ideology."[19] Though he does not cite his earlier critique, the fact that he returns to the base-superstructure problematic is not insignificant. "Few doctrines of classical Marxism have fallen into greater disrepute," according to Eagleton, "than the base/superstructure model" (*RW* 167). As a self-avowed "defender of the classical doctrine," Eagleton is therefore at pains to defend this model; indeed, as is clear from the rhetoric of the essay, it is a not-so-subtle defense of "classical Marxism itself." Which is to say an article of faith.

Now, the problem with the base-superstructure model is not so much "art" or "literature" as "history" or, more precisely, History. In other words, if it is not so difficult "to believe that one set of determinants alone ['material production'] has been responsible for the genesis and evolution of forms of social life" (*RW* 166), it is less easy to accept the consequences of this proposition: that "history has always worked according to the base/superstructure model" (*RW* 167). The sheer "historical reach" of the model is, for Eagleton, problematic

since just such reach would appear to presuppose a "static conception of history," which raises, in turn, the difficult question, "What is
it about history to date which Marxism believes to be static?" (*RW*
167). And yet, if one turns to Marx, *the* answer is "surely obvious":

> The reason why history to date has been fairly static, and so amenable
> to the kind of conceptual instruments [Marx] proposes, is that it has
> not really been history at all. It has been, as Marx comments, "pre-his-
> tory." History has not even started yet. All we have had so far is the
> realm of necessity—the ringing of changes on the drearily persistent
> motif of exploitation. History, or pre-history if one prefers, indeed dis-
> plays a remarkable self-identity from start to finish, presents a strik-
> ingly monotonous, compulsively repetitive narrative all the way
> through. What all historical epochs have in common is that we can say
> with absolute certitude what the vast majority of men and women
> who populate them have spent their time doing. They have spent
> their time engaged in fruitless, miserable toil for the benefit of others.
> Arrest history at any point whatsoever, and this is what we will find.
> History for Marxism is indeed, as Mr. Ford wisely commented, bunk, or
> at least the same old tedious story. (*RW* 166)

I have cited this passage from "Base and Superstructure in Raymond
Williams" not only because it is so extraordinary, rhetorically speaking, but because it constitutes the best single illustration of the difference between Williams's and Eagleton's work. In the final analysis, writing as he is from the Althusserian problematic (where
Theory is the Law), Eagleton needs the base-superstructure model to
legitimize *his* "eternal return" to Marx, the scientific, dialectical-his-
torical Marx: "man is historical; history is dialectical; the dialectic is
the process of (material) production; production is the very movement of human existence; history is the history of the modes of production, etc."[20]

Now, to be fair to Eagleton (or at least to attempt to be), his historicism and—to attend to the other pillar of his classical-Marxist
Imaginary—economism are not without their "pedagogical effect."
For instance: he argues persuasively that it is necessary to have some
account of determination and, true to form, "Base and Superstructure in Raymond Williams" pivots on this question. And yet, simply
to say that the base-superstructure "doctrine" turns on the "question
of determinations" is not really to say anything. To say, as Marx(ism)
does, that these "mutual" determinations are *asymmetrical*—"that in

the production of human society some activities are more fundamentally determining than others" (*RW* 169)—is another thing. Here
Eagleton's insistence on what he elsewhere calls "hierarchies of determination" is of real significance, especially from a political perspective, insofar as categories of hierarchy and asymmetricality are
absolutely crucial to any model, classical Marxist or otherwise, that
would refuse the lure of a "bad" egalitarian logic.[21]

This said, the problem with Eagleton's account of determination
is that the dominant instance that his ostensibly historical, asymmetrical model necessitates is always and only located in the base
(i.e., economy), a "vertical" posture that allows him to ignore—seemingly despite himself—both the "historical specificity" of the base-superstructure *metaphor* and historicity as such. Hence, even as he attempts to historicize his classically "base" reading of the model via a
horizontalization of the metaphor, history is, as it were, revertic-
alized:

> The "base" is that outer horizon or final obstacle against which a trans-
> formative politics continually presses up, that which resists its dynamic
> and exposes it as lacking. It is that which will not give way, whatever
> other achievements or concessions may occur, a final limit or thresh-
> old ceaselessly retrojected into our present struggles in the awareness
> that . . . "nothing has really changed." The base on this model, is not so
> much an answer to the question "What in the end causes everything
> else?" as an answer to the question "What in the end do you want?"
> (*RW* 175)

Having earlier, elsewhere, posed the question, recollecting Freud,
What do Marxists want?,[22] I can readily recognize the truth of Eagleton's assertion: in some real and profound sense we get, in the end,
what we want.

In fact, I have focused on Eagleton's most recent reading of
Williams because their projects constitute, it seems to me, very different answers to the question, What in the end do you want? Having
asked this question, Eagleton, for instance, observes that "there are
many sterile ways of being correct" (*RW* 175). Correctness, in other
words, is not all. There are also those like Williams—Eagleton adds,
echoing Milton ("heretic in truth")—who are "truthtellers in heresy,
deviating from a deadening orthodoxy in order to recover and revi-
talize what is of value in it" (*RW* 175). Thus, according to this logic,

Williams's "heretical truthtelling" would not have been possible without his "early break" with classical Marxism, an argument that would appear to represent a real recognition on Eagleton's part of Williams's project as, in some sense, the Other of classical Marxism. Yet one has only to register the rhetoric at work in the conclusion to "Base and Superstructure in Raymond Williams"—suffused as it is, like the essay as a whole, with the language of heresy and orthodoxy, a language that is anything but innocent—to recognize the doctrinal terms within which Williams's rehabilitation is effected. Indeed, given Eagleton's tortuous but ultimately canonical reading of Williams, it is hard to escape the feeling that Marxism for him is now essentially a theological position: you either believe in it or you do not. If in fact you believe, Marxism with its grand, classical consolations may well answer your needs. On the other hand, if you do not believe in it or, more to the point, if you do not believe that it is a matter of belief, then you must look elsewhere for theoretical satisfaction.

This is not, I cannot emphasize enough, a matter of somehow choosing between "Eagleton" and "Williams" or, less authorially, "classical Marxism" and "cultural materialism" (as if they were decidable, nondialectical terms) since the difference between the two is not original to either of them but is internal to the history of Marxism and its *disciplinary* history (and here the Foucauldian emphasis is absolutely apropos). Which is to say that the "discipline" of Marxism will only remain alive to the extent that it remains, like English, in crisis. From this perspective, Eagleton's reading of Williams is not only not surprising, it is the stuff out of which Marxism is, and has been, constituted as an object of knowledge. What *is* surprising is that the author of *Criticism and Ideology* is willing, wittingly or unwittingly, to reduce what should rightly be a debate about the future of Marxism to what in effect is a regressive, repressive evangelism—the gospel according to Eagleton.[23]

As Williams once remarked in "You're a Marxist, Aren't You?" (1975), there is something "fundamentally wrong" about a whole tradition such as Marxism being reduced to a "single name," "a single thinker"—even a thinker as "great as Marx" who, for Williams, is "incomparably the greatest thinker in the socialist tradition" (*RH* 66).

Need I add that even post-Marxism marks the ambivalence of this extraordinary patrimony, the Author as God-Father?

Given this "regime of truth" and *its* potentially authoritarian formation, it might not be too much to say that Williams's "invention" of cultural materialism is one instance of his endeavor to think Marxism in all its discursive, interrogative power without falling prey to the fascism of the patronym, the onanism of the One, and the fetishism of the Same. Though one might think—in fact, many "good" Marxists have thought—that the "desire for revolution" and the "good society" ("understood as the advent of communism") will free us from the "imaginary figures that haunt democracy," there is no escape, as the work of Claude Lefort continually reminds us, from (pre-)History: "Whoever dreams of an abolition of power secretly cherishes the reference to the One and the reference to the Same."[24] To continue to dream such a dream is to invite the kind of historical nightmares with which we are only too familiar.

Hegemony as (Social) Complexity: Emotion, Experience, and "Structure of Feeling"

> *I learned the experience of incorporation, I learned the reality of hegemony, I learned the saturating power of the structures of feeling of a given society, as much from my own mind and my own experience as from observing the lives of others. All through our lives, if we make the effort, we uncover layers of this kind of alien formation in ourselves, and deep in ourselves.*
>
> —Raymond Williams, "You're a Marxist, Aren't You?"

> *I have been pulled all my life . . . between simplicity and complexity, and I can still feel the pull both ways. But every argument of experience and of history now makes my decision—and what I hope will be a general decision—clear. It is only in very complex ways, and by moving confidently towards very complex societies, that we can defeat imperialism and capitalism and begin that construction of many socialisms which will liberate and draw upon our real and now threatened energies.*
>
> —Raymond Williams, "Two Roads to Change,"
> *Politics and Letters* (1979)

For all their specificity (and Murphy and Eagleton are admirably specific about, respectively, the institutionalization of English studies and the necessity of thinking the asymmetricality of social relations), both Murphy's account of the determinations of cultural materialism and Eagleton's countercritique of Williams's revision of the base-superstructure model display, it seems to me, an inarticulated sense of complexity. For Williams, on the other hand, determination is a *"complex* and interrelated process of limits and pressures" (*PM* 87 [italics added]).

This emphasis on complexity is not, needless to say, an isolated moment in Williams's work. In fact, the concept of "structure of feeling" represents just one, albeit privileged, instance of his effort to the, for him, irreducible "fact" of complexity. Not insignificantly, part of the complexity of this "structural" concept is Williams's characteristic stress on the "feeling" half of the equation ("it was a structure in the sense that you could perceive it operating in one work after another . . . yet it was one of feeling much more than of thought" [*PL* 159]), though it is precisely this stress on "feeling" or, more generally, "experience" that has drawn critical fire.

Thus, in *Politics and Letters*, the *New Left Review* interviewers refer to a "fetishization of experience" in Williams's work, arguing that his concept of structure of feeling is a not-so-original twist on the Leavis-*Scrutiny* theme of experience as "life" ("the living content of a work") as well as the tradition from which that theme derives: English empiricism. For the interviewers, experience is that which is "immediate," the "domain of direct truth," a "kind of pristine contact between the subject and the reality in which the subject is immersed" (*PL* 167).[25] Just such a notion of experience insinuates that Being precedes Language, that it is somehow possible to get at (the Truth of) Being without mediation, without what one might call the detour of discourse.

Against this reading, I would submit, first, that Williams's defense of experience should be seen at least in part as a critique of, and a strategic response to, the structuralist and, in particular, Althusserian elision of the subject (where experience is merely an effect of the system as "structure"[26]); and, second, that Williams's *"concept* of experience" is an affirmation of the "radical empiricism" that questions, à la Locke and Hume, "the existence of a knowing subject and unmediated access to reality."[27] From this perspective, Williams's concept of structure of feeling is an attempt, however successful, to avoid a vulgar-empiricist understanding of experience.

Accordingly, Williams observes in *Marxism and Literature* that an alternative definition of "structure*s* of feeling"—of those "specifically affective elements of consciousness" as well as those "characteristic elements of impulse, restraint and tone"—is "structures of *experience*" (*ML* 132). Though *experience* for Williams is the "better and wider word," he prefers the term *feeling* because it alludes both to the processual character of "*social* experience" and to "practical consciousness of a present kind, in a liberating and interacting continuity" (*ML* 132). Feeling, in other words, is not so much a matter of "private expression," a function of the individual subject, as a "form of sociality."

Less obviously but no less importantly, "structure of feeling" intimates that emotion, like imagination, has a history. Which is to say that emotion possesses a cognitive dimension and, hence, should not be treated as an epiphenomenon either of desire or ideology (to recollect Althusser's reading of Lacan). Williams himself suggests as much in the conclusion to *The Year 2000* (1983), where he recites the litany of negative, "materialist" objections against emotion in order to posit its irreducible value to a society predicated upon "livelihood" rather than production: "Emotions, it is true, do not produce commodities. Emotions don't make the account add up differently. Emotions don't alter the hard relations of power. But where people actually live, what is specialized as 'emotion' has an absolute and primary significance" (*Y* 266).

Still, given this (given, that is, Williams's polemical stress on "feeling," "emotion," and "experience"), Stuart Hall's criticism of the role that the concept of experience plays in Williams's work remains:

> The indissolubility of practices in the ways in which they are experienced and "lived," in any real historical situation, does not in any way pre-empt the *analytic* separation of them, when one is attempting to theorize their different effects. The ways in which everything appears to interconnect in "experience" can only be a starting point for analysis. One has to "produce the concrete in thought"—that is, show, by a series of analytic approximations through abstraction, the concrete historical experience as the "product of many determinations." (*RW* 62)

This Althusserian appeal to "production"—*theoretical* production, the formation of concepts—is not, Hall insists, to fetishize theory, since such a gesture would represent a mere reversal of Williams's supposed "fetishization of experience." Neither theoreticism, the fetishization of theory ("theory as judge and jury," "with a capital T"),[28] nor empiricism—an empiricism predicated, that is, on an "uninspected notion of 'experience'" (*RW* 62)—will suffice. Rather, analysis must "deconstruct the 'lived wholeness' in order to be able to think its determinate conditions" (*RW* 62).

Consequently, if, according to Hall, Williams's concept of structure of feeling is ultimately dependent on an "'experiential' paradigm" that has "disabling theoretical effects," how *is* one to think those "social experiences in *solution*" of which structure of feeling is a "cultural hypothesis"? More simply, if structure of feeling is theoretically unsatisfactory, what is there to replace or displace it? The answer to this question is, I would suggest, the concept of hegemony.

While this may not be a particularly radical suggestion,[29] it is a critical one inasmuch as hegemony is an indispensable concept for any cultural materialism worthy of its name. At the same time, it must I think be said that Williams's classism, like Gramsci's, ultimately prevented him from thinking hegemony in all its conceptual complexity.[30] For to think what Williams calls the "complexity of hegemony" is to think the social in all its "surplus." Thus, in *Hegemony and Socialist Strategy*, Laclau and Mouffe argue that "class politics" cannot be separated from—must, that is, be articulated with—the politics of race:

> That, in certain circumstances, the class political subjectivity of white workers in Britain is overdetermined by racist or anti-racist attitudes, is evidently important for the struggle of the immigrant workers. This will bear upon certain practices of the trade union movement, which will in turn have consequences in a number of aspects of State policy and ultimately rebound upon the political identity of the immigrant workers themselves. (*H* 141)

Having broached the question of the complex, overdetermined relations between the new immigrant class fraction and what one might call the old (white) working class, Laclau and Mouffe conclude after Gramsci that class struggle must be reconceived as "hegemonic struggle."

However, to accent the concept of "hegemonic struggle" is not to claim that the "new social movements" are *the* privileged point for the formation of a "socialist political practice," nor that such movements are necessarily "progressive" (since their political meaning is never given in advance). But it is to say that unlike Williams's "hegemonic" understanding of structure of feeling (with its characteristically proletarian, neo-Gramscian inflection),[31] Laclau and Mouffe's critical reinscription of hegemony—problematic as *it* is[32]—better enables one to think the dispersion, fragmentation, and indeterminacy of our postmodern moment. It is also to say that if questions of race and gender are not peripheral but central to the struggle for the kind of radical participatory democracy that Williams imagined, such an emancipatory political practice "can only come from a complex process of convergence and political construction to which none of the hegemonic articulations constructed in any area of social reality can be of indifference" (*H* 174).

Hegemony, in this sense, makes all the difference.

NOTES

The following abbreviations and editions have been employed for citations from Raymond Williams's work:

K   *Keywords: A Vocabulary of Culture and Society* (New York: Oxford University Press, 1983 [1976])

ML   *Marxism and Literature* (London: Oxford University Press, 1985 [1977])

PL   *Politics and Letters: Interviews with New Left Review* (London: Verso, 1980 [1979])

PM   *Problems in Materialism and Culture: Selected Essays* (London: Verso, 1982 [1979])

RH   *Resources of Hope: Culture, Democracy, Socialism*, ed. Robin Gable (London: Verso, 1989)

SC   *Sociology of Culture* (New York: Schocken, 1982 [1981])

WS   *Writing and Society* (London: Verso, 1983)

Y   *The Year 2000* (New York: Pantheon, 1983)

1. John O'Connor, *Raymond Williams: Writing, Culture, Politics* (Oxford: Basil Blackwell, 1989), p. 30.

2. "Raymond Williams: The Third Generation," *News from Nowhere*, no. 6 (February 1985). The abbreviation *NN* is used in subsequent citations in the text.

3. Terry Eagleton, ed., *Raymond Williams: Critical Perspectives* (Boston: Northeastern University Press, 1990). The abbreviation *RW* is used in subsequent citations in the text.

4. My reading of the rise of cultural studies is indebted to Terry Murphy; see "The Determinations of Cultural Materialism," *News from Nowhere*, pp. 58-72. For Williams's own sense of his relationship to Marxism-Leavisism, see in particular the important essay "Culture Is Ordinary" (1958) in *Resources of Hope*, pp. 7-10.

5. Terry Eagleton, "Mutations of Critical Ideology," *Criticism and Ideology: A Study in Marxist Literary Theory* (London: New Left Books, 1976), p. 21. The abbreviation *CI* is used in subsequent citations in the text.

6. Chris Baldick, "The Leavises," *The Social Mission of English Criticism, 1848-1932* (Oxford: Clarendon Press, 1983), p. 169. For an authoritative take on Leavisism and *Scrutiny* in particular, see Francis Mulhern, *The Moment of 'Scrutiny'* (London: New Left Books, 1979).

7. See *Politics and Letters*, where Williams remarks that the "decisive event" for him—

when, that is, he came "to believe that the centre of political gravity was not in the Soviet Union"—was neither the death of Stalin nor "Hungary in '56" but "East Germany in '53" (p. 88).

8. For a "standard" history, see René Wellek's *American Criticism, 1900-1950*, in *A History of Modern Criticism* (New Haven, Conn.: Yale University Press, 1986), in particular "The New Criticism," pp. 144-58.

9. Terry Eagleton, *The Function of Criticism: From the Spectator to Post Structuralism* (1984; reprint, London: Verso, 1985), p. 110.

10. To do justice to the relation between Williams and Leavis—a vexed and complex one—is beyond the scope of this essay. It is clear, however, that Leavis cannot, and should not, be reduced to Leavisism. See William Cain's *The Crisis in Criticism: Theory, Literature, and Reform in English Studies* (Baltimore: Johns Hopkins University Press, 1984), pp. 115-20 and 135-39.

11. See John Fekete, "Foundations of Modern Critical Theory," in *The Critical Twilight: Explorations in the Ideology of Anglo-American Literary Theory from Eliot to McLuhan* (London: Routledge and Kegan Paul, 1977), pp. 17-36.

12. Robert Hewison, for example, focuses on Hoggart's *Uses of Literacy* and Williams's *Culture and Society*; see Hewison's "Culture and Society," in *In Anger: British Culture in the Cold War, 1945-1960* (New York: Oxford University Press, 1981), pp. 177-80.

13. For a slightly different emphasis—for, that is, cultural studies as a counterdisciplinary practice—see Henry Giroux, David Shumway, Paul Smith, and James Sosnoski, "The Need for Cultural Studies," in *Teachers as Intellectuals: Towards a Critical Pedagogy of Learning* (South Hadley, Mass.: Bergin and Garvey, 1988), pp. 143-57.

14. See Tony Crowley, "Language in History: That Full Field," *News from Nowhere*, pp. 23-37.

15. I put "ideological state apparatuses" in quotations here in order to mark my non-"social reproductive" sense of this term. For Williams's critique of this Althusserian concept, see "Ideologists" in *Sociology of Culture*, pp. 222-23.

16. See Samuel Bowles and Herbert Gintis, *Democracy and Capitalism: Property, Community, and the Contradictions of Modern Social Thought* (New York: Basic Books, 1986), p. 3.

17. See, for example, Fredric Jameson, "Culture: The Cultural Logic of Late Capitalism," in *Postmodernism; or, The Cultural Logic of Late Capitalism* (Durham, N.C.: Duke University Press, 1991), pp. 1-54.

18. Paul Smith, "Visiting the Banana Republic," in *Universal Abandon?: The Politics of Postmodernism*, ed. Andrew Ross for the Social Text Collective (Minneapolis: University of Minnesota Press, 1988), p. 137.

19. On Eagleton's "aggressive survey" of Williams in *Criticism and Ideology*, see Lisa Jardine and Julia Swindells's "Homage to Orwell: The Dream of a Common Culture," in *News from Nowhere*, pp. 122-24.

20. Jean Baudrillard, *The Mirror of Production*, trans. Mark Poster (St. Louis, Mo.: Telos, 1975), p. 48.

21. See Ernesto Laclau and Chantel Mouffe, "Radical Democracy: Alternatives for a New Left," in *Hegemony and Socialist Strategy: Towards a Radical Democratic Politics* (1985; reprint, London: Verso, 1989), p. 141. The abbreviation *H* is used in subsequent citations in the text.

22. See my "The American Ideology: On Fredric Jameson" (forthcoming).

23. I am using *repression* here in the analytic sense in which Claude Lefort employs the

term in, for instance, "Marxism: From One Vision of History to Another," trans. Terry Karten, in *The Political Forms of Modern Society*, ed. John B. Thompson (Cambridge, Mass.: MIT Press, 1986), pp. 138–80.

24. Lefort, "Politics and Human Rights," trans. Alan Sheridan, in *Political Forms of Modern Society*, p. 270.

25. As Anthony Giddens observes in a review of *Politics and Letters*, the questions posed by the interviewers of *New Left Review* (Perry Anderson, Anthony Barnett, and Francis Mulhern) reflect a definite "house line," i.e., Althusserianism (*Profiles and Critiques in Social Theory* [Berkeley: University of California Press, 1982], p. 134).

26. For this paradigmatic "Marxist structuralist" critique of Marxist "culturalism," see Stuart Hall, "Cultural Studies: Two Paradigms," *Media, Culture and Society: A Critical Reader*, ed. Richard Collins et al. (London: Sage, 1986), p. 42.

27. John Higgins, "Raymond Williams and the Problem of Ideology," in *Postmodernism and Politics*, ed. Jonathan Arac (Minneapolis: University of Minnesota Press, 1986), p. 120.

28. Hall, "Two Paradigms," p. 44.

29. See, for instance, O'Connor, *Raymond Williams*, p. 114, and Patrick Parrinder, "Utopia and Negativity in Raymond Williams," in *The Failure of Theory: Essays on Criticism and Contemporary Fiction* (Totowa, N.J.: Barnes and Noble, 1987), pp. 80–81. For Williams's sense of "structure of feeling" as hegemony, see "Base and Superstructure in Marxist Theory," *Problems of Materialism and Culture*, pp. 37–40; "Hegemony," *Marxism and Literature*, pp. 108–14; and the entry for *hegemony* in *Keywords* , pp. 144–46.

30. With respect to Gramsci's classism, see, for example, Joseph Femia, "Proletarian Hegemony and the Question of Authoritarianism," in *Gramsci's Political Thought: Hegemony, Consciousness, and the Revolutionary Process* (Oxford: Clarendon, 1981), pp. 165–89; Laclau and Mouffe, "The Gramscian Watershed," in *Hegemony and Socialist Strategy*, pp. 65–71; and Carl Boggs, "The Theory of Ideological Hegemony," in *The Two Revolutions: Antonio Gramsci and the Dilemma of Western Marxism* (Boston: South End Press, 1984), pp. 153–98. To cite one of Gramsci's best English readers, Stuart Hall: "In spite of his attack on, say, class reductionism, there is no question that Gramsci regards class as the fundamental social division" ("Discussion," in *Marxism and the Interpretation of Culture*, ed. Cary Nelson and Lawrence Grossberg [Urbana: University of Illinois Press, 1988], p. 70).

31. For what I call Williams's "neo-Gramscian, proletarian understanding of hegemony," see "Base and Superstructure in Marxist Theory," *Problems in Materialism and Culture*, p. 43.

32. The theoretical usefulness of Laclau and Mouffe's *Hegemony and Socialist Strategy* —and it is, I feel, one of the most useful political-theoretical texts to appear in the last decade—does not diminish the need to interrogate its premises and analyses, critiques and claims. Though this is obviously not the place to begin such an interrogation, I would nonetheless invoke en passant Barbara Epstein's critique in "Rethinking Social Movement Theory" that Laclau and Mouffe's emphasis on socially constructed interest suggests that there are "no objective limits to politics, no structural framework that has to be taken into account in devising political action" (*Socialist Theory* 90 [1990: 53). Put another way: Laclau and Mouffe's antieconomism—bracing as it is (such is the depth to which some of us have internalized a certain Marx!)—results, paradoxically enough, in an underestimation of the question of *strategy*. For a similar critique, one that focuses on Laclau and Mouffe's insufficient conceptualization of the "relatively stable institutional structures of capitalism" as well as the "complex ways in which such structure[s] both set limits and provide

opportunities for strategic conduct," see Nicos Mouzelis's "Marxism or Post-Marxism?" *New Left Review* 167 (January/February 1988): 107-23.

Finally, for a critique of Laclau and Mouffe, see my "Post-Marxist Rhetoric, Rhetorical Marxianism: Discourse and Institutionality in Laclau + Mouffe and Resnick + Wolff" (forthcoming).

"The Longest Cultural Journey": Raymond Williams and French Theory

Michael Moriarty

I want to consider here the problematic relationship between the thought of Raymond Williams and the tendencies in French literary theory since the 1950s.[1] It was Williams himself who remarked that the crossing of the Channel must be one of the longest cultural journeys in existence by comparison with the physical distance.[2] In considering Williams's engagement with French thought of, broadly speaking, the structuralist and poststructuralist variety, we shall find an acute sense of that distance: a certain sympathy that is partly an antipathy to the enemies in Britain of that kind of thought, and partly perhaps a solidarity with some of those in Britain who make use of it, combined with a distrust of its potential to renovate the struggle with those problems of form and history in culture to which Williams's own work is so signal a contribution.

Increasingly, Williams moved back toward the Marxist tradition he had distanced himself from in his pathbreaking early works. In so doing, he was moving against the current. Just as many Marxists were beginning, in Lyotard's phrase, to "drift away" from the orthodoxy they had striven for, Williams began more and more to systematize his relationship to the Marxist tradition. Now, when the collapse of Marxism is being proclaimed all over the world, as a result of events that took place less than two years after Williams's death, losing him seems more and more tragic, and we lack his never-to-be-formulated analysis of the collapse of "actually existing socialism" in Eastern Europe.

For Williams, Marxist philosophy was above all a materialism, its

91

theme the inscription of social relationships not only in ideas but in the body, the nerves, the gut. In this, his work harks back to an earlier materialism, that of the eighteenth-century French writers like Diderot, for whom materialism was not only a set of theses about the place of mind and matter in the universe, but a philosophy of organic needs and pleasures, sensations and sensibilities. Almost no other writers in the Marxist tradition have stressed as Williams stresses that human beings' response to history is mediated not essentially through beliefs, or through discourses, but through feeling. "Structures of feeling": the category has been stigmatized for its imprecision, but it has this merit, that it is an attempt to affirm at once the intelligibility of history and the forces of desire and revulsion that traverse it. In his reservations about "structuralism," we can detect a suspicion that it is not, fundamentally, attuned to this vigilant materialism.

True, Williams's Marxism and "structuralism" can be seen as directed against the same ideological problematic of empiricist individualism. But part of the thrust of *Marxism and Literature* was directed against the enterprise of reinforcing Marxism theoretically by the formation of the "triple alliance" with structuralist linguistics and Lacanian psychoanalysis. And this is the important reason why the relationship of Williams to French thought should be studied. For the de facto collapse of structuralist Marxism makes it tempting to those whose primary loyalty is to the political and theoretical tradition that sees social consciousness as determined in various ways by social being and questions of culture as fundamentally questions of power and ideology to reject "structuralist" thought root and branch. The alluring prospect it seemed to offer in the 1960s of a general revolutionary theory yielded to the early-1980s spectacle of a "poststructuralism" that seemed to have become the willing accomplice of the North American literary academy's desire to burnish its traditional methods of close reading with an attractive philosophical gloss, and in so doing to ward off the intellectual challenge of Marxism. It is not surprising that one response to this was to look for an original sin that might explain this unexpected veering of theory away from revolutionary politics. The role of Adam here devolves on Saussure.[3] Now, it is tempting to cite Williams's prescient rejection of the Saussurean legacy as a dreadful warning of the dire results of having accepted it. What I want to do here is to complicate this picture by discussing Williams's critique of structuralism in detail. I am not principally concerned with vindicating the one against the other, but rather with establishing a kind of dialogue between the two positions.

I shall begin with a few brief observations on the related issue of Williams's attitude to psychoanalysis. The quarrel, before being with Lacan, is with Freud himself. Williams holds that the Freudian claim to scientificity is unsound. First, he subscribes to Timpanaro's critique of the *Psychopathology of Everyday Life* as acknowledging only its own procedures of interpretation, overlooking the fact that misreadings and misrememberings can often be explained by traditional philological methods involving no recourse to the unconscious (*PMC* 116-17; *PL* 331). Second, more broadly, he insists (as thinkers of quite different persuasions are beginning also to urge) that between the analytic experience and the finished case history intervenes the process of composition, accrediting the analysis by techniques not radically distinguishable from those of fictional narratives such as those of Strindberg or Proust (*PL* 332).[4] Third, he is visibly (and, one cannot help thinking, justifiably) impatient with the attempt to bring questions of desire and subjectivity within the ambit of materialism by effectively adopting Lacanian psychoanalysis lock, stock, and barrel, as if there were not other psychoanalytical and indeed psychological accounts of these problems (*PMC* 117-19; *PL* 331-33). Yet the fact that the motivation for the attempt is sound emerges from the following interesting passage, with its echoes of Freud's *Civilization and Its Discontents*:

> Although there are major features in the social structure which are barring intense experiences, which are certainly barring self-images of autonomy of being and feeling . . . the level of the most authentic protest seems separable from those more local historical structures. They lie very deep within the whole cast of the civilization which is, for its own deepest reasons and often while denying that it is doing so, repressing intensely realized experiences of any kind. (*WS* 162-63)

The difference is of course that Williams is speaking of "*the* civilization," rather than plain "civilization," and thus maintaining an openness to history.[5] And Williams condemns "the whole [Freudian] conception of the social order as a merely negative system of constraints and inhibitions" as tributary to "the most classical bourgeois theory" (*PL* 333).

I move on now to an area far nearer the main current of Williams's own work, the area of language, and in particular to his critique of Saussure. Detailed discussion of this criticism is somewhat problematic, because it is not always clear what Williams is referring to: whether to Saussure himself, insofar as his thought is represented in the *Cours de linguistique générale*, or to an identifiably Saussurean school of linguists (but then which ones?), or to a Saussurean vulgate or doxa, which has been historically influential but which may or may not be faithful to the positions of the *Cours*.[6] The problem emerges, for instance, when, having taxed Saussure (and, as it happens, Vološinov) for isolating "the sign," Williams writes that "most of the important work on relations within a whole system is therefore an evident advance," with the apparent implication that this is an advance on Saussure: as if the impossibility of considering adequately the individual sign outside its relationship to others were not one of Saussure's most characteristic emphases. It is possible, however, to summarize the main lines of Williams's critique of identifiably Saussurean positions, and this I shall initially do, returning to the salient points for individual consideration.

Williams treats Saussure as exemplifying a trend termed by Vološinov, to whom Williams is much indebted here, "abstract objectivism." Its errors are manifold. First, it misconceives the object of linguistics. Instead of beginning with "the living speech of human beings in their specific social relationships in the world," abstract objectivism treated this simply as exemplifying "a fixed, objective, and in these senses 'given' system, which had theoretical and practical priority over what were described as 'utterances' " (*ML* 27), and then identified this system (*langue*) as the object of linguistics. Second, the *langue-parole* antithesis takes the bourgeois distinction between individual and social for granted (*ML* 28). Third, the primacy of a closed system over the process of utterance, coupled with the thesis of the arbitrariness and fixity of the sign, banish history and activity from linguistics; Williams has identified these as the two crucial interests of a Marxist theory of language (*ML* 21). The superficial affinity of the primacy of the linguistic system with Marxism's insistence on the primacy of an economic system that escapes the control of individual agents (*ML* 28) provides a feeble counterargument for

those who would uphold an untenable synthesis between two profoundly antithetical currents of thought (*ML* 21, 35).

Before detailed discussion, another preliminary remark. "A definition of language is always, implicitly or explicitly, a definition of
human beings in the world" (*ML* 21; likewise, Barthes remarks that
"there is often nothing more *directly* ideological than linguistics").[7]
This is why Williams wishes to contest the ideological implications
of certain methodological approaches to language. Yet a theory of
language is also, more modestly, since the foundation of the discipline of linguistics, a theory of the foundations and objects of that
discipline (itself historically, socially, and ideologically determined,
to be sure). Roy Harris fairly observes that Saussure's appeal may
well be linked to the profound antihistoricism of the twentieth century, while also urging that its positions be understood first and
foremost in terms of the exigencies of an academic program.[8] Dark
mutterings, like those of Timpanaro, about the origins of structuralism in the "anti-materialist reaction" that began in the late nineteenth
century do not significantly further the criticism of it.[9]

Williams's first set of criticisms, however, of the *langue-parole*
distinction, are apposite and cogent. Saussure's formula according to
which *langue* is social while *parole* is "an individual act of will and
intelligence" does indeed overlook both variations of *langue* among
individual speakers and the fundamentally social nature of speech
(it does not, however, *preclude* a conception of the individual as so-
cialized).[10]

Moreover, Williams attacks the Saussurean view (not indeed confined to Saussure) of communication as the passing of a message *between* separate individuals, never seen as "*with* each other, the fact
of language constituting and confirming their relationship" (*ML* 32).
These inadequacies have, however, been noticed not only by a
Marxist linguist like Vološinov, but also by linguists manifestly indebted to Saussure like Jakobson and Benveniste. The latter above
all stresses that individual identity is constructed intersubjectively
through language, and he draws the corollary that once this is understood, the individual-society antinomy fades away.[11] Furthermore, as I shall argue later, the inadequacy of the binary Saussurean
distinction between social *langue* and individual *parole* finds a corrective response in Barthes's attempt to locate structures mediating
between them.

Within the context of the history of linguistics, Saussure's insistence on the arbitrariness of the sign makes sense as part of an effort to found linguistics as distinct from psychology. Its implication is that the structures of language do not reflect a metaphysical world order or universal human patterns of experience or psychology. To this extent, it might seem attractive from a materialist viewpoint. Williams, however, takes the implications of "arbitrary" rather differently, as cutting off language from society and history: "[the sign] is not arbitrary but conventional, and . . . the convention is the result of a social process" (*PL* 330). I shall come to this problem presently, noting, however, that de Mauro argues that Saussure eschews "conventional" deliberately, but for methodological not ideological reasons, because the word implies the preexistence of the two terms linked by the convention, and thus accredits the conception of a language as a nomenclature, a set of names assigned (by convention, on this hypothesis) to a set of things.[12] Only the insistence on arbitrariness allows Saussure to affirm the mutually constitutive relationship of signified and signifier, and the fundamentally differential character of language systems, seen as functioning in virtue of the relationships between terms within the system rather than between individual terms and things or processes in the world. Williams of course rejects both the conception of the sign and the conception of the language system as just stated. And this attempt to locate the assertion of arbitrariness within Saussure's theoretical enterprise of course leaves open the whole question of whether the relationship between languagesystems and the extralinguistic world is itself arbitrary (the question whose lack of answer in Saussure is censured by Eagleton). Again, this question may be considered in terms of a strategic move within the discipline of linguistics. Benveniste argues that the problem is fundamentally metaphysical, falling (for the present at any rate) outside the ambit of linguistics, and that to pose the relationship between sign and reality as arbitrary is a way for the linguist to keep that problem at arm's length, and moreover to forestall the response that the speaking subject spontaneously brings to it, that is, that word and thing are mysteriously linked.[13] Martinet's critique of the nomenclature theory admits the possibility that some differences between linguistic terms reflect differences in nature and contents itself with urging that to each language there corresponds a particular ordering of the data of experience, rather than seeking to divorce languages from the world of experience alto-gether.[14] Williams would presumably echo Sebastiano Timpanaro's claim that "there is a limit to the arbitrariness of the classifications which each language imposes on experience, and this limit is set by man's very psycho-physical structure, by his needs, by his responses to particular stimuli and by his cognitive-practical activities."[15] Yet this does not impugn the essence of the structuralist claim, which is that the structure of a language cannot be *read off* from the struc-ture of experience or of reality.[16] It is this claim, and the correspond-ing claim to autonomy of linguistics, that the thesis of arbitrariness serves to protect. But it has further implications that cast doubt on some of Williams's other criticisms of Saussure.

I shall leave these for a moment and return to the charge that the thesis of arbitrariness is an eviction of history. For Williams, it is be-cause it has a history that the sign is not arbitrary: it is "the specific product of the people who have developed the language in ques-tion" (*PL* 330). And the systematic character of language, which he does not deny, is the "result, the always changing result, of the activ-ities of real people in social relationships" (ibid.). To reduce linguistic activity to performance of a preexisting system "denies the possibil-ity of a constant process of significant present activity which is ca-pable of altering the system, which observably does alter the system of social language" (*PL* 331).

Of course, changes in the linguistic system are acknowledged by Saussure, and de Mauro takes the chapter on the mutability and im-mutability of the sign as the effective refutation of the claim that Saussure's conception is antihistorical.[17] On the contrary, "a particular language-state is always the product of historical forces," but the continuation is significant for Williams's argument: "these forces ex-plain why the sign is unchangeable, i.e., why it resists any arbitrary substitution."[18] In other words, history for Saussure implies immobil-ity. I shall quote three of his arguments in favor of this view. If the sign is intrinsically arbitrary, having no rational connection with the thing it refers to, then the notion of replacing one sign with another, supposedly more rational, cannot arise. Second, the system of a lan-guage is too complex for the speaking mass to modify it, and expe-rience shows that linguistic specialists have had no success in doing so. Third, the language is protected from change precisely because it involves the whole population of language users (whereas a social institution confined to a minority is the more open to modification by that minority). It is at this point that ideology surfaces most blatantly. For the claim is that the language "blends with the life of society" and that this is "inert by nature," and thus above all a conservative force.[19] The natural inertia of the life of the social mass is so taken for granted by Saussure that it can be adduced in a parenthesis. Yet the first two arguments are equally problematic. They both ignore the relationships between language and ideology. Let us suppose that the use of the masculine in English as a neuter form is purely the result of contingent historical shifts in grammatical paradigms; this would not alter the fact that it has ideological implications (the equation of the masculine with the normal and the universal). So that it makes sense to query this usage as feminists have done; and the usage itself is altering as a result. Again, intervention on the language system from above has not always been as ineffective as Saussure suggests. The seventeenth century in France and the eighteenth century in England show the contrary. In both, attempts were made to process the existing linguistic heritage so as to create a homogeneous ruling-class and metropolitan speech and writing. "The habits of a language are too strong," remarks Williams, "to be wholly altered by determined yet relatively ignorant teachers, but the mark of their effort is still on us, and the tension they created is still high" (*LR* 244). These last words implicitly address a point urged by Saussure in his demarcation of the diachronic and synchronic aspects of language: that the speaking subject ignores or is ignorant of the historical roots of his or her speech, and operates only with a synchronic system; that the linguist can therefore enter into the consciousness of speaking subjects only by suppressing the past, since for the speaking subject, the synchronic aspect of language is its true and only reality.[20] But the speaking subject may be far from unconscious of the *effects* of linguistic history: when that history that has promoted one (historically contingent) version of a system above others, no less and no more historically contingent, so as to identify it with the norm, the system as a whole; so that to learn to speak or to write ("correct") English may well be to learn to deny the speech habits of those with whom one grew up.[21]

Williams's final major criticism of Saussurean linguistics focuses on the concepts of sign and system with which it operates. First of all, he holds that "the relation within the sign between the formal element and the meaning which this element carries is . . . , crucially, . . . not fixed" (*ML* 37). The reality of the sign is as a "dynamic fusion of 'formal element' and 'meaning' . . . rather than as fixed 'already-given' internal significance" (*ML* 39). These remarks at least seem intended to cover Saussure, especially since the denial of the internal fixity of the sign in the first of the two passages just quoted follows directly on a denial of its arbitrariness (though, again, Williams's references to "formalist" linguistics [*ML* 38–39] are far from clear). Likewise, when he refers to the notion of language as "a closed, formal system" (*ML* 36), he seems to be talking of Saussure, perhaps among others, as he certainly is when he alludes to notions of language as "an objective system which is beyond individual initiative or creative use" (*ML* 40)—though the ease with which Saussure is here bundled into the same basket as mechanical and behaviorist theorists is disconcerting.

Yet this is where another aspect of the theory of arbitrariness comes in. It is because there is no natural bond linking signifier to signified that the link is determined by tradition (in other words, by history) and that the relationship between the two that constitutes the individual sign is open to change.[22] Saussure cites several examples of the historical variability of the relationship and concludes that "[a] language changes, or rather evolves, under the influence of all the forces which can affect either sounds or meanings."[23] As Barthes remarks, pursuing the Saussurean comparison of linguistics and economics: "Saussure's little tragedy is that, unlike the arrogant conservatives, he has confidence neither in the Sign nor in Gold: he sees clearly that the link between paper and gold, signifier and signified is shifting and precarious."[24] And this precariousness is precisely at the root of Saussure's conception of value, which serves to keep within bounds the shifting and indeterminate relationship between signifier and signified. For instance, he urges that a single word can convey quite different ideas (*adopt* in "to adopt a child," "to adopt a fashion"); and the fact that the comparison here is between literal and figurative uses shows that Saussure was not indifferent to the "creative" power of metaphor to modify the signifier/signified relationship. Again, the word *gentlemen* may within the course of a single speech be pronounced with striking variations of intonation and even meaning (it can express respect, servility, contempt).[25] Saussure then turns to value, the dimension of a sign's relationships with others in the system, as a means of pinning down its identity: but then in doing so he implies that that identity is variable and relative.[26]

There are two comments to be made on this. First, Vološinov correctly observes that Saussure's principal concern is with the problem of how we recognize a given unit among its variable semantic and phonic manifestations, whereas what speakers and listeners are concerned with is the sign's potential to be adapted to a given concrete situation.[27] To understand a sign, in particular, is to link it to that situation, not simply to recognize it as a stable entity. But one wonders how the sign could be adapted and its novelty in context assimilated if there were not some relatively stable unit there to be recognized: on the semantic level, "an effective nucleus of meaning but [which] has in practice a variable range," to adopt Williams's own formulation (*ML* 39); the compatibility of which, in itself, with Saussure's conception he seems unwilling to recognize, convinced as he appears to be of the fixity in Saussure of the signifier/signified relationship.

Second, however, Williams is unwilling to accept that the problem of the variability of the sign can indeed be reduced to that of the sign's relationships to other signs in the system. It must be linked to the social process of the creations of meanings (*ML* 42). True, the workings of this process are virtually ignored by Saussure, and this is no doubt partly the reason for Williams's claim that the Saussurean language system is essentially a closed one.

It has to be admitted that the text of the *Cours* is not univocal on this point. On the one hand, the notion of the value of a sign as determined by the relations between it and other signs leads Saussure to examine the associative relationships between a given sign and others with which it has something in common (two or more terms must have something in common for meaning to be able to arise from the difference between them). These relationships are intrinsically open-ended.[28] Moreover, de Mauro draws attention to Saussure's remark that a language at no time possesses a perfectly fixed system of units.[29] If this is so, the detailed study of shifts in meaning made, for instance, by Williams in *Keywords* does not preclude a certain Saussurean conception of a system as a temporary network of relationships between historically variable terms (the system, Saussure says, is never anything other than momentary).[30] Roy Harris, however, points to numerous other passages in the *Cours* that do indeed bear out Williams's assertion that the Saussurean language system is fixed and closed.[31] But to accept that these discrepancies exist within the *Cours* is not a further reason for jettisoning it. It is rather a reason for eschewing global gestures of acceptance or rejection, assertions of compatibility or incompatibility with Marxism (as if this too were not a profoundly divided and multiple current of thought).

I shall point to one of the tensions in the Saussurean system as a means of very tentatively suggesting a possible rapprochement between Williams's and Saussure's concerns. When a particular word is used, it is selected from a series of associated terms, stored in the individual brain.[32] Moreover, the listener's interpretation of the utterance presupposes his or her unconscious recourse to a similar, but not necessarily identical, storehouse. Now, if one accepts that the formation of these individual linguistic "storehouses" is in fact a social process, and a never-ending one, one can substitute for the notion of a homogeneous system, located in a homogeneous "speaking mass," the in itself quite un-Saussurean conception of a set of overlapping *langues*, in relationships of interdependence, competition, even hostility.[33] One then leaves room for the "intersecting of differently oriented social interests within one and the same sign community"—in short, for the class struggle in language alluded to by Vološinov.[34] It might of course seem easier for the Marxist involved in questions of language to adopt Vološinov lock, stock, and barrel. But that would be to cut oneself off from contact with the Saussurean legacy, and from significant currents of thought in domains other than language as such. It seems desirable, while granting the force of some of Williams's criticism of Saussure, to retain some kind of differential evaluation of different aspects of the Saussurean system, some sense of the productivity of its own internal tensions.

Against structuralist literary theory as such, the charge of indifference to history is repeated and narrowed down. Structuralism is indifferent to its own history, rooted in the antihistorical New Criticism. The application to literature of the model of language as an internal-rule-governed system Williams sees as "directly congruent" with New Critical procedures: Richards's thinking about the "isolated internal organization" of a poem, the North American analysis of a "specific verbal organization" (*WS* 206). There is a certain prima facie plausibility to this claim. Genette, for instance, accepts that, in its pro-motion of structure over substance, structuralism is more than a method: it is a general tendency of thought, what some would call an ideology. It belongs, he says, to the same movement away from positivistic historical and biographical discourse as the criticism of Proust, Eliot, and Valéry, as Russian formalism, French thematic crit-icism, and Anglo-American New Criticism. Genette even concedes that structural analysis can be considered in some sense an equiva-lent of "close reading."[35] The title of the article from which these re-marks are taken, "Structuralisme et critique littéraire," might be taken to bear out another of Williams's claims, that "literary criticism" is an Anglo-American term, its adoption in Europe a sign of American cul-tural preponderance (*PL* 337). And one might argue for a traffic of ideas in the other direction, from European formalism to a post-New Critical America. To American scholars committed to John Crowe Ransom's enterprise of founding literary criticism as an autonomous intellectual discipline (modeled explicitly on the structures of cor-porate capitalism: Criticism Inc.) exiled European formalists might conceivably have seemed the literary equivalent of German rocket technologists for NASA and the Pentagon.[36] Wellek and Warren, in their influential *Theory of Literature*, drew occasionally on Jakob-son, and even on Saussure (albeit for a rather insubstantial analogy), amid hosts of references to other critics, scholars, and theorists; and in equating literature with fiction, they might certainly be seen as at-tempting to uncouple it from nonliterary history and from ideol-ogy.[37]

But Williams is not content with this fairly plausible line of argu-ment, of a *congruence* between New Criticism and structuralism, but insists to a striking extent on a suppositious actual *influence* of the former on the latter. French structuralism, which may have looked so exotic an import in the 1960s, was only "a long-lost cousin who had emigrated from Cambridge in the late twenties and early thirties" (*WS* 206). The image of the cousin is restated in connection with the pronouncement that structuralism's development in France has been "deeply determined" by American New Criticism, of which it is simply a "more deeply alienated form." But X's cousin is not X's offspring: they are related by a common ancestor. Williams, how-ever, never identifies the ancestor, and the cousin image helps him to affirm the plausible affinity between New Criticism and structuralism (they look so alike they must be related), while by its reference to kinship structures suggesting a more problematic link of direct filiation (structuralism is the inheritor of the hereditary vice of the New Criticism, and the work of Barthes or Genette, say, is the culmination of a trend that started with the reactionary southern agrarianism of Ransom) (*PL* 337-38).

I think that the unstated structure of argument obscured by the metaphor goes something like this. Williams refers favorably to John Fekete's *The Critical Twilight* as a study of the ideology of scientific and antihistorical criticism (*PL* 337). Now, Fekete shows carefully how, in Ransom, for example, this ideology was developed as a means of coming to terms with a capitalist social order he had earlier rejected from the reactionary agrarian position. The agrarians had defended (their version of) culture against capitalism; the criticism had failed, partly because of shifts in the nature of capitalism itself, enshrined in Roosevelt's New Deal. By severing cultural values altogether from history, New Criticism then showed that they were not after all under threat from a social and political order now seen as unchangeable.[38]

Fekete then argues that structuralism also rationalizes the domination of an unchangeable system, an "epistemological strategy of technocratic rule." He does not, I think, claim that it is genealogically linked to the Anglo-American trends he discusses: rather, he speaks of "extending" his critique from the latter to the former. He is thus appealing to a likeness between them, a likeness doubtless rooted in a shared relationship to a world capitalist order. Having charted an Anglo-American narrative, he implicitly relates it, by the mention of French structuralism, to a larger narrative of capitalism and culture in the twentieth century. This in itself is unobjectionable. Williams, however, seems to want to include structuralism within Fekete's own narrative framework. The results are unfortunate.[39]

First, Williams offers no empirical or textual evidence for his account of the relationships between structuralism and the New Criticism. One could as plausibly claim that Jean-Pierre Richard must be a long-lost cousin of I. A. Richards. Genette's acceptance of a parallel does not, manifestly, imply a determinism; as well imply that Valéry or Proust was "deeply determined" by Eliot. True, in its formative years, French structuralism occasionally engages explicitly with North American or British debates and theorists. In their treatment of point of view and narration, both Genette and Todorov acknowledge the work of Percy Lubbock and Wayne Booth, but since they criticize it for its confusion of the two categories, it is hard to assert deep influence here.[40] As for Barthes, it is hard to believe that he ever heard of John Crowe Ransom: he never shows the slightest interest in, or even acquaintance with, Anglo-American criticism. In *Critique et vérité*, he asserts the fundamental ambiguity of the literary work, but I think we can accept his later statement that this really has nothing to do with the New Criticism, and is more a tactical and polemical move directed against the French academic orthodoxy.[41] Certainly, the open-ended plurality of the text as affirmed in *S/Z* has nothing in common with the organic unity that for the New Criticism transcends the ambiguities of the text; in his concept of the cultural code Barthes explicitly links the text to history and society through the discourses it quotes, presupposes, and conveys.[42]

One of the potentially misleading aspects of the assimilation of structuralism to New Criticism is in fact that it ignores the different status of the literary text in each. In general, New Criticism gives priority to the independence and uniqueness of the literary text, whether this is conceived, as by Richards, as the record of a complex experience or, as by Brooks and Wimsatt and Beardsley, as an autonomous self-contained object. Even when, as in the Eliot of "Tradition and the Individual Talent," the emphasis is on literature as an order, the components of that order are still individual texts. The focus, then, is on the work of literature as an end in itself, and its features are explained in terms of the relationship between its constituent elements, or between it and other works.

As such it may be contrasted with those schools of thought that see the work as the manifestation of "something else" besides itself, such as Marxism or psychoanalysis. But as Todorov points out, structuralist poetics belongs not to the former but to the latter category. Structuralist poetics deals not with the work in itself but with "literariness," what characterizes a discourse as literary, and the work is taken simply as an example of this.[43] This corresponds more or less to the goals Barthes allots to his postulated "science of literature," and to the approach he follows in his most characteristically structuralist work on literature, the "Introduction à l'analyse structurale des récits." The notion of "literariness" is no doubt itself problematic, although to affirm the specificity of literary discourse is not the same as to declare it autonomous.[44] But, this apart, the point at issue here is the tenability of Williams's claim of a determining influence, even indirect, of New Criticism on structuralism, and my argument is that not only is this historically unsubstantiated but it erases certain crucial theoretical divergences between the two. The assertion of a determination falls into the trap of reductionism Williams himself points to so tellingly in *Marxism and Literature*.

Again, it is worth noting that some of Williams's criticism of structuralism can be found in the mouths of "structuralists" or ex-structuralists themselves. One would not expect him to have been sympathetic to Barthes's rejection of the concept of the sign as tributary to Western theological metaphysics, but he might have echoed Kristeva's claim that a semiotics founded on the (Saussurean) linguistic model "restricts the value of its discovery to the field of practices which do no more than subserve the principle of social cohesions, of the social contract," even if again his alternative would not have been to privilege by contrast play, pleasure, desire.[45]

Williams's characterization of structuralism is thus questionable in certain important ways, but at the same time one must acknowledge its pertinence as an ideological diagnosis. It is wrong to reduce structuralism in general to nothing more than a high-tech New Criticism. But, in a given set of literary and cultural institutions, it could function in that way. The point is not altogether that structuralism loses its critical political edge on the journey from revolutionary France across the Channel or across the Atlantic, though that is partly true. Todorov or Genette, say, were never interested in harnessing literary structuralism to a revolutionary science of the sign (a few acerbic asides by Genette reveal a fundamental hostility to Marxist criticism).[46] And the practitioners of that science (Kristeva and Sollers leading the long-marching Maoist columns of *Tel Quel*, with Barthes as a fellow traveler) have by subsequent political and theoretical moves helped to discredit the global project Williams was challenging in *Marxism and Literature* and elsewhere: that of revitalizing Marxist theoretical and political practice by coupling it to structuralist linguistics and Lacanian psychoanalysis.

Yet, after all, the questions that project was addressing were genuine ones, and Williams least of all would have been satisfied with a simple counterinvocation of "history," a pious ejaculation aimed at silencing the tempting overtures of an idealist structuralism. The productive emphasis, on which he always insisted, was on a history of forms, and here his work converges with other strands of French-language theory to which the names of Barthes (mostly in his "early" period) and Goldmann can be attached.

Yet there is a sharp contrast in Williams's attitude toward these two. With Goldmann, there is a serious and patient engagement, the recognition not only of a shared project, but also of a theoretical debt on Williams's part; Goldmann's achievement is recognized even when his method is rejected as insufficiently materialist (*ML* 106). Toward Barthes, on the other hand, there is apparent indifference, at least in the published work.[47] Yet despite this one can point to significant elements of theoretical convergence between all three writers, going beyond the fact that the work of all three, as it took shape in the 1950s, can be seen as combating both the implicit ideology of orthodox literary and cultural discourses and the bankruptcy of the alternative orthodoxy of Stalinism. All three seek to rethink afresh the relationship of the literary text to history and to politics through a promotion of formal analysis against orthodox Marxist reflection theory.

I take Barthes first. In *Le degré zéro de l'écriture* he insists that the locus of political commitment is first and last in the writing. Between the national language and the singular inflections imposed on the writer by his or her irreducible bodily singularity, writing is the medium term:

> Every Form is also a Value; which is why between the language and style there is room for another formal reality: writing. In any literary form, there is the general choice of a tone, an ethos, so to speak, and this is precisely where a writer clearly individualizes himself, because this is where he commits himself.[48]

In so doing, with remarkable prescience, since his own reading or at least serious reading of Saussure postdates *Le degré zéro de l'écriture*, Barthes points to a significant absence in Saussure's *langue/parole* model of any mediating agency between the will and intelligence of the individual and the social product that is a language. Moreover, he shows that writing's contact with history is not or not only through the social and economic processes it does or does not represent, it is in the choice of an *écriture*, a moment of freedom that afterward functions as a constraint.

In *Le Degré zéro de l'écriture* Barthes does not specifically discuss reflection theory, but that he rejects it is plain from his dismissal of socialist realist writing. Whatever social processes or dilemmas it represents, it is tied by the linguistic and stylistic conventions it has assumed to the bourgeois literature that the bourgeois avant-garde has itself been forced by history to jettison as fatally compromised with the impostures of bourgeois ideology.

Barthes repudiates the Zhdanovist gesture that brands all concern with form as formalism, that is, bourgeois, indifferent to history and society. On the contrary, he insists that the more a system is defined through its forms, its codes rather than its signifieds, the more open it is to historical criticism.[49] In his essay on Lévi-Strauss, Barthes again asserts the "responsibility of forms" against the taboo on "formalism." Despite their apparent remoteness from history, Lévi-Strauss's ethnographical studies, revealing the logics in play in human beings' appropriation of the material world, offer models for the analyst of contemporary societies, enabling him or her to uncover the sociologic between the reasons and narratives offered by mass society.[50]

Ecriture in Barthes's sense comes under Goldmann's conception of human behavior in general as a significant response to a specific situation, which for both writers is a historically determined one.[51] And Goldmann develops this conception precisely to counter, or at least to qualify, reflection theory. The primary task of a sociologist of the novel is not to relate its content to social reality but to establish "the relationship between the *novel form* itself and the *structure* of the social milieu within which it has developed, that is to say between the novel as a literary genre and modern individualistic society."[52] To seek correspondences of content between the work and the collective consciousness or empirical reality is to focus on adventitious and heterogeneous aspects of the work, and to overlook its unity as a specifically literary production.[53]

Williams has paid eloquent tribute to this insight: "The most exciting experience for me, in reading Lukács and Goldmann, was the stress on forms," confirmation of his own conviction that

> the most penetrating analysis would always be of forms, specifically literary forms, where changes of viewpoint, changes of known and

knowable relationships, changes of possible and actual resolutions, could be directly demonstrated . . . and reasonably related to a real social history. (*PMC* 26)

Williams, however, registers an important caveat: "form, in Lukács or Goldmann, translates too often as genre or as kind" (*PMC* 27). And I think that Goldmann contents himself with this narrow conception because he needs it as a preliminary to narrowing down the object of formal analysis still further by an aesthetic evaluation; and that he wants to maintain evaluation, rather for the same reason as the Barthes of *S/Z*, as a counter to the indifference of bourgeois society to the qualitative.[54] And by the same token he does not in fact reject reflection theory en bloc. On the contrary, he argues that the reification and fetishism of capitalist society have deprived the collective consciousness of its active potential, transforming it into a mere reflection of economic reality. With the inevitable exception of Balzac, the novel proper (unlike the tragic drama of Racine) is not the expression of any collective consciousness at all but a transposition of the structures of daily life in capitalist society, originating in a nonconceptual affective resistance to it, and achieved, in formal terms, through a confrontation between a hero and a world both in discordance with authentic values. Goldmann stresses that these authentic values are immanent, not embodied in any one character or in the world, but surging into the discrepancy between the one and the other that emerges in the fundamentally ironic structure of the author's relationship to both.[55] Since the distinguishing character of a work of literature is, as we have seen, its unity, it is plain that most "novels," insofar as they embody a collective consciousness deprived of any active or creative role, are incapable of attaining this unity, and are thus not literature at all. They are therefore unworthy of the attention not just of the literary critic but also of the literary sociologist. Lacking form, they are nothing other than a congeries of stereotypes and notations of empirical data that give us no insight into the structures and workings of capitalist society.

The objections to this elegant argument are obvious enough. It is not just that, as Williams observes, the characterization of the novel as the confrontation between a "problematic" hero and a society whose limitations his fate reveals is derived from French and Russian novels, and seems to apply to few nineteenth-century English specimens of the genre (*WS* 161). The founding evaluations simply reproduce the value judgments of bourgeois literary consumption and criticism. Moreover, they involve a selective attitude to the historical and cultural material, a "substitution of epochal for connected historical analysis," and an indifference to actual cultural processes of production that confines analysis to already known history, structures, products (*ML* 106-7). Moreover, Goldmann's analysis of the disappearance of active collective consciousness depends on a view of the proletariat as incorporated into capitalist society (a view that can be paralleled in Barthes), which is deeply tempting to alienated intellectuals but whose temptations Williams rejects with impressive steadfastness.

What I want to suggest here is that the Barthesian concept of *écriture* is far less open to this kind of objection. Second, it provides a valuable complement to the notion Williams derives from Goldmann of the collective subject. This notion Goldmann defines in interestingly ambiguous terms. It is on one level a social group, constituting "a process of structuration that develops in the consciousness of its members affective, intellectual, and practical tendencies, towards a coherent response to the problems posed by their relationships to nature and by their inter-human relationships."[56] These tendencies are thwarted by the existence, in the individuals constituting the group, of conflicting tendencies deriving from their membership in other groups, hence the incoherence of the resulting artistic productions, saving those of the great writer.

It might be argued, of course, after Althusser, that this theory equates ideology with psychology, and that its stress on consciousness is insufficiently materialist for it to serve as effectively as a materialist contribution to the problem with which Williams links it: that of making sense of such historical configurations as romantic poets, Jacobean dramatists, and so forth. The objection is less applicable to another of Goldmann's formulations, in which the transindividual subject of cultural production is not a collection of individuals in a group, but a network of relationships in which the individual is only the immediate subject of the pattern of behavior in question.[57] But one would then have to incorporate into the network of relationships the raw materials on which the labor of cultural production operates: in this case, a language and a set of literary institutions. We should thus move nearer to the Althusserian concept of a mode of production as a combination of agents of production and instruments of production, not simply a set of relationships among agents. But we should also move nearer the terrain of Barthes's concept of *écriture.*

When Williams talks about such groups as romantic poets or Jacobean dramatists, he is less interested in chronological classification than in "a community of form which is also a specific general way of seeing other people and nature." What is important here is that in Williams's own terms it is the form that, so to speak, does the seeing, not, on this level, the minds of those who adopt it.[58] He knows (what Lukács and Goldmann seem less aware of) that writing is not the delivery of a consciousness into a transparent medium:

> The actual activity of almost all arts is a very material process indeed. . . . In the case of language, it is that experience of finding within what is often a quite resistant medium (indeed, what is not a medium at all—that misrepresents it), finding rather within what is a quite resistant stored area of language the possibilities of saying something quite specific which is not necessarily realized . . . until that process has been gone through. (*RH* 92-93)

Williams's own syntax, in this passage and elsewhere, drives, or rather winds, the point home, like someone bolting a metal plate into place, tightening the fit while constantly adjusting the alignment.

The medium that is not a medium presents itself to the writer in two ways. First, as a language, "which has entered into his own constitution long before he begins to write." And, second, as a form:

> Anyone who has carefully observed his own practice of writing eventually finds that there is a point where, although he is holding the pen or tapping the typewriter, what is being written, while not separate from him, is not only him either, and of course this other force is literary form.

His example is striking: nineteenth-century working-class writers, who wrote of their own lives not in the novel form, "virtually impenetrable to working-class writers for three or four generations," but in the autobiographical form they could relate to their experience of oral testimony (in religion or elsewhere) (*RH* 86). But what Williams is talking about here is not only genres but *écritures,* modes of writing within a genre or perhaps overrunning genre distinctions. And this point will appear if we read his essay "Forms of English Fiction in 1848" in relation to the notion of *écriture*.[59]

In this essay, Williams is seeking to make sense of the emergence of new forms of writing in more complex ways than are suggested by the claim that 1848 is the moment of the initiation in fiction of a characteristic bourgeois realism. For Barthes, too, 1848 is a dividing line with profound literary implications. It marks the splitting of a period of bourgeois hegemony that has lasted, in his view, for two hundred years. French society becomes visibly divided into three hostile classes, and bourgeois ideology no longer appears as a universal truth, but as one ideology among others. What emerges in place of the corresponding bourgeois *écriture* that linked together writers of different beliefs and persuasions within the gamut of bourgeois ideology is a multiplicity of different forms of writing, the study of which takes up the remainder of *Le degré zéro de l'écriture*. Clearly, the historical content of this analysis (leaving aside the question of its accuracy) is quite different from that of Williams's.[60] And Williams's concepts of interlocking class relationships, of "dominant," "residual," and "emergent" cultural forms, are far more subtle and sophisticated than the sociological categories Barthes brings to questions of cultural analysis.[61] What I want to stress is that both writers affirm that the question of literature and "1848" can only properly be put in terms of form. For Williams, as for Barthes, what the formal analysis reveals is the precise nature of the writer's, or group of writers', response to the historical situation, going beyond obvious features of class and ideological alignment. Barthes's analysis of the language of socialist realist novels undermined their claim to be considered authentically proletarian writing; Williams, operating to be sure with a different political agenda, is concerned to nuance a perception of the key mid-century "realist" English novels as embodying in fictional form "the emergence of a conscious, incorporating bourgeois culture" (*WS* 155).

The methodological affinities and discrepancies of Williams's concept of "form" with Barthes's of *écriture* will emerge from a few examples. Barthes draws attention to the verbal form and substance of the literary text: a set of historically variable relationships between a selection from the vocabulary of the language as a whole and a set of syntactic procedures. From the combination of these dimensions, which he will later call paradigmatic and syntagmatic, Barthes generates a remarkably subtle and flexible set of historical analyses. One of them deals with the incorporation into bourgeois fictional narrative of actual speech: at first, for decorative purposes, the dialects of bohemians, concierges, and thieves is quoted but kept at a safe distance from the reader, but in Proust and in Céline, the reproduction of different speech patterns comes to express the whole content of the social contradiction.[62] The parallel is striking with Williams's discussion of Elizabeth Gaskell, reproducing the dialect of the people she writes about, with careful annotations for the reader to whom, "in a culture as deeply divided into classes, especially on this issue of literature and book-learning," she knows it will be unfamiliar (*WS* 160). Again in *Vanity Fair*, Thackeray's placing of "a very remarkable socio-critical perspective within the half-playful, half-managing [narratorial] tone of an older kind of fictional form" (*WS* 159) may be linked precisely (despite the divergence of tone) with Barthes's discussion of the socialist realists' combination of proletarian subject matter and attitudes with the emphatic signs of an inherited literary language.[63] At the same time, when Williams wants to discuss those novels—by the Brontës, as it happens—that contain affirmations of intense personal experience, he draws on aspects of form (compositional technique, plot structure, and point of view) to which the notion of *écriture* as used by Barthes does not extend.

I am not, then, offering the notion of *écriture* as a catchall solution to the problems discussed by Williams. What I want to suggest is simply that it has a significant potential purchase on them, especially if it is linked to an analysis of the actual processes by which the knowledge of a language is reproduced in a given society, like that undertaken in the French context by Renée Balibar. Such an analysis could make it possible to develop the kind of insight I quoted earlier concerning the historical inaccessibility of the novel to working-class writers, since familiarity with the kind of linguistic codes necessary to the operation of the novel as conventionally understood can result only from a determinate social process of linguistic formation hard to separate from class subjection and incorporation.[64]

I have tried to argue in this essay that a wholehearted endorsement of Williams's critique of the French theoretical legacy known as structuralism is unhelpful, and that certain currents or moments within structuralism can be seen as profoundly suggestive from the point of view of a materialist criticism and theory. It was Williams himself who said that "a fully historical semiotics would be very much the same thing as cultural materialism" (*WS* 210). If the French theorists I have been considering did not or did not always succeed in, or even aspire to, linking the sign systems they studied with history, that is not an error likely to befall anyone responsive to the theoretical and critical writing of Raymond Williams.

NOTES

I refer to work by Raymond Williams in the text using these abbreviations, followed by page numbers:

LR *The Long Revolution* (Harmondsworth: Penguin: 1965 [1961])

ML *Marxism and Literature* (Oxford: Oxford University Press, 1977)

PL *Politics and Letters: Interviews with New Left Review* (London: Verso, 1979)

PM *The Politics of Modernism: Against the New Conformists*, ed. Tony Pinkney (London: Verso, 1989)

PMC *Problems in Materialism and Culture* (London: Verso, 1980)

RH *Resources of Hope: Culture, Democracy, Socialism*, ed. Robin Gable (London: Verso, 1989)

WS *Writing in Society* (London: Verso, 1984)

1. I use the word *French* for the sake of convenience. Of the French-language authors mentioned here, Saussure was Swiss and Goldmann Romanian; Todorov is Bulgarian.

2. *Resources of Hope*, p. 78. I shall hereafter refer to works by Williams in the text using the abbreviations shown above followed by the page number.

3. Thus Terry Eagleton, following Frank Lentricchia: Barthes's *Le plaisir du texte* "naïvely consummates a crippling repression of history born with Saussure's suspension of the referent and Husserl's bracketing of the empirical object" (*Against the Grain: Essays 1975-1985* [London: Verso, 1986], p. 53).

4. For a powerful study of relationships between theory and fiction, see Malcolm Bowie, *Freud, Proust and Lacan: Theory as Fiction* (Cambridge: Cambridge University Press, 1987).

5. The definite article in the German title of *Civilization and Its Discontents* (*Das Unbehagen in der Kultur*) has of course a generalizing, not a particularizing, value.

6. In a lecture published in *The Politics of Modernism*, Williams refers to the prevailing versions of Saussure as "misleading, even at times fraudulent" in their selectivity (p. 185; see also p. 171). He does not make clear the grounds for this view; though see Marc Angenot, "Structuralism as Syncretism: Institutional Distortions of Saussure," in *The Structural Allegory: Reconstructive Encounters with the New French Thought*, ed. John Fekete (Manchester: Manchester University Press, 1984), pp. 150-63. Williams refers in the lecture to this volume (*Politics of Modernism*, pp. 173-74).

7. Roland Barthes, "Saussure, le signe, la démocratie," in *L'aventure sémiologique* (Paris: Seuil, 1985), p. 222. The translation is my own.

8. Roy Harris, *Reading Saussure* (London: Duckworth, 1987), pp. 201-2.

9. Sebastiano Timpanaro, *On Materialism*, trans. Lawrence Garner (1975; reprint, London: Verso, 1980), p. 137. This is not to deny the serious and impressive character of Tim-

panaro's criticism of Saussurean linguistics as such, qualities one may fail to find in his treatment of French structuralism.

10. Ferdinand de Saussure, *Cours de linguistique générale*, ed. Tullio de Mauro (Paris: Payot, 1972), pp. 25–30; *Course in General Linguistics*, trans. Wade Baskin, with an introduction by Jonathan Culler (Glasgow: Fontana/Collins, 1974), pp. 11–15. For the criticism see Roman Jakobson, "Langue and Parole: Code and Message," in *On Language*, ed. Linda R. Waugh and Monique Monville-Burston (Cambridge, Mass.: Harvard University Press, 1990), pp. 81–109, especially pp. 90–93. I mention Jakobson rather than Williams's source, Vološinov (to whom Jakobson indeed alludes), in order to show that Saussure's inadequate formulation of the problem has been noted by non-Marxist thinkers about language.

11. Emile Benveniste, *Problèmes de linguistique générale*, vol. 1 (Paris: Gallimard, 1966, 1974), pp. 259–60. Compare Williams's formulation: "individuality, by the fully social fact of language . . . is the active constitution, within distinct physical beings, of the social capacity which is the means of realization of any individual life" (*Marxism and Literature*, pp. 41–42). On Jakobson, see note 10. This stress on the intersubjective creation of identity through speech is of course taken over by Lacan.

12. Saussure, *Cours*, p. 364.

13. Benveniste, *Problèmes*, p. 52.

14. André Martinet, *Eléments de linguistique générale*, rev. ed. (Paris: Armand Colin, 1980), pp. 11–12.

15. Timpanaro, *On Materialism*, p. 155.

16. Oswald Ducrot and Tzvetan Todorov, *Dictionnaire encyclopédique des sciences du langage*, (Paris: Seuil, 1972), p. 37.

17. Saussure, *Cours*, p. 448 n. 146.

18. Saussure, *Cours*, p. 105; *Course*, p. 72.

19. Saussure, *Cours*, pp. 106–8; *Course*, pp. 73–74.

20. Saussure, *Cours*, pp. 117, 128, 136; *Course*, pp. 81, 90, 96.

21. Williams makes this point powerfully in *Long Revolution*, p. 247.

22. Saussure, *Cours*, p. 108; *Course*, p. 74. See also *Cours*, pp. 448–49 n. 150.

23. Saussure, *Cours*, pp. 109–11; *Course*, pp. 75–76.

24. Barthes, "Saussure, le signe, la démocratie," p. 224 (my translation).

25. Saussure, *Cours*, pp. 150–51; *Course*, p. 108.

26. See Saussure's remarks on "redouter," "craindre," and "avoir peur" in *Cours*, p. 160; *Course*, p. 116.

27. V. N. Vološinov, *Marxism and the Philosophy of Language*, trans. Ladislav Matejka and I. R. Titunik (Cambridge, Mass.: Harvard University Press, 1986), pp. 67–68.

28. Saussure, *Cours*, p. 174; *Course*, p. 126.

29. Saussure, *Cours*, p. 234; *Course*, p. 171. See also *Cours*, p. 454 n. 176.

30. Saussure, *Cours*, p. 126; *Course*, p. 88.

31. Harris, *Reading Saussure*, pp. 221–22.

32. Saussure, *Cours*, p. 171; *Course*, p. 123.

33. These variations between different versions of the language, or different languages, would perhaps be predominantly semantic, but grammar and syntax would not be excluded.

34. Vološinov, *Marxism and the Philosophy of Language*, p. 23.

35. Gérard Genette, "Structuralisme et critique littéraire," in *Figures I* (Paris: Seuil, 1966), pp. 145–70.

36. Terry Eagleton remarks on the North American assimilation of structuralism in a form largely compatible with New Criticism (*Against the Grain*, pp. 52-53).

37. René Wellek and Austin Warren compare the distinction between "the poem as such" and "the individual experience of the poem" to that between *langue* and *parole* (*Theory of Literature* [Harmondsworth: Penguin, 1976], p. 152). This statement certainly does bear out Williams's view of the congruence between the structuralist conception of language systems and the New Critical view of the poem; but it would be odd to take Wellek and Warren's position as exemplary of French structuralism. On Wellek and Warren's identification of "literature" with "imaginative literature" or "fiction" see *Theory of Literature*, pp. 22-26.

38. John Fekete, *The Critical Twilight: Explorations in the Ideology of Anglo-American Literary Theory from Eliot to McLuhan* (London: Routledge and Kegan Paul, 1978), pp. 44-103.

39. Fekete's own attempt to place structuralism suffers from a certain lack of historical specificity. The movement "represents a motion in theory away from living praxis" and "rapidly becomes a major antagonist of dialectical humanism, the Marxist philosophy of liberation" (*Critical Twilight*, p. 195). It is hard to see the French Communist Party of the late 1950s as an incarnation of living praxis; and one of the key ideological motivations of "left" structuralism (Althusser, Barthes, *Tel Quel*) is, I think, the urge to rethink such notions as praxis, not necessarily so as to jettison them, but to get a clearer idea of their relationship to objective possibilities for revolutionary change. Fekete's more recent discussion, while still critical, allows more positive virtues to structuralism. See "Descent into the New Maelstrom: Introduction," in *Structural Allegory*, pp. xi-xxiii.

40. Tzvetan Todorov, "Poétique," in *Qu'est-ce que le structuralisme?* ed. Oswald Ducrot et al., pp. 99-166 (Paris: Seuil, 1968), pp. 116-23; Gérard Genette, *Figures III* (Paris: Seuil, 1972), pp. 203-5, where Cleanth Brooks and Robert Penn Warren are also criticized for the same confusion.

41. Roland Barthes, *Critique et vérité* (Paris: Seuil, 1966), p. 55; *Roland Barthes par Roland Barthes* (Paris: Seuil, 1975), p. 175. The stress on ambiguity may come from Jakobson, who does indeed call Empson to witness that the poetic text is intrinsically ambiguous ("Linguistics and Poetics," in *Language in Literature*, ed. Krystyna Pomorska and Stephen Rudy [Cambridge, Mass.: Harvard University Press, 1987], p. 85).

42. See, for instance, Barthes, "Analyse textuelle d'un conte d'Edgar Poe," in *L'aventure sémiologique*, p. 329.

43. Todorov, "Poétique," pp. 99-102.

44. Williams offers a minimal definition of literature as "the process and the result of formal composition within the social and formal properties of a language" (*Marxism and Literature*, p. 46), and stresses the historical and ideological variability of the uses of the term.

45. Roland Barthes, *Le bruissement de la langue* (Paris: Seuil, 1984), p. 81; Julia Kristeva, *The Kristeva Reader*, ed. Toril Moi (Oxford: Blackwell, 1986), p. 26. The stress on pleasure, however, does not at all exclude an investigation of the historical construction of bodily subjectivity; see Barthes, *Le plaisir du texte* (Paris: Seuil, 1973), pp. 98-99, and Christopher Prendergast's comments in *The Order of Mimesis* (Cambridge: Cambridge University Press, 1986), p. 77. This is something with which a materialist theory of ideology must come to terms.

46. Gérard Genette, *Nouveau discours du récit* (Paris: Seuil, 1983), pp. 15, 98-99.

47. *Le degré zéro de l'écriture* and *Mythologies* feature in the bibliography of *Marxism*

and Literature. Williams mentions Timpanaro's critique of Barthes and others with apparent approval in *Problems in Materialism and Culture*, p. 119.

48. Roland Barthes, *Le degré zéro de l'écriture* (Paris: Seuil, 1953), republished with *Nouveaux essais critiques* (Paris: Seuil, 1972), p. 14.

49. Roland Barthes, *Mythologies* (1957; reprinted, Paris: Seuil, 1970), p. 196; *L'obvie et l'obtus* (Paris: Seuil, 1982), p. 24.

50. Barthes, *L'aventure sémiologique*, pp. 241–42.

51. See Lucien Goldmann, *Pour une sociologie du roman* (Paris: Gallimard, 1964), p. 338.

52. Goldmann, *Pour une sociologie*, p. 35; Goldmann's italics, my translation.

53. Ibid., pp. 344–45.

54. Ibid., pp. 55–56, 47.

55. Goldmann goes beyond this immanentism, however, when, in contrast to his assertion that the critic or the reader is not the judge of authenticity (*Pour une sociologie*, p. 23), he identifies authentic values with transindividual ones (p. 55).

56. Ibid., p. 346.

57. Ibid., p. 339.

58. The essay of Williams's I am drawing on here, "Literature and Sociology" (in *Problems in Materialism and Culture*), is of course dedicated to the memory of Goldmann, and it is natural that Williams should wish to link his own thinking with Goldmann's in this context.

59. It is striking that Stephen Heath should have chosen two English "social" novels from the 1840s, *Mary Barton* and *Sybil*, to illustrate Barthes's notion of *écriture* (*Vertige du déplacement: Lecture de Barthes* [Paris: Fayard, 1974], pp. 36–38).

60. The general pertinence of Barthes's discussion of 1848 has been shrewdly criticized by Tony Pinkney in his introduction to *The Politics of Modernism*, pp. 6–8. His main objections echoes that of Williams to Goldmann, mentioned earlier: that Barthes discusses history in terms of epochs rather than connected developments (and, moreover, ignores any history other than literary after 1848). Pinkney also has some interesting observations on the "Brecht epoch" in radical theory from the 1950s on—to which, as he points out, Barthes's theater criticism made an important contribution (pp. 19–21)—and on Williams's self-distancing from it.

61. I have argued this in "Roland Barthes: Ideology, Culture, Subjectivity," *Paragraph* 11, no. 2 (1988): 185–209, and in *Roland Barthes* (Oxford, 1991), pp. 164–66.

62. Barthes, *Le degré zéro*, pp. 58–59.

63. Ibid., pp. 51–53.

64. I take my examples from class, but the question of women and ethnic groups' relation to the dominant culture and to literary culture is clearly bound up with all this.

Forgetting Williams
John Higgins

Since his sudden and unexpected death in January 1988, progressive intellectuals throughout the world have mourned the passing of Raymond Williams, perhaps the foremost British socialist thinker, intellectual, and cultural activist of the past fifty years. In the obituary columns of leading newspapers, at conferences and on television, and in the pages of special issues of academic journals, we have seen the public mourning of a figure who was, in Patrick Parrinder's words, "father-figure to thousands," who was, for Juliet Mitchell, "an intellectual and moral touchstone."[1]

We need to remind ourselves of the function that Freud ascribed to mourning. The aim of this difficult and painful process, *der Trauerarbeit*—the *work* of mourning—is to forget; and, paradoxically, to forget through remembering. Freud argues that the work of mourning seeks to reduce the intense libidinal cathexis that the subject still invests in the newly lost beloved object and, in reducing it, to frame that lost one as memory image only. The lost one as memory image is severed from the world of presences just as a photographic image is.[2] The memory image is, as it were, smaller in scale, two-dimensional, diminished; it reminds us of the lost or absent one and at the same time confirms the loss. Yet in its framing and consequent reduction, the image makes the loss bearable by finding a way to represent it; the image makes it bearable through representation. We remember, but for a moment only, before we turn our attention back to the world and seek other objects for our regard: "The fact is," writes Freud, "that when the work of mourning is completed the ego becomes free and uninhibited again."[3] The production of memory in the work of mourning diminishes the intensity of libidinal attachment and enables the subject, once the work of mourning is complete, to take up and develop new attachments in the world of presences.

The work of mourning is a work of representation, a work of mourning and memorializing, and one of its central aims is forgetting the lost one. Has our public mourning of Williams shared some of the same dynamic of this private mourning? An analysis of the valedictory editorial of the British journal *New Formations* suggests that this is so. For here, to the precise extent that Williams is remembered and mourned, the interest of his work is reduced to such an extent that it might as well be forgotten.

The editors first acknowledge their debt to Williams: "the intellectual and political space" of the journal was, they write, "pioneered" by him ("pioneered" already preparing the reader for his supercession). Williams "would doubtless have resisted the way that many of our articles draw on radical post-structuralism." For them, Williams "remained a 'prophet of culture'" and although "his work constituted a sustained critique of the *content* of the Arnold-Mill-Leavis tradition, he retained from it a paradigm of the *form* of culture which made him reluctant to question the integrity of identity as such." Against Williams, after Williams, *New Formations* places Stuart Hall's "vision of a radical pluralism" and Homi Bhabha's "account of an agonistic political fluidity." These, the editors assure us, "are certainly more fragmented and, if you like, more 'post-modern' than Raymond Williams's Enlightenment ideal of a common culture."[4]

The terms of this remembering of Williams are at the same time the terms that enable us to forget him, in the sense of decreasing the interest of his work and diminishing its value, worth, and relevance. The process of mourning is completed once Williams's work can be named, can be remembered, and then through that naming and remembering can be seen to belong to the past, can be safely forgotten. What troubles me here is not so much the inexactness of the reference to "Williams's Enlightenment ideal of a common culture"— a reference that glosses over the ins and outs of some thirty years of Williams's thinking on the subject, and all the twists and turns of its specific development—but its characterization of Williams's *objec-

tions to "radical post-structuralism." For objections there certainly were to the poststructuralist theories that Williams dubbed "the New Conformism" in his final essays. But here Williams is described as "reluctant to question the integrity of identity as such"; he would doubtless have *resisted* . . . radical post-structuralism." Such a characterization, by representing intellectual disagreement as a matter of some personal "reluctance" and "resistance," makes impossible any real debate of the central theoretical issues. To remember Williams in this way, as the last of the Enlightenment thinkers, amounts to little more than an invitation to forget his work by consigning it to vaults of memory dusty enough never to be opened again.

The *New Formations* editorial in fact rejects the rapprochement between radical semiotics and cultural materialism that Williams had suggested as a possibility in March 1981. Here, in a provocative analysis of the history of literary studies and the terms of his own troubled and troubling relation to Cambridge English, Williams spoke of the possible convergence between the two. "To our mutual surprise," he noted, "my work found new points of contact with certain work in more recent semiotics. . . . I remember saying that a fully historical semiotics would be very much the same thing as cultural materialism."[5] After all, they shared an opposition to the still dominant paradigm of "Cambridge English"—a paradigm in which works of literature are considered in isolation from the means and conditions of their production. Williams's "surprise" at this newly discovered closeness turned particularly on the related questions of psychoanalysis and language. "There were still radical differences," he maintained, "especially in their reliance on structural linguistics and psychoanalysis."

Certainly a central element in any account of Williams's "reluctance to question the integrity of identity as such" would be his well-attested hostility toward psychoanalytic theory, the theory that, particularly in its Lacanian form, has done most to question any such integrity. What in fact were Williams's criticisms of psychoanalysis? And to which of many Freudianisms were they addressed? Do they apply to that version of psychoanalytic theory espoused by the *New Formations* mode of "radical poststructuralism"? These are questions that any serious assessment of Williams's work have to address.[6]

Williams had planned to devote a chapter of *Culture and Society* to Herbert Read and the British Freudians, but it was apparently removed for reasons of space.[7] Nonetheless, the substance of Williams's criticisms can be gathered from his remarks in *The Long Revolution*, where, following Christopher Caudwell, he sees psychoanalysis as trapped in the confining categories of bourgeois social theory. It is unable to go beyond the sterile opposition of "individual" to "society" and therefore unable to grasp the reality of social process. Its central concept is sublimation, understood as the necessary adaptation of the individual to his or her society, and this stress on adaptation is in itself reactionary. Its claims to understanding artistic creativity are too reductionist to have any substantial explanatory value.[8]

This largely negative assessment (Williams does admit that psychoanalysis had focused a new and needed attention on the family) seems little altered from the evidence of his remarks on psychoanalysis some twenty-five years later, in the extraordinarily extensive interviews conducted by the *New Left Review* and published as *Politics and Letters*. Williams is still hostile to any claims psychoanalysis might have for being a "special method" of interpretation, and still rejects the idea of sublimation as "not very serious thinking."[9] In response to the question "What is your view of attempts to conjoin psychoanalysis with Marxism?" he replies:

> I do not want to reserve Marxism from what I think is a major challenge to it—the importance of fundamental human drives which are not an idealist human nature, but which are simply biological, material conditions. But I don't think that Freudian instinct theory, or the notion of geno-types by which Caudwell was briefly very taken, provide a possible basis for an explanation of this area that has been unexplored in historical-materialist terms. I have never felt that Freud and Marx could be combined in that way. There can be no useful compromise between a description of basic realities as ahistorical and universal and a description of them as diversely created or modified by a changing human history. Though the biological data may indeed be universal, our relevant actions are *biological and cultural*, and neither can be reduced to the other.[10]

That Caudwell should be the first name to come to Williams's mind is in itself instructive. What of Reich, Adorno, Marcuse, Sève, or, more to the point in the context of the *New Left Review* discussion, Althusser? As well as the substance of Williams's criticisms of psychoanalysis, here we have some indication of their limits. For even in its own terms, the passage betrays a crucial hesitation in Williams's conceptual vocabulary: psychoanalysis is both a theory that recognizes the importance of "fundamental human *drives*" and "Freudian instinct theory." "Drive" and "instinct" are alternative translations for the German *der Trieb*, while "instinct" is the usual translation for *das Instinct*. The *Standard Edition* gives "instinct" as the translation for both German terms. Most commentators now question the *Standard Edition*'s choice on the grounds that an important conceptual distinction—implicit if never explicit in Freud's usage—is lost. The distinction is between the conceptual force of the two terms *Instinkt* and *Trieb*. This is a crucial distinction for any argument such as Williams's—which is concerned with the nature of Freud's debt to biology.[11]

For Laplanche and Pontalis, in their painstaking *The Language of Psychoanalysis*, instinct is traditionally "a designation for behaviour predetermined by heredity and appearing in virtually identical form in all members of an individual species."[12] Any reliance by Freud on instinct taken in this sense would clearly support Williams's suspicions that psychoanalysis is essentially and of necessity an ahistorical theory. But Laplanche and Pontalis go on to draw a distinction between this idea of instinct—for which, they say, Freud always uses the German *der Instinct*—and Freud's use of *der Trieb*. This they define as "a pressure that is relatively indeterminate both as regards the behaviour it induces and as regards the satisfying object."[13]

Freud's first substantial uses of the term are in the *Three Essays on the Theory of Sexuality* (1905). One of Freud's main achievements in this work is the distinction he works between human and animal sexuality. While animal sexuality is powered solely by the needs of biological reproduction, human sexuality is constructed psychically and socially, forever swerving from the biological. The aim of human sexuality is pleasure rather than reproduction, not the result of a biological urge but rather the attempt to satisfy a psychic pressure. Sexuality is not instinct but drive.[14]

Yet William's rejection of psychoanalysis rests precisely on an identification of psychoanalysis with a biologically given "instinct theory." "Was I wrong to have referred to Freud mainly in terms of the later works?" asked Williams. "Surely it is in these that his more general propositions about human history, about the character of civilization, or about the nature of art are to be found?"[15] But what weight should be given to these "more general propositions"? Freud himself referred to many of his later works as "speculative," indicating the hypothetical nature of his arguments; radical semiotician Christian Metz has argued that there was no reason to suppose that Freud himself should be best suited to articulating the precise import of his own theory of the unconscious for the social sciences. Indeed, argues Metz, it is in later works such as *Beyond the Pleasure Principle*, *Moses and Monotheism*, and *Civilization and Its Discontents* that Freud's "psychologism" comes through most strongly, and where he betrays the precision of his own insights into the unconscious.[16] The answer to Williams's question is that it was a mistake to base his assessment of the implications of psychoanalysis for social theory on those later works.

And what of Williams's account of the unconscious, perhaps the most crucial term in the vocabulary of psychoanalysis? In *Keywords*, Williams shows considerable skepticism toward what he sees as the psychoanalytic notion of the unconscious. "The more difficult but now most extended use came in the work of Freud," he writes, and suggests that "the original definitions imply that what becomes *unconscious* was once (but too painfully) *conscious*." He then criticizes what he sees as a move away from this specificity "to a generalized condition: the *unconscious* and especially *the unconscious mind*," where the "dynamic sense of something being made *unconscious* is often replaced . . . by the assumption of a primary and autonomous *unconscious* mind or being" as in "Jung's hypothesis of *the collective unconscious*." In other uses, the unconscious as "taken not only as stronger than *conscious* mental and emotional activity, but as its true (if ordinarily hidden) source" for Williams represents a "powerful modern form of IDEALISM."[17] As such, it is implied, the idea of the unconscious should be rejected.

The casual conflation of the Freudian with the Jungian notion of the unconscious immediately betrays a further lack of conceptual precision in Williams's account.[18] It comes as no surprise that some of the most critical remarks directed at Williams in the course of the *New Left Review* interviews refer to the *Keywords* account:

> The way you've spoken about the unconscious is always in terms of an inner zone of silence, of pure repression. Whereas in Freud the unconscious is always active in speech; it is not so much a blank area that

is not operative, that is completely repressed out of existence, as something like the hidden side of everything which is manifest. For him the
cases of real repression are those where the normal processes of communication of the unconscious to the conscious are blocked, and the
result is a determinate system of disturbance which can be traced in
the conscious—there is an abnormal displacement. When you speak of
the unconscious, it is as if it were a reserved sector, a special enclave,
which can be created by certain kinds of social prohibitions, whereas
for Freud it is coextensive with the conscious. The effect of your account of unconscious processes is to reduce their qualitative significance enormously, by comparison with that of Freud for whom the
unconscious is an active structure which is at work in everything that
we do. The idea of the unconscious as a central psychological structure
is separable from the particular map Freud drew of it, which is often
very crude. Would you assent to it as such?[19]

Where Williams suggested that conscious and unconscious were
understood as oppositional categories in Freudian thought, the *New
Left Review* team suggests that they are better understood as coextensive, interwoven: the unconscious is "the hidden side of everything which is manifest . . . an active structure which is at work in
everything we do." What they stress, against Williams's account, is, in
a word, the Lacanian "rereading" of the unconscious as that "active
structure."

Williams's reply—"Sure, that is a more acceptable way of putting
it"—amounts to a spectacular evasion of the conceptual issues at
stake. For it is not a question of one "particular map" of the unconscious being better than another. They are not different maps of the
same terrain so much as different maps of different conceptual territories. The "Freudian" notion of the unconscious that Williams criticizes, derived as he says from his readings of Freud's later works
and Caudwell's notion of "genotypes," is conceptually incommensurable with the Lacanian version put forward by the *New Left Review.*[20] And, as Charles Taylor has pointed out, incommensurable
means rival rather than alternative.[21] The Lacanian concept of the
unconscious is a rival to, not just different from, the unconscious of
Williams's account. Williams therefore cannot "accept" the different
(Lacanian) map offered by the *New Left Review.* Since to do so
would entail, if not giving up and rejecting his own criticisms of psychoanalysis, at the very least addressing them more specifically to

the work of Lacan—and particularly to its deployment in Althusser's own attempted conjunction of Marxism and psychoanalysis.

That Williams does not do so becomes clear in his remarks at the end of this section of interviews, where he repeats his fundamental skepticism toward psychoanalysis as it has been taken up by feminism: "I feel especially uneasy about psychoanalysis now because of the intensity with which sections of the women's movement . . . have turned to it. I am wholly reluctant to oppose them, but some of their formulations are self-evidently hasty." In particular, he criticizes the "rush for instant authorities to provide the 'scientific account' of what is happening inside them" as "a condition of abject dependence."[22] Williams does not specify which of their formulations are "self-evidently hasty," but it is difficult not to believe that this must include the feminist emphasis on the construction of identity in and through language derived from Lacan.[23]

What does Williams have to say of Lacan? Very little, as such. Williams mentions Lacan twice in *Politics and Letters*, and each time the burden of his remarks is the same: Lacan's work is important, but it should not be accepted uncritically and unquestioningly as a simple "confirmatory authority."[24] Elsewhere, Williams objects strongly to the ways in which

> one can be asked, in the same mode as for an opinion of a film or a novel, whether one 'accepts the findings of Freud or of Skinner or of Lacan', without any significant realization that all such 'findings' depend on criteria of evidence and on the (contested) theoretical presuppositions of both the evidence and the criteria. . . . The grasp at fluently learned systems is no way, and certainly no materialist way, of 'resolving' the problems of such 'findings'.[25]

We can distinguish three levels of Williams's criticism of and opposition to psychoanalysis. First, there are the relatively precise criticisms of psychoanalysis as Williams understood it from his reading in the forties and fifties—the criticism of psychoanalysis as an instance of bourgeois social theory, as a biological theory of the instincts that cannot be combined usefully with Marxism. The problem with these criticisms for the reader in the nineties is that they do not directly address the now-dominant Lacanian version of psychoanalysis, which itself sets out to attack many of the same concerns.[26] Second, there are Williams's general criticisms of the authority that psychoanalysis—including the influential Lacanian "rereading" of Freud—has been given, uncritically, by feminists and Althusserians. It is just this skeptical attitude toward the authority of theory that is absent from the *New Formations* account; and, in terms of Williams's understanding of any real commitment to materialist analysis, is damagingly absent.[27]

This second level of criticism—Williams's skepticism concerning the strictly scientific authority of psychoanalysis—is connected to a third important strain in his thinking: the theory of the subject as constructed in language and as divided by language, the theory that I take *New Formations* to invoke in the reference to the "fragmented subject." For while Williams never addressed the question of the *New Formations* "fragmented subject" in any direct relation to the internal complexities of Lacanian theory, he did address some of its central conceptual components elsewhere. While it is undoubtedly correct to suggest that Williams never met the challenge of "radical poststructuralism" on the terrain of psychoanalysis, it would be quite wrong to imply that Williams never met the challenge at all. With characteristic obliquity, Williams chose for this confrontation his own conceptual field: the richly conflictual history of theories of language.

Marxism and Literature, published in 1977, was originally conceived as a series of lectures for the English faculty at Cambridge in the early 1970s.[28] They mark a distinct change in the focus of Williams's critical attentions, for their target is no longer the traditional literary and cultural criticism that had been the object of Williams's work from *Reading and Criticism* (1950) through *The English Novel from Dickens to Lawrence* (1971) to what most regard as his masterpiece, *The Country and the City* (1973). The new target is closer to home. *Marxism and Literature* was directed

> against the limits of the newly dominant mode of critical structuralism, because this was taken as Marxist literary theory all over Western Europe and North America . . . [and against] a mode of idealist study claiming the authority of Marxism and the prestige of association with powerful intellectual movements in many other fields.[29]

At the very least, the object of Williams's criticisms in *Marxism and Literature* can be seen as the forerunners or predecessors of *New Formations*'s "radical poststructuralism"; I suggest that these criticisms have a continued relevance, particularly in relation to the *New Formations* project. For we are now in a position to recognize that a central feature of this "mode of idealist study" was its focus on the constitutive relations between language and subjectivity. In retrospect, this focus, emphasis, and concern was apparent in such diverse and competing fields of inquiry and debate as Althusser's theory of ideology, Michel Foucault's discussions of power, knowledge, and the Panopticon, and Derrida's multiple attacks on "logocentrism," not to mention Barthes's third-period writings, work in the school of Lacan, feminisms both European and Anglo-American, and the work of literary critics, historians, and cultural analysts on both sides of the Atlantic. Surely it should be recognized that at least some of the questions raised by Williams are still relevant to much of our best intellectual and political analyses, including the work of *New Formations*.

Early versions of the study contained nothing on the theory of language, noted Williams, "whereas now it is the longest section of the book, and I would say the most pivotal. . . . There particularly I felt the limitations of length, because by then I could have written a whole book on that subject alone."[30] "Pivotal" then because it is here that he addresses most directly the key question of the constitution of the subject in and through language.

In a dense survey of debates from Vico to Vološinov, Williams is particularly concerned to identify, and to argue against, two pervasive ways of thinking about language as a distinctively human faculty. First, the common idea of language as expression, of language as a purely instrumental faculty, totally under the conscious and creative control of the individual human will. And second, an opposing position, the idea of language as a totally given system, with its associated notion of the totally subordinated human subject. Against these two ideas, and their related versions of individual and subject, Williams asserts the necessity for a fully social understanding of language, one that he argues would revise our usual notions of both expression and the language system and entail a consequent revision of our ideas of human linguistic agency. If the first can perhaps be most readily seen in the romantic theories of expression that underlie the theories of practical criticism in a Richards, a Leavis, or an Eliot (theories that Williams had already addressed in works such as *Culture and Society* [1958] and *The Long Revolution* [1961]), then the

second can best be seen in those twentieth-century theories of language that seek to align themselves with the natural sciences.[31]

In an insight generated by the procedures of his own practice of
cultural materialism, the analysis of all forms of composition in relation to their means and conditions of existence, Williams remarks an
"unnoticed consequence" of the position that the linguistic observer
sought to occupy in deference to the idea of scientific objectivity.
Williams rejects any easy assumption of such objectivity and stresses
the positionality of the linguistic observer who

> was observing (of course scientifically) within a differential mode of
> contact with alien material: in texts, the records of a *past* history; in
> speech, the activity of an alien people in subordinate (colonialist) rela-
> tions to the whole activity of the dominant people within which the
> observer gained his privilege. This defining situation inevitably re-
> duced any sense of language as actively and presently constitutive.[32]

For Williams, this practice of supposedly external and neutral observation could produce only a "reified understanding," blind to the
pressures of its own social and political construction. Decisively and,
for Williams, disastrously, language comes to be represented as a
system whose speakers have only passive access to it, while all
agency is credited to the side of the "neutral" observer. In the observer's understanding, and in the observer's understanding alone,
the system is actively grasped as a unity.

What most concerns Williams in this is the "ironic relation" and
"apparent affinity" between this linguistics—which was to become
the structural linguistics of Saussure—and Marxism, and particularly
the modish structural Marxism of Louis Althusser. The theories
share "the assertion of a controlling 'social' system which is *a priori*
inaccessible to individual acts of will and intelligence,"[33] save the
grasping intelligence of the theorist. For both structural linguistics
and structural Marxism, the subject—but never the theorist—is constituted by the system of language.

According to Williams, any such conception represents a significant reduction of the constitutivity of language. For those we might
call linguistic idealists, human subjectivity is entirely constituted by
language; human consciousness is entirely an effect of language.
Language precedes human consciousness, not just in the sense that
the system of language exists prior to any individual's access to or

participation in it, but as the totally determining ground of human consciousness. Thinkers as diverse in their interests as Althusser, Foucault, and Derrida share a common ground in this linguistic idealism.[34] In Williams's view, any such theories are mistaken in the logical priority that they give to language over human consciousness, and in their consequent reduction of human consciousness to an effect.

Classical materialists have fared little better in Williams's opinion. He cites "a modern authoritative view" that declares, "First labour, then articulate speech, were the two chief stimuli under the influence of which the brain of the ape gradually changed into the human brain." For Williams, the problem is again one of logical and temporal priority. In this crude Marxist view, language is secondary to the activity of labor, relegated to the status of "reflection." The most crucial aspect of the constitutivity of language is once again missed—language as an "*indissoluble* element of human self-creation,"[35] neither secondary and reflective nor primary and determining, but rather enabling and reflexive. Williams turns to the work of the Soviet thinker V. N. Vološinov for a more adequate theory of language, one that avoids the Scylla of idealism and the Charybdis of reflection theory.

Vološinov's "decisive contribution" lay in his rejection of language seen either as secondary reflection or as constituting system. For Williams, Vološinov was the first to see "'activity' (the strength of the idealist emphasis after Humboldt) as social activity and to see 'system' (the strength of the new objectivist linguistics) in relation to this social activity and not, as had hitherto been the case, formally separated from it."[36] For Vološinov as for Williams, language was "necessarily a social action, dependent on a social relationship."[37] Williams sums up Vološinov's positive contribution in terms of his notion of the sign and, in particular, in the related ideas of the sociality of language and the concept of the usable sign:

> The usable sign—the fusion of formal element and meaning—is a product of this continuing speech-activity between real individuals who are in some continuing social relationship. The 'sign' is in this sense their product, but not simply their past product, as in the reified accounts of an 'always-given' language system. The real communicative 'products' which are useable signs are, on the contrary, living evidence of a continuing social process, into which individuals are born and

within which they are shaped, but to which they then also actively contribute, in a continuing process. This is at once their socialization and their individuation: the connected aspects of a single process which the alternative theories of 'system' and 'expression' have divided and dissociated. We then find not a reified 'language' and 'society' but an active *social language*. Nor (to glance back at positivist and orthodox materialist theory) is this language a simple 'reflection' or 'expression' of 'material reality'. What we have, rather, is a grasping of this reality through language, which as practical consciousness is saturated by and saturates all social activity, including productive activity. . . . It is of and to this experience—the lost middle term between the abstract entities, 'subject' and 'object', on which the propositions of idealism and orthodox materialism are erected—that language speaks. Or to put it more directly, language is the articulation of this active and changing experience; a dynamic and articulated social *presence* in the world.[38]

Of course, this passage could easily be read as evidence for the "irrelevance" of Williams's arguments to "radical poststructuralism," as testimony to his hopeless immersion in and adherence to a humanist theory of the subject. *New Formations* would surely see the passage as an expression of Williams's "Enlightenment" theory of the subject, of his clinging to an empiricist version of unified subjectivity. Williams refers to "real individuals" rather than to subjects, while reality is "grasped" through language rather than constructed by language. Language is the "living evidence of a continuing social process"; it is "'the articulation of this active and changing experience; a dynamic and articulated social *presence* in the world." The final emphasis on *presence* seems a willful rejection of the deconstructive and poststructuralist critiques of the self-presence of the subject in language. After all, didn't Derrida, once and for all, elucidate for us the impossibility of language as "a dynamic and articulated social presence in the world" showing how language could never articulate the presence of the subject? And didn't Althusser, for all the faults of his epistemology, at least show us the limitations of any theoretical reliance on any concept of "experience"?[39]

But such a reading—one that reacts to the key words of those "fluently learned systems"—would be blind to Williams's central point in this passage: his distinction between the *socializing* and the *individuating* effects of language. For Williams, these are "the connected aspects of a single process which the alternative theories of 'system' and 'expression' have divided and dissociated" and which poststructuralism, in its obsessive critique of human identity, has largely ignored.

When *New Formations* asserts that Williams was "reluctant to question the integrity of identity as such," there is an implicit and entirely unargued assumption that such questioning is necessary, that such questioning goes without saying. But a questioning that goes without saying falls easily into pure dogmatism. Is the "integrity of identity as such" one concept, one category that can be considered, and then immediately rejected, "as such"? Examining the question in a little more detail in the light of Williams's position is worthwhile.

A great deal of poststructuralism's challenge to "the integrity of identity as such" might be summed up by Lacan's dictum "a signifier represents a subject for another signifier," where the subject appears as the effect rather than the cause of signifying practices. A central feature of Lacan's work was his persistent challenge to the integrity of identity, to the apparent unity and primacy of the subject announced in the essay that represents the earliest formulation of his revisionary challenge. Lacan argues that his central concept of the mirror stage sheds light "on the formation of the *I* as we experience it in psychoanalysis. It is an experience that leads us to oppose any philosophy issuing directly from the *Cogito*."[40]

A favored point of reference and analogy for Lacan's arguments in this regard is the division in linguistics between the "sujet de l'énoncé" (the subject of the enounced) and the "sujet de l'énonciation" (subject of the enunciation).[41] For Lacan, philosophy can only deal with the subject at the level of the *sujet de l'énoncé* because it deals only with the conscious ratiocination identified with the Cartesian *Cogito*. Philosophy rejects from the outset and is unable to assimilate any idea of the unconscious. The recognition by linguists of another level to language, the level of enunciation, is used by Lacan to assert the existence of the unconscious, which philosophy constitutionally resists. In *The Four Fundamental Concepts of Psychoanalysis*, Lacan refers to the Cretan Liar's paradox in order to show that the logical paradox only exists for a subject that insists on the unitary and undivided nature of the philosophical subject.

Here Lacan "purposely distinguishes the level of the enunciation from the level of the enounced," and goes on to explain the use of this distinction:

Its use can be illustrated from the fact that a too formal logical thinking introduces absurdities, even an antinomy of reason in the statement *I am lying*, whereas everyone knows that there is no such thing.

It is quite wrong to reply to this *I am lying*–If you say, *I am lying,*
you are telling the truth, and therefore you are not lying, and so on. It
is quite clear that the *I am lying*, despite its paradox, is perfectly valid.
Indeed, the *I* of the enunciation is not the same as the *I* of the
enounced, that is to say, the shifter which, in the enounced, designates
him. So, from the point at which I state, it is quite possible for me to
formulate in a valid way that the *I*–the *I* who, at that moment, formu-
lates the enounced–is lying, that he lied a little before, that he is lying
afterwards, or even, that in saying *I am lying*, he declares that he has
the intention of deceiving.[42]

Psychoanalysis deals precisely with this division in subjectivity
between conscious and unconscious thinking–a division that, according to Lacan, is impossible for any philosophy of consciousness,
the impossibility illustrated by the logical paradox presented by the
Cretan Liar. For Lacan, there is a truth of which the divided subject is
necessarily unconscious through the very fact of that division, and
yet this truth is manifest in all the subject's utterances. In the analysts's concern for truth, he or she is concerned with the subject at
the level of the total enunciation rather than with the conscious subject of any particular enounceds. Psychoanalysis thus questions the
integrity of the subject both in the fact of the division between the
subject of the enounced and the subject of the enunciation, which
embodies the division between conscious and unconscious thinking,
and in the consequent question of the truth of the subject's utterances, which remain, as Lacan puts it, a matter of "profound ambiguity."[43]

But it is important to recognize the limits of this questioning of
the integrity of the subject's identity. For what Lacan is here concerned with is the division of the subject in and at the moment of
enunciation. The critique is above all directed at the synchronic moment that Lacan identifies as the moment of the *Cogito*, breaching
the apparent unity of that moment, and with it the identity and integrity of the subject. Here the subject's identity is understood *syn-
chronically*, and Lacan is not concerned with its *diachronic* aspect,
the problem of personal identity, the question of the self understood
across time in a history of the subject.

Yet it would be absurd to suggest that psychoanalysis is not concerned with this diachronic dimension. Take, for instance, the example of the Rat Man's "principal magic word": "He had put it together out of the initial letters of the most powerfully beneficent of his prayers and had clapped an 'amen' at the end of it." The word was *Glejisamen* or *Glejsamen*. Borrowing Lacan's terms, we can see how the subject of this enounced is unaware or unconscious of its true meaning, and has indeed an explanation of the term to offer Freud. To the consciousness of the analysand and, as it were, at the level of the enounced, the word refers to *gleichlich* (happy)—"let me be happy"—while the *amen* is the end of his "prayer," though the other elements are obscure to him. But Freud does not accept this explanation and is well aware that another meaning is to be found at, to borrow Lacan's terms, the level of the enunciation:

> When he told it me, I could not help noticing that this word was in fact an anagram of the name of his lady. Her name contained an 's', and this he had put last, that is, immediately before the 'amen' at the end. We may say, therefore, that by this process he had brought his 'Samen' ('semen') into contact with the woman he loved; in imagination, that is to say, he had masturbated with her. He himself, however, had never noticed this very obvious connection; his defensive forces had allowed themselves to be fooled by the repressed ones.[44]

The *Glejisamen* example can be used as evidence for the division in the subject between conscious and unconscious thinking, and certainly reveals the fragmented nature of the Rat Man's subjectivity and the play inherent in all signification. But it also points to the necessity of understanding the history of that subjectivity and the grounds of that play. The linguistic expression of that fragmentation, evident on the level of the enounced, can only be understood by reference to the subject's particular history, by the name of his girlfriend (Gisela) and so on. The play of language has specific grounds in the personal identity—however fragmented—of the Rat Man himself. Whatever the concern with the fragmentation of the subject's synchronous identity, psychoanalytic interpretation nevertheless has to deal with the diachronic level. Whatever the strategic value in emphasizing the division of the subject, in criticizing the kind of self-identity that Lacan associated with American ego-psychology, even Lacanian psychoanalysis still had to deal with personal identity.

It seems to me that there is a major problem implicit in *New Formations*'s criticisms of Williams that is associated with a more general difficulty posed by much poststructuralist thinking. This problem is the failure to distinguish between the synchronic moment of self-identity and the diachronic duration of personal identity, and therefore to assume that the critique of the synchronous unity of the subject, of self-identity, can apply directly to personal identity, to the history of the subject through time. Indeed, is it not true to say that the poststructuralist critique of the integrity of identity neglects the diachronic dimension entirely? If so, it repeats an overemphasis on the synchronic dimension increasingly remarked by commentators.[45] Perry Anderson has described the obvious problem with his usual brisk acuity:

> The supremacy of *langue* as a system is the cornerstone of the Saussurean legacy: *parole* is the subsequent activation of certain of its resources by the speaking subject. But the priority of the one over the other is of a peculiar sort: it is both unconditional and indeterminant. That is to say, an individual speech-act can only execute certain general linguistic laws, if it is to be communication at all. But at the same time, the *laws* can never explain an *act.* . . . Language as a system furnishes the formal *conditions of possibility* of speech, but has no purchase on its actual *causes.* . . . The extrapolation of the linguistic model by post-Saussurian structuralism, however, typically proceeded to a tacit conflation of the two types of intelligibility. Conditions of possibility were systematically presented 'as if' they were causes.[46]

As Anderson puts it, in an insight that would doubtless have appealed to the Williams of *Marxism and Literature,* the "characteristic immobility of language as a structure is accompanied by a no less exceptional *inventivity* of the subject within it: the obverse of the rigidity of *langue* is the volatile liberty of *parole.*"[47] In Williams's terms, language not only socializes because it determines identity by creating its conditions of possibility; language also makes possible the individuation involved in the history of any subject, makes possible personal identity.

What most concerned Williams regarding such theories can be summed up by the first sentence of his chapter on language in *Marxism and Literature*: "A definition of language is always, implicitly or explicitly, a definition of human beings in the world."[48] There is always a politics implicit in theory, a "definition of human beings in the world"; and Williams was disturbed by the politics implicit in much poststructuralist theory, a politics that he aligned with the general movement he refers to in his final essays as the New Conformism.[49]

In these essays, Williams attacked what he called the New Conformism in the general context of debates in and around the meanings of modernism and the avant-garde. Williams distinguished two faces of modernism: the first, "the innovative forms which destabilized the fixed forms of an earlier period of bourgeois culture" and the second, the New Conformism that had in its turn managed to restabilize these originally radical forms "as the most reductive versions of human existence in the whole of cultural history":

> The originally precarious and often desperate images—typically of fragmentation, loss of identity, loss of the very grounds of human communication—have been transferred from the dynamic compositions of artists who had been, in majority, literally exiles, having little or no common ground with the societies in which they were stranded, to become, at an effective surface, a 'modernist' and 'post-modernist' establishment.[50]

While the essays in the collection deal most specifically with drama, there are many sideswipes at contemporary theory, and it is important in this sense to see *The Politics of Modernism* as carrying on the debate with structuralist and poststructuralist theory begun in *Marxism and Literature.*

In the essay "Language and the Avant-Garde," strategically delivered at the Strathclyde conference on language and linguistics, Williams attacks the selective version of modernism peddled by much contemporary literary theory. Contemporary theoretical polemics, argues Williams, have appropriated or misappropriated the actual complex history of modernism, and the "most serious consequence of this appropriation is that what are actually polemical positions, some of them serious, on language and writing, can pass, however ironically, as historical descriptions of actual movements and formations." He emphasizes:

> Even at their most plausible—in a characteristic kind of definition by negative contrast, where the main stress is put on a common rejection

of the representational character of language and thence of writing—there is not only an astonishing reduction of the diversity of actually antecedent writing practices and theories of language, but a quite falsely implied identification of actual Modernist and avant-garde writing—with convenient slippages between the two loose terms—as based on attitudes to language which can be theoretically generalized, or at least made analogous, to what, borrowing the classifications, are themselves offered as modernist or avant-garde linguistic and critical positions and methodologies.[51]

For the New Conformists, he argues, "the fragmented ego in a fragmented world has survived as a dominant structure of feeling."[52] It is difficult not to include poststructuralist theory as a part of that same moment.

While *New Formations* might wish to criticize Williams for his use of the phrase "the fragmented ego" (does it not betray his relative ignorance of psychoanalysis?), I have tried to show that there are still serious grounds for paying some attention to Williams's arguments regarding language and the theory of the subject, particularly in the light of Williams's idea that theory too is a question of representation, that every theory of language involves a representation of the social world. How radical, in the end, is the "radical poststructuralism" offered by *New Formations* if it is unable to distinguish between self-identity and personal identity? What Williams's arguments demonstrate, in the last ten years of his life, is that the conjunction between semiotics and progressive cultural analysis is not so easily made. I believe that his arguments in this regard should not be too easily buried under any memorial that represents him as the superseded pioneer, the last Enlightenment thinker. Forgetting Williams by naming him in this way is a mistake we do not need to make.

NOTES

1. See, for example, *The Independent*, January 28, 1988 (Terry Eagleton and Frank Kermode), *The Guardian*, January 29, 1988 (Frances Mulhern), *The Nation*, April 1988 (Edward W. Said and Edward P. Thompson). The British journal *News from Nowhere* devoted a special issue—*Raymond Williams—Third Generation*—to Williams in February 1989. Patrick Parrinder's remark is drawn from *London Review of Books*, February 12, 1988, and Juliet Mitchell's from my report on the National Film Theatre forum Raymond Williams—Towards 2000 (June 30, 1989), published as part of my own memorial essay, "Raymond Williams 1921-1988" in *Pretexts: Studies in Writing and Culture* 1, no. 1 (1989): 79-91.

2. Compare Bazin's essay "The Ontology of the Photographic Image," in *What Is Cinema?* ed. Hugh Grey (Berkeley: University of California Press, 1967) and Barthes's *La chambre claire: Note sur la photographie* (Paris: Gallimard, 1980) for a probing of the relations between death and the photographic image.

3. See Freud, "Mourning and Melancholia," in *The Standard Edition of the Complete Psychological Works of Sigmund Freud*, 24 vols., ed. James Strachey (London: Hogarth, 1953-74) 12:245.

4. *New Formations*, no. 5 (Summer 1988): 3-4.

5. Raymond Williams, *Writing in Society* (London: Verso, 1984), p. 210.

6. For a step toward such an assessment, see my essay "A Missed Encounter: Raymond Williams and Psychoanalysis," *Journal of Literary Studies* 6, nos. 1 and 2: 62-76. The following section of the present essay adapts and borrows from material that first appeared there.

7. Raymond Williams, *Politics and Letters* (London: Verso, 1979), pp. 99-100.

8. See Raymond Williams, *The Long Revolution* (Harmondsworth: Penguin, 1961), especially pp. 96-97, 48-64.

9. Williams, *Politics and Letters*, p. 333.

10. Williams, *Politics and Letters*, pp. 183-84. Emphasis in the original.

11. See Freud, *Standard Edition* 1:xxiv-xxvi for a discussion of the difficulties posed by the translation of *der Trieb*. Strachey acknowledges that his rendering of it as "instinct" "has been attacked in some quarters with considerable, but, I think, mistaken severity. The term almost invariably proposed by critics as an alternative is 'drive.' . . . It is not the business of a translator to attempt to classify and distinguish between Freud's different uses of the word." Frank J. Sulloway's *Freud and Biology* (New York: Basic Books, 1979) is the most thorough—and polemical—account of Freud's indebtedness to biology.

12. Laplanche and Pontalis, *The Language of Psychoanalysis* (London: Hogarth, 1973), p. 214.

13. Ibid.

14. Lacan's "rereading" of Freud first sought to draw attention to this crucial distinction. See, for example, *The Four Fundamental Concepts of Psychoanalysis* (New York: Norton, 1978), especially chapters 12-15, where some of the benefits of Lacan's creative rereading of Freud can be seen. For an excellent historical analysis of the significance of Freud's discussion in the *Three Essays on Sexuality*, see Arnold Davidson, "How to Do the History of Psychoanalysis: A reading of Freud's 'Three Essays on Sexuality,'" *Critical Inquiry* 13, no. 2: 252-77.

15. Williams, *Politics and Letters*, p. 333.

16. See Christian Metz, *The Imaginary Signifier* (London: Macmillan, 1982), p. 24: "Freud's discovery in its breadth is of concern to virtually all fields of knowledge, but only if it is suitably articulated with the data and exigencies peculiar to each of them, and notably to those whose object is directly social: nothing guarantees that the 'discoverer' (the father), just because he is the discoverer, should be best placed to carry out this readjustment in domains of which he had sometimes no fundamental knowledge. . . . It is at this weak point that the 'psychologism' to be found in Freud (but not in his central discoveries) and for which he has been justly criticised, bursts through." For a thorough discussion of the nineteenth-century context of Freud's discussions of cultural history, see Rosalind Coward, *Patriarchal Precedents* (London: Routledge and Kegan Paul, 1983).

17. Raymond Williams, *Keywords* (London: Fontana, 1976), pp. 271-72. Emphasis in the original.

18. For an excellent discussion of the divergences between their respective accounts, see John Forrester, *Language and the Origins of Psychoanalysis* (London: Macmillan, 1980), pp. 96-122.

19. Williams, *Politics and Letters*, p. 182.

20. Indeed, Caudwell's notion of the genotype may well belong to an entirely different conceptual universe. Caudwell's definition may be found in *Illusion and Reality* (London: Lawrence and Wishart, 1958): "When we speak of 'man' we mean the genotype or individual, the instinctive man as he is born, who if 'left to himself' might grow up into something like a dumb brute, but instead of this he grows up in a certain kind of society as a certain kind of man—Athenian, Aztec or Londoner. We must not think of the genotype as completely plastic and amorphous. It has certain definite instincts and potentialities which are the source of its energy and restlessness. Men differ among themselves because of inborn characteristics. . . . This genotype is never fround 'in the raw'" (p. 136). Williams's annoyance with it is scarcely surprising; but it hardly represents very adequately any very definite concepts of psychoanalytic theory. In *Culture and Society* (Harmondsworth: Penguin, 1990), Williams sniffs that "this version of the 'genotype' interacting with 'external reality' is some way from Marx" (pp. 278-79).

21. See Charles Taylor, "Rationality," in *Philosophy and the Human Sciences: Philosophical Papers II* (Cambridge: Cambridge University Press, 1985), where Taylor observes, apropos of Peter Winch's famous discussion of Zande witchcraft, that "incommensurable activities are rivals; their constitutive rules prescribe in contradiction to each other" (pp. 145-46).

22. See Williams, *Politics and Letters*, pp. 184-85.

23. For a classic account, see Juliet Mitchell, *Psychoanalysis and Feminism* (Harmondsworth: Penguin, 1974); for a discussion of some of that text's strange silences with regard to Lacan, see Jane Gallop, *Feminism and Psychoanalysis: The Daughter's Seduction* (London: Macmillan, 1982), pp. 1-14. See also *Feminine Sexuality*, ed. Juliet Mitchell and Jacqueline Rose (London: Macmillan, 1982).

24. See Williams, *Politics and Letters*: "I have great respect for the work of Lacan, but the totally uncritical way in which certain of his concepts of phases in language development have been lifted into a theoretical pediment of literary semiotics is absurd, in a world in which there is current scientific work of a non-philological kind with which all such concepts have to be brought into interplay" (341). "In the same way the work of Lacan today should not be taken as a confirmatory authority, the provision of a framework within which other compositions are read, but rather as itself a composition which we all believe to be important" (332).

25. Raymond Williams, *Problems in Materialism and Culture* (London: Verso, 1980), pp. 117, 118-19.

26. Althusser drew attention to many of these features in his essay "Freud and Lacan," originally published in 1964. See *Essays on Ideology* (London: Verso, 1988), especially pp. 15-25.

27. David Macey's challenge, that "*Screen*'s appropriation of Lacan rests . . . upon a series of unproven assertions and unfounded assumptions" needs, in particular, to be squarely faced, given the importance of this particular synthesis of Marx and Freud for progressive cultural analysis in the seventies and eighties. See his *Lacan in Contexts* (London: Verso, 1988), especially pp. 15-25.

28. Williams, *Politics and Letters*, p. 324.

29. Ibid., pp. 339-40.

30. Ibid., p. 324.

31. See especially *Culture and Society* part 1, chapter 2, "The Romantic Artist," and part 3, chapters 3 and 4; and *The Long Revolution* part 1, chapter 1, "The Creative Mind." For a comparable account that, like Williams, stresses the relations between language as constitutive and the opposition to scientism, see Charles Taylor's "Language and Human Nature," in *Human Agency and Language: Philosophical Papers II* (Cambridge: Cambridge University Press, 1985).

32. Raymond Williams, *Marxism and Literature* (Oxford: Oxford University Press, 1977), p. 26. Emphasis in the original.

33. Ibid., p. 28.

34. That, at least, is my contention. Though there is no space here to discuss this in detail, it may be worth remarking how in Althusser's theory of ideology—for all its stress on the materiality of ideological practices—the human subject is no more than the bearer or support of those practices, its consciousness an effect of an interpellation modeled on and ultimately conceived of as linguistic; how, for Michel Foucault, it is not that power works on and against individuals, that power subordinates individuals, but rather that the very existence of the individual consciousness is to be conceived of as the product of the discursive networks through which power flows. For Derrida, the self-consciousness of the moment of utterance is an illusion, the effect of a play of signifiers, the effect of *différance*. For an interesting discussion of both Foucault and Derrida, see Peter Dews's stimulating *Logics of Disintegration* (London: Verso, 1987). I discuss the case of Althusser in "Raymond Williams and the Problem of Ideology," in *Postmodernism and Politics*, ed. Jonathan Arac (Minneapolis: University of Minnesota Press, 1986).

35. Williams, *Marxism and Literature*, p. 31.

36. Ibid., p. 35.

37. Ibid., p. 36.

38. Ibid., pp. 37-38. Emphasis in the original.

39. For now classic statements of such positions, see Althusser, *Reading Capital* (London: Verso, 1979), pp. 34-40; and Derrida, "Différance" in *Margins of Philosophy* (Chicago: University of Chicago Press, 1982), pp. 1-27.

40. Jacques Lacan, *Ecrits*, trans. A. Sheridan (London: Tavistock, 1977), p. 1.

41. The major figure for Lacan here is Emile Benveniste, whose *Problèmes de linguistique générale* (Paris: Gallimard, 1966) should be consulted, especially pages 225-88. A useful survey of debates about enunciation can be found in the *Dictionnaire encyclopédique des sciences du langage*, ed. D. Ducrot and T. Todorov (Paris: Seuil, 1972), pp. 405-10.

42. Lacan, *Four Fundamental Concepts of Psychoanalysis* (Harmondsworth: Penguin, 1974), pp. 138-39. Translation modified; emphasis in the original.

43. See Lacan, *Four Fundamental Concepts of Psychoanalysis*: "We now find ourselves at last—in the very act of the commitment to analysis and certainly, therefore, in its first stages—in maximum contact with the profound ambiguity of any assertion on the part of the patient, and the fact that it is, of itself, double-sided. In the first instance, it is as establishing itself in, and even by, a certain lie, that we see set up the dimension of truth, in which respect it is not, strictly speaking, shaken, since the lie as such is posited in this dimension of truth" (p. 138).

44. See "Notes on a Case of Obsessional Neurosis," in *Standard Edition*, 10:105.

45. For a provocative general survey, see Anthony Giddens, *Central Problems in Social Theory* (London: Macmillan, 1979), particularly chapters 1 and 2. Giddens argues that the

"pressing task of social theory today is not to further the conceptual elimination of the subject, but on the contrary to promote *a recovery of the subject* without lapsing into subjectivism. . . . In their endeavour to dissolve the subject, structuralism and positivism thus have an important element in common, and in the context of the social sciences in the English-speaking world it is all the more necessary to insist that the de-centring of the subject must not be made equivalent to its disappearance. Any form of social theory which merges the de-centring of the subject, as a philosophical tenet, with a propadeutic of the end of the individual as either a desireable, or inevitable movement of contemporary social change, becomes subject to the charge of ideology that critics are so fond of levelling against structuralism" (pp. 44–45). Manfred Frank, in his *What Is Neostructuralism?* (Minneapolis: University of Minnesota Press, 1989), similarly remarks: "Against Derrida I would object that . . . one would necessarily fall into the absurdity of denying the subsistence of something like familiarity with ourselves. But that would not only be contradictory to what he himself gives as his intention (namely, wanting only to explain self-consciousness *differently* than is done by metaphysics); it would ultimately come down to a denial of the fact that we can associate a meaning with the terms 'the self,' 'consciousness' and 'the I' in our everyday language. The functioning of language itself contradicts this" (pp. 280–81). Following Frank, Dews also argues that Derrida's theory of *différance* ultimately leaves him "unable to explain how the experience of meaning is able to occur at all" (*Logics of Disintegration*, p. 98). It seems time for a careful reassessment and revision of our notions of—and critiques of—personal identity. For a first step in that direction, see my "Derrida, Hume and the Politics in Personal Identity," in *Historicising the Body Politic: Nation and Individual in C18,* ed. John Higgins and Lesley Marx (Human Sciences Research Council Press, 1994).

46. Perry Anderson, *In the Tracks of Historical Materialism* (London: Verso, 1983), p. 38.

47. Ibid., p. 44.

48. Williams, *Marxism and Literature,* p. 21.

49. See *The Politics of Modernism: Against the New Conformists,* ed. Tony Pinkney (London: Verso, 1989). Another important formulation, unfortunately absent from Pinkney's collection, can be found in Williams's 1987 lecture "Country and City in the Modern Novel," published in *Pretexts: Studies in Writing and Culture* 2, no. 1 (1990): 3–13.

50. Williams, *Politics of Modernism,* p. 130.

51. Ibid., pp. 65–66.

52. Ibid., p. 93.

Part II

History, Politics, Literature

Raymond Williams on Tragedy and Revolution
Kenneth Surin

It is difficult to deny that *Modern Tragedy* (1966) was a work of signal importance in the development of Raymond Williams's thought.[1] Issues both practical and theoretical regarding history, politics, culture, literature, socialism, and so forth were treated in this book with a commitment to a version of revolutionary socialist struggle that was to become palpably evident in such later works as *Marxism and Literature* (1977) and *Towards 2000* (1983)—a commitment that, prior to *Modern Tragedy*, had been displayed in a much more qualified way in *The Long Revolution* (1963) and was merely nascent in *Culture and Society* (1958). Even so, *Modern Tragedy* has been virtually overlooked in the veritable flood of material on Williams and his work that has appeared since his unexpected and premature death in 1988. These discussions have tended invariably to focus on the more "canonical" *Culture and Society, Marxism and Literature*, and (to a lesser extent) *The Country and the City*. In many ways this is only to be expected, though this apparent oversight has had the effect of blocking the realization that *Modern Tragedy* was always one of the most pointed and decisive of Williams's theoretical and practical "interventions" (as they say in Britain these days).

It is clear from the *New Left Review* interviews with Williams published as *Politics and Letters*[2] that *Modern Tragedy* was produced as something of a response to George Steiner's *The Death of Tragedy* (1961). Steiner's elegy was framed on the assumption that tragedy as a dramatic system was sustainable only in societies with an irreducibly hieratic character, and since modern societies have effectively consigned the divinities and their orders to silence, they, as "post-tragic" societies, can no longer accommodate in any profound or creative way this particular dramatic form. Williams did not attempt a direct refutation of Steiner's position. Instead, without even mentioning Steiner by name, he sought to identify and delineate the historical and social conditions of possibility for the various kinds of tragic experience and their associated dramatic forms, and to show that an argument of the kind mounted by Steiner necessarily privileged, and this in a quite arbitrary way, the particular "structure of feeling" that subtended Greek tragic art (this being the paradigmatic tragic mode for Steiner—tragedy properly so called had for him to be congruent with the typical conventions and principles of Greek tragic drama). It was not too difficult for Williams to show that Steiner's argument was vitiated both by a propensity to universalize in a specious way what was really a very particular and specialized rendition of tragic experience, and by an understanding of the history of a set of artistic forms that failed to take that history's variety and complexity sufficiently into account. The upshot was a narrowing of the scope of the tragic: situations and personages that could not be pressed into this Greek tragic schema—with its own very distinctive conceptions of the destruction of heroic and noble figures, the catastrophic violation of a metaphysical or sacerdotal order, the engaging in an irreparable action, and so forth—had necessarily to be seen as lacking in "tragic significance." And yet, as Williams pointed out:

> [The] events which are not seen as tragic are deep in the pattern of our own culture: war, famine, work, traffic, politics. To see no ethical content or human agency in such events, or to say that we cannot connect them with general meanings, and especially with permanent and universal meanings, is to admit a strange and particular bankruptcy, which no rhetoric of tragedy can finally hide. (*MT* 49)

My purpose in this essay is not, however, to delve into the intricacies of this debate on the alleged demise of tragedy. Nor do I wish to imply that Williams's own positions are entirely beyond criticism. Why, after all, invest so much in the category of the tragic? And is it not possible to resituate discourses invoking this category in other quite different, and possibly more productive, frames (such as that of a discourse of the sublime)? Morever, as Williams and others have since acknowledged, the terms of this exchange on the nature of tragedy were those of an intellectual politics very specific to the teaching of English in Cambridge in the 1950s and 1960s. Broader and (for me) more important concerns regarding tragedy and related issues are broached in *Modern Tragedy*, and it is to some of these that I want now to attend. In particular, I want to consider Williams's treatment of the relation between tragedy and revolution. No one in this century, unless one is tempted to make a case of sorts for Lukács, thought more deeply and powerfully about this relation than Raymond Williams.

The context for the discussion of revolution and tragedy in *Modern Tragedy* is supplied by Williams's sense that something like a new "structure of feeling" was being put in place during the time that elapsed between the writing of the first edition and the publication of revised editions of this text (the period roughly between 1962 and 1979). This is evident from the several references in it to the Cuban Revolution, the Vietnam War, the independence struggles of the emergent nations of the so-called Third World, the Prague Spring of 1968 (and what that portended for an assessment of the historical outcomes of the Bolshevik Revolution), the radical student movement of the 1960s, and so on. Thus the 1979 afterword contains a perceptive characterization of the rise of several political and economic developments that reached their culmination in Britain and the United States in the 1980s and 1990s:

> Managed affluence has slid into an anxiously managed but perhaps unmanageable depression. Some political consensus has held but the social consensus underlying it has been visibly breaking down, and especially at the level of everyday life. Managed transitions from colonialism have been profitably achieved but are increasingly and fiercely being fought in a hundred fields. The balance of terror is still there, and is yet more terrifying, but its limited and enclosed stabilities are increasingly threatened by the surge of wider actions. It is then not surprising that the dominant messages are of danger and conflict, and that the dominant forms are of shock and loss. (*MT* 208)

What Williams has identified here can be further described and analyzed in terms of more than one set of theoretical notions—hence, some would perhaps be disposed to say that Williams has fastened onto the moment of transition between "Fordist" and "post-Fordist" strategies of accumulation; others that he is recognizing the manifestations of what can now be seen as the emergence of a new "cultural logic," namely, that of "postmodernism"; and yet others that he is perhaps registering the emergence of a new economic and cultural dispensation, that of a globalized cultural order increasingly characterized these days as that of a "postcoloniality" (as opposed to a predecessor "coloniality" that extended from about 1870 to the 1960s).[3] Whatever we may want to say, whether in agreement or disagreement, about Williams's account of this new "structure of feeling," it has to be noted that the emergence of a decisive conjuncture of this kind is for him the moment par excellence for the creation and intensification of tragic experience:

> Important tragedy seems to occur, neither in periods of real stability, nor in periods of open and decisive conflict. Its most common historical setting is the period preceding the substantial breakdown and transformation of an important culture. Its condition is the real tension between the old and the new: between received beliefs, embodied in institutions and responses, and newly and vividly experienced contradictions and possibilities. (*MT* 54)[4]

Williams thus believes that it is possible to look for "the structure of tragedy in our own culture," though we have in the process to eschew any search "for a new universal meaning of tragedy" (*MT* 62). He locates the search for this present-day "structure of tragedy" in a historical trajectory that extends back to the French Revolution: from that time onward "the action of tragedy and the action of history have been consciously connected, and in the connection have been seen in new ways" (*MT* 62). But, Williams goes on to say, the nineteenth century saw the development of two opposing tendencies on this question of the relation between tragedy and history. One, which encompasses both Hegel and Schopenhauer and Nietzsche, separated the movement of consciousness from the movement of history—Hegel by providing what was in effect a flawed (because idealistic) doctrine of reconciliation (i.e., a theodicy of history) and Schopenhauer and Nietzsche by offering an understanding of tragedy motivated by their respective secular mythographies of fate (and for Williams this was yet another baneful manifestation of idealism). The other tendency, to be associated with Marx, brought history and tragedy into a conscious relation. Williams, as one would expect, aligns himself with the latter tendency and proposes to see tragedy in our time as "a response to social disorder" (*MT* 63).

The proposal that tragedy be viewed as "a response to social disorder" runs into an immediate difficulty (as Williams himself acknowledges). The preceding tradition of reflection on tragedy had very great difficulty in viewing tragedy as a response to social crisis. And then, according to Williams, there has been in this century a widespread perception that the idea of tragedy is "itself defeatist," that existing conditions will be changed only by the exercise of our own powers, that tragedy is pervasively "ideological" because it compels us to understand suffering as an always present, unalterable condition. Today, therefore, "we cannot recognise social crisis as tragedy . . . [and] the idea of tragedy . . . has been explicitly opposed by the idea of revolution" (*MT* 63). Williams sets himself the task of undoing this opposition between tragedy and revolution:

> What seems to matter, against every difficulty, is that the received ideas no longer describe our experience. The most common idea of revolution excludes too much of our social experience. But it is more than this. The idea of tragedy, in its ordinary form, excludes especially that tragic experience which is social, and the idea of revolution, again in its ordinary form, excludes especially that social experience which is tragic. And if this is so, the contradiction is significant. It is not a merely formal opposition, of two ways of reading experience, between which we can choose. In our own time, especially, it is the connections between revolution and tragedy—connections lived and known but not acknowledged as ideas—which seem most clear and significant. (MT 64)

Williams's suggestion that our received ideas of revolution "exclude too much of our social experience" is to be found in a number of his other writings. Certainly it is present in *The Long Revolution*, where "the long revolution" is depicted as "a genuine revolution, transforming men and institutions; continually extended and deepened by the actions of millions, continually and variously opposed by explicit reaction and by the pressure of habitual forms and ideas."[5] The "long revolution" is thus understood to be a "cultural revolution," though as such it is not to be separated in principle from other revolutionary processes.[6]

Revolution is a complex, many-staged process for Williams. At one level it is "a whole action," a "total practical activity," of living human beings: here it constitutes a slow, uneven, and even barely perceptible series of cumulative transformations that extend over a "long duration" invariably subtended by a not always apparent violence and disorder. At another it is the specific crisis of this more comprehensive process of disorder, a process that, despite its disordered state, can nonetheless possess its own stability. Revolution in this case is the transmutation of this underlying, extended disorder into an explicit crisis, a crisis that can then have the character of an insurrection.[7] Tragic experience, in one form, is experience of this pervasive disorder, in any one of its many dimensions, and this even though the disorder in question may not in this instance have manifested itself in an explicit way as a rebellion. Revolution is thus not necessarily to be identified "with violence or with a sudden capture of power" (*MT* 76). In its other characteristic form, tragic experience is rooted in the revolutionary insurrection itself and its outcomes. But even this particular kind of tragic experience is compatible with a constructive activity, because for Williams there is scope for processes of reconstruction and reconstitution in all but the most (tragically) devastated societies. These processes of transformation are available, if not at the level of specific social institutions and structures, then (just as significantly where Williams is concerned) at that of a deeper and more radical "structure of feeling." The tragic action is therefore a confrontation with, and a resolution of, this disorder. It is a confrontation that typically takes the form of a struggle, revolution being "the disordered struggle against disorder" (*MT* 83). The implication is clear: tragedy is possible because it is *we* who constitute the disorder, we who perpetrate the tragic horrors of revolution. Any ensuing liberation does not annul the terror, since the liberation and the terror are connected, often in immensely complicated ways:

> We see indeed a certain inevitability, of a tragic kind, as we see the struggle to end alienation producing its own new kinds of alienation. But, while we attend to the whole action, we see also, working through it, a new struggle against the new alienation; the comprehension of disorder producing a new image of order; the revolution against the fixed consciousness of revolution, and the authentic activ-

ity reborn and newly lived. What we then know is no simple action:
the heroic liberation. But we know more also than simple reaction, for
if we accept alienation, in ourselves or in others, as a permanent condition, we must know that other men, by the very act of living, will reject this, making us their involuntary enemies, and the radical disorder
is then most bitterly confirmed. (*MT* 83)

The crucial question for Williams (at this juncture) is the form of
an adequate reflection on these processes of development and transformation. Here he is explicit in his repudiation of "mechanistic" and
"unilinear" models of change. In dealing with this question Williams
identifies a nineteenth-century tradition of thought that extends
from liberalism and culminates in naturalism (though naturalism is
in an important sense a theoretical arrestation of liberalism). Naturalism, as a "tendency," promoted a conception of change and development based on evolutionary, as opposed to revolutionary, principles. Williams is worth quoting on this substitution:

> [Behind] the idea of social evolution was an unconscious attachment to
> the development of a *single* form. Social development was uncon-
> sciously based on the experience of one type of Western society, and
> its imperialist contacts with more 'primitive' societies. The real social
> and cultural variation of human history was thus reduced to a single
> model: unilinear and predictable. Even Marxists took over this limited
> model, and its rigidity has been widely experienced in some twentieth-
> century communist practice. A more adequate understanding of both
> natural and cultural evolution would have made so mechanical and
> unilinear a model untenable, for it would have emphasized both varia-
> tion and creativity and thus a more genuinely open and (in the full
> sense) revolutionary future. (*MT* 70, n. 1)

The outcome was a "mechanical materialism" that enjoined "the separation of historical development from the action of the majority or
even, in its extreme forms, from all men" (*MT* 70). Society came to
be viewed as "an impersonal process, a machine with certain built-in
properties" (ibid.). This substitution was therefore "theoretically and
factually a mystification of real social activity, and as such discred-
ited reason itself" (ibid.). Naturalism, and its accompanying model of
society, succumbed in this way to a powerful irrationality. It was
not the only nineteenth-century intellectual movement to do this
(according to Williams)—romanticism was the other. But Williams's

treatment of romanticism, as a general movement, is highly problematic and even inadequate, as I shall now try to indicate.[8]

Romanticism always seemed to exist for Williams solely in its English version. It is certainly a bit of a surprise to the historian of tragedy that Williams, who generally was so unfailingly alert in this area, should fail to engage seriously with the immense speculative interest in tragedy (and especially Greek tragedy) shown by the thinkers who constitute the movement known as German idealism and (theoretical) romanticism. For it is quite well known that Hegel, Schiller, Schelling, the Schlegel brothers, and Hölderlin were at some point in their careers enthusiastic supporters of the French Revolution (Hölderlin in fact never wavered in his commitment to social and political revolution), and it is also commonly known that these thinkers used a variety of conceptions of tragedy and the tragic to reflect on what was for them the historically exigent question of the politics of revolution. On reflection, though, it is perhaps not so surprising that Williams, the few pages he devotes to Hegel in *Modern Tragedy* notwithstanding, should largely overlook the writings dealing with tragedy and politics produced by these thinkers. They wrote in a highly abstruse philosophical idiom, and this includes even Hölderlin, who of course is commonly regarded as the great lyric poet of the German language, but who also produced a number of essays in philosophical aesthetics that have retained their importance to this day. It would probably take someone trained as a philosopher to engage in any depth or detail with the more speculative writings of German idealism and romanticism, and Williams, for all his very considerable gifts and accomplishments, was not, and indeed did not see himself as, a philosopher. Nevertheless, it is the case that in the writings of German idealism and (speculative) romanticism we have the most substantial treatment of the subject of tragedy provided by any fully fledged movement of intellectuals in the so-called age of modern revolutions. This work on tragedy was of course invariably undertaken by these thinkers as part of a wider, and "thoroughly philosophical," reflection on the function of art as a medium of (absolute) reflection. It would therefore be appropriate for someone with an interest in the history of philosophical aesthetics to pay his own quite unworthy tribute to Raymond Williams by examining what German idealism and romanticism had to say about

tragedy and revolution through its reflections on art and the absolute.[9]

A consideration of the subject of tragedy and revolution is arguably very much in order these days for another reason. There appear to be some significant affinities between recent times (1989
being the decisive marker)—a period which has come to be dominated by an inexorable consciousness of the failure of the revolution of 1917—and the time (roughly 1790 to 1830) of German idealism
and romanticism, when of course the French Revolution and its aftermath constituted for the thinkers of that generation an event of
undeniable world-historical dimensions.[10]

The French Revolution represented for the thinkers of German
idealism and romanticism another speculative "moment" in tragedy's
continuing history as an ideological form. I have noted that it was
Williams's great accomplishment in *Modern Tragedy* to have recognized, at a time that saw, in Britain at any rate, shameless declama-
tions of the "death" of tragedy, the continued persistence of tragedy
as an ideological form. In so doing Williams insisted that we are
today still confronted—though assuredly not in the same ways as
our predecessors—by the question, the question posed quintessentially for tragedy, of the necessity and possibility of reconciling freedom and nature (or necessity). And it is precisely this question that
was central for German idealism and theoretical romanticism; it was
this question that this movement addressed so uncompromisingly
under the rubric of tragedy. Williams, however, gave no indication
in *Modern Tragedy* that romanticism, and especially German romanticism, addressed this question more powerfully and productively than any other intellectual movement. The historical narrative
provided in *Modern Tragedy* speeds straight from Hegel (who, as
we have seen, was regarded by Williams as an unregenerate theodi-
cist) to Marx and his followers (who, more plausibly for Williams,
viewed the tragic conflict of ethical forces spoken about by Hegel as
the outcome of a prior and more decisive antagonism between historical and social forces). This hasty progress from Hegel to Marx in
itself militates against a productive assessment of romanticism, and
especially of German romanticism, since such an assessment demands an almost immediate complication of the narrative of *Modern Tragedy*: if there is a royal road that leads from Hegel to Marx
(and I am not necessarily denying that there is one), then any road

that leads to, or through, German romanticism will represent something of a detour from this itinerary. One of the initial presuppositions of this essay is that this detour merits a deeper study than is perhaps allowed for in Williams's book. Hegel's relationship to romanticism is complex (*ambivalent* is perhaps the better word) in any case, and it could further be argued that Williams was precluded from giving an adequate characterization of this particular aspect of German romanticism by his tendency in *Modern Tragedy* (though not elsewhere) to assimilate the several (some would say the many) romanticisms to one particular manifestation—the English—of this always quite diverse movement.[11] Williams perhaps succumbed to one of the pitfalls that attends any attempt to identify Hegel (or anyone else, for that matter) as a paradigmatic figure in the history of tragic discourse: in such a scheme of things, Hegel inevitably comes to be abstracted, and thus isolated, from the rest of German idealism and romanticism. There is also the danger here of an assimilation of a real diversity of theme and emphasis to that which happens to be seen as the singular, exemplary instance (in this case Hegel). Williams was thus mistaken in his implication that there is somehow a basic incompatibility between the attempt to delineate the speculative "moment" of tragedy and the endeavor to use tragedy as a resource for understanding the character of revolution (a character that is necessarily social and political). He seemed to believe that any effort to "think" tragedy in its speculative "moment" results inevitably in the transmutation of tragedy into a metaphysical or spiritual principle à la Hegel, whereas (or so *Modern Tragedy* implies) what is essential to any adequate conception of revolution (and this obviously includes the attempt to reflect on it in the form[s] of the tragic) is something of a different (i.e., "nonmetaphysical") order, namely, "the recognition of revolution as a whole action of living men" (*MT* 65).

But these are harsh words if they are not immediately qualified by the acknowledgment of the even-handedness with which Williams conducted his critique of romanticism. The section on romanticism in *Modern Tragedy* contains the admission that romanticism was "profoundly liberating," at least in its early stages (*MT* 71). However, Williams goes on to say of romanticism that "partly because of the inadequacy of any corresponding social theory, and partly because of the consequent decline from individualism to subjectivism, it ended by denying its own deepest impulses, and even reversing them" (ibid.).[12] The suggestion that romanticism betrayed itself by a retreat into "subjectivism" may be true of English romanticism, but it is not so true if one thinks of its German counterpart, and especially of Hölderlin. If, as Williams contends, the romantics failed because they were not able to develop an adequate social theory, then it may be that the subsequent development of such a theory will make possible a rereading of romanticism, and not only that, but also reactivation of its "deepest impulses," impulses, which, as Williams himself points out, have as their "object" an indubitably revolutionary politics.[13]

It is widely agreed that the text titled *Das älteste Systemprogramms des deutschen Idealismus* (The earliest system-program of German idealism) is crucial for any understanding of the theoretical and practical course taken by German speculative idealism and romanticism.[14] The authorship of this text, written, it is commonly thought, in 1796, has been a matter of considerable and always inconclusive debate since it was published by Franz Rosenszweig (one is strongly tempted to add the adjectives *irrelevant* and *futile* to those used to characterize this debate). The "System-Program" text survives in the form of a copy made in the handwriting of Hegel, though in addition to him, its other possible authors have been alleged to be Schelling or Hölderlin.[15]

The primary theses adumbrated in the eight paragraphs of this historically significant document are as follows:[16]

1. All metaphysics will eventually be supplanted by ethics. The ruling idea of this ethics is "the representation of myself as an absolutely free being."
2. A new "physics" will have to be devised to deal with the question, How must a world for moral being be constituted?
3. The state has to be destroyed because it cannot be what it is without curtailing the freedom of human beings.
4. Neither God nor immortality must be sought outside of humanity.
5. The highest form of reason is the aesthetic, and truth and

goodness are united in beauty. Philosophy must perforce become an aesthetic philosophy.

6. A "religion of the senses" is needed by "the masses" and the philosopher alike. The creation of this new *homo religiosus* will involve a "monotheism of reason and of the heart," and a "polytheism of the imagination and art."

7. A "new mythology," one that is a "mythology of reason" at the service of "the ideas," will also be needed.

For all its explicitly political radicalism, some of the features of this manifesto (and this should not be too surprising) show it to reflect patterns of thought widely current in German intellectual life at that time. The "System-Program" invokes, for example, in a fairly direct way, Winckelmann's imaginative vision of an ideal Hellas (possessing all the excellences that modernity appeared to lack), a vision that German idealism and romanticism regarded as an indispensable ethical spur for contemporary political transformation.[17] Accompanying this appeal to the myth of a primordial Greece is a commendation—one just as common as this myth of an ideal and beautiful Greece representing "*die Totalität der Gattung*" (Schiller) —of the aesthetic act as that which is uniquely suited to repairing the breach between subject and object that modernity had created.[18] The "System-Program" also maintains that a transformation of consciousness is the necessary precondition of social and political change, a principle that had been upheld by Fichte and Schiller (who of course had been among the most influential of the preceding generation of thinkers).[19] Also very much in evidence in this text is the intellectual legacy of Kant's critical philosophy—the project of a "new moral metaphysics" that the "System-Program" proposes is explicitly stated to be of a Kantian provenance by its authors, who moreover declare that the "System-Program" will undertake to fulfill the task of "collapsing" metaphysics into ethics that Kant had inaugurated but did not complete. The "System-Program," however, departs from Kant's philosophy in at least one major respect: it proposes a "religion of the senses" for the philosopher (and not just the masses), whereas Kant had been the proponent of a rational religion that he believed was the one ordained by the "telos" of human progress.[20] We could enumerate many other influences, not mentioned so far, that intersect in this unusual document. It is a text that, for all its concision, provides as productive a topology for under-standing the project of modernity as, say, Hegel's *Phenomenology* or Nietzsche's *Untimely Meditations* (I have in mind especially the meditation titled "Vom Nutzen und Nachteil der Historie für das Leben") or Marx's *Eighteenth Brumaire of Louis Napoleon*—and not just the project of modernity because what many people now call postmodernity is perhaps usefully to be understood as the realiza-tion, "coming after modernity," that "crisis," this "crisis," is the (seem-ingly) inexorable culminating point of modernity.

The "System-Program," in two nonidentical but virtually inseparable "moments," expresses both the "crisis" of modernity and the mode(s) of its resolution. Its stipulation that neither God nor immortality must be sought outside the domain of the human—a notion first de-livered for German idealism by the "Transcendental Dialectic" of Kant's first Critique—amounts to an appropriation of the powers of the divine by the citizens of modernity. This stipulation accompa-nies, and this very much in order to certify, the birth of a new *homo religiosus* who represents "himself" as "an absolutely free being" (*Wesen*) and who, under the sign of this freedom, will undertake to create "an entire world" (a creation that the "System-Program" calls "the one true and thinkable creation out of nothing"). The human is now the bearer of the infinite. But the "System-Program" also carries, in its first two paragraphs, the distinct implication of the impossibil-ity of presupposing the infinite: as H. S. Harris notes, these para-graphs "are part of a theory of practical reason, and of rational faith in the Kantian sense,"[21] and the core of this rational faith (the bounds of which are charted in the "Transcendental Dialectic" of *The Cri-tique of Pure Reason*) lies in its consignment of the infinite to the realm of absolute indetermination ("the noumenal"). At the same time, it is true that this particular legacy of the first critique—its "problematizing" of the infinite—is taken up in *The Critique of Judgement*, where, in the section titled "The Analytic of the Sub-lime," Kant poses for the imagination (as opposed to the under-standing) this very question of the representability of the infinite. The "System-Program" continues along Kant's path by posing this question for the "new" mythology it advertises.

The new *homo religiosus* of the "System-Program" is indubitably a tragic figure: this new being must be (a) god and yet "he" cannot be (a) god. Under the auspices of modernity, "he" cannot be that which "he" must be, or perhaps even more pointedly, this personage cannot be the very thing "he" has become. It is therefore not surprising that German speculative idealism and romanticism should address this "crisis" of modernity via a whole series of reflections on tragedy and the tragic—not merely by reflecting on the subject of tragedy, for as we have indicated, it sought to broach the question of this "crisis" at a wider level of generality, by constructing a theory of antiquity, a wholly paradigmatic antiquity.[22]

Modernity gave to its denizens the task of reimagining the infinite, the illimitable, and through this reimagining to traverse the schisms (between subject and object, sensuousness and intelligibility, history and nature, etc.) that constitute its "crisis." The "System-Program" proposes a revolutionary rereading of the relations between the elements of these schisms. Schelling and Hegel did this by resorting to a philosophy of nature (Schelling) and an account of a vast transcendental subjectivity that has as its "telos" the reassimilation of the plenitude of objective determinations (Hegel). Hölderlin, however, refuses this dialectical idealism, this "philosophy," of Schelling and Hegel (the quotation marks are needed here because what Hölderlin proposes amounts to a complete recasting of "philosophy," indeed something very like its "disorganizing" or "ending," its mutation into a thought without categories, "aesthetics"). Hegel would subordinate the aesthetic to the philosophical by maintaining that it is only philosophy that can say what art is, art not being able to say this about itself; and Schelling, while conceding more to aesthetics than Hegel did by accepting that philosophy was unable "to lend meaning to art," nevertheless came to hold that only philosophy could express "in ideas" what the aesthetic sensibility could only "intuit" (i.e., cognize without an awareness of its reason) in the concrete work of art.[23] Hölderlin, however, realized that it was impossible—in principle—for philosophy to undertake this regulative and/or expressive function for its counterpart discourses. Philosophy was, irresolvably, a problem unto itself, and so could not be the means (i.e., the conceptual means) whereby subject and object, sensuousness and intelligibility, and so forth are reunited.

In his longest theoretical essay, "Verfahrungsweise des poetischen Geistes" ("On the Operations of the Poetic Spirit"),[24] Hölderlin argues

that no unity can be so absolute that it amounts to something entirely insusceptible to difference and differentiation: if this were so,
Hölderlin maintains, there would be no unity because there could
be no "bringing together" of anything in such a state of pure undif-
ferentiatedness, or at least there would be no difference between
this alleged unity and what Hölderlin calls "an empty infinity." On
the other hand, if in a commerce or alternation of opposites there
did not remain something "integral and unified," then there would
be nothing but "an infinity of isolated moments (a sequence of
atoms, as it were)." To obviate this second danger of total fragmentation, the poetic spirit has to transform each temporal moment into
a point positioned within an organic whole, so that this spirit can
monitor the movements backward and forward of all such moments. The mediation of poetic spirit is therefore necessary for any
overcoming of division. In which case, however, the reconciliation
achieved by this "poetic" mediation is always exterior to the pro-
gressus of the moments in question. Unity can never be intrinsic to
the ebb and flow of moments; it is accomplished in what is necessarily an exteriority supplied by the mediation of the poetic spirit.
The intuition that confers unity does so by operating on a fundamental and insurmountable separation between reflection and
Being. Or to put this in more contemporary parlance: for Hölderlin
the moment of unity can never be primordial because "difference"
interposes itself, ubiquitously, between intuition and object, and so
reconciliation is always potentially "deferrable." Philosophy cannot
sustain the notion of an originary unity, and this impossibility (i.e.,
the unavoidability of "difference") is itself a condition of the possibility of philosophy.[25] It would seem that Paul de Man was therefore
essentially right to portray Hölderlin as the poetologist/poet of "deferral."[26]

The Hölderlinian denial of anything approximating a primordial
unity, however, is not necessarily what de Man takes it to be, that is,
a philosophical procedure for forestalling or postponing all premature reconciliations. We can "read" this procedure in a quite different
way (while acknowledging in the same breath that de Man is not
mistaken in holding that there is a philosophical safeguard in
Hölderlin against excessively hasty attempts to override "difference").

Hölderlin's safeguard can be viewed, *pace* de Man, as a proposal precisely for returning the project of reconciliation to the historical, political, social, and economic places of its construction. Hölderlin's great achievement is to have shown us that reconciliation, if it takes place, is not something that is fated to occur: it comes about only when we, in "a defiance of reason and poetry" (to appropriate from another context a phrase of Toni Negri's), ceaselessly reinvent this (reconciled) reality. Hölderlin is the proponent of a dynamic and liberating materialism, even as he invokes the transcendental imagination as the "essential" source of the constructiveness of being: indeed, the very existence of this imagination is taken by him to be the complement of any materialism, since it is the imagination that enables materialism to retain its constructive power in the very moment that materialism has lost its hope. The poetic imagination, in this Hölderlinian account, is nothing less than the indomitable power to reinvent reality continually—a reinvention and reinventing that, even as it is generated by the "projective" power of the imagination, is harnessed to material forces through its being positioned, irremovably, in a "space" of desire, and (further) by virtue of being so positioned is at the same time a revolutionary movement of freedom and happiness. Though, we should add, it is not necessarily a revolution that is taking place now, in the sense of being a revolution that has found its politics. Hölderlin teaches us that there is always a revolution that is still to find its politics, and that, in a very profound sense, it is the poet who registers the reality of this revolution and thereby opens a "space" for the politics that is to come.

Toni Negri, in a discussion of Spinoza and Leopardi, has shown us how a previous politics, a politics that did not survive the "crisis" of modernity, tried to teach us to hope so that we may live for a better future.[27] This politics did not survive the loss of that hope. A "new" politics, one of the deliverances of the poetics of Hölderlin, will be one that instead taught us to live, for it is by living (and by living we of course mean more than merely surviving) that we are taught hope.

Living (and so resisting or "escaping" in the sense made well known by Deleuze and Guattari?).[28] Hölderlin speaks elsewhere of our "need" for "a monotheism of the reason and of the heart," and for a "polytheism of the imagination and art."[29] The context of this need is not specified by Hölderlin, though there would almost certainly be something counterintuitive if we did not connect it with the "time of universal freedom and equality" that was a kind of irremovable horizon for Hölderlin's philosophy of life.

But what is the relation of tragedy and the tragic to this "time of universal freedom and equality"? If tragedy were here understoood in Hegelian terms, then the answer to this question would be relatively easy to provide. Where Hegel is concerned, this time of unbounded happiness would be when the oppositions and diremptions that lie at the heart of tragic conflicts are finally and decisively "sublated" (that is, overcome without being abolished) by the higher unity that is absolute spirit.[30] For Hegel, the opposition of finite beings, while it is not eliminated, is nonetheless reconciled in Spirit (namely, self-consciousness) as the supreme identity of identity and difference. Hegel's is thus, unreservedly, a philosophy of the mastery of difference. Hölderlin, by contrast, repudiates the presumption of identity that underlies this (Hegelian) mastery over ontological difference (to lapse into a Heideggerian idiom): as we have seen, his essay "On the Operations of the Poetic Spirit" indicates that difference can never be incorporated—"dialectically"—into a totality that retains difference if only in order to resolve it within the higher unity constituted by this totality. There is no (reconciling) Absolute in Hölderlin's thought, or if there is an Absolute in his system, it is one that is ceaselessly multiplied.[31]

Hölderlin, like Leopardi, provides us with a reconstructive materialism, one still grounded in the tragedy of Being, but a materialism that also offers the hope of rediscovering happiness, a hope of overcoming and transcending this tragedy in what Josef Chytry, in his *The Aesthetic State: A Quest in Modern German Thought*, succinctly calls "a post-tragic age of republican harmony and poetic dwelling."[32] The coming of this age is to be associated with the birth of a new kind of consciousness, an essentially poetic consciousness. This would be a consciousness that, unlike the one depicted by Hegel, when it reaches the stage of final reconciliation, would still retain the primacy of the sensuous and the principle of difference. Hölderlin provides the image of postrevolutionary political order that will be coextensive with the "space" of a new and different kind of desire ("sensuousness"). The creation of this "space" is associated by Hölderlin with the indwelling of the infinite or unbounded in the domain of the finite. But this is not an "intact" Absolute that permeates or unfolds within the realm of the finite (in the manner of Hegel): Hölderlin's indwelling infinite is this by virtue of the very dissolution of the boundaries between finite and infinite, and he thus renders impossible in principle a dialectical overcoming of these boundaries (again as in Hegel). The unbounded, the infinite, can only manifest itself in the multiplicity, in the unstoppable but "nonagonistic" proliferation of difference and discontinuity that marks this "space," the "space" of a new social collectivity. It is the abyssal source (which is not the same as an "origin") of this multiplicity.[33]

The times beyond the dialectic of the old and the new, that is, the time that some call postmodernity, is "post-tragic," although in saying this, we have to note in the very same breath that there is a sense in which this new dispensation is also ineluctably "tragic" (in the manner specified by Philippe Lacoue-Labarthe, that is, that this is an order in which there takes place the "ruin of the inimitable and the disappearance of models"). Hölderlin speaks for and to this new order because he is the first exponent of a new kind of "writing" (as they say nowadays) that has effectively dispensed with what is frequently termed "the Platonic-Cartesian" understanding of truth, that is, the conception of truth that relies fundamentally on the distinction between (original) "model" and (replicated) "copy," and that defines truth in terms of the adequation between original and replica. If the tragic is associated with this loss, then there is a sense in which our age can have no need for tragedy, understood here as some kind of optic or horizon through which we come to have knowledge of our world or condition or whatever. Our time, or rather our "space," simply *is* tragic. And this because all we have now are localized points of indetermination, of endless multiplicity. The standard or classical conception of tragedy was articulated in terms of such categories as the irrevocable, the irreconcilable, and so forth. But a world of essential incompletions (so that in principle all "completions" are instituted by a particular politics), of the infinitely deferrable limits (so that in principle all "limits" are again impositions enacted by a particular politics), and so forth, is not one that can accommodate categories associated with traditional conceptions of tragedy and the tragic. What is tragic about this world is exactly this—that there is no place in it for notions of the unredeemable, the irresolvable, the immutable. It is the tragedy of an absence, in this case the absence of tragedy. However, it is precisely the (poetic) vision of such a world that Hölderlin regards as the basis of a barely utterable but fabulous hope, the hope that in this new world we will have come to be so different that it is not possible anymore for us to tell who the gods are: they and we are mutually indistinguishable because "we" (but what new form is signified by this "we"?) have become something that does not make us either like or unlike the gods. Hölderlin has effectively undone any opposition between "theological" and "anthropological" predicates. This dismantling of the opposition between the divine and the human, or the theological and the anthropological, represents a repudiation on Hölderlin's part of a dialectical conception of tragedy. Tragedy, on this account, cannot thus be understood as the loss, the final and irretrievable loss, of some kind of primordial unity. Hölderlin may have begun his examination of tragedy with a typically "Greek" or dialectical conception of tragedy in front of him, but he can perhaps justifiably make for himself the claim that Nietzsche advanced on his own behalf in *The Will to Power*, namely, that "[it] is I who discovered the tragic, even the Greeks misinterpreted it."[34] Tragedy ceases to be negative; it is no longer to be understood as a Hegelian or quasi-Hegelian supersession of contradiction or difference. In Hölderlin's vision the tragic has acquired the character of the sublime. His poetics is thus a new cartography of the sublime.

In drafting what amounts to a cartography of the sublime that displaces a traditional or classical theory of the tragic, Hölderlin provides the lineaments of an understanding of the sublime that came to be very influential in this century. This is a view of the sublime that merges its obvious aesthetic features with a recognition of what was until very recently its generally less prominent function as an almost indispensable category for the historical imagination.[35] So prominent is this reflection on the sublime nowadays that there is hardly a major contemporary philosopher who has not produced at least an essay on this subject: Derrida, Lacoue-Labarthe, Lyotard, Deleuze, and Hayden White come readily to mind as thinkers who have employed, and in some cases have interrogated as well, the category of the sublime.[36] These notable discussions of the sublime—identified by all these thinkers as the "unpresentable"—pose the difficult, the intractable question of its relation to the tragic. This question has been addressed specifically by Lacoue-Labarthe, who is unapologetic in his claim that the tragic (as portrayed by Aristotle) has in our time come to be subsumed by the sublime.[37] But it may not really be necessary for us to deal with the question of the relation between the sublime and the tragic. Hölderlin, in any case, dismantles this distinction in his poetics of tragedy precisely by asserting that it is the very unpresentability of the infinite—its "sublimity," in our terms—that makes for tragedy. This is the crisis of modernity (or so we have said): the unpresentability of the infinite creates a state of affairs, a "contingency," that demands a reimagination of the horizon of the infinite. Hölderlin indicated that it is the task of poetry to reimagine this horizon. He also knew, however, that the infinite and the eternal can become historical actualities only if ethics (which here is inseparable from politics) brings about their insertion into the historical. Hölderlin is thus inescapably utopian, or "impossibly" utopian, as Lukács would indeed subsequently, and mistakenly, contend. I want to conclude by making some remarks about the nature of such a "utopian" politics, in connection with what Raymond Williams had to say about the politics to come.[38]

> It is not some unavoidable real world, with its laws of economy and laws of war, that is now blocking us. It is a set of identifiable processes of realpolitik and force majeure, of nameable agencies of power and capital, distraction and disinformation, and all these interlocking with the embedded short-term pressures and the interwoven subordinations of an adaptive commonsense. It is not in staring at these blocks that there is any chance of movement past them. They have been named so often that they are not even, for most people, news. The dynamic moment is elsewhere, in the difficult business of gaining confidence in our own energies and capacities.
> . . . It is only in a shared belief and insistence that there are practical alternatives that the balance of forces and chances begins to alter. Once the inevitabilities are challenged, we begin gathering our resources for a journey of hope. If there are no easy answers there are still available and discoverable hard answers, and it is these that we can now learn to make and share. This has been, from the beginning, the sense and impulse of the long revolution.
>
> —Raymond Williams[39]

It has been my contention in this essay that the "System-Program" manifesto and Hölderlin's philosophical writings on tragedy provide the lineaments of a poetical ontology (or ontological poetics) of revolutionary transformation, a "materialist" ontology/poetics that can productively be used to understand the processes that constitute the current political, social, and economic conjuncture. And if it is accepted that the politics of transformation that Williams sought to formulate under the rubric of "the long revolution" is (very broadly) in accord with the constitutive features of this present conjuncture, then, at the very least, there exists the real possibility of bringing about a useful rapprochement between this romantic ontology/poetics and Williams's conception of a "long revolution."

But what is the character of this current conjuncture? And (to ask a question that Williams would perhaps have insisted on raising in this connection) what is its associated "structure of feeling"?[40]

Williams posed the question of "the current conjuncture" in a number of essays in the 1970s and 1980s and also in *Towards 2000*. In these essays and in *Towards 2000* he came more and more to recognize the increasingly abstract and "diagrammatic" nature of present-day capitalism, to see that it is only by submitting itself to such processes of abstraction that capitalism can ensure that any and every kind of production (even those whose forms are "precapitalist") is mediated by it and placed at the disposal of accumulation. Williams had a profound appreciation of the import of this transformation, namely, that because the forms of capital were now so mobile and diverse, the sites of power in our current social realities, and the irreducibly complex and unstable movements of force positioned at these sites, were too varied, and too constitutively uncontained, to be managed by a politics of the kind that existed in the last two hundred years. He resorted to Gramsci's notion of "hegemony" in his efforts to reflect on this development, and he shared Gramsci's conviction that the forces that created revolutions were cultural and political rather than economic, so that, for instance, it was not possible (if not before then certainly not now) to make an overschematic distinction between (economic) "base" and (cultural) "superstructure."[41] There is a sense in which he went even further than Gramsci (who did not after all relinquish the base-superstructure distinction, but merely reconfigured it)—for Williams the economic, the political, the social, and the cultural spheres merge into a seamless totality, and in late capitalism especially, any revolution would have to extend unevenly along the many fronts that constituted this whole. Its course would be circuitous, its duration "long." Hence, there would always be the possibility of alternative responses within the same "structure of feeling" (*MT* 208).

This is the time of an integrated world capitalism (to use a phrase of Toni Negri's) that is essentially "paranational" in form. In this situation, the many and various functions of the state have come increasingly to be devolved into the apparatuses that it comprises, so that what we are seeing is a kind of "withering away" of the state.[42] This decomposition of the institutional assemblage that is the state makes possible the emergence of new and different collective subjects, associated with the growth of new social movements, their social agents, and an attendant "micropolitics."[43] This is a space of "heterotopia," a "heterotopia" that is unfolding, though not necessarily "progressing" politically, because its politics is a politics that is yet to come, yet to be achieved. Williams evinced an acute sense of all this in his last writings.

What the poetical ontology discussed in this essay furnishes in this context is the rudiments of a theory of subjectivity not predicated on a philosophy of the will, that is, a philosophy that affirms the principle of an interiority (traditionally understood in terms of the will and its cognates, e.g., the soul or consciousness or whatever). With the repudiation of this philosophy of interiority, it is no longer possible to understand political change in terms of a "bending" of the will or the getting of many wills to act in whatever kind of concert. Unlike the subject of this philosophy of the will or interiority, the collective subjectivities of this poetical ontology are the loci of a multiplicity of powers and potentials. The typical and appropriate mode of organization for this kind of collective subjectivity will be what Henri Lefebvre has called "generalized self-management" and Williams a "new orientation of livelihood: of practical, self-managing, self-renewing societies."[44] In this "new orientation of livelihood" the interests of the collective subjectivities will be presented, expressed, rather than represented in the way that the politics of the last two hundred years has purported to do.[45] There is a sense in which this "politics" of self-management is the "postpolitics" of the creativity of living labor, a creativity that cannot in principle be managed by the adversary of this self-construction and self-renewal, namely, capitalism. It cannot be managed by capital because, as Toni Negri has pointed out, the process of this new form of social cooperation is ontological: it is constituted through the multiple and uncontainable stratifications of memory, of desire, of struggle.[46]

Intrinsic to this process of self-construction is the emergence of a structure that makes it possible for us to enter into a relation with new forms and modes of becoming—forms that for the ontological poetics supplied by the "System-Program" manifesto are designated neither by "theological" nor by "anthropological" predicates. Forms whose "syntax," as we have seen, is that of an unbounded or illimitable finitude, or rather, that of an "indwelling" of the absolute or infinite in the realm of the finite, and this precisely because the boundary between finite and infinite has been deconstituted or deconstructed. A finitude that is compatible with the constitutive power of our freedom, despite what theology and anthropology may declare, and this in the name of a certain "dialectical" rendition of the tragic.

All this prompts me to pose the following question: Did Raymond Williams really manage to avoid this "dialectical" version of the tragic? That is, did he not, despite all his efforts to the contrary, remain within the dialectic between theology and anthropology that has been at the heart of all preceding conceptions of tragedy and the tragic? He seemed to view tragedy very much as the tragedy of limits and boundaries, whereas Hölderlin regarded tragedy as precisely the absence of such limits and boundaries, as the multiplication of the absolute. Of course we are dealing here with very different discourses: Williams was certainly not concerned to formulate an ontology of the tragic in the way that Hölderlin was; his interest was in a certain kind of empirical-conceptual claim about the relation between a particular way of experiencing and thinking (the tragic vision) and the social and cultural forms that subtended that quite specific mode of experience and thought. But if my argument in this essay has been plausible, then the new and emergent historical conjuncture that Williams himself had begun to identify even in *Modern Tragedy* is one that lends itself to a "theorization" in terms of the cartography of the tragic-sublime provided by German speculative romanticism and idealism. Williams was not wrong when he claimed that romanticism lacked a social theory. Today, however, that defect or oversight can be remedied, and indeed is being remedied, in the writings of such thinkers as Negri and Deleuze and Guattari.

In my account, then, *Modern Tragedy*, for all its moments of bril-

liance, is in the end theoretically broken-backed. Williams had recognized in this work and elsewhere the emergence of a new historical and social conjuncture, but was unable to respond to it except in
terms of a reconstructed version of the old "dialectical" conception
of tragedy. In German speculative romanticism and idealism, however, we find a basis for understanding the tragic sublime that is resolutely nondialectical. This poetics/ontology of the tragic, when it is
harnessed to the characterization of the current conjuncture provided in some of Williams's later works (most notably *Towards
2000*), does, in my view, lead to a more productive conception of
what this conjuncture seems presently to be about.

NOTES

I am indebted to Gail Hamner for discussions that helped in the writing of the final version of this essay.

1. The first edition of *Modern Tragedy* work was published in London by Chatto and
Windus. The revised edition, with an added afterword, was published in London by
Verso in 1979. Unless otherwise stated, all page references in the text will be to the re-
vised edition, identified by the abbreviation *MT.*

2. Raymond Williams, *Politics and Letters: Interviews with New Left Review* (London:
Verso, 1979).

3. These respective sets of theoretical notions are not necessarily mutually exclusive; if
anything, they complement each other as overlapping ways of characterizing one or
more of the constituents of the same emergent economic, historical, and social conjuncture. On "Fordism" and "post-Fordism," see especially Michel Aglietta, "World Capitalism in
the Eighties," *New Left Review*, no. 136 (1982): 5–41, and Alain Lipietz, "Towards Global
Fordism?" *New Left Review*, no. 132 (1982): 33–47. On "postmodernism" as a "cultural logic,"
see Fredric Jameson, *Postmodernism; or, The Cultural Logic of Late Capitalism* (Durham,
N.C.: Duke University Press, 1991), especially chapter 1. On "postcoloniality," see, for instance, Gayatri Chakravorty Spivak, *Other Worlds: Essays in Cultural Politics* (London:
Methuen, 1987), and *The Post-Colonial Critic: Interviews, Strategies, Dialogues*, ed. Sarah
Harasym (London and New York: Routledge, 1990).

4. In a 1975 essay, Williams talks about this new and emergent "structure of feeling" in
the following terms: "What we thought we saw emerging in the 1960s was a new form of
corporate state; and the emphasis on culture . . . was an emphasis, at least in my own
case, on the process of social and cultural incorporation, according to which it is something more than simply property or power which maintains the structures of capitalist
society. Indeed, in seeking to define this, it was possible to look again at certain important
parts of the Marxist tradition, notably the work of Gramsci with his emphasis on hegemony. We could then say that the essential dominance of a particular class in society is
maintained not only, although if necessary, by power, and not only, although always, by
property. It is maintained also and inevitably by a lived culture: that saturation of habit,
of experience, of outlook, from a very early age and continually renewed at so many
stages of life, under definite pressures and within definite limits, so that what people
come to think and feel is in large measure a reproduction of the deeply based social order

which they may even in some respects think they oppose and indeed actually oppose. And if this is so, then again the tradition of Stalinism and the tradition of Fabianism are equally irrelevant." See "You're a Marxist, Aren't You?" in *Resources of Hope* (London: Verso, 1989), pp. 74–75. I have quoted this lengthy passage because it sets the terms that governed Williams's thinking on social and cultural change for the rest of his intellectual career.

5. Raymond Williams, *The Long Revolution* (New York: Columbia University Press, 1961), p. x.

6. Ibid., p. xi.

7. On this, see *Modern Tragedy*, p. 61. Williams draws a distinction between "political revolution" or rebellion and "a general human revolution" (p. 76). The latter would correspond to his sense of a "long revolution."

8. The following sections on German romanticism and speculative idealism have been taken in large part from my so far unpublished paper "Rethinking Tragedy? Reimagining Revolution?" My thinking on this subject has benefited from the comments of James Rolleston.

9. In suggesting that the "philosopher" is able here to accomplish something that is perhaps beyond the compass of the historian of literature, I do not mean to endorse Hegel's claim, made in the introduction to his *Lectures on Fine Art*, that there is a passage from art to philosophy, and that romanticism was not able to chart this supersession of art by philosophy because its thinkers were not successful in elaborating a genuinely *philosophical* "prose of thought" as a result of their weddedness to a Fichtean "principle of absolute subjectivity," a commitment that led them to view substantial content (*Gehalt*) as a mere "posit" of the genius of the individual artist. See Hegel, *Aesthetics: Lectures on Fine Art*, trans. T. M. Knox (Oxford: Oxford University Press, 1975), vol. 1, pp. 64–69. Williams was concerned to combat precisely this Hegelian disposition to make the theory of tragedy into "a system of ideas"; see *Modern Tragedy*, p. 36. I have no desire to fault Williams for failing to be genuinely "philosophical" (whatever that is). An engagement with German romanticism of a kind not undertaken by Williams is all that is proposed here, not the "sublation" by "philosophy" of an "unphilosophical" Williams. Williams's criticism of Hegel is well taken, but there were currents in German intellectual life contemporaneous with Hegel that are overlooked by Williams in his desire to make Hegel into a paradigmatic figure in the theory of tragedy. Michael Moriarty has provided an excellent analysis of Williams's fraught and ambivalent relationship with French literary theory, and pretty much the same characterization can be provided of Williams's engagement with German thought. For Moriarty, see "The Longest Cultural Journey: Raymond Williams and French Theory," *Social Text*, no. 30 (1992): 57–77.

10. Where the nineteenth century is concerned, the crisis was the general crisis of a number of other, more specific, crises: the failure of the French Revolution to produce a transformed social and political order when it was commandeered by Bonapartism; the increasing transparency of the "dialectic" of the *Aufklärung* (in the sense identified by Adorno and Horkheimer in their delineation of the dialectic of "enlightenment"); and, related to this, the growing heteronomy of the ends of the Enlightenment project. For exemplary general surveys of this aspect of German cultural life, to which I am indebted, see Josef Chytry, *The Aesthetic State: A Quest in Modern German Thought* (Berkeley: University of California Press, 1989), and the chapter titled "Aims of a New Epoch" in Charles Taylor, *Hegel* (Cambridge: Cambridge University Press, 1975), pp. 3–50. I am also indebted to the following more specifically historical studies: Franz Gabriel Nauen, *Revolu-*

tion, Idealism and Human Freedom: Schelling, Hölderlin and Hegel and the Crisis of Early German Idealism (The Hague: Martinus Nijhoff, 1971), and W.H. Bruford, *Culture and Society in Classical Weimar* (Cambridge: Cambridge University Press, 1962).

I owe to Philippe Lacoue-Labarthe the point that absolute idealism was founded on the paradigm of tragedy. See his *Typography: Mimesis, Philosophy, Politics*, trans. Christopher Fynsk (Cambridge, Mass.: Harvard University Press, 1989), p. 209.

11. This is not the right place in which to deal with the question of Hegel's relation to romanticism. His own criticisms of it in the *Aesthetics* notwithstanding, it could be maintained that Hegel did give expression to his "own" romanticism in some of his texts prior to the publication of *The Phenomenology of Spirit.* Alexander Kojève cites the *Lectures* of 1805-6 as one such text. See G. W. F. Hegel, *Jenenser Philosophie des Geistes* in *Sämtliche Werke*, ed. Johannes Hoffmeister (Leipzig: Meiner, 1931), vol. 20, pp. 180-81. For Kojève's claim, see *Introduction à la lecture de Hegel* (Paris: Gallimard, 1947), p. 573. Kojève's depiction of the Hegel of these *Lectures* as a romantic is upheld by Georges Bataille in "Hegel, Death and Sacrifice," trans. Jonathan Strauss, *Yale French Studies*, no. 78 (1990): 9-28. See especially pp. 9-10.

Williams's tendency to make its English manifestation determinative for any understanding of romanticism is evident in *Modern Tragedy*, pp. 71-73. Particularly problematic is the claim that romanticism, unlike utilitarianism, "sought liberal values in the development of the individual" (p. 71). This may have been true of British romanticism, but it definitely does not hold in the case of its German counterpart, which had a deep fascination with a certain "nonliberal" mythology of the ancient Greek polis.

12. Williams goes on to say: "Romanticism is the most important expression in modern literature of the first impulse of revolution: a new and absolute image of man. Characteristically, it relates this transcendence to an ideal world and an ideal human society; it is in Romantic literature that man is first seen as making himself" (Modern Tragedy, p. 71).

13. A somewhat lengthy detour through German romanticism will be undertaken in the next few sections. I believe this to be necessary not only because it is important to show what Williams might have missed because of his propensity to assimilate the various "romanticisms" to their English version, but also because German romanticism furnishes a poetical ontology or ontological poetics, with an attendant conception of revolution, that is highly congruent with Williams's understanding of revolution and political failure.

14. Rainer Nägele, for instance, argues that Walter Benjamin's essay "Über das Programm der kommenden Philosophie" ("Program of the Coming Philosophy") is very much an attempt to take up the "System-Program." For the English translation of Benjamin's essay, see *The Philosophical Quarterly* 15 (1983): 41-51. Nägele's claim is made in "Benjamin's Ground," in Nägele, ed., *Benjamin's Ground: New Readings of Walter Benjamin* (Detroit: Wayne State University Press, 1988), p. 24.

15. The various claims about its authorship are mentioned in Chytry, *Aesthetic State*, p. 124, n. 36. It is not important to detain ourselves over the merits of these claims. Most informed commentators agree in any case that the "System-Program" was the decisive intellectual springboard for Hegel, Hölderlin, and Schelling alike; and that even if it had been written by Hegel or Schelling, the dominant influence behind its production was undoubtedly Hölderlin.

16. I have used the translations of the "System-Program" given in Thomas Pfau, ed. and trans., *Hölderlin: Essays and Letters on Theory* (Albany: State University Press of New York, 1988), pp. 154-56; and H. S. Harris, *Hegel's Development: Toward the Sunlight (1770-1801)* (Oxford: Clarendon, 1972), pp. 510-12. Both Pfau and Harris make their trans-

lations from Fuhrmans's text in Hölderlin's *Sämtlicher Werke* (Grosse Stuttgarter Ausgabe), ed. Friedrich Beissner (Stuttgart: Kohlhammer, 1943-85), vol. 4, pp. 297-99.

17. On the immense influence exerted by Winckelmann on the thinkers of this period, see Chytry, *Aesthetic State*, especially pp. 11-37. See also Philip J. Kain, *Schiller, Hegel, and Marx: State, Society, and the Aesthetic Ideal of Ancient Greece* (Montreal: McGill-Queen's University Press, 1982). Kain, however, argues that Hegel is an apparent exception to this tendency to idealize ancient Greece. According to him, Hegel holds that alienation can be overcome not by reestablishing a spiritual unity with nature ("the Greek ideal"), but by the attainment of a higher mode of freedom that comes about only when alienation (which Greek civilization was fortunate never to know except during the time of its final decline) is overcome at the level of consciousness, that is, "rationally" and not "aesthetically" (the ancient Greeks never managing in Hegel's eyes to get beyond a mere *Kunstreligion*). Freedom for the modern human being is thus the kind of laborious undertaking it never was for the Greeks because of their indifference to "subjectivity"; see especially pp. 34ff. Kain is right about Hegel, but he somewhat overstates his point because all the major figures of German idealism and theoretical romanticism who subscribed to the myth of an ideal Hellas (including Goethe and Schiller) posited in one way or another a decisive rupture between that antiquity and (their) modernity. Hegel may have been exceptional in the stress he placed on this break and in the sense he had of the limitations of the Greek ideal, but it would be misleading to infer from this that his counterparts "idealized" Greece while he did not. Hegel did assert that the trajectory of Absolute Spirit had to take it beyond the "schöne Sittlichkeit" of classical Greece, but this realization is not incompatible with the ascription to it of virtues and qualities that modernity allegedly does not possess. I find the accounts provided by Chytry and H. S. Harris of Hegel's attitude to the classical polis to be more judicious than Kain's. See, respectively, *Aesthetic State*, pp. 178-218, and *Hegel's Development: Night Thoughts* (Oxford: Clarendon, 1983), in particular pp. 241-42, 404, 505, 515-16, and 557-58.

18. The author(s) of the "System-Program" had important immediate precursors when it came to according a decisive importance to the aesthetic act: Kant's *Critique of Judgement* and Schiller's *Letters on the Aesthetic Education of Man* initiated a veritable tradition in German idealism and romanticism.

19. For Fichte, see *The Science of Knowledge* (*Wissenschaftslehre*), trans. Peter Heath and John Lachs (Cambridge: Cambridge University Press, 1982), pp. 29-85. For Schiller, see the Seventh Letter in *On the Aesthetic Education of Man*, trans. Reginald Snell (New York: Continuum, 1989), p. 47. Excellent commentary on the intellectual relationships between Fichte and Schiller and Hölderlin, Hegel, and Schelling is to be found in Nauen, *Revolution, Idealism and Human Freedom*.

20. Hegel, Hölderlin, and Schelling were well acquainted with the work of Herder, and so would have been familiar with what Charles Taylor has described as his "expressivist" anthropology, one of the primary tenets of which was the inseparability of knowledge and sensation. For this tenet, see Herder, *Vom Erkennen und Empfinden der Menschlichen Seele*, in *Herders Sämmtliche Werke*, ed. Bernhard Suphan (Berlin: Weidmann, 1877-1913), vol. 8, p. 199. Taylor's valuable discussion of Herder is to be found in *Hegel*, pp. 13-27.

21. See H. S. Harris, *Hegel's Development: Toward the Sunlight*, p. 249.

22. Lukács identifies the world-historical conjuncture that prompted the creation of this paradigm of antiquity: "The model of antiquity was the necessary political ideal of the bourgeois class struggle for its independence and for political power. More and more the

ancient *polis* became the political model of the bourgeois revolutionaries, until the development found its practical fulfilment in the great French Revolution. It was a practical fulfilment, to be sure, which revealed in a blatant manner the difference between ancient and modern society and showed vividly to what extent the ancient *polis* and the ideal of the *polis* citizen were unable to provide either the content or the form of the modern bourgeois revolution and of modern bourgeois society; to what extent they were simply the (necessary) vestment, the (necessary) illusion of its heroic period. 'Robespierre, St.-Just, and their party perished,' Marx says, 'because they confused the ancient, *realistic-democratic community*, based on real slavery, with the modern *spiritualistic-democratic representative state*, which is based on the *emancipated slavery of bourgeois society*'"; see Lukács, "Schiller's Theory of Modern Literature," in *Goethe and His Age*, trans. Robert Anchor (New York: Howard Fertig, 1978), pp. 102-3, emphases in the original. It should be stressed that Lukács nonetheless believes this "illusion" to be "clearly a progressive movement" because "the return to a remote past in this case is a progressive utopianism" (ibid.). See also Roy Pascal "'Bildung' and the Division of Labour," in *German Studies Presented to Walter Horace Bruford* (London: Harrap, 1962), pp. 14-28.

23. Hegel makes a well-known distinction between the three forms of absolute spirit—art, religion, and philosophy—and claims that art only provides sensuous knowledge of spirit, whereas religion presents the Absolute to consciousness in the form of "pictorial thinking," and philosophy surpasses both art and religion because it, and only it, is "the free thinking of absolute spirit." See *Aesthetics*, pp. 91-105, especially p. 101. For Schelling's slightly more restrained depreciation of aesthetics in relation to philosophy, see *The Philosophy of Art*, trans. Douglas W. Stott (Minneapolis: University of Minnesota Press, 1989), p. 11.

24. "On the Operations of the Poetic Spirit," in Pfau, ed. and trans., *Friedrich Hölderlin*, pp. 62-82; see especially pp. 70ff.

25. A similar conclusion regarding the unavoidability of "deferral" can be also be drawn from Hölderlin's essay 'Urtheil und Seyn' ("Judgement and Being"), in Pfau, ed. and trans., *Hölderlin*, pp. 37-38.

26. See de Man's "The Image of Rousseau in the Poetry of Hölderlin" and "Wordsworth and Hölderlin" in *The Rhetoric of Romanticism*, trans. Andrej Warminski and Timothy Bahti respectively (New York: Columbia University Press, 1983), pp. 19-46 and 47-66; and "Heidegger's Exegeses of Hölderlin," in *Blindness and Insight: Essays in the Rhetoric of Contemporary Criticism*, 2d ed. (Minneapolis: University of Minnesota Press, 1983), pp. 246-66.

27. Antonio Negri, "Between Infinity and Community: Notes on Materialism in Spinoza and Leopardi," trans. Michael Hardt, *Studia Spinozana* 5 (1989): 151-77.

28. See Gilles Deleuze and Félix Guattari, *Kafka: Toward a Minor Literature*, trans. Dana Polan (Minneapolis: University of Minnesota Press, 1986), p. 59, where it is said of the "line of escape" that it is "finding a way out, precisely a way out, in the discovery that machines are only the concretions of historically determined desire. . . . [To] dismantle a machinic assemblage is to create and effectively take a line of escape." Deleuze and Guattari distinguish between an "escape" (which does not require an act of negation on the part of the escapee, in the way that, say, the slave of Hegel's notorious "master-slave" dialectic has to negate his master in order to become free) and a "freedom" (which requires precisely such a negation, but in the process imposes a specific, and thus delimiting, horizon—that of a relation to the master—on the slave's quest for liberty).

29. See Pfau, ed. and trans., *Hölderlin*, p. 155.

30. For Hegel's account of the resolution of tragedy in a higher unity created by absolute spirit, see *Phenomenology of Spirit*, trans. A. V. Miller (Oxford: Oxford University Press, 1977), pp. 443ff.

31. I owe this way of putting things to Toni Negri, "Between Infinity and Community," p. 158.

32. Chytry, *Aesthetic State*, p. 174.

33. For this reason I would maintain that Hölderlin's "infinite" has powerful affinities with a Spinozan or Deleuzian "substance." I am grateful to Gail Hamner for compelling me to be more explicit and precise in my reading of this "infinite."

34. Nietzsche, quoted in Gilles Deleuze, *Nietzsche and Philosophy*, trans. Hugh Tomlinson (New York: Columbia University Press, 1983), p. 11. I am deeply indebted to this work for the account of tragedy given in this essay.

35. See the valuable survey of the different conceptions of this historical or political sublime in Gary Shapiro, "From the Sublime to the Political," *New Literary History* 16 (1985): 213–36.

36. For Derrida, see the long essay titled "Parergon," in *The Truth in Painting*, trans. Geoff Bennington and Ian McLeod (Chicago: University of Chicago Press, 1987), pp. 37–82. For Lacoue-Labarthe, see "On the Sublime," trans. Geoff Bennington, in *Postmodernism: ICA Documents*, ed. Lisa Appignanesi (London: Free Association Books, 1989), pp. 11–18; *La poésie comme expérience* (Paris: C. Bourgois, 1986), pp. 123–29; and "Sublime Truth (Part 1)," trans. David Kuchta, *Cultural Critique*, no. 18 (1991), pp. 5–31. For Lyotard, see "Complexity and the Sublime," in Appignanesi, ed., *Postmodernism*, pp. 19–26; "The Sublime and the Avant-Garde," trans. Lisa Liebmann, Geoff Bennington, and Marion Hobson, in *The Lyotard Reader*, ed. Andrew Benjamin (Oxford: Blackwell, 1989), pp. 196–211; and "After the Sublime: The State of Aesthetics," in *The States of "Theory": History, Art, and Critical Discourse*, ed. David Carroll (New York: Columbia University Press, 1990), pp. 297–304. For Deleuze, see the passages that deal with the "cinema of the sublime" in *Cinema 1: The Movement-Image*, trans. Hugh Tomlinson and Barbara Habberjam (Minneapolis: University of Minnesota Press, 1986), passim. For Hayden White, see "The Politics of Historical Interpretation: Discipline and De-Sublimation," in *The Politics of Interpretation*, ed. W. J. T. Mitchell (Chicago: University of Chicago Press, 1983), pp. 119–44.

37. Lacoue-Labarthe says that "there is a condensation around the notion of the sublime of a certain number of problems and questions which for Aristotle and the Greeks were questions which concerned tragedy"; see his "On the Sublime," in Appignanesi, ed., *Postmodernism*, p. 17.

38. A fuller treatment of Hölderlin's poetics along the lines indicated in this essay is to found in my so far unpublished paper "Rethinking Tragedy? Reimagining Revolution?"

39. Raymond Williams, *Towards 2000* (Harmondsworth: Penguin, 1985), pp. 268–69.

40. A form of this question was posed earlier in this essay when, albeit briefly, the issue of the context of the discussion of revolution and tragedy in *Modern Tragedy* was raised.

41. I refer here of course to Williams's well-known 1973 essay "Base and Superstructure in Marxist Cultural Theory," republished in *Problems in Materialism and Culture* (London: Verso, 1980), pp. 31–49. See also "Marx on Culture," in *What I Came to Say* (London: Hutchinson Radius, 1989), pp. 195–225.

42. I discuss this more fully in my "Marxism(s) and 'The Withering Away of the State,'" *Social Text*, no. 27 (1990): 35–54.

43. This is indicated in following passage from the 1973 essay "The City and the World": "For there is nothing now more urgent than to put the fundamental idea—the problem of

overcoming the division of labour—to the tests of rigorous analysis, rigorous proposal, and rigorous practice. It can be done only in new forms of cooperative effort. If what is visible already as the outlines of a movement is to come through with the necessary understanding and strength, we shall have to say what in detail can be practically done, over a vast range from regional and investment planning to a thousand processes in work, education, and community.

. . . The last recess of the division of labour is this recess within ourselves, where what we want and what we believe we can do seem impassably divided. We can overcome division only by refusing to be divided. That is a personal decision—but then a social action." See "The City and the World," in *What I Came To Say*, p. 89.

44. See Henri Lefebvre, *The Survival of Capitalism: Reproduction of the Relations of Production*, trans. Frank Bryant (London: Alison & Busby, 1976), p. 125. For Williams, see *Towards 2000*, p. 266.

45. Lefebvre, *Survival of Capitalism*, p. 125.

46. On this, see Antonio Negri, "Twenty Theses on Marx: Interpretation of the Class Situation Today," trans. Michael Hardt, *Polygraph*, no. 5 (1992): 136-70.

Antipictorialism in the English Landscape Tradition: A Second Look at *The Country and the City*

Peter de Bolla

It is now almost twenty years since the first publication of Williams's *The Country and the City*, which makes it almost overdue for some form of reappraisal. I would like to make some first steps toward a reassessment by concentrating on what I take to be the core of Williams's argument, his account of the changing structures of feeling that accompanied the alterations in land use and ownership throughout the eighteenth century in Britain. Williams, we should recall, moves between high and low literary productions that were simultaneous with this "agrarian revolution" and juxtaposes these writings with good measures of social and economic history. I shall recap the argument as I see it more fully, but before getting to his account I would like to make one or two caveats about my own approach.

First, it would be ungenerous in the extreme to forgo acknowledgment of the breadth and scope of Williams's book. As in all his writing, Williams is here at pains to ensure that scholarly evidence and critical sensibility resonate with real lived experience. This is a constant feature of *The Country and the City*, which memorably opens with an autobiographical account of Williams's own move and estrangement from the countryside in which he was born. To focus on a very specific part of the argument may seem, then, somewhat niggardly and in a spirit directly counter to Williams's entire project. But, as I hope to show, the developments in scholarship since Williams first began to work on these materials extend his own vision even as they revise some of his insights. Nevertheless, I would not want this essay to be understood as an academic quibble or taken in the spirit of a correction to Williams's now outdated scholarship, since this would be to seriously misread both my own intentions and what I take to be Williams's. Williams never lost sight of the working people whose proximity to the land sustains them, creating a lived experience of the country very different from that of the city dweller (and in this case that of the academic city dweller), and this attentive pressure is always conjoined to a very explicit political agenda that seeks to improve the conditions of working people. For this reason Williams's version of the *representation* of agrarian improvement in mid-eighteenth-century Britain is mediated through a politics that is highly attuned to the conditions of the dispossessed. The processes of dispossession were not started during the period on which I focus (a point well made by Williams himself), nor have they reached their conclusion. For this reason, if for no other, I want to stress that the following comments are made in the spirit of sharpening the divisions between the landscape as aesthetic form and land use as productive source of sustenance. If at times my counterexamples seem to redress the balance back in favor of landowners against those dispossessed of their land, I offer them only to make even clearer the divisions between these competing uses of the land.

Second, not only is Williams's argument broad in scope and mine restricted, but where mine shall be extremely closely tied to a specific historical moment, Williams's ranges over a vast expanse of time. I shall have nothing to say about this grand historical narrative, about the ways in which the distinctions between country and city have persisted or mutated over time, so in this sense my comments are to be taken as partial in regard to the full scope of the book. There are, though, benefits to be gained from this since close attention to the crucial mid-eighteenth-century context will yield the possibility for greater precision at the margins of the argument.

The Country and the City

Let us begin by recalling what I have termed the central argument of Williams's book, which begins by addressing what Williams takes to be a pretty constant feature of our Western tradition: the troping of the country-city distinction in terms of a pastoral ideal versus a corrupting urban environment. Wherever we look throughout the literary tradition, we will find a disconsolate city dweller yearning for the simpler and more fulfilling pleasures of the country. This yearning is almost always temporalized, positing a "golden age" in which either the divisions between country and city were not marked in such a fashion or in which life could be happily led without moving to the city. Such a time never existed, of course; the invocation of fictitious past times is merely a figurative maneuver. Thus, when Goldsmith complains of the destruction of agrarian communities, he is, Williams contends, doing nothing different from Massinger's contrasting of the new commercial ideology of early-seventeenth-century England with the "old landed settlement."[1] But this, again, is no different from Thomas More complaining in 1516 about the destruction of another old order, which is nothing different from Langland's complaint in the 1370s, and so on.

Williams is certainly correct in identifying this trope: it is one of the most basic ways in which we figure to ourselves historical change and continuity. This basic human experience, which we commonly associate with forms of nostalgia, could be said to be the primary topic of investigation in the book. It is a mark of Williams's honesty that an associated human experience, the guilt we feel when we fail to wax nostalgic, is also examined. Having said this, however, I shall argue that the historical is more contingent than this broad argument allows, which is to say that there are indeed differences between Massinger's complaint and Goldsmith's, or between Langland's and More's. In other words, while tropes may well stay the same over time—that is to say, while the *ways in which we figure* the past in relation to the present, an idealized pastoral mode in relation to a lived urban one, may remain constant—*what is being figured* does change. Thus one may use a standard figure in accounting for the differences between one age and the present, but the constancy of the trope does not attest to the invariance of the relations being described. I shall argue, then, that the mid-eighteenth century did witness changes that ought to be understood in terms that distinguish this period from both those preceding and those following it.

It is slightly misleading to set up my argument in this manner since Williams, by implication, holds to something like this view.

This can be adduced from his lengthy attention to the period I have just mentioned and from the central position given in the book to discussion of the agrarian revolution. However, this sense of historical specificity must also be balanced against another invariant in Williams's argument: the structure of feeling that is the touchstone for the "real" lived experience of the land. Williams puts this in the following manner:

> The detailed histories indicate everywhere that many old forms, old practices and old ways of feeling survived into periods in which the general direction of new development was clear and decisive. And then what seems an old order, a 'traditional' society, keeps appearing, reappearing, at bewilderingly various dates: in practice as an idea, to some extent based in experience, against which contemporary change can be measured. The structure of feeling within which this backward reference is to be understood is then not primarily a matter of historical explanation and analysis. (48)

This inaccessibility to historical explanation is in part caused by the fact that the trope we have been examining, the figuring of an idealized past as nostalgic golden age, is one of the primary ways in which we understand historical change itself. Because of this, the "real relations, to past and future, are inaccessible" (99). The question that is rather loudly begged here is what these "real relations" are if they too are not figured in some way. In other words, Williams is at pains to distinguish a kind of false consciousness that is figured as history, as our experience of the past and future, from the real lived experience constituting a "structure of feeling" that is clearly supposed to be in some sense more authentic. The pressure around the term *real*, which is everywhere present in the book, testifies to this rather awkward resistance to a more thoroughgoing relativism. At the end of the day what is absolutely invariant is an authentic relation to the land that can only be understood via an experience of a life lived in extreme proximity to the land that sustains it.

There is, then, a difficulty in relation to how the argument moves from *representations* of the country-city distinction and all that is implied by them to these structures of feeling that somehow exist independent of the need to be within representation. They are, indeed, lived experience itself. We shall return to this difficulty when we turn to historical examples.

Having outlined the mythical invocation of golden ages, the argument moves toward the historical period in which the country-city distinction takes on special significance, the mid-eighteenth century, via a discussion of the particular literary topos of the country house poem. The discussion at this point has been rightly praised as some of the finest writing on the subject.[2] The treatment of Jonson's *Penshurst*, for example, has become the standard critical commentary on the poem. As Williams approaches the historical epoch, we shall dwell in some detail on the argument that begins to broaden out to include not only literary representations of the countryside but also social and economic history. The first thing to be said about this concerns the intervention Williams makes here into the standard literary history of the period. Alan O'Connor has written about how this book emerged as a response to the ways in which this literary tradition had heretofore been taught (most especially under the aegis of the Cambridge English Tripos).[3] The country house poem had primarily been examined within an autonomous literary context that endeavored to demonstrate the coherence and consistency of a tradition; such autonomous literary history sees one poem as a response to a previous poem, which is itself an encounter with a previous one, and so forth. Williams puts his objection with scathing irony:

> Where poets run scholars follow, and questions about the 'pastoral' poetry or the poetry of 'rural retreat' of our own sixteenth to eighteenth centuries are again and again turned aside by the confident glossing and glozing of the reference back. We must not look, with Crabbe and others, at what the country was really like: that is a utilitarian or materialist, perhaps even a peasant response. Let us remember, instead, that this poem is based on Horace, Epode II or Virgil, Eclogue IV; that among the high far names are Theocritus and Hesiod: the Golden Age in another sense. (29)

Williams comments on this parody of the standard line: "It is time that this bluff was called" (29). In so doing, he opens out the context for reading his chosen literary texts. It is all too easy to forget now that the environment in which Williams was working and teaching was deeply resistant to anything except intrinsic readings of literature. The meld of social and economic history that forms the background to the core of the book was, therefore, relatively speaking a new departure. From our later perspective, however, the range of materials Williams chooses to present is still rather narrow: the literary texts are still taken primarily from the great tradition of Goldsmith, Pope, and Wordsworth (although Williams is truly a pioneer in his attention to the almost completely forgotten writings of Stephen Duck and Robert Bloomfield). The argument is, therefore, fully within a rather traditional conception of "literature": it is poetry, primarily, that constitutes this tradition.

It might be objected to this comment that since Williams sets out to discuss the country house poem tradition, it is hardly surprising that the body of materials he presents is drawn from that tradition. It might also be said that even granted this, the argument is nevertheless far broader in its scope and range of reference than alternative contemporary accounts. While both of these objections are sustainable, my purpose in taking this line is to open out Williams's discussion to allow an ever greater latitude in the trawl of "literary" examples. To this end I would suggest that the structure of feeling Williams is at pains to describe can be approached through the variety of writings on the landscape to be found not only in "high" literary forms such as poetry but also, and perhaps more importantly, in accounts of visits to country seats, garden manuals, and aesthetic writings of the period. For this reason, I shall discuss some of these alternative sources.

In turning to these slightly different literary forms, we shall be both extending Williams's fundamentally accurate analysis of the representations of the country during the period and subjecting the interlacing of literary texts with social and economic history to some scrutiny. Again, while it may seem ungenerous to criticize Williams's work for what it does not set out to do, there is, nevertheless, something at stake in the level of accuracy we might aspire to concerning the interrelations between contemporary representations and our own social and economic historical analyses. The purpose of undertaking a reassessment of *The Country and the City* is not only to revise Williams's crucial insights in the light of recent scholarship, but also to add our own more skeptical contemporary sense of the ways in which social and economic historical data may be brought to bear on representations taken from a past epoch.

This last point can be made very tellingly as we return to the sequence of Williams's own argument. After having discussed the country house poem in its larger historical frame, Williams turns to "Young's eighteenth century," which, along with the transition via Wordsworth into the industrial cityscape of the early nineteenth century, occupies the next hundred or so pages. In the first instance Williams wishes to demonstrate how the early eighteenth century contains a number of competing or contradictory responses to changes in rural England. These he calls "attitudes rather than feelings" (87), and they are the result of two distinct traditions of representation that are both undergoing transition and causing friction. As Williams puts it:

> We have then to distinguish two phases of the transition from reflection to retrospect. There are the poems which celebrate what, to borrow their characteristic language, we must call humble and worthy characters, in a country setting, in a more or less conscious contrast with the wealth and ambition of the city and the court. And then there are those which develop this ethical contrast, in which the contrast of country and city is as it were an atmosphere or a determining climate, into an historical contrast, in which the virtues are seen as unmistakably past, in an earlier and lost period of country life. (9)

And from this friction there is going to emerge a new structure of feeling that can be best exemplified by Goldsmith's *Deserted Village*. It is in this poem that the full measure of rural change begins to be represented in all its contradictory force, and it is here that Williams's own political convictions begin to be unleashed with disturbing accuracy. Goldsmith's poem is, according to Williams, recording a "social process" that "is in fact one of clearance, of eviction and evacuation, to make way for a mansion and its grounds" (96). There follows a long and detailed reading of Goldsmith's poem that brings to the surface a number of deeply embedded contradictions in Goldsmith's relation to and representation of the lost countryside. These contradictions are as much about being a poet, or about poetry itself, as they are about "real relations" to the land. In this Williams has taught us all a great deal about the complicated position any writer is placed in when he or she attempts to convey, reveal, or represent feelings that are held as a part of lived experience. These complications only compound when the writer speaks on behalf of others whose experience may or may not coincide with the writer's own.

The course of the argument is, nevertheless, far from complicated: Williams points out in no uncertain terms that the "naturalising" of the English landscape that took place throughout eighteeenth-century England was effected at the cost of depriving those whose lives depended upon the land for sustenance of their rights to the countryside. This point is made not only in terms of the economic and political arguments of enclosure and engrossing—were this the case Williams's argument would certainly not have been a new departure—but also, and far more importantly, in terms of a new way of seeing the land. It is this stress on how representations of the landscape go hand in hand with new structures of feeling and seeing that I want to investigate further. Consequently, as Williams remarks in commenting on some lines of verse by Crabbe, "This is an alteration of landscape, by an alteration of seeing" (110).

This change in how the landscape was *seen* has traditionally been understood in pictorial terms. The standard scholarship on this, from Elizabeth Manwaring to John Barrell, has outlined the ways in which landowners began to construct landscapes that conformed to the pictorial criteria of Italian landscape painting.[4] Williams sketches the argument in the following way:

> The main argument is well known. Eighteenth-century landlords, going on the Grand Tour and collecting their pictures by Claude and Poussin, learned new ways of looking at landscape and came back to create such landscapes as prospects from their own houses: create, that is, in the sense of hiring Brown ('the peasant') or Kent or Repton. Certainly we have to notice a change of taste in the laying out of decorative grounds under French and Italian and Dutch influence to the park landscapes of the eighteenth-century improvers. (152)

This story has become the absolute orthodoxy, but as I hope to demonstrate, its truth is only partial. In contrast to this pictorial tradition there is also at least one other strongly developed aesthetic that was self-consciously antipictorial and, furthermore, this alternative tradition was clearly affiliated with a different social class and served different ends in relation to land use. This will, of course, merely strengthen Williams's argument, but there are also further gains to be had from the greater accuracy of the picture.

Once again I do not wish to distort Williams's argument for the sake of my own, so it becomes necessary to add that Williams himself qualifies the standard story as I have related it. He claims, rightly, that many landscapes consciously set out to imitate Claudian views, and that this version of "nature" was entirely fabricated by both a traditional landowning class in possession of a new aesthetic and a newly monied class with considerable capitalist interest in the new skills required to create such "natural" landscapes. In this sense the aesthetic goes hand in hand with capital growth. But, as Williams points out, this collusion between the aesthetic and the exploitative produced only one way of seeing; there remained differently motivated aesthetic responses, differently slanted ways of seeing. As Williams writes of the high bourgeois aesthetic: "We must insist on this central character even while we also notice that caught up and used and enjoyed within this social composition were many real ways of seeing landscape which had different motives" (155).

In illustration of this point he goes on to quote from Dyer, Thompson, Cowper, and Coleridge in a kind of miniature history of how this aesthetic of the pictorial will mutate by the end of the century into a recognizably "romantic" form of the natural. The problem here is that this rather truncated chronology leaves behind those who were developing concurrently with Pope and Thompson a countertradition, a fact that would have become evident if only Williams's brief had been slightly wider and included examination of the agricultural texts and gardening manuals that would have supplied him with this evidence. It is in these texts where we find a real struggle over the possession of the land, from the perspective not only of the dispossessed (Williams's major focus) but also of those who began to find employment in this new-found land. In other words, it was not only working people who depended upon the land who were affected by this wholescale attempt to redesign the landscape, not only those who were physically moved from their homes who were faced with a new structure of seeing (which they were both excluded from and required as props for), but also a new group of working people who constructed these landscapes, maintained them, and, as we shall see, in some cases had considerable say about how they looked. Here we do well to remember that the overwhelmingly influential architect of this massive reorganization of the English landscape—Capability Brown—came from yeoman farming stock and began his career as a humble gardener in the employ of Sir William Loraine. That Brown came to epitomize the "aestheticizing" attitude I have associated with the pictorial tradition only serves to emphasize the full complexity of the mid-eighteenth-century struggle over ways of seeing the land and constructing the landscape.

Eighteenth-Century Landscape: Another View

In the remarks that follow I shall endeavor to deepen and extend Williams's account of how the mid-eighteenth-century reorganization of land use led to alterations in seeing the landscape. My primary focus will be the literature about the landscape generated within the context of "garden literature"—manuals of landscaping, tours, and visual aesthetics.

Manuals and treatises concerning the layout and construction of gardens began to be published in Britain during the second decade of the eighteenth century.[5] The interest in gardens and landscape aesthetics manifest in more "philosophical" writers such as Shaftesbury also dates from around the same period, and as the century drew toward its middle years, a number of writers both imaginative and occasional, such as Pope and Addison, made considerable contributions to this growing tradition. It is not, however, until relatively late into the century, the 1770s, that a conscious evocation of a tradition becomes evident in the writings of the two authors who created the eighteenth century's own history of its landscape arts: Horace Walpole and Thomas Whately. This history, which is highly contingent and mediated by all kinds of ideological filiations, has by and large been responsible for almost all subsequent versions of what happened to the English countryside during the period.[6]

Perhaps the most aggressive aspect to Walpole's *The History of Modern Gardening* (1771 and 1780) is its strenuous attempts to claim for the landscape garden a specifically national heritage: the English created this form in contradistinction to the French or Dutch, and it closely embodies and mirrors the political correctness of the English. The landscape, then, is unfettered, free, just as all freeborn Englishmen are. In the comment from the *History* that gets quoted in all the secondary literature, Walpole proclaims that it was the genius of Kent that transformed our landscape: it was Kent who "lept the fence, and saw that all nature was a garden."

It is very rarely remarked how far this comment epitomizes what Williams discerns as a paternalistic attitude to the land: whatever lies in prospect before one has the potential for being "naturalized"—turned into an aesthetic experience. When Walpole notes that "all nature was a garden" we should pause a moment to translate his comment thus: the productive uses of the land no longer dominate its aesthetic uses. In making this translation, however, we are in fact participating in the Walpolian ideological reading of eighteenth-century landscape. It is true to say that this ideology existed and determined the views of many landowners throughout the century, but it is also the case that as many, if not more, landowners continued to work the land and to include functioning farms as a part of a re-modeled landscape park.

It is nevertheless the case that the construction of the typical Brownian park was understood in terms of this elite cultural ideology that proclaimed nationalist pride in the liberty taken to be ex-emplified by the "natural" look of English landscape. The pictorial analogy is also, of course, a crucial part of that ideology since only a small section of the population had access to the modes and procedures of education in how to look at pictures—namely, the grand tour. Kent, then, is taken by Walpole to exemplify this pictorial tradition as well as represent the culminating point of a specifically English art.[7] What is left out of Walpole's calculations is precisely Williams's alerations in seeing, which were happening all around and permeating all strata within society. This resulted in a number of inroads into the privileged class domain of high art, specifically in relation to the education of the spectator. Many gardens and parklands were necessarily caught within this permeation of class boundaries as the increasing tourism of the age brought various groups into contact with the landscape and with each other.

Both designers and those who actually worked the land were also a part of this educational environment, so that what has most often been taken as a change in "taste" from the emblematic garden to the expressionist—which is to say from one full of classical illusion requiring some measure of education in order to "see" the landscape to one in which a "feeling" response was all that was required—need not be taken only in these restricted terms. Gardens embody ways of looking, structures of how to look, and those structures increasingly took account of the variety of lookers and also began to propose specific schemes of instruction into how to look.

Walpole's quite specific analogy of Kent's designs for the landscape with painting—"he realised the compositions of the greatest masters in painting"[8]—is merely the very deliberate sign that the Whig history of landscape arts wishes to elevate this peculiarly English art to the status of oil painting. Furthermore, once in this pantheon, everything can be subordinated to its engrossing aesthetic. As Walpole tells us, "An open country is but a canvas on which a landscape might be designed." There was, however, an antipictorialist argument mounted during the period that spoke for a different constituency and promoted another, rather different, alteration in ways of seeing the landscape. I now turn to this less familiar tradition.

Perhaps the clearest example of this antipictorial tradition is to be found in William Marshall's *Planting and Ornamental Gardening*, published in 1785. Marshall was an agriculturalist, not the son of one of the most powerful politicians of the age, who became interested in "improvement" from a rather different perspective. Where the painter "arranges" the landscape to suit an aesthetic theory, the agriculturalist is at pains to allow nature its own nature. Marshall's critique is succinctly and tellingly put, and I quote it at length:

> In a picture bounded by its frame, a perfect landscape is looked for: it is of itself a *whole*, and *the frame must be filled*. But it is not so in ornamented Nature: for, if a side-screen be wanting, the eye is not offended with the frame, or the wainscot, but has always some natural and pleasing object to receive it. Suppose a room to be hung with one continued rural representation,—would *pretty pictures* be expected? Would correct landscapes be looked for? Nature scarcely knows the thing mankind call a *landscape*. The landscape painter seldom, if ever, finds it perfected to his hands;—some addition or alteration is almost always wanted. Every man, who has made his observations upon natural scenery, knows that the Mistletoe of the Oak occurs almost as often as a perfect natural landscape; and to attempt to make up artificial landscape, upon every occasion, is unnatural and absurd.[9]

This is an alternative liberation of nature, only this time it is from the constraints of the painterly straitjacket that Walpole and his followers would wish to impose. Connected to this liberating move is the insistence on Marshall's part that the viewing experience is not an isolated aestheticized form of high art appreciation—viewing the landscape as if it were hung on a wall in front of one's face—but a temporal form that takes in the full range of sensory experience we encounter in the open air. This experience is, we should note, sensitive and sensitized to the full variety of stimulus encountered in the "real" of looking. As Marshall writes, "In viewing natural scenery . . . almost every sense is engaged. . . . The eye . . . is acted upon by a varied light . . . [and] irritated by the motion of animals."[10]

Not only the eye, however, registers this multiplicity of objects: "the ear, too, is engaged in living pictures; the lowing of kine, the neighing of horse, the bleating of the flock, the coarse *barking* of the deer" (82). This kind of synesthesia will become even more deliberately constructed in the romantic experience of the natural world, but here it stands as a reminder to us of the sensitivity to the productive capacities of the landscape that competes with Walpole's Whig aestheticization.

Before we leave this antipictorialist tradition I would like to cite one further example, since it begins to call the bluff of the painterly in rather interesting ways. George Mason published his *Essay on Design in Gardening* in 1768 and a revised edition in 1795. In that second edition we find a review of Price's *Essay on the Picturesque*, in which Mason complains about the analogy between painting and landscape. He writes:

> I freely declare, that very few of Claude's pictures (even of his best-chosen subjects) ever excited in myself an ardent desire of being transported to the spots, from which they were taken. They always seemed to me rather wonderful combinations of objects by an effort of genius, than what were likely to have existed anywhere in reality.[11]

Here the entire question of "vraisemblance" and the "real" of looking is raised; this is something that is never addressed in the standard Walpolian "history." The point I wish to take from all this is that the painterly look represents only *one* possibility for the spectator. Furthermore, similarly motivated forms of seeing were generated throughout the various stratifications of eighteenth-century society, and this included not only landowners and dispossessed laborers but all in between as well. Thus for example, in the massive tour literature of the period the increasingly mobile "middling" sort began to stake a claim for their own structures of seeing and feeling. One of their number, Joseph Heely, left us with one of the finest accounts of three eighteenth-century gardens, Hagley Park, Enville, and the Leasowes, in which such a claim can be found expressed.

I do not wish to examine in any detail his account, but merely to note in passing that not only are his own class or social affiliations problematic, but he sees them that way himself. Thus, visiting the Leasowes, Heely complains about the presence of other tourists, people who are presumably precisely in his own social milieu, but who represent for the upwardly aspiring Heely the uneducated class he wishes to distance himself from. Yet, having said this, Heely is also caught by his own middle-class aspirations and recognizes that the viewing experience is fully capable of educating those without education. As he tells us: "Each [Hagley, Envil, and the Leasowes] may be called a school for taste."[12] It is precisely this educative function that we might term a middle-class territorialization of the landscape; it certainly rides roughshod over laboring experiences, which, it might be said, were less in need of education than reenfranchisement.

We may now return to Williams's inflection of this tradition and to the political purposes behind his account of the rural revolution that transformed the English countryside during the course of the eighteenth century. I have very briefly pointed toward some of the complexities of the eighteenth-century tradition in order to extend Williams's analysis to include more than the elitist tradition we find represented in the poetry of the period. While the dispossessed rarely left behind representations of similar standing (although the "unlettered" tradition is fuller than one might expect), and the upwardly mobile tended to write pragmatic texts such as gardening manuals rather than high literature, there nevertheless remains a problem over the relations between any of these representations and the "real" lived experience we take it to mediate.

Williams is surely correct in asserting that these new forms—of the landscape, of poetry, of seeing the land—participated in the creation of a new "structure of feeling," but this structure is both more heterogenous and more widely disseminated than Williams suggests. Furthermore, the forms in which the representation of the land took place were not innocent in regard to the particularities of specific ideologies informing different structures of feeling. The alteration in the ways in which a Joseph Heely or a William Marshall saw the landscape were equally compromised in regard to a "real" lived experience and equally determining of that supposed "reality." For a Heely or a Marshall the sense of such a "real" experience was no more or less authentic than for a Stephen Duck or, more significantly, for an unknown laborer. To conclude here is to invoke one of Williams's repeated gestures—toward complexity—and to acknowledge how much we owe to the breadth of his humane vision.

NOTES

1. Raymond Williams, *The Country and the City* (St. Albans: Grenada, 1975), p. 20. Subsequent page references appear in the text.

2. See Laurence Lerner, "Beyond Literature: Social Criticism Versus Aesthetics," *Encounter* 41 (July 1973): 61-65.

3. See Alan O'Connor, *Raymond Williams: Writing, Culture, Politics* (Oxford: Blackwell, 1989), p. 25.

4. See Elizabeth Wheeler Manwaring, *Italian Landscape in Eighteenth Century England: A Study Chiefly of the Influence of Claude Lorrain and Salvator Rosa on English Taste 1700-1800* (Oxford: Oxford University Press, 1925), and John Barrell, *The Idea of Landscape and the Sense of Place 1730-1840: An Approach to the Poetry of John Clare* (Cambridge: Cambridge University Press, 1972).

5. It is customary to take Stephen Switzer's *Ichnographia Rustica*, which was published in 1718, as the first book devoted entirely to this project.

6. It is only very recently indeed that garden historians have begun to reexamine this standard history critically and to see it for what it is, an aggressive fiction claiming to be fact. See Stephen Bending, "Politics, Morality and History: The Literature of the Later Eighteenth-Century English Landscape Garden," Ph.D dissertation, Cambridge, 1991.

7. This is to conveniently forget that many of Kent's landscapes are equally at home in another, less prestigious tradition: scenery for in the theater, a social environment far less rigidly divided by class filiations.

8. Horace Walpole, *On Modern Gardening*, ed. I. W. U. Chase (Princeton, N.J.: Princeton University Press, 1943).

9. William Marshall, *Planting and Rural Ornament*, 2 vols. (London, 1796), vol. 1, p. 271. Emphasis in the original.

10. William Marshall, *A Review of "The Landscape," also of "An Essay on the Picturesque"* (London, 1795), p. 81.

11. George Mason, *An Essay on Design in Gardening*, 2d ed. (Lodon, 1795), p. 199-200.

12. Joseph Heely, *Letters on the Beauties of Hagley, Enville and the Leasowes*, 2 vols. (London, 1777), vol. 2, p. 231.

Raymond Williams and British Colonialism
Gauri Viswanathan

The failure of the British left to conceptualize cultural practices in relation to imperialism is most pronounced in its unproblematic conflation of the terms *national* and *imperial.* One would least expect to find this tendency in such works as Brian Doyle's *English and Englishness* (1989), Alan Sinfield's *Literature, Politics, and Culture in Postwar Britain* (1989), or Robert Colls and Philip Dodd's *Englishness* (1987), where the "naturalness" of English culture is rejected as a false premise obscuring a history of invented discourses and disciplines. But the ways of reading the invention of "national culture" are as varied as the discourses themselves, and when English "national" culture is read almost exclusively as ideologically motivated by social currents and institutional developments within England (as it is by these critics) it acquires a narrow and limited definition whose generative events are safely circumscribed within local boundaries. This restriction makes it possible, for instance, for Brian Doyle to argue that English studies "embodied not only the high culture of 'polite society' but also the 'national' character," to the point where the discipline of English came to be promoted as "uniquely suited to a mission of national cultivation,"[1] and for Sinfield to observe that the cultural monuments of England served as an instrument of "national domination" elsewhere.[2]

What makes imperial culture possible, both Doyle and Sinfield suggest, is an already existing national culture that is itself a product of mediation between local class tensions. For these critics, the success of national culture abroad is attributable to a comparable negotiation of competing demands in a colonized population—a population that has been reorganized to correspond to English class structure. According to this interpretation, if English culture can be understood as the combatively achieved set of ideas of the English elite—the assertion of the elite's hegemony over the masses—the success of British rule in the colonies is equally an effect of this won hegemony (the domestication of native classes being merely an extension of the domestication of English lower classes). When one is confronted with paradoxes in British imperialism, one explains them away by drawing comparison to practices in England. For example, the moral content of instruction in British colonies far exceeded the immediate and practical requirements of bureaucratic management and efficiency. This fact has been explained by equating the colonial "natives" with the "ignorant" English lower classes (and thus retaining the English context as a fixed point of reference); no attempt has been made to probe into the composition of the indigenous societies and the historical conflicts between secular and sacred instruction that might have produced such a moral emphasis (an emphasis that also served a utilitarian framework of bureaucratic efficiency). In British India, specifically, there was a clear-cut recognition by British authorities of the authoritative position held by the learned classes and of their potential usefulness as intermediaries for diffusion of Western principles (even through the vernacular languages) to the masses. The immediate objective of British colonial policy was not so much to reenact the regulation of the British working classes in colonial territories as to evolve localized strategies for coping with perceived differences between British and native social structures, strategies that would have the desired effect of management. If those strategies had more universal application than originally intended, it is not the genuine parallels between Britain and India that compel attention but the critics' process of trying to homogenize the two.

One of the unfortunate effects of conflating *national* and *imperial* is the elimination of important historical distinctions that would make a simple equation between class and racial ideologies more difficult, if not impossible. When, for instance, the tensions between secular and religious tendencies in British culture are studied from outside the parameters of English society, it soon becomes apparent that British class conflicts do not fully explain those tensions, and that they do not satisfactorily constitute the only or primary point of reference. The explanation for the growth of English studies as a product of middle-class ascendancy and containment of lower-class aspirations is only a partial one, and it fails to take into account the use of the colonies as a test site for secular experiments in education, such as training in practical skills for conducting ordinary bureaucratic transactions. Such secular experimentation, lacking in the moral content that traditionally informed education in England (which was still largely dominated by the aristocratic and clerical orders), was both actively contested by missionary groups already present in British-controlled India and unmasked by them as a function of mercantile interests. The effect of such contestation was that secular education entered into a unique dialectical relation with imperatives of moral and religious instruction. Given the fact that the Bible was officially debarred by British colonial policy, which scrupulously adhered to postures of disinterestedness in matters concerning religion, that dialectic of religious and secular motives impelled the disciplinary formation of English literature as we know it today. The importance of the colonies for diffusing, maintaining, and redefining conflicts that have hitherto been identified primarily as English class conflicts thus makes it all the more urgent to consider English culture first and foremost in its imperial aspect and then to examine that aspect as itself constitutive of "national" culture. Such a project challenges the assumption that what makes an imperial culture possible is a fully formed national culture shaped by internal social developments; it also provokes one to search for ways to reinsert *imperial* into *national* without reducing the two terms to a single category.

The tendency to work with *national* and *imperial* as interchangeable terms is noticeable in the work of Terry Eagleton, Chris Baldick, Brian Doyle, and Alan Sinfield, among others. But we would have to go back to Raymond Williams to trace the genealogy of a critical approach that consistently and exclusively studies the formation of metropolitan culture from within its own boundaries. Williams has written on Western culture with such brilliant insight and illumination that to cast aspersions on his work for its neglect of imperial influences might seem churlish at best. My intent in this essay is not to harangue Williams for his failure to account for imperialism's shaping hand in English culture—indeed, there is no novelty or originality in finding fault with Williams on this point—but to examine how and why Williams's analysis of sociocultural pro- cesses in nineteenth-century England, with its primary focus on Eng- lish class formation, left a nebulous space that at one level seemed to allow for the potential broadening of that analysis of English to in- clude colonizer-colonized relations but at another implicitly resisted such further refinements. My view is that Williams's "silence" about imperialism is less a theoretical oversight or blindness than an inter- nal restraint that has complex methodological and historical origins. These origins require illumination and explication, since they are symptomatic of persistently obstinate problems in the serious study of imperialism and culture.

In this essay I locate Williams's methodological difficulties in his conflicting models of interpretation that approach culture in terms of process and as an internal social development of English life while, in reverse fashion, presenting imperialism as a full-blown en- actment of economic motives that are encompassed by a larger sys- tem of economic determination. Further, I propose that these con- flicting methodologies can be explained in terms of Williams's own analysis of the historical development of British Marxism, which he describes as a cross between Marx and English romanticism; this cross produces a liberal-humanist strain in British Marxism that as- signs a dynamic value to culture as an instrument for activating so- cial consciousness, even while conceding its dependence on eco- nomic structures. I suggest that Williams's work partakes of this double strain, alternately giving more weight to the fluidity and un- decidability of social process on the one hand and, on the other, to the implacable operation of a system of economic forces. The set- ting up of the terms *culture* and *imperialism* in mutual opposition must be seen as offering one possible explanation for culture's tenu- ous relation to imperialism in Williams's theory.

In recent years Williams's alleged ambiguity about culture and im- perialism has been subjected to a fair amount of critical scrutiny, provoking questions that have as much to do with the study of im- perial discourse as with the modes of cultural analysis opened up by Williams: Does such ambiguity mean that his cultural theory is flawed to begin with? Are the intellectual paradigms for discussing imperialism simply unavailable to him? Can Williams offer an effec- tive alternative to studying culture exclusive of imperial relations?[3]

At first glance it would seem that these questions lose some of their contentious edge in the context of Williams's *The Country and the City*. This work stands out as the exemplary text linking English social formation with the economics of imperialism, which it does through the characterization of the metropolis as the site of political and economic control. The connection between empire and city, colonies and country, however, is built on more than simply the power of analogy. If the city's relation to the country can be understood as replicated in the relation of the imperial metropolis to the subject colony, then the capitalist accumulation at the metropolitan center—or what Williams calls "the extension to the whole world of that division of functions which in the nineteenth century was a division of functions within a single state"—points in the direction of the appropriation of global economic power by one and the same class. As Williams asserts: "The model of the city and country, in economic and political relations, has gone beyond the boundaries of the nation-state. . . . What was happening in the 'city', the 'metropolitan' economy, determined and was determined by what was made to happen in the 'country': first the local hinterland and then the vast regions beyond it, in other people's lands."[4]

And yet, as Williams is quick to point out, *colonial territory* does not function merely as an analogous term to *country*. Williams takes great care to stress that the relation of the metropolis to the country, on the one hand, and its relation to the colonies, on the other, cannot be understood as interchangeable. Quite the contrary: Williams emphasizes that colonial developments had a more direct and immediate effect on the ascendancy of the metropolis, contributing in the long run to the eventual decline of England's rural base. As an instance, he cites the profits that were generated by the new rural economy of tropical plantations and the whole organized colonial system of which it was a part, successfully transforming Britain into an industrial and urban society. Williams insists on the inseparability of the decline of England's rural areas from these developments in the colonies. That decline, he notes, was further hastened by newly created problems of poverty and overcrowded cities, in partial solution to which the colonies acquired new significance as places of emigration.

At this point Williams appears to be on the brink of exploring the symbolic and reciprocal relation of the colonies to British domestic difficulties; of probing into an analysis of how far-flung territorial possessions acquire new meanings in English culture and society as the release of geographical space that was progressively being closed off in England because of increasing urbanization. But having reached this important recognition of the sociology of empire building, Williams's analysis goes no further. Searching though his critique of imperial extension may be, Williams cannot offer more concrete, material testimony to colonial presence, despite the theoretical status accorded the colonies as vital influences on British society. Not only is the relation between British imperialism and culture *not* further theorized; wherever connections are suggested between the two, they tend to take the form of ironic observation, as for instance when Williams traces the way that the colonies are constructed in nineteenth-century literature as at once the source of the problem of rural decline and urban overcrowding and the solution to it. A tone of understatement and paradox governs his description of selected works of British fiction in which emigration functions thematically as the point marking the novel's dissolution (the point where characters whose lives were not compatible with the British system were "put on the boat"). Williams interprets this pattern as a simple strategy for resolving the conflict between personal ethic and social experience while at the same time obviating any further questioning of either the ethic or the experience.[5] The effect of such an interpretation, however, is to render colonial territories without material presence or substance. The colonies as actual places impinging on the lives of English characters in powerfully direct, immediate ways cannot be accommodated by Williams's location of dramatic conflict in the self-delusions of characters; the colonies, in his reading, are turned into a vanishing point, the symbolic space for dissolving all problems that cannot be solved at home.

In critiquing the novel's propensity to find convenient solutions, often at the cost of sidestepping the complexities of colonial relations, Williams's own criticism fails to highlight those relations as being in themselves critical problems that must be unraveled and foregrounded in cultural analysis. To theorize the relation of imperialism to those developments—be they urban overcrowding or rural poverty—requires us to consider further the ways that the colonial arena is reconstructed to serve as a potential site for the resolution of problems that cannot readily be solved in the home country.

How the composition and general character of the colonized society is represented and often refigured in nineteenth-century discourse, both administrative and literary, can surely *not* be kept apart from, for example, analysis of emigration as a theme in fiction of that same period. Whether we are discussing Charles Kingsley's Chartist hero in *Alton Locke*, who is dispatched to America, or the characters of Elizabeth Gaskell's *Mary Barton*, who make their way to Canada, we encounter that curious and disturbing presentation of the lands to which these characters proceed as *empty spaces* to be newly populated and settled. Perhaps even more disturbing is Williams's participation, howsoever unintentional, in the homogenization of the societies that receive these English characters, even in so simple and innocuous a statement as this one: "In the new lands there was a great need for labourers."[6]

Williams's description of imperialism as one of the "last models" of city and country further obfuscates the precise nature of its relation to British economic production and, by extension, its cultural formations, because it proposes that British influence extended outward rather than that the "periphery" (that is, the colonies) had a functional role in determining internal British developments.[7] At some points, as for instance when he alludes to the country-house system built on the profits of European expansion in the sixteenth and seventeenth centuries, Williams acknowledges that British local developments were vitally affected and shaped by imperial activity. But by and large his understanding of imperial influence is limited to the *effects* of economic profits, and his commentary rarely gets beyond a description of British global involvement as an extension of socioeconomic developments that had already been set in motion within nineteenth-century England. This is all the more remarkable in light of the fact that he is aware that events in the "peripheries" reshaped and determined domestic relations; for example, he writes in *The Country and the City* that "from at least mid-nineteenth century, there was this larger context [of colonial expansion] within which every idea and every image was consciously and unconsciously affected."[8]

Given this insight, why does Williams refrain from studying those ideas and images as factors shaping not just the economic organization of English society but also the particular forms in which metropolitan culture was expressed? If, as Williams himself points out, the

idealization of empire following rural decline and urban concentration constitutes the structure of many industrial novels of mid-nineteenth-century England,[9] why does his own discussion of these novels in *Culture and Society* and elsewhere exclude empire? Is his
reticence an expression of self-imposed limits, a concession to the
practical difficulties of orchestrating a sustained cross-referential
analysis of English and imperial culture? Or is there some complex
inhibition that restrains him from speaking about English culture
and the culture of its imperial possessions simultaneously, as if
speaking about them in the same breath were tantamount to simpli-
fying or, worse still, distorting their relations? To put it another way,
what is entailed in analyzing these relations that will make that effort more than a juxtapositional exercise and will produce not
merely description but also explanation of the particular forms in
which English culture came to be expressed?

As these questions suggest, some of Williams's internal restraints
are related to problems of methodology. Edward Said has drawn attention to Williams's methodological self-consciousness, citing the latter's comments on Lucien Goldmann as an instance of Williams's
troubled awareness that certain theoretical frameworks that had
powerful local appeal were too elusive to offer genuine insight into
a global view of cultural politics: "There was this obvious difficulty:
that most of the work we had to look at was the product of just this
work of reified consciousness, so that what looked like the methodological breakthrough might become, quite quickly, the methodological trap."[10] What impresses Said most about this passage is that
Williams, "as a critic who has learned from someone else's theory . . .
should be able to see the theory's limitations, especially the fact that
a breakthrough can become a trap, if it is used uncritically, repeti-
tively, limitlessly."[11] Perhaps the thorniest problem for Williams was
how to grapple with those forms of analyses, both liberal and Marxist, that rely on cause-effect models for explanations of cultural and
social phenomena. Base and superstructure, to take one example, are
two terms that, for Williams, are heavily implicated in theories of
causal relations, and he is acutely aware of the difficulties of pursuing a project that seeks to go beyond nondeterministic explanations
of society while at the same time remaining bound by an obligation
to retain some of the more useful features of such Marxian categories. Williams's own particular contribution to cultural criticism is

his construction of culture and society as activity, through which he challenges the reading of base-superstructural relations as fixed abstractions. In insisting on a more fluid description of base, Williams set out to study culture and society as active process, taking as his point of departure the idea that economic structures (on the one hand) and superstructural institutions and forms of consciousness (on the other) have a mutual, *reciprocal* influence. Ideally, his approach has the capacity to release critical theory from adherence to notions of predetermination and also from descriptions of culture and society derived exclusively from within the parameters of that same society. Indeed, Williams's criticism of Lukács in "Base and Superstructure in Marxist Cultural Theory" is aimed precisely at the latter's hermetic approach to social systems. Williams makes it clear that he has no use for a static or highly determined, rule-governed model in which the rules of society are highlighted to the exclusion of social and historical process.

No doubt, the specific relevance of Williams for colonial discourse studies derives from his long-standing quarrel with Lukács and other materialist critics, a quarrel that led to his questioning of economic structures as the sole determining factor of cultural formation and his favoring a model of contestation between dominant and subordinate classes. It will be recalled that Williams's project in *Keywords* was to increase our awareness of the hidden conflicts covered over by words like *democracy* and *culture.* He reminds us:

> The book was organized around the new kinds of problem and question which were articulated not only in the new sense of *culture* but in a whole group of closely associated words. Thus the very language of serious inquiry and argument was in part changed and changing, and my purpose then was to follow this change through in the writing of the very diverse men and women who had contributed to this newly central argument.[12]

Contestation as Williams presents it is embedded in the very language of intentions. In "Base and Superstructure" Williams stresses that the specific organization and the structure of society are directly related to certain social intentions, "intentions by which we define the society, intentions which have been the rule of a particular class."[13] But though *intentionality* as Williams uses the word may seem merely another term for determination, it would be a mistake to infer that by this he means prefiguration or control. Rather, he sees the determinative principle in intention as more closely allied with the notion of "setting of limits" and "exertion of pressure." By defining intention in these terms, Williams sought to get away from the crudely reductive idea that the direction a society takes is already prefigured and that it is merely following the course laid out for it at some prior, indeterminate, untraceable point. Also, his reading of intention as a "setting of limits" allows for the possibility of conflict, because the crucial nodes where constraints are placed are more readily identifiable as the places where resistance may occur against the gross "exertion of pressure." Indeed, Williams's main contribution is in offering a dynamic model that will permit one to study culture and society in terms of how social will or intention (the terms are interchangeable) is engaged in an unceasing activity of circumscribing human behavior, on the one hand, and diluting resistance to the authority that it represents, on the other. To know the "social intentions" by which a society is defined is thus to identify not only the potential places where the collective will seeks to assert itself, but also where it is most subject to the fracturing and dissipation caused by extreme pressure.

Williams's chief insights lie, I think, in pointing to the inherent instability of hegemony, particularly its vulnerability to external assaults and its defensive mechanisms for establishing authority. Hegemony, Williams reminds us, is never monolithic or uncontested; he emphatically states that "it is misleading to reduce all political and cultural initiatives and contributions to the terms of the hegemony."[14] But in a seriously inhibiting way, Williams's model does not adequately incorporate the dynamics of his proposed cultural materialism, as is especially evident in his reluctance to extend his notion of contestation to transcultural or cross-referential situations. While his theory of culture has the potential to produce a reading of England's colonial adventure, his cultural analysis is seriously inhibited by the framework of economic determinism within which that reading is produced. Suspending contestation altogether, Williams's scattered comments on empire in *The Long Revolution* and *Culture and Society* suggest that Britain had achieved dominance through the power of a fully formed cultural and institutional system whose values were simply transplanted to the colonies. That system is subsequently identified as the "national" culture, but it partakes little of the contingencies of the colonial situation it confronts, and it remains hermetically sealed from the continually changing political imperatives of empire. What is quite striking is that Williams, while appearing eager to break away from the weaknesses of Marxian theory (and indeed he does come uncannily close to proposing a method of analysis of nineteenth-century culture that would have to incorporate empire to be complete), remains peculiarly reticent in pursuing imperialism as that single crucial factor that would invalidate totalizing descriptions of any kind and favor process over system—two critical objectives to which Williams has otherwise shown himself to be seriously committed.[15] Instead, what has the potential to be a liberating methodological insight and a critical tool for resetting the boundaries of cultural study across societies remains curiously undeveloped by Williams in his own critical practice.

For it must be emphasized that the nature of British imperialism, which crucially depended on securing the consent and acquiescence of its would-be subjects and, consequently, on developing strategies of maneuver—strategies that included joining culture to political aims to negotiate the distance between a politics of noninterference and untrammeled domination—is too fluid and volatile to be easily accommodated to base-superstructural explanations or totalizing models of economic behavior. One of the earliest histories of education and culture under British colonialism, N. N. Law's *The Promotion of Learning in India by Early European Settlers* (1915), points out this irony of modern times: increased commercial activities alone did not spur British imperialism as much as did involvement in the education of the "natives," culminating in English schooling, the inculcation of British manners, the reshaping of "native" identities, and so on; subsequent educational histories have made a similar observation. But the crucial point is not so much that there is a strong connection between cultural interventions and the growth of colonialism (few will now dispute it), but that each gave the other a powerful reinforcement by means that far transcended the purely economic. Even an influential critique like Martin Carnoy's *Education as Cultural Imperialism* (1974) focuses almost exclusively on the economic function of education to fit individuals for roles in society that are of material benefit to the colonizer. In this reading, "cultural imperialism" has no deeper meaning than the transplantation of the values of one culture to another. However, such a defin-

ition cannot possibly account for the persistent appeal of the colonizer's culture after the colonial ruler has withdrawn. And the repeated allusion in British historical documents to English art and literature as "lasting monuments of our dominion," even after the
formal conferral of independence, bespeaks a culture whose authority derived from imperial activity, more particularly from the
cumulative strategies of securing "native" allegiance that by no
means excluded contestation with indigenous cultures. If rejection
of British rule proved easier than rejection of the culture it left behind, the "whole way of life" that it affected is a concrete reality that,
as Williams is the first to acknowledge in *Culture and Society*, cultural criticism would have to contend with, not by isolating elements (of which the economic is only one) as single determinants of
the whole but by studying the interaction of all elements—political,
legal, economic, philosophical, religious, and so forth. Later in the
essay I will briefly discuss what I consider an exemplary work of intellectual history that interweaves the formation of English political
doctrine and the practical governance of empire, at every step of
which proposed changes in local customs and usages through legislation provoked further modification of and resistance to doctrine
(in England as much as in British-controlled India).

Williams's cultural materialism attempts to include imperialism in
its sphere of discourse, but it is inherently incapable of accounting
for imperialism as a function of metropolitan culture. Williams is
pulled in two directions: on the one hand, he wishes to dispense
with the rigidity and two-dimensional abstractness of certain Marxian analytic categories, such as base and superstructure, but at the
same time he is interested in saving what he considers to be some of
their more useful insights. Though he rejects the *language* of base
and superstructure, he retains its interpretive value in yielding historical understanding. Consequently, Williams's reading of Britain in
relation to global power suffers from the reintroduction of both the
language and the concepts of economic and ideological determination. Despite Williams's lifelong commitment to contesting purely
abstract categories of analysis that draw on theories of system rather
than on history, his critical practice paradoxically reproduces those
abstractions in the context of imperialism.

The contradictory impulses in Williams's work run parallel to
what he perceived as the central contradiction of British Marxism,

which he describes as a "historical interaction" between romanticism and Marx whereby culture is valued for its supposed role in the "activation of energy" and the creation of individual consciousness, while at the same time it is thought to remain passively dependent on economic and social development.[16] Singling out Christopher Caudwell as the worst offender, Williams takes British Marxists to task for their unwitting defense of liberal-humanist ideas of cultural value in response to what they saw as Marx's diminution of the value of intellectual and creative activity. Linking Marxism as practiced in England with the romantic tradition of the poet as creator of consciousness, Williams brilliantly reveals how British Marxism has always sought to give a high value to culture by adhering to a dynamic view of art as an active instrument for uncovering a suppressed history.[17] Williams considers it pertinent to interrogate English Marxists "who have interested themselves in the arts whether this is not Romanticism absorbing Marx, rather than Marx transforming Romanticism."[18]

But what Williams may not have realized is that his own work reflects aspects of the romantic temperament, especially with regard to the reading of English culture as process. From the volatile, uncertain middle ground of history, art is conceptualized as both reflecting the economic structure and affecting attitudes toward reality that "help *or hinder* the constant business of changing it."[19] In continuing to work with concepts like "consciousness" and "agency" to describe the transformation of society and individual experience by nineteenth-century social forces (including those of industry and democracy) Williams reveals that he is interested in salvaging the more useful aspects of the romantic idea of culture as a site of resistance without having to subscribe to the romantic belief in the power of art to change human beings and society as a whole. Because Williams sees art as occupying a middle ground, he is able to read in the industrial novels of Dickens, Kingsley, and George Eliot the possibilities for social action, not through legislation (which is bound to be doomed) but through what Williams calls "the instinctive, unintellectual, unorganized life" against which the hegemony of industrial life must contend.[20] At such points in *Culture and Society* Williams clearly oscillates between a view of culture as coeval with social process, always fluid and indeterminate in its meanings and definitions, and a more obdurate, antiromantic reading that gives more power to the forces of economic change.

Empire further dramatizes the tensions in Williams's cultural theory. In his analyses of British culture Williams radically questions that same analytical framework of economic determinism by which he simultaneously explains British imperialism. Time and again Williams undertook close readings of Marx and Engels to show how these two thinkers themselves resisted crude economic reductionism. In *Culture and Society* Williams quotes a significant passage from Engels to illustrate his point:

> According to the materialist conception of history, the determining element in history is *ultimately* the production and reproduction in real life. More than this neither Marx nor I have ever asserted. If therefore somebody twists this into the statement that the economic element is the *only* determining one, he transforms it into a meaningless, abstract and absurd phrase. . . . There is an interaction of all these elements [political, legal, and philosophical theories, religious ideas, etc.], in which, amid all the endless *host* of accidents (i.e. of things and events whose inner connection is so remote or so impossible to prove that we regard it as absent and can neglect it) the economic element finally asserts itself as necessary. Otherwise the application of the theory to any period of history one chose would be easier than the solution of a simple equation of the first degree.[21]

As Williams understands this passage by Engels, the task for cultural criticism is to accept seriously the challenge of dealing with what is concretely manifest—the "way of life" as a whole—without isolating economic elements from the totality or interpreting economic change as occurring in neutral conditions. Williams claims that the "one vital lesson which the nineteenth century had to learn—and learn urgently because of the very magnitude of its changes—was that the basic economic organization could not be separated and excluded from its moral and intellectual concerns."[22] If Williams was openly hostile to the *Scrutiny* version of culture as the guarded possession of a minority isolated from the general society, he was equally critical of the totalizing tendencies of Marxian analysis (see his critique of Lukács). In work after work Williams repeatedly attacked static descriptions of culture as unilaterally determined by economic conditions, and he even went so far as to say that there can be no such thing as an *already existing culture* "because culture cannot be democratized without thereby being radically changed."[23] That is to say, the consciousness of a whole society is too diverse and disparate to be circumscribed by the self-definitions of the economically dominant class.[24] The "whole way of life" thus is both determined and determining, and it is to that, rather than to the economic system alone, that literature has to be related.

Yet there remains the peculiar paradox of Williams's critical position: at the very moment he sought to disengage culture from deterministic explanations, he was locked into a reading of imperialism as the end point of European market forces. The element of creative tension present in his interpretation of English cultural formation is displaced by more deterministic modes of explanation in his discussion of empire. Is it any wonder, then, that, having defined culture and imperialism in noninteractive terms, and through mutually exclusive analytical categories, he should so detach one from the other? In wishing to suspend economic determinism in his analysis of English culture, while at the same time adopting its theoretical argument to account for Britain's imperialistic involvement, Williams is caught in a methodological trap of his own making from which there is no escape.

Given the conflictual ways in which Williams's cultural materialism is worked out, it is not surprising that he has so little to say about British imperialism and its effects on English culture. To advance a different but related argument, his reticence in naming colonialism as a shaping factor in English cultural formation can be interpreted as a reluctance to consider the economics of imperialism as having a final determining power over culture. This is by no means to make apologies for Williams's omission of colonialism, but it is to gesture toward the enormously complex situation Williams finds himself in as a result of a commitment to a revision of Marxian analytical categories that refuses to comply with notions of economic determinism as fully explanatory of culture. Williams's uneasiness in working with exclusively economic categories causes him to give scant attention to the reciprocal and determinate relation between culture and imperialism, which he mistakenly reads as the end point of established economic motives that get transplanted from Britain to its colonies, rather than as a test site for a culture in formation. But that same uneasiness, we have to remind ourselves, is responsible for his studying English culture and society as historical process rather than as the end result of fixed economic imperatives. We can only conclude that if Williams chooses to "ignore" imperialism, it is because the terms of his analysis impel him to do so.

Williams's peculiar reticence in naming imperialism restricts him to a form of essentialism that robs his cultural model of much of its potency. At the most basic level, his failure to incorporate the historical reality of empire into both his theoretical analyses and his readings of literary texts exposes a conception of society that is rendered in isomorphic terms, and cultural ideas appear in Williams as if they were self-generated rather than produced by external conditions. This is glaringly apparent in his account of the origin of national culture and character, which he locates in the Germano-Coleridgean school.[25] Williams reads the distinctions made by Coleridge between culture and civilization as an attempt to interweave a philosophy of society with a philosophy of history and so to root human perfectability in social conditions. But by introducing the notion of "cultivation," Coleridge, and Williams as well to some extent, reworks culture into a general condition or habit of mind. As a genealogy of culture, *Culture and Society* wavers unsteadily between the two critical positions with which Coleridge comes to be associated in Williams's reading: culture as process and history (subject to flux, discontinuities, modifications), which is set against culture as social value (expressed independently of radical change and historical disjunctions). Standards of perfection acquire two meanings: in the first instance they are drawn from society and in turn influence it, but in the other, they are set apart to judge it. This movement of culture from social process to social arbiter, which Williams undertakes to chart as the history of English culture, seriously limits him to a model of structural continuity. Even though Williams militates against a model of continuous, organic history, that is precisely the kind of impression his work produces, for in tracing culture—prefigured as "English"—from its own conceptual base as the pursuit of perfection, Williams's description precludes the possibility that its foundations exist outside it. A historical practice such as imperialism can appear merely as a context for the promotion of culture, not as a condition for its generation or as a determinant of its content and shape.

The trap closes in on Williams more definitively at this stage. Having chosen to conceive of culture and social process as products of the same society, Williams frees himself from the obligation of tracing their development through contexts other than those in which (he presumes) they originated, contexts that would inevitably have led him (in the deepest historical sense) to imperial relations. To take a very simple example from educational history that Williams discusses in *The Long Revolution*, industrial schools were set up in the first quarter of the nineteenth century to provide manual training and elementary instruction in the Bible and other moral subjects. Williams reports on a revolution in teaching method that came to be known as the Lancaster and Bell monitorial system of instruction; this method consisted of the use of monitors and standard repetitive exercises, which allowed fewer numbers of teachers to teach greater numbers of pupils. Education in an era of mass democracy had found its first effective medium, observes Williams, documenting the growth in enrollments—and moral selves—that had been made possible by what many of us today might consider a fairly mundane innovation. The new pedagogy marked a significant moment in British social history, writes Williams, for "a national system of elementary schooling . . . had been set going."[26] The monitorial system, which rests on the concept of the few teaching the many, is a raw prototype for the more developed Arnoldian formulations of a hegemonic culture filtering downward through the agency of a carefully chosen elite.

What Williams fails to note is that the success of the Lancaster and Bell method in managing and controlling a mass population was partly assured in England because *it had been introduced and tested elsewhere.* The experiment began almost fortuitously in colonial India, where the problems of governing a large population were greatly exacerbated by the fact that there was limited English manpower available for the task. Dr. Andrew Bell, who had been an Anglican chaplain in the Indian Army, tried to cope with his many duties as superintendent of the orphan asylum at the Egmore Redoubt at Madras and as chaplain to five regiments. Frustrated by the meager resources available to him, he employed a better than average pupil to teach his fellow pupils to write and draw in the sand of the classroom floor. The boy proved as capable a teacher as he had been a student. Bell publicized this "discovery" in *An Experiment in Education* (1797). The Madras system was introduced into the Charity

School of St. Botolph's, Aldgate, in 1798 and in the Kendal industrial schools the following year. But the system made little headway until Joseph Lancaster began in 1801 to use it in his one-room school in London where he taught over a thousand children through a system of "drafts not classes" and published his results in *Improvements in Education as It Respects the Industrial Class of the Community* (1803).[27]

I do not mean to suggest, by citing this example, that for every social or cultural movement enacted in England there was a corresponding event that preceded it in the colonies. (It would be equally disastrous to infer, from these transfers of movements and ideas, that sustained analogies can be drawn between class relations and colonizer-colonized relations in the two societies.) Nor do I wish to imply that all errors of omission are ideologically motivated. But I do think that the fact of omission itself suggests a problematic relation between theory and history, or system and process, of which Williams could not have been ignorant. *The Country and the City* goes a long way toward establishing the fact that the changes wrought on English culture and society are more than the product of internal developments. But as I suggested earlier, theorizing the relation of imperialism to those developments—be they excessive urbanization, rural poverty, or the need for mass literacy—requires an additional step in the direction of establishing how the colonized society gets refigured and redrawn to serve as a potential arena for the working out of ideas and solutions that are as yet only partially or insufficiently developed in the home country.

Eric Stokes's *The English Utilitarians and India* is a paradigmatic work that offers a powerful approach to conceptualizing relations between domestic and imperial spheres. Stokes relocates the utilitarian ideas of Bentham and the two Mills from their English context to their use in the governance of India and in the general shaping of British imperialism. In his opening statement Stokes points out that British rule overseas "was not a disconnected and meaningless fragment of English history" but reflected the English character and mind "in a way that often escapes the Englishman confined within his domestic setting."[28] In the dialectic of empire and home, utilitarianism is shown to be a construction of imperial rule, its principles of governance being constantly tested and challenged in the flurry of exchange between the East India Company's court of directors and the governor-general and his council in India.

Two striking discussions in Stokes's work suggest a potentially useful hermeneutic for dealing with problems of cultural analysis that emerge in Raymond Williams's work. First, in his incisive commentary on the conflicting agendas of English liberalism and Burkean conservatism as they were played out in British India (the latter's Orientalist call for salvaging and protecting "native" culture against British commercial incursions clearly opposing what it saw as an interventionist, assimilationist program of cultural change), Stokes reveals how these conflicts in colonial India sharply divided the supporters of liberalism in England, producing doubts about its viability as a nonauthoritarian philosophy of change. The inflexible will of Lord Cornwallis, governor general from 1786 to 1793, and the aggressive policy of administrative reform that he promoted further exacerbated English fears (particularly among the conservative members of the London-based court of directors) that liberalism was a thinly disguised veil for the ambitions of self-aggrandizing individuals appointed to serve in the East. The effect of this interaction between the worlds of colonizer and colonized was to produce resistance to political doctrine where there was none before, a splitting and confusion of liberal aims where, previously, reformist tendencies appeared to be in the ascendancy.

The other great achievement of Stokes's book is its insistence on the need to break through the forced homogenization of native cultures that underlies official British discourse on the colonies; to restore to heterogeneous populations modes of self-definition that include, among other things, custom and usage—self-definitions that were systematically effaced in British juridical discourse to produce contrived categories of racial and religious identity, such as "Hindu," "Christian," "Mohammedan," "Eurasian," and the catchall but empty category of "Native." In a brilliant chapter titled "Law and Government" Stokes minutely details the reorganization of governmental machinery in early-nineteenth-century British India that sheared subordinate presidencies of their independent legislative, financial, and diplomatic powers and invested the governor-general and his council with more centralized authority. The Benthamite fondness for efficiency and smooth functioning of government encouraged the trend toward concentrating decision making in a few experts rather than diverse constituent assemblies. Proposals to set up a legislative council and a law commission to develop a uniform civil code governing the disparate groups of the subject population were only one indication of how the exercise of utilitarian principles required a homogenization of existing native laws and customs. During his tenure with the East India Company, James Mill issued several important dispatches that aimed at bringing the "native" government under a common law that would not at the same time be entirely synonymous with English law. (For instance, that Mill was cautious about tampering with the fabric of indigenous society was apparent in his reluctance to alter existing property laws, but his recognition of individual property rights in the soil was a clear challenge to indigenous modes of traditional joint ownership and communal control.)[29] The question for research as it is addressed by Stokes is why such efforts at securing uniformity were resorted to with such constancy and regularity, and what implications these efforts had for the shape of English culture and English philosophy in general.

Nonetheless, the leveling of disparate cultural identities in far-off lands seems to go unchallenged in Williams's work, as does the primacy of the economic category. Earlier I suggested, taking my cue from Williams, that the contradictions in his position on imperialism can be read as internalizations of historical contradictions inherent British Marxism, with its origins in the cross-fertilization of Marx and romanticism wherein culture is understood as alternately controlled by and independent of economic structures. This double focus on passive dependence and active contestation puts culture in the position of either affirming those structures or, in an enabling exercise of individual will, challenging them. The ambivalence of culture's trajectory is what Williams liked to think of as process or history, and his readings of English culture are informed by his sense of the dynamic interplay of event with social and economic reality.

But if the legacy of romanticism left an uneasy mark on British Marxism, which responded by moving in the direction of theory and system building to restore the primacy of economic determinism, the legacy of British Marxism thus construed left a similar mark on Williams. He too has shown a tendency to move toward system when he is unable to contend with the historical fluidity of economically engendered realities such as imperialism. Aware of the impossibility of accommodating system *and* process, Williams addresses the reciprocal relation of culture and imperialism in arbitrary and fragmented ways, producing in turn a systematic failure to recognize "Englishness" as an imperial construct.

As in the work of his successors, "national" culture in Williams takes the place of imperial formations, but this turns out to be a choice that creates new problems for cultural analysis: the fully constituted character of "national" culture obscures the heterogeneous fragments out of which it was originally constructed.[30] As Williams must have been aware, one of the unfortunate outcomes of an approach to English culture as self-generated is the fact that cultural identity as a value takes precedence over the historical discontinuities and asymmetrical developments from which it emerged. In the end, what we are left with is a disturbing reminder that there is, after all, no view like the one from the *other* country.

NOTES

1. Brian Doyle, *English and Englishness* (London and New York: Routledge, 1989), p. 12.

2. Alan Sinfield, *Literature, Politics, and Culture in Postwar Britain* (Berkeley and Los Angeles: University of California Press, 1989), p. 130.

3. Some of these questions are implied in several recent critiques of Williams. See Edward W. Said, "Intellectuals in the Post-Colonial World," *Salmagundi*, nos. 70-71 (1986): 44-64; Benita Parry, "Problems in Current Theories of Colonial Discourse," *Oxford Literary Review* 7 (1987): 27-58.

4. Raymond Williams, *The Country and the City* (London: Chatto and Windus, 1973), p. 278.

5. See *The Long Revolution* (New York: Columbia University Press, 1961), pp. 66-67, for Williams's all too abbreviated account of the Empire as a place of emigration to solve working-class problems at home. In *Culture and Society* (1959; reprint, New York: Columbia University Press, 1986) Williams discusses Gaskell's *Mary Barton* more closely to show that the emigration to Canada with which the book closes is a feeble solution proposed by its author, a "cancelling of the actual difficulties and the removal of the persons pitied to the uncompromised New World" (91). In reading emigration as a form of negation, Williams reinforces the idea of the insubstantiality of territories abroad. See also Raymond Williams, *Politics and Letters: Interviews with New Left Review* (London: Verso, 1979).

6. Williams, *Long Revolution*, p. 66.

7. It is true that in *The Sociology of Culture* (New York: Schocken, 1982) Williams attempts to account for the contribution of twentieth-century immigrants to metropolitan formations, but his indecisiveness about the status of these contributions is unsettling: do new groups from "peripheral" regions cause ruptures in "national tradition," or do their intellectual and creative activities become identified with the dominant culture? Williams's difficulty in answering this question must surely be related to his framing it within the context of a "single national social order."

8. Williams, *Country and the City*, p. 281.

9. Ibid.

10. Williams, *Problems in Materialism and Culture* (London: Verso, 1980), p. 21; also cited in Edward W. Said, *The World, the Text, and the Critic* (Cambridge, Mass.: Harvard University Press, 1983), p. 239.

11. Said, *The World, the Text, and the Critic*, p. 239.

12. Raymond Williams, *Culture and Society* (1958; reprint, New York: Columbia University Press, 1986), p. ix.

13. Raymond Williams, "Base and Superstructure in Marxist Cultural Theory," *New Left Review*, no. 82 (1973): 7.

14. Raymond Williams, *Marxism and Literature* (Oxford: Oxford University Press, 1977), p. 113.

15. See Edward W. Said, "Traveling Theory," in *The World, the Text, and the Critic*, p. 241, for an illuminating discussion of Williams's critical recognition of the answerability of theory to historical and social situations. See also "Media, Margins, and Modernity: Raymond Williams and Edward Said" in Raymond Williams, *The Politics of Modernism* (London: Verso, 1989) for further elaboration of this theme in relation to alternative cultural analyses, and Edward W. Said, *Culture and Imperialism* (New York: Knopf, 1993), for a refilling of those spaces left empty by Williams.

16. Williams, *Culture and Society*, p. 280.

17. For a recent reassessment of the recovery of value in Marxist critical theory, see Frank Kermode, *History and Value* (Oxford: Clarendon, 1988). Kermode points out that though Marxist literary theory attempts to repudiate transcendental notions of value in art, the archaeological activity it endorses implicitly locates value in the hidden or suppressed quality of literature's material relation to historical process. Kermode hastens to say that there is nothing wrong in considering value in terms that render art a document in the class war. But why, he asks, do even the most uncompromising of Marxist critics like Terry Eagleton find it so difficult to get away from the idea that there is something in art that makes it art and *not* a mere document in the class war? Kermode demonstrates how Marxist and liberal humanist theories of art converge on this point. He suggests that Marxist literary theory is no less essentialist, no less able to escape history's mediation of value in its assumption that there is a "real history" that is covered over by false ideological versions of it. By insisting that value lies in the historical conditioning that is concealed by aesthetic expression, Marxist theories of art paradoxically save the value of past art. For art produced even under "old abhorrent dispensations" (now superseded) can legitimately claim value because of its usefulness in uncovering a suppressed history. Even Marx and Engels were susceptible to this current of thought, as the great esteem in which they held Balzac proves.

18. Williams, *Culture and Society*, p. 274.

19. Ibid., emphasis in the original.

20. Ibid., p. 95.

21. Engels, letter to J. Bloch, September 21, 1890, in *Selected Correspondence*, p. 475. Quoted in *Culture and Society*, p. 267, emphasis in the original.

22. Williams, *Culture and Society*, p. 200.

23. Alan O'Connor, *Raymond Williams: Writing, Culture, Politics* (Oxford: Basil Blackwell, 1989), p. 58.

24. In "Culture Is Ordinary" Williams personalizes the idea of culture as encompassed by a "whole way of life" to distinguish between cultural and educational institutions, which

as bastions of privilege are the purveyors of a single culture, and "English" or lived culture, which is possessed by working classes and upper classes alike. In Raymond Williams, *Resources of Hope* (London: Verso, 1989), p. 7.

25. Williams, *Culture and Society*, pp. 61–63.

26. Williams, *Long Revolution*, p. 137.

27. Joseph Lancaster, *Improvements in Education as It Respects the Industrial Class of the Community*, 2d ed. (1803), excerpted in *Education and Democracy*, ed. A. E. Dyson and Julian Lovelock (London: Routledge and Kegan Paul, 1975), p. 40. See also *Educational Documents: England and Wales 1816–1963* (London: Chapman and Hall, 1965) for extracts of commission reports on popular education alluding to the success of the Lancaster and Bell system. A plaque honoring Andrew Bell's contribution to English education hangs in Westminster Abbey, describing Bell as "the eminent founder of the Madras system of education who discovered and reduced the successful practice of mutual instruction founded upon the multiplication of power and division of labour on the moral and intellectual world which has been adopted within the British Empire as the rational system of education of the children of the poor." For further illustration of the crossover of educational theory and practice from the colonies to England, see my *Masks of Conquest: Literary Study and British Rule in India* (New York: Columbia University Press, 1989).

28. Eric Stokes, *The English Utilitarians and India* (1959; reprint, Oxford: Oxford University Press, 1989), p. vii.

29. Stokes notes Bentham's strong influence on Mill on this point, adding that "while asserting the universal applicability of his principles of law, Bentham admitted that the details would require modification to suit local conditions. It was important in his eyes that the law should as far as possible harness popular prejudices to its service so as to strengthen its influence" (*English Utilitarians*, p. 69). Stokes refers his readers to Bentham's essay in *Works*, vol. 1, titled "Of the Influence of Time and Place in Matters of Legislation."

30. Patrick Parrinder, in *The Failure of Theory* (Sussex: Harvester, 1987), has accused Williams of narrowly national concerns, and I think there is some truth in the charge that Williams sought to discover the possibilities of "commonness" and "solidarity" rather than to affirm multiple cultures in a multicultural society. Williams's historical interest may have been in the sources of fragmentation and dissolution of identity, but that interest metamorphoses into a project for recovering and reuniting identity. Williams's eagerness to achieve a common culture may partly explain his inability to take a structurally disjunctive view of cultural formation. Parrinder interprets Williams's increasing emphasis on national culture as evidence that he is more interested in addressing the historical experience of a nation accustomed to the rigors of war than one experiencing insulation from military aggression (p. 323).

"What We Have Again to Say": Williams, Feminism, and the 1840s

Cora Kaplan

No decade has been more associated with Raymond Williams's developing method of cultural analysis, or is more indelibly stamped for our future understanding with his idiosyncratic focus, than the 1840s in England. Williams's reading of that troubled historical moment, initiated in his chapter on "The Industrial Novels" in *Culture and Society 1780-1950* (1958), remained remarkably constant over time, but his exemplary use of it would shift in significant ways between his two major, related treatments of it in "The Analysis of Culture" in *The Long Revolution* (1961) and in "Forms of Fiction" (1977).[1] These two essays, together with the chapter entitled "Charlotte and Emily Brontë" in *The English Novel from Dickens to Lawrence* (1970), foregrounded what he elsewhere called "that remarkable generation of women novelists" as the most significant creators of the "emergent" fictional forms of the decade in which the subjective or personal voice, the bearer of "intense feeling," became the prime mover of narrative.[2] It is this emergence of a particular kind of individual voice from the turbulent social upheavals of the forties that intrigued and increasingly disturbed Williams; what is intriguing and disturbing in turn to his feminist readers is his unwillingness, except briefly and ambivalently in his essay on the Brontës, to name that voice as female and to instance its development as the effect of historical changes in the meaning of sexual difference. For if in his wider oeuvre, as Morag Shiach has suggested, women are significantly missing as historical agents and as cultural producers, in

211

Williams's writing on the mid-nineteenth-century they are only too powerfully present.[3]

Williams's characteristic displacement of gender and sexuality as categories of analysis both diffused and defused the central place he ascribed to women novelists in the nineteenth century. Sexual difference did not therefore become an invisible referent in Williams's strategic use of women's fiction—the effect of displacement in psychoanalytic terms is typically a shift in focus and affect. Rather, its unexplored presence, amounting often to a kind of disavowal that both admitted and denied its importance, allowed him the freedom of a sleight of hand in which women's narratives were simultaneously representative of a general strand in the "structure of feeling" of the time and bore an eccentric, at times even pathological, but always undiagnosed relationship to it. Both displacement and disavowal of the determining role of sexual difference structured Williams's interpretation of the subjective voices and narrative modes created chiefly by women in the mid-nineteenth-century. He believed the emergence of these new forms of fiction, and of what we would be more likely than he to call "subjectivity," to be crucial elements of the profound cultural shifts taking place in the whole social formation at the time. If we keep in mind that this period was the historical conjuncture through which he chose to test through "actual analysis" many of the key concepts of what he came to call "cultural materialism," it may make it easier to see why gender—even women—as a complex presence rather than as a structuring absence has implications for his work as a whole. And whether sexual difference was an explicit or suppressed referent in his writing, the pattern of Williams's negotiations of its meanings for the 1840s forms an illuminating kind of objective correlative to the uneasy, guarded, sometimes defensive, but rarely hostile responses he made in later life to questions about the relationship between his own work and contemporary feminism.[4]

Williams's untimely death has allowed those feminists deeply indebted to his writing but somehow reluctant to cite or challenge it in his lifetime out of a combination of politeness and anger to break their silence in essays that read like productive if critical acts of mourning.[5] In this elegiac mode they are able to explore the effects of Williams's silences and resistances around issues of gender while overcoming their own by articulating the ways in which his thinking can continue to enrich feminist analysis. I intend this essay to be a contribution in that genre, for in working through the paradoxical place of women, sexuality, and gender in Williams's arguments about the 1840s, I have come to see how his perspectives and those of feminist critics and historians often run parallel and occasionally dovetail, both in their critique of an older Marxist analysis of culture and in their interest in and reservations about structuralist and post-structuralist theory. This convergence may indeed partly explain the long silence of feminism about his work and influence and, conversely, his own reticence and reservations about feminism, for it often seems as if these analyses—both where they intersect and where they differ—are in a kind of unacknowledged competition for the same ground.

This is especially true of the troubled relationship that both Williams and socialist feminists have had to the "emergent" forms of subjectivity of the mid-nineteenth century. For Williams's and for certain feminist analyses, although in somewhat different ways, the seductive and terrifying shapes of female subjectivity, realized most vividly in the writing of the Brontës, have been a fateful staging of modernity created through social and political struggle. Cast (in my view, miscast) as the primary agents and bearers of all that is most disturbing about modern individuality, they come to represent its most ethically problematic effect.[6] The narrow task of this essay is to reembody gender in Williams's writing on the 1840s as a way of locating its place in his wider analysis. Though limited in scope, this paper I believe forms a necessary prologue to the larger task of pinning down and exorcising the phantom figure of bourgeois femininity as it haunts, in turn, the projects of cultural materialism and of materialist feminism.

The Politics of Identification: The Case of Mrs. Gaskell

That shadowy figure begins to take shape as early as Williams's discussion of Elizabeth Gaskell's *Mary Barton* (1848) and *North and South* (1855) in *Culture and Society*. It is adumbrated in his illuminating comments on the "change of emphasis" and of title that Gaskell made from *John Barton* to the published work, *Mary Barton*, a change from an admirable but ultimately unstable identification with John Barton, "'my hero, *the* person with whom all my sympathies went'" (*CS* 100) to the focus on "the daughter," as Williams insisted on calling Mary Barton. This shift marked, for Williams, the decline from what might have been "a great novel of its kind," in which "sympathetic observation" combined with "a largely successful attempt at imaginative identification" (*CS* 100), to a fiction dominated by "the familiar and orthodox plot of the Victorian novel of sentiment . . . of little lasting interest" (*CS* 101). This first novel, Williams suggested, cannot be written because the murder John Barton commits, a political murder atypical of working-class response to "grave suffering," was a "dramatization of the *fear of violence*" that the middle and upper classes felt "and which penetrated, as an arresting and controlling factor, even into the deep imaginative sympathy of a Mrs. Gaskell" (*CS* 102). While this fear was a general one, its productive expression in *Mary Barton* was, Williams thought, specific to the act of writing itself. For it is the author, he reminded us, who "planned the murder, herself, and chose, for the murderer" her hero, an imaginative choice that is a projection of the general fear that is followed by a "recoil," which has "the effect of ruining the necessary integration of feeling in the whole theme" (*CS* 102).

Never once did Williams overtly suggest that Gaskell's "recoil" is overdetermined by her gender as well as her class position, but that implication is immanent if unstated in the structure of his analysis. The murder, Williams argued early in his essay, puts John Barton "beyond the range of Mrs. Gaskell's sympathy (which is understandable), but more essentially, beyond the range of her powers" (*CS* 101), which turn out to be so much more appropriately attuned to the novel of domestic melodrama and sentiment that "it now seems incredible that the novel should ever have been planned in any other way. If Mrs. Gaskell had written 'round the character of Mary Barton all the others formed themselves,' she would have confirmed our actual impression of the finished book" (*CS* 101). This judgment *preceded*, by a page, Williams's astute analysis of the psychosocial effect of Mrs. Gaskell's identification with her murderer, and it implied that except for the author's extradiegetic comment on the making of her story and its first protagonist, readers would never know that John Barton was a heroic figure for his creator. This is, however, manifestly untrue. Both novels, if we want to accept Williams's firm separation of them, are there in the *Mary Barton* we still read; the text's sympathetic identification with John Barton and its recoil need no authorial gloss. Williams's account of the in-evitability of its failure in political and artistic terms, insofar as this was encoded in the inadequacy of Mrs. Gaskell's "powers" or the welcome ease with which she allowed herself to be diverted "to Mary Barton" and the sentimental, all clearly inscribed an essential and devalued, but never discussed, notion of the feminine. Insofar as Mrs. Gaskell was an ungendered representative of the liberal bour-geoisie, Williams *almost* said, her unwritten book might have suc-ceeded; insofar as she was a woman, he never quite said, it was bound to fail.

This unstated difference structured too Williams's incisive argu-ment about the book's two stages of magical resolution. The first of these, the reconciliation between *men*—murderer and industrialist—and the move of employer and employees toward "efforts at im-provement and mutual understanding," what Williams called the "characteristic humanitarian conclusion" of the times, "must certainly be respected" (*CS* 102). Mrs. Gaskell did not leave it at that, however, and neither could Williams. He was deeply critical of her second piece of narrative closure, which, I want to argue, is what he saw as the "feminine" ending. Williams concluded his discussion of *Mary Barton* by noting that the characters who were "the objects of her real sympathy"—Mary Barton, Jem Wilson, Mrs. Wilson, Margaret, Will, Job Leigh—were transported to Canada, a "devastating conclu-sion," he felt, as a comment on the "actual situation" of the forties, but one "with which the heart went" (*CS* 103). A failure of emotional nerve and will was implied here that the "minister's wife" even with her "deep and genuine" response to suffering and her "pity" could not transcend (*CS* 102). The "confusing violence and fear of vio-lence" (*CS* 102) that Williams believed joined pity in this "structure of feeling" enacted another kind of violence on the narrative of class struggle, a "writing-off" without a social or political resolution that killed off John Barton and allowed his friends and kin to emigrate. At every stage of Williams's argument about *Mary Barton*, there-fore, gender acted as a suppressed but present determinant, ethically and aesthetically dividing the most liberal end of the bourgeois imagination, orchestrating the different registers of the idea of "cul-ture" that Williams argued came into play in this period: "culture" as response and alternative to the forces of industrialization, "culture"

as a concern with "the new kinds of personal and social relationships," "culture" as a "complex and radical response to new problems
of social class," and lastly "culture" as it is a "reference back to an area
of personal and apparently private experience, which was notably
to affect the meaning and practice of art" (CS 17).

These interactive definitions come from Williams's remarkable introduction to *Culture and Society*, which set so much of his subsequent analysis in motion. Feminism could use his reading of *Mary
Barton*, which remains for me the single most illuminating critical
analysis of the novel, to reweave these various elements of culture.
We might then see more clearly how the two narratives with their
male and female protagonists and their generic alterity coexist in the
same novel. If we were to allow the transgressive, cross-class, cross-
gender identification of the "minister's wife" with her working-class
hero and murderer to be as "real" as her sympathy with its women
characters and the less violent working men, then we might be able
to admit that what is projected into John Barton's murderous act is
not simply undifferentiated bourgeois fear but rather bourgeois
women's anger, evoked not only by sympathy with the starving
poor but also as a complex of empathetic and correlative rage at the
indifference of men of her own class, from which, as Williams
rightly pointed out, she must recoil. And if we resist the move that
"writes off" the narrative that is about women, the move through
which Williams relegated the representation of Mary Barton's experience of cross-class sexuality and of sexual politics within the working class to second-rate genre—the stock sentimental—we may be
able to come to a reintegrated reading of the novel as one whose
narrative, sympathies, and political analysis were both symptomati-
cally split along the lines of class and gender and expressively *about*
those social fractures. Similarly, Williams provided us with exactly
the right question about the double resolution: why the emigration
of surviving working-class men and women if masters and men can,
within fictional convention, come to "mutual understanding"? Again,
the answer may be in the unspoken anger in Gaskell's novels that
centered a critique of contemporary masculinity—class specific in its
particulars but transclass in its effects—as part of its focus on class
conflict. It is perhaps that protofeminist anger that projectively created the social violence of the male Carsons and informed Gaskell's
identification with, and initial idealization of, their social adversary

John Barton. Williams helps us to see what he could neither quite see nor say, that the "minister's wife" may not have had much faith in the "humanitarian solution" imagined only as a pact between men. In this sense the emigration of a symbolic fragment of the whole working-class community may be both more utopian and less pusillanimous than Williams suggested: as near, perhaps, as the middle-class woman's idea of a radical alternative could come in the 1840s to the oppositional social revolution she wished "at heart" to avert. Read like this, with the gender categories and analysis fully established and acknowledged, *Mary Barton* textualizes all the new meanings of "culture" that Williams laid out, without the negative valences his interpretation of class and gender difference assigned to women.

A bare page of Williams's chapter on "The Industrial Novels" dealt with *North and South* (1855), a novel that interested Williams much less because its protagonist was in the "actual position" of the author, and its emphasis was on "attitudes *to* the working people, rather than on the attempt to reach, imaginatively, their feelings about their lives" (*CS* 103). Williams accords a somewhat grudging "respect" to the novel's union of the practical and sensible in the marriage of "Northern manufacturer" and "Southern girl"—a union in which female "influence" "humanizes" Thornton and leads to his attempt to improve the "human relations in industry" (*CS* 103). But Williams drew the line when Gaskell gave Margaret economic control over Thornton, for it was only through her legacy and "under her patronage" that Thornton was to be able to make his experiment at "'cultivating some intercourse with the hands'" (*CS* 103). This working out through money from "elsewhere," the device that "solved so many otherwise insoluble problems in the world of the Victorian novel," Williams characterized as yet again an "outside" solution to the "insupportable" relations between classes (*CS* 104), its "outsideness"—of region, gender, and materialism—damningly compounded because it comes from a southern woman's money. Class relations are once again figured as the province of men, and a solution that gives a bourgeois woman too much economic, political, and moral power over her husband is read as external to the real dynamics of the historic situation and the shifts in consciousness and practice that might change it: therefore "adventitious" (*CS* 104). Yet the Thornton-Hale liaison was a pretty ordinary kind of economic relation in a period when women's money shored up the business of husbands, brothers, and sons.[7] Williams's discomfort was, rather, based on *North and South*'s emphatic rewriting of the relative hierarchy of men and women, a fact emphasized by his characterization of Margaret's "patronage," the word implying a kind of grating aristocratic ascendency, which, in the novel, it definitively is not. Williams's assessment of Gaskell was shot through with a sense of discomfort that may be, at its core, with the very centrality of her role in the genre of the industrial novel. In one fiction she reached beyond her "powers" by trying and failing in her creative imagining of the lives of the poor; in another she gave the female protagonist with whom she is closely identified too much power altogether in the reformation of the industrial bourgeoisie. Although this was Williams's only lengthy treatment of Mrs. Gaskell, her work figured strongly in his later analyses of the fiction written in, and about, the forties. What is embedded so distinctively in the narrative perspective of *Mary Barton* in its final form and in both protagonist and narrative in *North and South* is the way in which women and their point of view became arbiters, within the life of the text at least, not only of the "insupportable situation" of the Two Nations of rich and poor but also of the divided and unequal worlds of men and women. This narrative process is deeply inscribed in all the novels of the decade that most interested Williams. *Dombey and Son*, *Wuthering Heights*, and *Jane Eyre* all have in common with *North and South* resolutions in which women come to dominate rather than simply influence the ethical worlds of the novel.

Gender and the Structure of Feeling: *The Long Revolution*

In the interviews in *Politics and Letters* Williams notes that *The Long Revolution* (1961), intended as a sequel with a different kind of theme and emphasis to the largely well received and much discussed *Culture and Society*, was greeted with a highly critical, overtly hostile response. *The Long Revolution* enraged readers on the right, Williams remembered, because they saw it as bringing back into postwar literary analysis those "social questions" so prominent in the 1930s.[8] Part of that response must, in retrospect, have had to do with the very different mode of narration in the two books.

The studies did have, of course, a dynamic continuity, but while the first focused on texts and authors, the second explored the shifting organization and forms of cultural production as they articulated the meaning of, and were themselves part of, social and political change. *The Long Revolution* did not proceed through a familiar, traditional close reading of writers and texts but critiqued and radically reworked the selective traditions in which they had been framed, arguing directly against a traditional "mysticism" in the making of canon and value and for the self-conscious responsibility of cultural critics to understand and reveal the contemporary and historical grounds for their "active choices" (*LR* 70). Williams called attention to the intellectual and political process that is always involved in the changing constellation of selective traditions; in so doing he cut away at "Time, the abstraction" as the arbiter of the universal (*LR* 70). The notion of atemporal value or the assumed wholeness of a society was also challenged in his development of the categories of the "social character" and "structure of feeling" of an age. The first primarily described the abstracted ideals and rules of the dominant group competing with those of other classes, and the latter, a much more slippery concept, the lived sense of a historical moment, which drew from the "real conflict" and competition between social characters as well as the "life lived in its shadow" (*LR* 80, 79). A "structure of feeling is not uniform throughout the society; it is primarily evident in the dominant productive group" but it "has to deal not only with the public ideas but with their omissions and consequences, as lived" (*LR* 80).

The extended definition of these these two important concepts—social character and structure of feeling—in the first part of "The Analysis of Culture" in *The Long Revolution* marks out the critical distance Williams took at this point in his writing from the Marxist theorization of culture with which he was familiar, a distance very thoughtfully elaborated in chapter five of *Culture and Society.*[9] We can see in his distinction between social character and structure of feeling his argument with any unified, undifferentiated notion of bourgeois ideology, and in his refusal to use a model of base and superstructure his quarrel with the existing theories of the determination of culture. Yet it is evident in *The Long Revolution* that Williams was still deep in conversation with these theories of culture, working out his own problematic in relation to the issues they posed. In the second half of "The Analysis of Culture" he took the 1840s as the exemplary site of his paradigm.

I have laid out Williams's framework in some detail because it is crucial to any understanding of the presence and elision of gender in this groundbreaking essay, which sets out an agenda for analysis of the period not yet realized by cultural critics or historians. His consideration of the forties ended rather than began with the fiction that he thought articulated "at a level even more important than that of institutions . . . the real relations within the whole culture" (*LR* 84, 85). The literary field that must be taken into account included the most popular writers and the fiction bought from W. H. Smith's stalls by railway travelers in 1848, a constituency that included significant numbers of "'persons of the better class'" (*LR* 72). Smith's 1848 best-seller list included a great deal of sentiment and adventure, with few recognizable names from the selective tradition we read today, but it is notable, though Williams did not highlight the fact, for its almost equal representation of male and female authors, who stood six to four in its tally. The broad literary terrain that Williams described included the new popular periodicals representing writers like G. W. M. Reynolds and the recently established popular Sunday press, as well as the family magazines that Williams explained were the precursors of women's magazines today. It is in relationship to this wide field of writing that centrally involved, as Williams's gender-neutral documentation nevertheless makes clear, the shifting nature of women's readership, that we must, he argued, think about the particularity of certain "good" novels. These must be considered through the realization that genre fiction—"the now disregarded popular" and what we now hold to be more "literary" productions—characteristically shared the same devices of character and plot: orphans, heiresses, cross-class romance, legacies, and emigration (*LR* 84). These elements were combined in all kinds of fiction—as Williams had suggested they were in Mrs. Gaskell's—to develop conservative closures for the social conflicts they textualized (*LR* 84). Exceptional fictions may stand out, in this frame of reference, by the way in which "ordinary situations and feelings are worked through to their maximum intensity" or "one element of the experience floods through the work, in such a way as to make it relevant in its own right, outside the conventional terms" (*LR* 85). The novels and novelists that do this preeminently are *Wuthering Heights*, the "early parts of *Mary Barton* . . . Charlotte

Brontë, taking lonely personal desire to an intensity that really questions the conventions by which it is opposed," and Dickens, especially in those fictions that center on the orphan or exposed child (*LR* 85). Moreover, although these novels too "grasp" at magical solutions, "in the end" the "intensity of the central experience is on record and survives them" (*LR* 85).

It is these fictions, most of them by women and about them, with their "lonely exposed figures," the ungendered "orphan," "child" as well as the "governess, the girl from a poor family" (*LR* 85), fictions that are often the "ones less concerned with the problems of society" (*LR* 84), that most fully expressed through an "irresistible authenticity," "a *general* judgement of the human quality of the whole way of life" (*LR* 85). These fictions, Williams argued, exemplified the "reality" that lay below the confidence that is assumed by the social character—they acted, we may say, extending Williams's own argument a little, as a kind of oppositional "structure of feeling" though, as he said, with the connection to the "ordinary structure of feeling" still visible (*LR* 8). What these fictions of female isolation and male infantile helplessness (itself syntagmatically allied with the experience of women) textualized was, in fact, nothing less than "Man alone, afraid, a victim . . . the enduring experience." Overwhelmingly it was women's writing, and often, though not exclusively, women's narrative within the text, that expressed a transclass, transgendered condensation of the fears differentially engendered in the poor and the well-to-do by the social conflicts and social changes that Williams, earlier in the chapter, marked out as the defining events of the decade.

If we go back to the "seven features" that he saw as dominating the "general political and social history" we can now see what an extraordinary claim he was making for these particular texts. These features were: the repeal of the Corn Laws, the re-creation of the Tory Party under Disraeli, Chartism, factory legislation, the amendment of the Poor Law, the Public Health Act of 1848, and the "re-involvement of the churches . . . in social conflict" (*LR* 74). Each of these featured events and the narratives attached to them, from today's feminist vantage point, were gendered narratives, carrying momentous implications for the lives of women. I myself would want to argue that most of Williams's "seven features" were overtly textualized in Brontë's *Jane Eyre* together with issues of race, nation, and empire that were significantly absent from Williams's sketch of the period's social and political landmarks. That was not, however, the argument *he* was making. For him *Jane Eyre* was primarily the story of "lonely personal desire," and it is in such stories that the symbolic anxieties of those who live in the "shadow of the social character"—or to put in another equally melodramatic way, in the chasm opened by a structure of feeling that implied that "there could be no general solution to the social problems of the time" (*LR* 84)—were most fully, intensely expressed.

In a sense this structure of feeling and this generic human response was the reverse of a romantic megalomania that saw, as Williams said elsewhere, "the poet as legislator" (*CS* 265). It was as Williams situated it, but not as he described it, the emergence of an individuality perversely marked by romantic abjection vis-à-vis the social, its loneliness and isolation a function of its desperation at the level of social and psychic need. A feminist rereading of Williams's analysis, one that adds the category of gender to his remarkable documentation of its presence, might well *want* to argue that this position in the 1840s was most forcefully and intensively represented across the fractures of class and gender by the liminal figure of the governess, or by the ailing Paul Dombey and his neglected sister Florence, that the abjection of the starving adult poor and the frightened bourgeoisie *does* necessarily find its generic figuration in what is culturally marked as the feminine. But such a reading would have to go on to grapple with that movement noted earlier in women's fiction in the period toward the protofeminist assertion of women's authority—the move that had made Williams so uneasy in his reading of Mrs. Gaskell. That agressive and aggrandizing trajectory is suppressed in "The Analysis of Culture" on behalf of a more abstract and idealized version of these fictions.

For Williams too in this essay, the representations of women in the generic popular fictions read, if not always written, in the decade were dominated by a kind of willing abjection; in these texts women are "weak, dependent, and shown as glad to be so" (*LR* 81). It is significant that he saw the forties as the *end* of a period when both an older model of the "cultivated gentlemen" and the new masculine hero, "the successful exponent of self-help," can still "burst into public tears, or even swoon" (*LR* 81). This observation, which he carried forward into several of his responses to questions about gender in the 1980s, was Williams's single negotiation, in this essay, of historical changes in the representations and relations of men and women. In a sense, however, the whole trajectory of his argument, which gave fiction by and about women such a transcendent role in articulating the human suffering and the anxiety set in motion by the social crisis, mirrored the change he was describing. Through their expressive rendering of a suffering both obliquely and overtly coded as feminine, these novels articulated a general anguish that male writers and grown men, especially heroes, conforming to shifts in the social character would find it increasingly difficult to represent. *Dombey and Son*, the odd male text in this group, was the kind of exception that proved the rule, for its story writes the tragic and pathological effects of a dominant masculinity without tears. Yet if for Williams it was female anomie, anguish, and abjection that in the 1840s expressed a generic human condition, and in so doing created a fiction of "radical human dissent" that put "the intensity of the central experience on record" (*LR* 85), it was vital to avoid making the gendered nature of this development too explicit. The function of these "creative" texts in Williams's analysis was to represent something of the social totality, to go beyond the decade's confrontations and alterities to an experience shared, however unevenly, by the culture as a whole. Conceptually the "structure of feeling" made some of these connections, but as Williams conceived it, it was neither unifying in its effects nor constant in its intensities (*LR* 80, 85). The word *general* is repeated again and again toward the end of the essay in the course of Williams's search to find a contemporary form that will capture it, for the general could not, in his view, be simply the donnée of the interpreting historian. Insofar as he did find an example of the general, it was in *Wuthering Heights*, a fiction "in which the complicated barriers of a system of relationships are broken through" by an "absolute" if transgressive "human commitment" (*LR* 86). Yet for this novel to embody "radical dissent" in the broader terms Williams sought here, the sexual and gendered nature of its revolt and its commitment could not be directly named.

The veiled and slightly overwrought climax of this important essay cannot help but evoke a certain impatience, read today. It seems slightly ludicrous that *Wuthering Heights* should be drafted to represent a symbolic narrative of the common potential for social transformation, transcending abjection and succeeding where *Mary*

Barton, for instance, had so significantly failed. It is maddening to watch Williams as he produced yet another abstraction of the novel, especially one that is so peculiarly withholding about the sexual and emotional register of its rebellions and commitments. Must there be fictions, after all, that stand witness to a "general" condition in any historical conjuncture? From a fully Marxist or feminist position there need not be, probably cannot be, such a "general" condition or text; nevertheless, a stubborn desire for such an inclusive representation is a tension within reforming, utopian, and revolutionary projects. Even acknowledging that recalcitrant desire, if we engage gender and sexuality as deeply contested and shifting terrains in the 1840s it will be hard to press the work of Charlotte, Anne, or Emily Brontë into such symbolic service.

Almost all of the argument in "The Analysis of Culture" would, in "Forms of Fiction" be translated or reworked into Williams's version of Marxism. But this longing for some material embodiment of the "general," within the historical moment, working through and past the lived structures of feeling that too often insisted, gloomily, that "there is no general solution" to social conflict, could not be so revised, although they remained a constant leitmotiv in Williams's work. In "The Analysis of Culture" the remarkable refusal to designate the arena of conflict in which the "radical dissent" of the Brontës was fought became almost tantamount to a refusal of sexual difference itself. Here the conceptual disavowal of difference allowed the male critic the kind of unstable identification—in the other direction both of class and gender—that Mrs. Gaskell made with John Barton. This identification could remain intact, as long as it was couched in terms of the "general" and rendered either as the abjection of extreme need or as a commitment so extreme that, like Cathy and Heathcliff's, it could only be "realized through death." In this identification the boundaries of the self could be threatened or dissolved as long as that self did not have to acknowledge a difference and conflict between the sexes that, like so many other differences and conflicts, might not admit of a general resolution. In its own way Williams's condition for the elevation of these texts was his version of the magical resolution that he so neatly exposed elsewhere, its sleight of hand effecting a premature sublation that masked the terms of struggle in the society of which it spoke.

The Fiction of the Forties Meets Contemporary Feminism

The essays so far explored, from the late 1950s and early 1960s, were written in that historical period between first- and second-wave feminism when the position of women was almost wholly kept out of socialist and progressive agendas. Williams's work on the mid-nineteenth century, as we have seen, was remarkable in that it brought the question of gender forward through the heightened attention he gave to women's writing; his most important and iconoclastic move was to draw the novels of the Brontës, those novels "less concerned with the problems of society," into a vital relationship with the social changes and crises that shaped the decade. Yet the cost of that connection was that the overt themes of the novels—sexuality, sexual difference, and gender—appeared for an instant only, and then in the most gnomic reference possible, before they were abstracted to a generic plane where they virtually represented the universal human condition—"man alone."

By 1970 and 1978, when Williams published again on the Brontës and on the 1840s, such unqualified effacement of the sexual politics in these novels was no longer quite possible. Williams's essay "Charlotte and Emily Brontë" in *The English Novel* was a liminal text, an essay crafted from lecture notes made and delivered between 1961 and 1968 and written up in 1969, the year in which, roughly speaking, the women's movement came to Britain, catching the political imagination of, among others, just those socialist women intellectuals for whom Williams's work was so fundamental. The main thrust of Williams's essay was clearly to correct, clarify, and unpack the claims he had made for the Brontës' fiction in *The Long Revolution*, to rationalize the relationship between these fictions of "passion" and "desire" and the effects of "industrial dislocation." In doing so he firmly rejected "symbolic" readings of *Wuthering Heights* that emphasized the mystical, melodramatic, or romantic (*LR* 64); he turned away too from Marxist critics' wholesale attempt to render the novel as a social text of class conflict with Heathcliff as the proletariat. He argued that

> social experience, just because it is social, does not have to appear in any way exclusively in these overt public forms. In its very quality as social reality it penetrates, is already at the roots of, relationships of

every kind. We need not look only, in a transforming history, for direct or public historical event and response. When there is real dislocation it does not have to appear in a strike or in machine breaking. It
can appear as radically and as authentically in what is apparently,
what is actually personal or family experience. Any direct reference of
Wuthering Heights to that transforming social crisis seems to me then
displaced, for this exact reason: that its real social experience is then
explicitly reduced. . . . What we have again to say is that social experience is a whole experience. Its descriptive or analytic features have no
priority over its direct realisation in quite physical and specific personal feelings and actions. (*LR* 65)

"What we have again to say . . . " In the years following 1970 feminism would be saying something quite like this, glossing and elaborating the phrase that, more than any other, distinguishes the perspectives of the second wave of the women's movement: "the
personal is political." Williams himself was moving on a kind of parallel track—parallel but never convergent, for "personal" and "family"
cannot stand in for the particular, historical experience of women or
substitute for an analysis that makes gender and sexuality a primary
determinant of culture. In this 1970 essay he initiated the argument
that was elided in his earlier discussion of the Brontës, now highlighting the specific focus of these novels of "intense personal feeling" on love and desire; moreover, he rooted these emotions as they
were expressed in the 1840s within a world where the social and
psychological have not become separate categories. This world for
Williams was "the world of Blake: a world of desire and hunger, of
rebellion and of pallid convention: the terms of desire and fulfill-
ment and the terms of oppression and deprivation profoundly connected in a single dimension of experience" (*LR* 60). The genealogical linking of the Brontës with male romanticism, with Blake, Keats,
Shelley, and Byron, made in the first two pages of the essay, was, as
Williams might say, decisive, for it allowed Charlotte and Emily
(Emily especially) to become speakers in a radical tradition in which
the unmet needs and desires of men and women existed—if only in
Blake and only there in a "unity" the poet could "barely maintain"—
in a "single dimension of experience" (*LR* 60, 61). In the pages that
follow this opening, Williams attempted, in a half-hearted, half-
baked way, to set up a historical framework for looking at gender,
specifying first the changes in masculine training and behavior

through which men "learned not to cry" (*LR* 62, 63). In this new culture of "rigidity," which included "public soberness of dress," it was up to the women writers, from the Brontës through George Eliot, inscribing themselves in the dominant "masculine mode," to "keep alive" and "newly affirm" the world of feeling, which Williams asserted was not only "keeping a woman's world going" but a "human world" (*LR* 62). The problem for women writers as seen through the eyes of the "male middle-class," which are hard to distinguish in this particular passage from Williams's own eyes, was largely a matter of their breaking through the "repressive, unfeminine, dowdy" image of the governess, an image of asexuality (*LR* 63).

In this essay, then, the Brontës became both the keepers of an idealized and unified world of intense feeling that is integrally social as well as personal and the initiators of new modes of expression for those feelings lost, somewhere just after the mid-century, to men. "Multipersonal and varied in consciousness," set in what he tellingly called a "border country," *Wuthering Heights* was Williams's favorite fiction in this mode. He approved Cathy's "central affirmation—not desire *for* another but desire *in* another" (*LR* 66) and touchingly memorialized the psychic dislocation that is the effect of Heathcliff's "mourned loss" of her. This novel that Williams thought "might seem . . . a novel without a history: a novel without precedents or descendants" (*LR* 63) he reread as a fiction of origins, framing it as the lost world of

> reciprocated feeling, literally a relationship: that kind of relationship which is truly given rather than taken, which is there and absolute before anything can be said. In its quality as given—here in a childhood, a shared childhood in a place—it is where social and personal, one's self and others, grow from a single root. (*LR* 67)

This figuring of the maternal (for what other love is like the one just described, and so distinct from the more adversarial and sexual relationship of Cathy Earnshaw and Heathcliff?) and its merging with the communal, the world of childhood in another border country, unintentionally revealed the place of *Wuthering Heights* in Williams's own lost and longed-for utopia. *Wuthering Heights* was the "multipersonal" text that represented the idea of "one's self and others" generated from a source, the "single root" both phallic and maternal, "where the light falls from so many directions, in so many accents, on an intensity of stated relationship which is examined and lasts, persists, through the intricacies of observation and of time" (*LR* 73).[10]

Williams sharply distinguished this generative and productive world from that created by Charlotte Brontë's "subjective single and immediate" (*LR* 71) voice, the voice that "stands . . . at the head of a tradition" initiating in its narrative method "the fiction of special pleading" (*LR* 73). For while, in Williams's analysis, the "connecting power of Charlotte Brontë's fiction is in just this first-person capacity to compose an intimate relationship with the reader," he argued that this power is used to construct a "secret sharing," with distinctly conspiratorial overtones, so that there are "things the reader knows but the others—the other characters, the outside world—do not" (*LR* 69). What Williams was overtly describing was an innovative reading relation, the invention of voice and address through which Charlotte Brontë's texts invited, defined, and positioned an audience; his eloquent and precise description of these textual effects, however, seems driven by an admiration crossed with fear. In Charlotte Brontë, in *Jane Eyre* but especially in *Villette*, he found this intensity terrifying in both its inclusions and its exclusions. The "'I' of the novel and the subjective position—the only available position" (*LR* 69, 70) of the reader he rendered as

> private confidence, this mode of confession: the account given as if in a private letter, in private talk; the account given to a journal, a private journal, and then the act of writing includes—as it were involuntarily, yet it is very deliberate and conscious art—the awareness of a friend, the close one, the unknown but in this way intimate reader: the reader *as* the writer, while the urgent voice lasts. (*LR* 70)

The absence of choice in the matter of readerly identification that this subjective mode constructs—an identification in this case of the male reader with the female writer/speaker and its suffocating, almost claustrophobic quality, implied in Williams's insistent repetition of *private* in conjunction with *confidence, confession,* and *intimate*—constitutes this imposed identification as both scary and, in some awful way, unwilling and involuntary; the reader is forced, by a "deliberate and conscious" artistic seduction, not only to listen to but also to *be* the urgent voice of "special pleading." The generic power of that "private" voice is tipped toward the traditionally feminine modes of discourse—the letter, the conversation, the journal—never meant to be exposed in the public sphere. At the risk of over-reading this passage, its tone, itself so affectively urgent and in excess of its rhetorical analysis, carries for me something distinct if undefined of the coercive rather than generative side of the maternal relation, a trace of the mother's insistence that the child listen to and identify with *her*. Certainly it is in direct contrast with the pleasurable voluntary identification with Emily Brontë's voice or, perhaps more specifically, a woman's identification—"desire in another"—both willing and involuntary, with her man. At a somewhat different but not unrelated level, Charlotte's particular deployment of the subjective voice represented for Williams the dark side, the morally corrupt and politically questionable, even the mad side, of that historically developing interiority, the self-conscious evocation of a monstrous individuality, here specifically *female* individuality, in which "the persons outside this shaping longing demanding consciousness have reality only as they contribute to the landscape, the emotional landscape, of the special, the pleading, the recommending character" (*LR* 74). At the end of the essay his own prose fell apart in an extraordinary way, miming the imploring, staccato stream of consciousness he cited from Charlotte Brontë. Stigmatizing that consciousness as providing a rationale for manipulation and abuse, he claimed that

> some extraordinary things have been done in its name: use of others, abuse of others; a breakdown of discourse—and with discourse so much else, so many other needs and realities—as the all-including voice, the voice pleading for this experience, for understanding of it, for the exclusion of alternatives—alternative voices, alternative viewpoints—comes through and creates its own world. (*LR* 74)

This attack, which itself feels both "involuntary" and "deliberate and conscious," bears some ironic similarities to Williams's insight into the half-conscious reasons for Mrs. Gaskell's creation of John Barton as murderer. In "Charlotte and Emily Brontë" Williams projected onto the composite figure of Charlotte Brontë/Lucy Snowe a violence he first creates and then judges. In this passage it is obliquely implied that certain aspects of the claims of expressive female agency—those that insisted on the value of the private, of psychological interiority, and, perhaps, of the particularity of women's experience of them—demanded a kind of singular identification that, in excluding "alternatives," was murderous of "others." It seems eerily to prefigure and to condense both in its choice of target and its specific accusations much early and still existing reaction against elements in contemporary feminism, a reaction mainly but by no means exclusively male. I want to pause for a moment to read it, anachronistically, as an early if unacknowledged form of that response. We can trace the escalation of its critique from Brontë's secrecy and solipsism, shared only with readers/friends narcissistically imagined as the self, to her unreasonable demand for empathy, to her supposed destruction of all competing "needs and realities" and "viewpoints"—which we may conjecture are those of class as well as of gender. As a critique of feminism—one that, we must emphasize, Williams never overtly made—it has been an especially harsh judgment when it has come from progressive men: socialist men aiming, like feminists, to imagine and enable an alternative world more democratic, integrated, and communal. If I am right in suggesting that something of this critique is encoded in "Charlotte and Emily Brontë," it is enlightening to understand that in Williams's case it came not only from a projection of fear but also from a prior sympathetic, even idealizing identification with "lonely personal desire." We can recognize too in the terrain this essay opened up about desire and identification, as well as in its defensive and aggressive moves across it, an agonized understanding that a mutual identification across gender lines was at stake in the historical process through which modern subjectivity was made. The importance of this insight, which in very simple as well as very complex ways also produced Williams's "recoil," cannot be underestimated, although it has taken some time for feminist theorists and historians to see it as central. Neither should we be tempted to read Williams's reaction as a reflex outside history. As I hope Williams himself might accept (although this hope is a form of impossible desire) it is the historically specific context of that "recoil" as well as of the emergence of Charlotte Brontë's idiosyncratic and emblematic voice that needs—even now—further interrogation.

The first time I heard Williams speak was to my knowledge the last time he formally considered the 1840s in any detail. The occasion was the 1977 Sociology of Literature Conference at the University of

Essex, an annual meeting of socialist literary and cultural critics. Our theme was the year 1848. In a small way it was a historic event for me and for the nine other attending members of the Marxist-Feminist Literature Collective, for we collectively presented the distillation of two years' work, a collectively written paper on "Women's Writing: *Jane Eyre, Shirley, Villette, Aurora Leigh*."[11] Standing together at the front of the conference in plenary session we each read, in turn, a short section of the paper to a somewhat incredulous audience. Our presentation was both a display of power and a spectacular demonstration of our critique of the "isolated individualistic ways in which we operate in academic spheres" (*LR* 185). In the paper we attempted a synthesis of Marxism and psychoanalysis, making use of Althusser, Lacan, Kristeva, and Macherey in order to challenge English male Marxist critics in both their marginalization of women writers and their lack of an analysis of gender or sexuality. Only Terry Eagleton's book on the Brontës, *Myths of Power: A Marxist Study of the Brontës* (1975), is directly cited as an interpretation we critiqued; we were concerned to confront men of our own generational structure of feeling. Less interested in celebrating the emergent bourgeois voice of the woman writer (although we noted its development in this period), we were attempting to use structuralist and poststructuralist strategies to reintegrate psychic and social analysis. Through an exploration of the subordination of women in the kinship systems of the mid-nineteenth century we highlighted the importance of understanding the assertion of female desire within and against its exploitative terms. That paper was a crude collage—our cosmetic term was "polyphonic"—and it begged as many questions as it asked, not least about the theory we were deploying, but it did succeed, I think, in trying out a new set of questions. To what extent our feminist academic chorus line incited or dispelled male anxieties about contemporary feminism, a reflex well established by 1977, it was hard then and harder now to tell.

I place us in this scenario because our somewhat disruptive presence was a documentation of the shift in the structure of feeling of my generation about the question of sexual politics—and here I am using Williams's term in its most useful but elusive sense as the lived affect of a time, its dynamic, ephemeral stories that hold and revise the contradictions between its competing ideologies and between these and their radical oppositions and alternatives. I could read our presence at this event as both oppositional and alternative and our piece as completely at odds with Williams's "Forms of Fiction," which was, I believe, the closing talk. But this was not the case; our affiliations at the conference were more complicated, even paradoxical. In our rather awkward use of French theory we were, for example, part of what Williams feared was becoming the new, and he felt conservative, theoretical orthodoxy. Not of course an enemy of theory, but a skeptic when it came to some of its conjunctural embodiments, he could, as in "Crisis in English Studies" (1981), eloquently defend the importance of even those developments with which he was least in sympathy.[12] Yet his critiques of structuralism and of Lacanian versions of psychoanalysis around this time are often severe. He saw them as, among other things, reifying the historic divisions that had inexorably formed between the social and the psychological, as reducing the dynamism and complexity of a constantly changing and interactive set of effects by examining them in a synchronic framework, and as setting up separate histories that ought to be considered relationally. The closest paper to our own at the conference, both in theoretical sympathies and in its mode of tackling gender, although we disagreed with its argument, was not any of the other women's papers on women writers but Terry Eagleton's Lacanian reading of masculinity in Tennyson's *The Princess*.[13]

Williams's talk, "Fictions of Form," was for me the most intellectually memorable event of the conference, although some of it is a repetition and much a reworking of "The Analysis of Culture" and the essays on Dickens and the Brontës in *The English Novel*. His argument about old and new discourses was now rearticulated in the categories of the residual, dominant, and emergent culture, a more precise but also more emotionally distant paradigm. He used the occasion of this talk to refine his distinctions between the different modalities of "subjectivist intensity" in Dickens, Gaskell, the Brontës, and Thackeray, rendering them in terms of their different kinds of enunciation, and through the appropriation of the concept of "deep structure." He was remarkably generous toward those emergent forms, commenting on

> the finitely significant openness of certain of the new impulses . . . for these, as new content, and as new forms of the content, are genuinely

> emergent elements . . . attempting to lift certain pressures, to push
> back certain limits, in a fully extended production, bearing the full
> weight of the pressure and limits, in ways which simple forms, the
> simple contents, of mere ideological reproduction never achieve. (*FF*
> 290)

His emphasis here was on the plurality of strategies within the
larger category of the "autobiographical" or personal. Urging us to
take the time to explore the oppositions and connections within the
emergent, he argued strongly against the reductive move that would
inscribe all these texts as the same version of bourgeois ideology.
The Brontës do not figure quite so prominently in this piece; they
are part of a larger, more finely tuned arrangement of emergent
voices, and Charlotte's "special pleading," which he mentioned
briefly and critically again, did not appear as such a dangerously en-
gulfing and aggrandizing solo. I speculate now that for Williams
feminism as part of a public discourse was much less threatening—
or intriguing—than in its shaping personal registers in the nineteenth-century novel. Reading this essay next to its predecessors,
one is struck, after acknowledging the brilliance of its nuanced, original discussion of form, by how very abstractly the social, the psychic, and even the political and literary are figured, as if the grounds
of the discussion, the turbulent history of the 1840s or the contro-
versal texts themselves, no longer need to be imaginatively called
up because they are presumed to be so well known and so worked
over by critic and audience.

But it seemed more than that, too. I remember that in listening to
the talk I was frustrated by its unwillingness to spell out the "radical
intensities," to give them emotional and material specificity. Questions of form and address displaced the troubling contents that, in
1970, Williams struggled to engage. All three of his discussions of the
1840s cry out for a more exact and probing understanding of subjectivity, of the psyche, of sexual difference, yet after all they unfolded
for feminism as the work of no other writer on the period has done,
a landscape for our further exploration. Although he would engage
generously if critically with feminist work, notably in his reviews of
Barbara Taylor's *Eve and the New Jerusalem* and Carolyn Steedman's *Landscape for a Good Woman*,[14] it never became a focus of
interest in later years. Still, it is as if in some way that could never,

for reasons I have offered in this essay, be brought fully to consciousness or enunciation, he carried those issues in embryo with
him and they found their articulation, as he often pointed out such
shaping, inchoate questions do, in the form and emphases of these
pieces discussed here that so powerfully center women's writing. By
1977 other voices had provided an articulation of the issues, at odds
with his own, but nevertheless out there, attempting, as he suggested about earlier forms of the emergent, "to lift certain pressures,
pushing back certain limits, in a fully extended production, bearing
the full weight of the pressure and limits" (*FF* 290). Perhaps this explains in part why "Forms of Fiction" itself lacked just those "radical
intensities" of his earlier work on the 1840s, when he was working
this vein freshly and with more intellectual elbow room. For all its
brilliance, this last essay, especially at its close, feels somewhat hol-
low and gestural. The passage from the end, twice quoted here, performs a kind of poetic hydraulics that fails to indicate *what* weight
is being redistributed—as if Williams had, with some relief perhaps,
abandoned the struggle to find a language of theory or of feeling, or
even a historical narrative that could convey concretely what actually *was* so progressive in the subjectivist mode initiated in the 1840s.

Yet if, in conclusion, we return to the kind of historic parallels I
have been drawing between Williams's own intellectual and political trajectories and those of second-wave feminism, we can see how
the paradoxes crystallized for him in those emergent female voices
of the nineteenth century are intimately related to the problems
they have come to pose for contemporary feminist analysis. The
breakup of a class-based politics in Britain, well advanced by 1977,
together with the fragmentation of the women's movement under
the pressure of Thatcherism, weakened the socialist-feminist project
of integrating the "personal" into old and new collective social agendas. More generally, in the anglophone left's autocritique of its failure to resist the ascendance of right-wing governments and ideologies, the "personal" and psychological paradigms of social movement
politics were frequently elided with the triumph of a reactionary individualism. At the same time, British and American feminism,
under pressure from its left wing for a more developed class analysis, and from black and postcolonial feminism for a fuller history of
the relationship between feminism, gender, and imperialism, began
to read its eighteenth- and nineteenth-century origins in a less cele-

bratory mode. By the mid-1980s an interrogation of the bourgeois and imperialist origins of anglophone feminism was under way—one in which what Gayatri Chakravorty Spivak has memorably called the "cult" texts of the Brontës have figured prominently. This ongoing genealogical exploration has become more historically located and politically nuanced, complicating its early ethical stance and therefore its implications for contemporary feminism. What we might highlight here, apropos of the parallels I have been tracing, is that this new critique initially denied to these writers and their fictions both the gender-specific radicalism of their protofeminism—the theme of 1970s feminist interpretation—and the generalizing power of their subversive, if subjective, opposition to convention, the positive pole of Williams's analysis. Following its distinctive logics, feminism has, surprisingly, reproduced in certain aspects of its revaluation of its origins its own version of Williams's impasse, the product of his most pessimistic thinking, which argues that the subjective voice offers the fullest symbolic expression to the most general forms of human alienation, repression, and subordination while acting, in its very emergence as a particularly gendered voice, as a destructive force that not only breaks up or challenges other solidarities and perspectives, but also threatens to efface them. The appearance *within* feminist debate of that paralyzing paradigm in which gender functions primarily as a device for describing classic oppositions needs to be explained—and resisted—in the broader context in which contemporary cultural analysis has developed, through an analysis of the imbrication of its several strands. Looking back, Williams seems only too prescient in his early and unhappy intuition that the subjective voice of modernity, identified as a woman's voice, might remain, rightly or wrongly, a disturbing register of the contradictions and paradoxes of the modern.

NOTES

1. See Raymond Williams, *Culture and Society 1780-1950* (Harmondsworth: Penguin, 1963), chapter 5; *The Long Revolution* (Harmondsworth: Penguin, 1965), pp. 57-88; and "Forms of Fiction," in *1848: The Sociology of Literature: Proceedings of the Essex Conference on the Sociology of Literature, July 1977*, ed. Frances Barker et al. (Wivenhoe: University of Essex, 1978), pp. 277-90. Subsequent references to these sources are cited in the text as *CS, LR,* and *FF.*

2. Raymond Williams, *The English Novel from Dickens to Lawrence* (London: Hogarth, 1984), pp. 60-74; "that remarkable generation . . . " from "Media, Margins and Modernity:

Raymond Williams and Edward Said," *The Politics of Modernism*, ed. Tony Pinckney (London: Verso, 1989), p. 195.

3. Morag Shiach, "A Gendered History of Cultural Categories," chapter 2 of this volume.

4. These responses are discussed by Morag Shiach in chapter 2 and by Carol Watts in "Reclaiming the Border Country: Feminism and the Work of Raymond Williams," *News from Nowhere* 6 (1989): 89–107. The longer passage from "Media, Margins and Modernity" cited earlier is of particular interest because it focuses on the 1840s.

5. Morag Shiach notes in chapter 2 that "the silence is eerie, though whether it is polite or angry is hard to tell."

6. See especially Nancy Armstrong, *Desire and Domestic Fiction: A Political History of the Novel* (New York: Oxford University Press, 1987), chapter 4; Gayatri Chakravorty Spivak, "Three Women's Texts and a Critique of Imperialism," in *"Race," Writing and Difference*, ed. Henry Louis Gates Jr. (Chicago: University of Chicago Press, 1986), pp. 262–80. Carolyn Steedman brings Williams and Armstrong usefully together on this issue in an essay in part to do with Williams and gender: "Culture, Cultural Studies, and Historians," in *Cultural Studies*, ed. Lawrence Grossberg, Cary Nelse, and Paula Treichler (New York: Routledge, 1992), pp. 613–21.

7. See Leonore Davidoff and Catherine Hall, "'A modest competency': Men, Women and Property," *Family Fortunes: Men and Women of the English Middle Class, 1780–1850* (London: Hutchinson, 1987), chapter 4.

8. Raymond Williams, *Politics and Letters: Interviews with New Left Review* (London: New Left Books, 1979), part 2.

9. Williams, "Marxism and Society," *Culture and Society*, pp. 258–75.

10. It is also figured as the ideal world of passive, receptive femininity, "a country waiting to be entered" (*Long Revolution*, p. 66).

11. In *1848: The Sociology of Literature*, pp. 185–206.

12. *New Left Review* 129 (1981), reprinted in *Writing in Society* (London: Verso, 1983). See especially his comment on psychoanalysis that "Marxism had been generally weak in this area of the problems of subjectivity, and there might be a radical new dimension of enquiry, testing evidence and propositions in this area which is so evidently important in the production of meanings and values" (p. 210).

13. "Tennyson: Politics and Sexuality in 'The Princess' and 'In Memoriam,'" in *1848: The Sociology of Literature*, 97–106.

14. "The New Morality," *Guardian*, March 17, 1983, p. 16; "Desire," reprinted in Raymond Williams, *What I Came to Say* (London: Hutchinson, 1989), 295–313. See Morag Shiach's discussion of these pieces in chapter 2 of this volume.

Raymond Williams and Marxism
John Brenkman

Reds

For twenty years Western Marxists looked back to two historic moments to guide our theoretical work on society and culture: 1917 and 1968. As symbols, as historic watersheds, as reminder and conscience of political struggle, the Russian Revolution and then the events in Prague, Paris, and Mexico City and in the United States at the Democratic convention in Chicago and at Columbia University stimulated important work in every field of social and cultural theory.

As each generation of Marxists has faced coming to terms with Stalin, "Soviet Marxism," or "actually existing socialism," it has developed various explanations for the fate of the Russian Revolution. And at each turn there have been attempts to consolidate—and withstand—the criticisms of the Soviet Union by renewing the notion that 1917 remained a starting point and a benchmark for socialism in the twentieth century.

The proximity of the uprisings in Paris and Prague in 1968 gave a new twist to these resurrections of the Russian Revolution, namely, the belief that the struggle against Western imperialism and capitalism and the struggle against state socialism and Soviet hegemony were two sides of the same coin. The challenge to Western capitalism, we believed, would turn out to belong to the same struggle as the challenge to Soviet totalitarianism. From this perspective, the Russian Revolution could once again become a revolutionary starting point. From this conjuncture flowed Rudolph Bahro's critique of actually existing socialism.

The sentiment that the revolutionary legacy had a future pervades a good deal of writing throughout the 1970s and into the 1980s, but the future began to dim as the decade of Thatcher and Reagan took hold tooth and claw. The 1980s rapidly eroded the whole project in which Marxist theory attempted to preserve the expectations and transformations of the 1960s.

An emblem of Marxist theory in the Thatcher-Reagan decade is furnished in the film written by Hanif Kureishi, *My Beautiful Laundrette.* Omar's Papa is a Pakistani journalist and socialist. Ailing and alcoholic, he lies bedridden in London watching his son trim his toenails for him. He berates Omar for succumbing to his rich uncle's enticements and admonishes him, "You've got to study. We are under siege by the white man. For us education is power." The socialist's son, however, is smitten with Thatcherite ambition and wants only to make money managing his uncle's laundrette. When Papa stumbles into the laundrette's grand opening hours late and encounters Johnny, Omar's long-time friend, a former skinhead turned entrepreneur, he can only shake his head and sigh, "The working class is such a great disappointment to me."

When this decade of greed and social regression in the West then culminated, so unexpectedly, in the revolutions of 1989 in the East, critical Marxism found itself, I believe, at an ultimate impasse. There were of course last gasps: "Now that the Soviet perversion of socialism has collapsed the West can finally have a genuine debate on socialism!" "The events in Eastern Europe finally prove that even actually existing socialism contained an inner dynamic propelling it toward change!" Despite such absurd claims, the liberation of Eastern Europe *from* socialism has shattered the mythological value of the Russian Revolution. It is no longer a meaningful starting point for envisioning social and political change. When the Berlin Wall fell, Humpty-Dumpty could not be put back together again.

The very project of critical or Western Marxism has been thrown into question. I do not mean to suggest that it is implicated in the fallen regimes. The differences in political conviction between Western and Soviet Marxism, or between critical and scientific Marxism, ran deep. What counts, rather, is that Western Marxism could not provide the intellectual tools or the political vocabulary that the peoples and movements of the former Soviet Union and Eastern Europe—let alone China—needed to struggle for their freedoms and rights and for justice within their societies. Western Marxism proved irrelevant to the great revolutionary moment at the end of the twentieth century.

As a result, socialism has been left to appear antithetical to democracy. Conversely, the anachronistic notion that capitalism is the cradle of democracy has gained prestige worldwide. Thatcherism and Reaganism have scored an unanticipated ideological victory that will continue to influence the processes of social and political renewal going forward in Eastern Europe and the former Soviet Union.

What then does it mean today to take up the topic of Raymond Williams's contribution to Marxism? It cannot be a matter of looking to his works simply for paths out of the current impasse. As regards Marxism itself, I believe the impasse is permanent. The need is for a rearticulation of socialism and democracy. And Williams's contribution to that theoretical and political task, which requires a critique rather than a renewal of Marxism, was immense.

As a novelist, Williams found sources for this articulation of socialism and democracy in his own earliest experiences as the child of working-class parents. As a political thinker, he sought to link socialism and democracy by interrogating the meaning of revolution and the vocabularies of modern politics. As critic and teacher, he revitalized socialist thought through his commitments to the democratization of culture. Through this multiplicity of his writing—fiction, politics, criticism—there emerges, I hope to show, a profound working through of some of the most urgent political and cultural issues of our time.

In the Name of the Father

It is significant that Williams's own historical benchmarks were not 1917 and 1968. They were 1926 and 1966, the year of the General Strike in Great Britain and the year that the Labour Party's return to power revealed how intent it was to make its pact with capitalism, NATO, and American imperialism. In 1926 Williams's father joined the General Strike at great risk to his own well-being and his family's. In 1966 Williams himself left the Labour Party, with a pained and ominous sense that the future of socialism had just become far more difficult and far riskier.

Williams's most important intellectual contributions to literary and cultural studies were, I will argue, efforts to keep faith with these two historic moments and with the choices he and his father made in their drastically different circumstances. I am not thereby restricting the relevance of his thought to its national context—as though to explain what makes his Marxism *so British*—nor am I suggesting that the biographical benchmarks limit the import of his work. On the contrary, these pressures coming from his own political experience animate his thought and are key to its broader validity. Historical thinking cannot test its validity except against history, a history that is concrete and pressing.

Williams was five years old, his father barely thirty, at the time of the General Strike. The nation's miners were locked out when they refused a contract calling for dramatic wage cuts; the owners also sought a longer working day and the power to replace nationwide contracts with local agreements. The government of Prime Minister Stanley Baldwin, whose Tories had been brought to power by a red scare in 1924, refused to sustain the miners' wages through subsidies to the coal industry. When talks between the government and the Trades Union Congress broke down, the TUC called for a national strike in support of the beleaguered miners. More than 3 million workers struck for nine days before retreating; the miners suffered utter defeat and were eventually forced to accept the coal industry's conditions.[1]

Williams explored his own relation to these events, and to the continuing importance of the strike in his own life, in his 1962 novel, *Border Country*. He later told an interviewer, "The chapter which describes the Strike is very close to the facts."[2] The autobiographical novel weaves together two stories. Matthew Price, historian and academic, has returned to his family's village in Wales at the time of his father's stroke. In the other, flashed-back strand of the story, the life story of the father, Harry Price, is told in the context of family and community life.

In 1926 Harry Price is a signalman in Gynmawr along with two other men, Morgan Rosser and Jack Merideth. Instructions come from the union to begin a work stoppage on Tuesday morning. Morgan is the local secretary of the railwaymen's union and a dedicated socialist who sees in a general strike a weapon against the capitalist order. "'We're saying we're the country,'" he tells Harry. "'We're the power, we the working class are defying the bosses' government, going to build our own social system.'"[3]

Harry not only resists this view but warns Morgan that it will only backfire in trying to enlist Merideth in the strike. And indeed Merideth does refuse to strike. His is the last shift before the stoppage, and he refuses to sign out until another man comes on. He refuses to shut down the signal box. All three signalmen and their stationmaster, Tom Rees, are in the box that Tuesday morning, stalemated so long as Merideth does not sign out. Finally, Rees tells Merideth he will take over himself. It seems to be the act of a company man taking over his striking subordinate's duties, but as soon as Merideth signs out, Rees himself initiates the strike by closing the box.

By dramatizing the divergent opinions and motives of the three signalmen, Williams attempts to ground his story in their specific experiences of community and work. The men never "represent" ideologies. Harry is not motivated by any of the larger aims, but by his sense of allegiance: "'I'll stand by the miners, if it comes to it.'"

The anticipation of a long strike throws him headlong into efforts to provide for his family. He is desperate to avoid debt. He resolves to pay the rent with a pound from his strike pay and then replenish that with the advance he hopes to get on his monthly one-pound payment as groundskeeper of the village's bowling green. His other savings he had recently spent "on a new honey extractor and a season's supply of jars." How precarious the family's finances might become, how the strike threatens to strain the villagers' reliable relationships with one another, how sullen Harry becomes under all the stresses he bears but refuses to express—all this Williams portrays through a series of small events that occur during the nine days of the strike.

Complicating the texture of this essentially naturalistic narrative is the mixing in of the young son's perspective. His *knowledge* of the events is sharply limited because of his age, and he is shown pursuing his normal activities with friends, school, and church. His *moral experience*, on the other hand, is somehow caught up in the crisis of the strike. Indeed, the specific actions Williams recounts involve guilty actions: a misdeed and a false accusation.

After receiving a book for his part in a church school program, Will (as Matthew was called in childhood) hurls the book into a stream in plain sight of the congregation. His father retrieves it, and the family pass by the gathering of churchgoers, including their landlady, and walk home. The father says not a word until they reach the cottage, and then tells his wife, referring apparently to the humiliations of the community's gaze, "He's got his punishment.'" What Will does not witness is his father's encounter the next day with the landlady, when Harry brings her the rent and apologizes for his son's behavior:

> Mrs Hybart put down the iron, and went across to the fire, "Well, they always say, boy. Like father like son."
> "I don't know what you mean."
> "The father goes on strike, the boy throws the book away."
> "That's altogether different. I'm not apologizing for the strike."
> "Well you ought to. Such daftness."

Having registered her opinion on the strike, Mrs. Hybart then perplexes Harry by refusing to take the rent. "'When it's all over, boy, you can pay me then.'" Her parting words—"'Forget this old strike.'"—reiterate her disapproval. Harry, as though declaring his intention to keep up his commitment to her *and* to the strike, retorts, "'I shan't forget anything.'"

The pound Harry intended for the rent figures in Will's other episode as well, which happened the day before the book-hurling episode. Just after Harry had calculated how he would use his strike pay for the rent and replenish it with his earnings from mowing, he learns that Will has lost the one-pound note a neighbor had given him to buy her groceries. With, as always, determined silence, Harry looks for the money without success, and then takes the family's rent money down to the store, buys the groceries, and delivers them and the change to the neighbor. It turns out, however, that the neighbor had never in fact put the money in the pouch she gave Will. He had been falsely accused of losing it. The scene's denouement includes father, mother, and son:

> "I'm sorry. Honestly, I'm sorry," Harry said, and bent forward so that his head touched the boy's shoulder.

"Not for you to be sorry, Dada," Will said but pushed the head away.

Ellen came in behind them, quietly.

"I got the pound, Harry. And the twopence she made me bring, for Will's sweets."

"I don't want her old twopence," Will shouted.

"Leave it all," Harry said, sharply, and got up. "I'll hear no more about it. Now get the lamp lit, and we'll have some food."

Ellen, suddenly quiet, obeyed.

What began with the accusing father's regret ends with the husband's irritated commands. Harry's money worries toss him from paternal remorse to male authoritarianism. He is caught in the panic of his fear of debt in the midst of the community's ethic of mutual obligation. At the same time, he makes displays of authority to salve his wounded sense of his ability to provide.

While these typical pathologies of working-class men in crisis are rendered crisply as well as sympathetically, Williams's portrayal of Will's moral experience is more complex. What connects the false accusation and the misdeed, the missing money and the damaged book? I think the key lies in how much happens out of Will's earshot. He does not hear Mrs. Hybart compare him to his father. Yet it is by means of this identification of the son with the father on the basis of their misdeeds that the narrative creates a moral reverberation between the childhood memory and the historical record. The child's experience becomes implicated in historical events. In the other episode, the moral resonance lies in the fact that the son is accused of losing money just at the time of the family's greatest need. His negligence not only adds to the father's worries but also intensifies his sense of failure. By the same token, the son's guiltiness is itself very like the father's fear of failing in his responsibilities, and the falseness of the accusations ends up resembling the unjustified scorn the striking father has encountered from the schoolteacher and the landlady. Once again father and son are reflected in one another. Yet all these implications, too, lie just beyond Will's consciousness, since he is not privy to the difficult calculations his father was making at the very moment he himself supposedly lost the money.

The complex tie between the son's experience and the father's resides, therefore, in the connections the *writer* makes, not in those Will could have directly felt. The moral tropes that decisively connect the son's experience to the father's have been constructed in the process of writing. They have been, to use a phrase from Williams's own critical lexicon, actively composed. If the novel is read naturalistically, such constructions are a kind of allegorical overlay. If it is read autobiographically, however, these fabricated parallels between father and son create, retrospectively, the son's *moral* tie to the father's *political* decision.[4]

The trope that makes the son mirror the father also fashions Williams's own relation to 1926. It links the writer and the story, and in turn links past and present in the shape of a moral commitment to the politics of the General Strike. Williams takes on a responsibility to keep faith with the strikers in his own political-intellectual activities, just as he continually pays homage to family and village. When he delivers a commemorative lecture on the fiftieth anniversary of the strike, he barely even alludes to the strike's causes and outcomes. Looking past the strike's failure, he instead stresses the political learning processes it unleashed in the consciousness of ordinary workers. From this perspective, what happened in the Welsh village where his father was a railway signalman becomes a crucially typical rather than peripheral event, the key to a continuing heritage rather than an isolated moment lost in the past.

Heritage of Revolt/Mythology of Revolution

Williams knew in his bones how important it is to keep faith with actual moments of rebellion, with histories of resistance and revolt. Such historical moments are filled with meanings without which our own search for social justice would be lost. The messages they send forth, however, are seldom obvious. Forty or fifty years later, what should be the political form of fidelity to the General Strike? Williams felt that question to be so urgent and so difficult that he had to write a novel to begin working it through. And he continued to work it through in each new political context he faced. Keeping faith requires a recurrent struggle with the meaning of the past as well as the present.

An ambivalence runs through Williams's responses to the resonance between 1926 and contemporary situations and problems. On the one hand, he draws from the General Strike the insight that people's politicization and their readiness to govern themselves follow the arc of their everyday relationships and understandings. He carries this insight into his criticism and teaching. It informs his whole commitment to the democratization of culture. On the other hand, Williams also falls back on a mythology of revolution to interpret the General Strike, casting its brief flowering of direct popular power as a prefiguration of socialism. This interpretation, I will argue, distorts his political reflections on democratic and revolutionary traditions.

Paradoxical as it sounds, his fidelity to the General Strike radicalizes his commitment to the democratization of culture even as it confuses his political understanding of democracy and revolution. First, the problem of Williams's political reflection on democracy and then, in the next section, his contribution to the democratization of culture.

Williams starts out with a cogent account of the impact of the General Strike on the railwaymen, whom he considers genuinely industrial workers even though they were scattered throughout the country and lived in villages and on farms. Their participation in the strike, he argues, led them to see themselves as a force within society as a whole:

> The part of the history that most needs emphasis, and that was actually very evident in that country station and in thousands of other places up and down the country, was the growth of consciousness during that action itself. What began with relative formality, within a representative dimension, became, in its experience, the confidence, the vigour, the practical self-reliance, of which there is so much local evidence; and this was not just the spirit of a fight; it was the steady and remarkable self-realization of the capacity of a class, in its own sufficient social relations and in its potentially positive social and economic power.[5]

This legacy of class consciousness was still palpable to Williams in 1977. A few months after his lecture at the National Union of Mineworkers' anniversary conference at Pontypridd, he wistfully recalled how at that commemorative event "it seemed incredible that there had not been socialism in Britain for fifty years."[6]

In his writings between 1966 and 1977, Williams tends to mythify the leap in consciousness experienced by his father and the other striking workers of 1926. He wants the workers' intensified sense of their power within society to translate, more or less directly, into a vision of a socialist future. Accordingly, the striking railwaymen's self-reliance is made to prefigure—and prepare—what Williams considered the key to socialism: "the direct exercise of popular power."[7]

So what is wrong with this resoundingly democratic slogan? Assuredly, a general strike is a challenge to capitalist enterprises *and* to the government that supports them. There is strong evidence that when British workers confronted the government as an antagonist in 1926, they saw themselves as a class and glimpsed how they might shape the nation. And indeed the concerted collective action that workers undertake in a general strike can prefigure radically widened and deepened participation in political institutions.

The direct exercise of popular power is short-lived, however, whether it succeeds in its immediate goals or not. Direct popular power cannot establish, let alone instantiate, the *forms* of democratic participation. It can create the space for new democratic institutions, and it can bring new participants into the political sphere. But "direct popular power" cannot itself be institutionalized. Increased popular participation requires increases in the mediations, the complexity, the diversity of various decision-making bodies composed of different constituencies, driven by different needs and interests, and probably guided by varying principles and values. Democracy has to guarantee, even foster, plurality.

Williams was too enamored of the moment of class unity briefly embodied in the General Strike. It became the benchmark for his understanding of socialist democracy, especially in *Politics and Letters* and *Keywords* and even in the political essays from the 1980s collected in *Resources of Hope.* He does not fully appreciate the countervailing need for democratic institutions to fracture and diversify power. The solidarity of embattled workers and the bonds of rural communities so dominate Williams's image of socialism that he onesidedly privileges the goal of social unity. Neither individual rights nor the plurality of social life finds an adequate place in his conception of socialist democracy.

The undervaluation of plurality and right is compounded by Williams's antipathy to the electoral process in Western democracies. His attitude congealed in the aftermath of his break with the Labour Party in 1966. Labour had won a hundred-seat majority in Parliament but proceeded to chart a conservative course. Prime Minister Harold

Wilson set out to break a seamen's strike and shortly afterward responded to a currency crisis by devaluing the pound sterling and cutting social programs. These events finalized Williams's sense that "the Labour Party was no longer just an inadequate agency for socialism, it was now an active collaborator in the process of reproducing capitalist society."[8]

Williams joined with E. P. Thompson and Stuart Hall to write the *May-Day Manifesto* in 1967-68. Under its aegis they helped form a national commission of leftist groups. "There was real unity," Williams recalled in his 1976 interviews, "against the Labour government's trade union legislation, against the emergence of Powellism, against the Vietnamese war." But in 1970 the group split four ways and collapsed in response to upcoming national elections. Williams belonged to a group that wanted to run Left Alliance candidates, an alternative that Left Labourites, the Communist Party, and other groups participating in the commission found unacceptable.

The bitterness Williams still felt six years later over the commission's demise expressed itself in a vituperation against elections:

> It never reassembled. A movement which had managed to sustain a significant amount of left unity disintegrated over the electoral process—over whether it was permissible to make electoral interventions to the left of the Labour Party. *A strategy of common activity could survive anything except an election.*[9]

The blame is misplaced, however much the scheduling of elections can be a tactic to blunt opposition. The more salient issue is that the *Manifesto* commission was not yet ready to act in concert in a crisis that tested the various groups' loyalty to the ideologies, programs, and allegiances they had brought with them in the first place. Time never stands still politically, and new political identities always have to ripen in unpredictable weather. There is nothing unique about the electoral process's ability to nip political plans in the bud. Fluctuations in the economy, public opinion, or war can just as unexpectedly deplete or fuel an incipient process of political organization.

Williams's response stems, I believe, from his anger at Labour's betrayal of the legacy of 1926 in 1966. The party of our fathers had sold out the past. It had broken faith with the political traditions that led back to the General Strike. What, then, did it now mean to keep faith in a context where no organization could legitimately claim to be the instrument of workers or the site of their unity?

Deeply troubled by this question, Williams responded with his interpretation of the General Strike as a prefiguration of revolution and socialism. He also began to revise his important concept of the long revolution—by which he had meant that social transformation was never a punctual event but a protracted process of change through many-layered social relationships and feelings. He dissociated the long revolution from electoral politics altogether. And, finally, he moved considerably closer to a kind of rejectionist critique of liberal democratic values.

The new critique of liberal democracy offers itself as a correction to the assumptions behind *The Long Revolution*, published in 1961. "In *The Long Revolution*, I did start to develop a distinction between representative and what I called participatory democracy," he says in reply to a fairly aggressive question from *New Left Review* about the difference between "bourgeois democracy" and "socialist democracy." "However, I certainly had not at that time developed a full critique of the notion of representation, which it now seems to me in its common ideological form is fundamentally hostile to democracy. I think the distinction between representation and popular power has to be now put very sharply."[10]

The opposition between mere representative democracy (equated with electoral politics) and genuine popular power (equated with the General Strike) thematizes, in theoretical terms, the rupture between 1966 and 1926. Williams's important discussion of "democracy" in *Keywords* is flawed precisely to the extent that it employs this theoretical opposition. He construes a polarity in the modern meaning of democracy between socialist and liberal alternatives:

> In the socialist tradition, **democracy** continued to mean *popular power*: a state in which the interests of the majority of the people were paramount and in which these interests were practically exercised and controlled by the majority. In the liberal tradition, **democracy** meant open election of representatives and certain conditions (**democratic rights**, such as free speech) which maintained the openness of election and political argument. These two conceptions, in their extremes, now meet each other as enemies.[11]

This antagonism at the extremes of meaning seems to refer to the cold war confrontation between NATO and the Soviet bloc, at the level of their political systems and of their legitimating rhetorics:

> If the predominant criterion is popular power in the popular interest, other criteria are often taken as secondary (as in the **People's Democracies**) and their emphasis is specialized to "capitalist democracy" or "bourgeois democracy." If the predominant criteria are elections and free speech, other criteria are seen as secondary or are rejected.

The sense of symmetry obfuscates an important difference. The Western democracies actually have elections and various guarantees of free speech, but the regimes of the Soviet Union and Eastern Europe (the "people's democracies") in the 1970s were in no way advancing or institutionalizing "popular power in the popular interest." By failing to account for the specific cynicism and emptiness of Soviet rhetoric or to distinguish its duplicities from those of Western cold war rhetoric, Williams created the impression that the tension between the liberal and socialist understandings of democracy was as stalemated as the cold war itself.

The semantics of extremes grossly oversimplifies the liberal tradition. Western denunciations of the Soviet system in the name of freedom, democracy, or rights have run a complex gamut from demonization to engaged critique. Hannah Arendt, Claude Lefort, and George Konrad cannot be thrown in with the Richard Nixon of the 1950s or the Ronald Reagan of the 1980s.

When Williams turns to spell out what criteria of democracy are subordinated or rejected in the liberal tradition (in symmetry with Soviet denunciations of "bourgeois democracy"), he skips the intricacies of anti-Soviet discourse altogether. Instead, he portrays the liberal tradition quite narrowly in its Tory guise as a repressive force against British labor:

> If the predominant criteria are elections and free speech, other criteria are seen as secondary or are rejected; an attempt to exercise popular power in the general interest, for example by a General Strike, is described as **anti-democratic**, since **democracy** has already been assured by other means; to claim economic EQUALITY . . . as the essence of democracy is seen as leading to "chaos" or to **totalitarian democracy** or *government by trade unions.*

The polarization of Toryism and the working class within Great Britain is thus made parallel to the cold war polarization of West and East, and both are then said to embody the fate of the modern liberal and socialist meanings of "democracy." What gets completely lost is the fact that the liberal and socialist traditions have themselves developed complex, ambiguous understandings of democracy.

The semantic promiscuity of "democracy" bothers Williams. Everybody uses it. "**Democracy** was," he writes, "until the 19th century a strongly unfavourable term, and it is only since the late 19th and early 20th century that a majority of political parties have united in declaring their belief in it."[12] Faced with the many hypocritical and propagandistic uses of the term, Williams concludes with a strange lament that harks back to a supposedly simpler time when "democracy" could have been appropriated with a cleaner, unambiguously oppositional meaning since it was mostly used negatively by ruling classes to express their contempt for the very idea that the multitude of poor might rule: "It would sometimes be easier to believe in democracy, or stand for it," Williams writes, "if the 19th-century change had not happened and it were still an unfavourable or factional term. But that history has occurred, and the range of contemporary sense is its confused and still active record."[13]

"Its confused and still active record"—Williams has painted himself into this corner. For the idea that socialism stands for an unequivocal sense of democracy is an illusory effect of his polarization of the liberal and socialist traditions. As he otherwise demonstrates so powerfully in *Keywords*, lexical problems *are* political problems. And the difficulties of meshing socialism and democracy are profound. They do not arise because liberals have misappropriated the term *democracy*. Socialism has tremendous antidemocratic potential that cannot be dispelled by appeals to egalitarianism. This antidemocratic potential is just as intrinsic to socialism as it is to capitalism, and just as dangerous and damaging.

I reread Williams's remarks on the Chinese Cultural Revolution with sorrow:

> It is an indispensable condition of socialist democracy that the division of labour should be challenged by regular participation of everyone in ordinary labour. The fact that the Chinese did not fully put it into practice or that certain people were exempted from it doesn't change the fundamental principle at all. That principle has never been so

clearly and powerfully enunciated as in the Cultural Revolution. I do not think that anyone should manage or administer any form of labour without the knowledge that they themselves will perform it, as well as, preferably, having come from it. When I heard pathetic stories about professors being taken from their libraries and laboratories and sent to help bring in the harvest I felt totally on the side of the revolutionaries.[14]

These remarks are all the more striking because they come in a passage of the *New Left Review* interviews where Williams had just warned about the capacity of Western leftists to display more political passion about distant or long past struggles than about their own: "A particular kind of political alienation can occur when people opt for revolutionary processes which have happened elsewhere, coming alive more when they are relating to those than when they are engaging with the drabness of their own situation."[15]

In the next breath he glorifies the Chinese Cultural Revolution as though it was pointing the way through the thorny problem of squaring freedom and equality at the level of the division of labor. What reveals a more poignant "political alienation" than a Western intellectual dubbing the Cultural Revolution an exemplar of *socialist democracy*?

And yet Williams's attitude was widely shared in the mid-1970s. I made Mao's *Four Essays on Philosophy*, especially "On Contradiction," a central text in the first seminar I taught on theory in 1975, buoyed by the *Tel Quel* project and Althusser's *For Marx* and *Lenin and Philosophy*. In the immediate wake of the 1960s, "cultural revolution" seemed to name a generalized set of processes transforming societies worldwide. Our hopes for radical political transformation in the West had been dashed, and yet we had an ongoing experience of significant transformations in everyday life and in culture. Much of the impetus for the initiatives in cultural theory in the mid-1970s was a desire to consolidate the gains and redeem the losses of the 1960s through a concept and practice of cultural revolution.

Many of us too easily lost our moral-political bearings in this context regarding the People's Republic. Ignorance of what was really going on found a convenient alibi in the complexity of events and in the Western supposition of Chinese inscrutability. The romance of revolution effortlessly transformed the Great Proletarian Cultural Revolution into a symbol of radical political renewal. The Red

Guards through whom the Chinese leadership wielded power became an icon of the European and American student movements as their own political potential was dissipating.

There is a haunting irony in the fact that a *student* movement in the West could symbolize its highest aspirations in the repression of intellectuals and the programming of young people's thought in China. As the *New Left Review* interviewer put it in a pointed rebuke of Williams's comment, "It is far more important in China today that everybody should have equal access to political information than that professors should bring in the harvest."

Against Distinction

I want to turn now to the alternative trend in Williams's fidelity to the General Strike of 1926. He saw that the whole process that altered the strikers' consciousness of themselves and their society was a development from, not a break with, their everyday experiences, relationships, and forms of communication. Culture was a resource for their critical awareness of society and their vision of a fuller participation in its institutions.

Williams kept faith with this insight in the whole project of his literary and cultural criticism, embodying it in a commitment to the democratization of culture quite unparalleled in the Marxist tradition or in contemporary theory more generally. In the topics and methods of his criticism he sought out paths to demonstrate how the production of culture is the result of the accumulated learning, coordinated efforts, and shared understandings of human beings in their social relationships.

He experimented with concepts like "structure of feeling" to explain how even the most innovative moments in literary history are evidence of some emergent set of social perceptions, dispositions, or attitudes shared by a group. He was seeking an alternative to the concept of ideology, which, since Marx, was laden with the assumption that culture is merely a distorted consciousness of real social practices. He increasingly distanced himself from Marxism. By the time he wrote *Marxism and Literature* he was systematically detaching his own cultural and literary criticism from the concept of ideology.

He had gravitated much closer to the sense of culture introduced by the early Marx and then abandoned, namely, the notion that culture is a set of material-social practices that are not categorically different from the material-social practices typically designated as "economy" or "material production." This notion runs directly counter to the basic paradigm of Marxist cultural theory. Marxism categorically separates "society" and "culture," whether the two terms are then conceptualized as base and superstructure or material reality and consciousness or social relations and representation or the economy and the symbolic. Williams shows how the key models of Marxist cultural and literary interpretation—reflection, mediation, typification, homology, correspondence—remained in thrall to the base-superstructure model at the heart of Marx's own theory of ideology.[16]

Williams rejects the idea that social classes in capitalist society have radically distinct or separate cultures (bourgeois culture, proletarian culture). The developed forms of the modern public sphere, citizenship, and education leave no social group utterly insulated from the dominant culture. At the same time, Williams rejects the notion that the dominant culture itself is merely imposed on subordinate groups and classes. The dominant classes are not so singly the authors of the culture, and the subordinate classes are not so passive as the model suggests. The prospect or the possibility of a *common culture* has, in Williams's view, been irreversibly planted in the development of modern Western societies.

The new forms of multiculturalism in contemporary society may well have sounded the death knell for the ideal of a common culture, and they are undoubtedly posing a new challenge to the relation between plurality and equality. But to understand Williams it is crucial to see how a common culture served as an ideal in his work. He did not presuppose that there already was a common culture, let alone that, as in F. R. Leavis, it could be comfortably located within the habits and prejudices of a particular stratum of society.

It was primarily in the domain of educational reform that Williams advanced the idea of a common culture as a goal. He advocated several measures together designed to radically reform education. The scope of the minimum education provided every child in elementary and secondary school should be expanded; tiered or tracked systems of schooling up to the age of sixteen should be broken down; students should be trained in democratic deliberation and decision through "their participation in the immediate government of the institution they attend"; instead of being pressured to quickly acquire specific credentials for an intended occupation or profession, young people age sixteen to twenty-five should be given a wide range of postsecondary education options and the freedom to revise or experiment with their choices; some form of continuing education should be guaranteed for all adults, and employers should be required to make provision for it. With his call for "a public education designed to express and create the values of an educated democracy and a common culture," Williams turned the arrogant, traditionalist, class-bound idea of a common culture into a radical, open-ended vision of people's widening participation in changing forms of literacy and learning.[17]

The same preoccupation informs the most basic premises of Williams's literary criticism and theory. He approached literature as part and parcel of the history of literacy. Literature/literacy—there is no more basic ground, etymologically or empirically, on which to understand literary history or the relation between literature and society. Yet literacy long remained a marginal topic of literary studies. Williams not only makes it central but also construes "literature" more broadly than any modern critic. The phrase he chose to title his most important collection of essays—"writing in society"—might well serve as his definition of literature.

The connections between literature and literacy cut two ways. Since reading and writing have to be taught in an organized manner, "the introduction of writing and all its subsequent stages of development are intrinsically new forms of social relationship." By the same token, the social relationships that shape literacy shape writing: "It was only at some point in the nineteenth century, very late in the record of English literature, that the majority of English people could read and write. It is impossible to imagine," Williams dryly asserts, "that this had no effect on what was written and what was read."[18]

The social unevenness of literacy and learning not only shapes what is written and read and how it is written, it also shapes how it is read. As Pierre Bourdieu has shown, social classes in capitalist society use their education and orchestrate the whole range of their cultural preferences, from eating to musical taste, to differentiate themselves from others, or to accept their differentiation from others, on the basis of *distinction*.[19] In the specific domain of literature, confirming one's social distinction is ingrained in the motives and rewards of reading. The "social conditions of the education of readers—and, more generally, of interpreters—affect the way they read the texts or the documents they use."[20]

As a critic and teacher, Williams devised various strategies for cutting against the grain of distinction in the reading of texts. He sought to give the reinterpretation and appropriation of literary traditions a contrary value. Reading should be a learning process in which the potential leveling of social hierarchies becomes palpable; it should sharpen the perception of both the elements of commonality and the elements of domination—the civilization and the barbarism—in cultural creations.

Always alert to the institutional context in which he worked, Williams inflected his democratizing strategies with interestingly different emphases when it came to elite and nonelite education. Several of his early books—*Culture and Society, 1780-1950, Drama from Ibsen to Eliot, The English Novel from Dickens to Lawrence*—grew directly out of his years of teaching adult education. His aim was to enable adult working students to lay hold of the intellectual and literary traditions that, in the complex history of social exclusion and cultural distinction, had become the prevalent trends in cultural criticism, drama, and the novel. Students were not being invited to an exercise in abject appreciation. They were, rather, being provided with the competence and mastery needed to understand, on their own terms, just those texts that the culture of distinction continually tried to put beyond their grasp.

A red thread running through these early books is the modern debate over culture and society. His adult students were being invited to see themselves as participants in that debate. "In speaking of a common culture," Williams wrote, "one is asking, precisely for that free, contributive and common *process* of participation in the creation of meanings and values, as I have tried to define it."[21]

Williams demystifies without denigrating the complexity and learning accumulated in texts by Dickens or Ibsen or Eliot. His criticism tends to describe forms by breaking down the various means of expression or "composition" or construction the authors employ. He tends to show how dramas and novels get made, but he roman-

ticizes neither genius nor craft. Nor does he cast the reader's deci-
pherments as heroic acts of unconcealing or demythologizing.
Rather, he tends to put the writer's process of artistic construction
and the reader's process of interpretive reconstruction more nearly
on the same footing. Reading and writing become the two sides of a
shared competence. Williams theorized this reciprocal relationship
in *Marxism and Literature* in terms of the sociality of language: "It
is a socially shared and reciprocal activity, already embedded in active relationships, within which every move is an activation of what
is already shared and reciprocal or may become so."[22]

Shared competence and reciprocal relationship do not imply unexamined consensus. By foregrounding the continuing modern debate over culture and society as well as the social relationships
within which literature is produced, Williams linked culture to critical reflection. He was readying readers to participate in those debates and in the active making and remaking of culture.

An essay that reflects these pedagogic and critical values is the introduction Williams wrote in 1969 to a volume of the *Pelican Book
of English Prose*. A sketch of the social origins and education of writers in English literary history alerts his readers to the role of the social divisions running through British culture:

> It is still quite clear in Britain today that there is not only a marked in-
> equality of representation in writers, as between different social
> groups, with the majority of writing still coming from a highly orga-
> nized middle class; but also, in relation to this, a definition of interest
> which has to do with their quite common educational background,
> which only a few share with the majority of their potential readers.[23]

The essay's accent falls on opening this majority's access to a literature not written for them. While society controls access to education
and participation in the public sphere, the resulting literature also
holds out the prospect of an experience that is not wholly bound by
these contours of social exclusion and hierarchy. Writing and reading are a social transaction that can displace or realign the social relationships within which the writing was produced. While "society determines . . . the writing of literature," it is also the case that

> the society is not complete, not fully and immediately present, until the
> literature has been written, and that this literature, in prose as often as
> any other form, can come through to stand as if on its own, with an in-

trinsic and permanent importance, so that we can see the rest of our living through it as well as it through the rest of our living.[24]

What can sound to more jaded postmodern ears like a simple faith naively expressed is in fact Williams's significant and principled stand for the idea that every literate citizen is but a few semesters away from a capacity to engage literature amply and critically, and to do so by bringing his or her own experience to the act of reading.

Williams held to a humanism in his understanding of textuality and reading. It kept him at a distance from the antihumanism of theorists like Althusser, Foucault, and Derrida. Like the radical Puritans of the seventeenth century and today's liberation theologists, Williams believed the interpretation of even the most complex and sacred texts is within everyone's reach. To put it in their grasp is the responsibility of writers and teachers in struggles within all the institutions and discourses of culture.

A democratizing appropriation, making the culture one's own, is also necessarily fraught with ambivalence. It needs to be an articulate ambivalence. A model is Williams's own *The Country and the City*. His project is to connect English literature's complex history of nature poetry, pastorals, and country settings to the crushing history of feudal and capitalist exploitations of the land and the landless. Those exploitations of the past are still visible in the beautiful landscapes and architecture of the English countryside. Visible, but not immediately recognized. The history of social relationships is easily effaced from consciousness even as it fills the whole visual field of consciousness. Monuments of civilization are also monuments of barbarism. It is the task of criticism then to appropriate and protest at the same time.

Williams, the Welsh railway signalman's son, analyzes country-house poems and the place of the country estate in British fiction through a fiercely personal assessment of English mansions:

> Some of them had been there for centuries, visible triumphs over the ruin and labour of others. But the extraordinary phase of extension, rebuilding and enlarging, which occurred in the eighteenth century, represents a spectacular increase in the rate of exploitation: a good deal of it, of course, the profit of trade and of colonial exploitation; much of it, however, the higher surplus value of a new and more efficient mode of production. It is fashionable to admire these extraordi-

narily numerous houses: the extended manors, the neo-classical mansions, that lie so close to hand in rural Britain. People still pass from village to village, guidebook in hand, to see the next and yet the next example, to look at the stones and the furniture. But stand at any point
and look at that land. Look at what those fields, those streams, those
woods even today produce. Think it through as labour and see how
long and systematic the exploitation and seizure must have been, to
rear that many houses, on that scale. See by contrast what any ancient
isolated farm, in uncounted generations of labour, has managed to become, by the efforts of any single real family, however prolonged.
And then turn and look at what these other "families," these systematic
owners, have accumulated and arrogantly declared. It isn't only that
you know, looking at the land and then at the house, how much rob-
bery and fraud there must have been, for so long to produce that degree of disparity, the barbarous disproportion of scale. The working
farms and cottages are so small beside them: what men really raise, by
their own efforts or by such portion as is left to them, in the ordinary
scale of human achievement. What these "great" houses do is to break
the scale, by an act of will corresponding to their real and systematic
exploitation of others. For look at the sites, the facades, the defining
avenues and walls, the great iron gates and the guardian lodges. These
were chosen for more than the effect from the inside out; where so
many admirers, too many of them writers, have stood and shared the
view, finding its prospect delightful. They were chosen, also, you now
see, for the other effect, from the outside looking in: a visible stamping
of power, of displayed wealth and command: a social disproportion
which was meant to impress and overawe.[25]

The physicality of the class society persists down into the present
not only in the presence of the country houses but also in the modern reclamation of them. For every house turned to "some general
use, as a hospital or an agricultural college" others have become "the
corporation country-house, the industrial seat, the ruling-class
school."

The *New Left Review* editors would later scold Williams for
"eclips[ing] history seen as a cumulative development of forces of
production and division of labour, which in and through the very
forms of social stratification and exploitation has been responsible
for the growth of real human gains." Yes, yes, of course, he replied,
the country house or the cathedral was built as part of an earlier period's perhaps inevitable form of creating wealth and developing
society. Nevertheless, he added:

The nature of their power does not necessarily end, in the tidy way the simplest kind of Marxism suggests, with its epoch. The cathedrals are not just monuments to faith, the country houses are not just buildings of elegance. They are constantly presented as "our heritage," inducing a particular way of seeing and relating to the world, which must be critically registered along with our acknowledgement of their value.[26]

The struggle over what our heritage shall be, and how it will be used, is the critic and teacher's daily battleground. The work that flowed most directly from the context of adult education stressed the mastery of forms and the learning of history. Williams's emphasis changes with his appointment to Cambridge in the mid-1960s. New problematics arise, in particular, over how to apply the aesthetic and intellectual understanding of the past to the present. In short, what are the alternatives to "distinction" in the appropriation of culture within elite education?

Williams tells a marvelous, self-mocking anecdote about how he came to write *Modern Tragedy*, a book the editors of *New Left Review* among others consider his "most militant text." His first lectures at Cambridge were to be a course on modern tragedy. To avoid having to prepare, he decided to rip off and recycle his 1952 book, *Drama from Ibsen to Eliot*:

> But in the process of giving the lectures, with a particular awareness now of the more general debate over the nature of tragedy, they became transformed. It was as if I went into the lecture room with the text of a chapter from *Drama from Ibsen to Eliot* in front of me, and came out with the text of a chapter from *Modern Tragedy*. The same authors are discussed in the two books, the same themes developed, the same quotations used—which is the key point of continuity.

Faced with students for whom "the idea of revolution had—if not the impact of the late sixties—already a significant resonance," Williams transformed a textbook on dialogue and staging into a treatise on tragedy and revolution! What had been practical criticism for workers and adult students became ideology critique for radicalized elite students. "It is a curious fact," he muses, "that I was being a relatively sound academic before I was in academia. Once I was in it—. I think the connection isn't accidental."[27]

The chapter entitled "Tragedy and Revolution," written in 1965, is

one of Williams's most searching essays. He marshals a whole reading of tragic drama and of the relevant traditions of the idea of
tragedy and then brings that cultural heritage to bear on the understanding of contemporary history. The use of heritage is for critical
reflection on the present. In inaugurating his Cambridge teaching
with this project, Williams challenged the culture of distinction and
turned a kind of knowledge acquired by social privilege to a new
task.

In substance the essay works out a tragic-revolutionary view of
modern history. On the one hand, Williams insists on the tragic character of modern political and social transformation. On the other
hand, he affirms his commitment to the transformation of capitalist
society. He holds a decidedly humanistic and moral perspective on
societies. A society is in need of revolution to the extent that "the incorporation of all its people, *as whole human beings*, is in practice
impossible without a change in its fundamental form of relationships." The source of the society's disorder, the violence already
wound into its institutions and structures, is the product of social division and exclusion. In such a society, the everyday acquiescence to
disorder is called order:

> We expect men brutally exploited and intolerably poor to rest and be
> patient in their misery, because if they act to end their condition it will
> involve the rest of us, and threaten our convenience or our lives. . . .
> We have identified war and revolution as tragic dangers, when the
> real tragic danger, underlying war and revolution, is a disorder which
> we continually re-enact.

For Williams, the forms of tragic drama illuminate the nature of
modern social transformation: "The tragic action, in its deepest sense,
is not the confirmation of disorder, but its experience, its compre-
hension and its resolution."[28]

In a strategy strikingly different from the building of cultural
competence in adult education, Williams's Cambridge lectures on
tragedy mobilize the intellectual and aesthetic resources of Western
tragic drama for a pointedly oppositional interpretation of history
and society. He sought to displace the culture of distinction with a
tragic-revolutionary appropriation of the cultural heritage.

There are, then, perhaps three registers of Williams's criticism. In
Modern Tragedy, the knowledge of a tradition is turned from a

badge of social distinction into an instrument of political reflection. *Culture and Society* or "Notes on English Prose," in contrast, reconstructs the intellectual and aesthetic skills of reading, imparting to new readers a capacity to experiment with active cultural-political interpretation, to join the debate on culture and society in the very act of appropriating traditions into their own life world. And, finally, in a third register, *The Country and the City* asks how a society's forms of wealth and power are embodied in its structures of feeling and its modes of expression; cultural forms, from poems to the cultivated landscape, are found to be ambiguous ciphers of human achievement and human violence.

These three registers of Williams's criticism are not united methodologically. Each took shape in the context of particular institutions and practices. Each proceeds from a distinct assessment of criticism's role in the public sphere. Moreover, as a critic, Williams continually plunged into new empirical complexities before completing his theoretical clarifications. Nevertheless, his diverse projects share a common intent: to challenge the culture of distinction by deepening and broadening the democratization of culture.

Heretical Empiricist

Williams was ultimately of two minds when it came to the meaning of revolution and social transformation. Debating revolutionary theory with *New Left Review,* he oscillates between a latter-day Leninist vision of revolutionaries capturing state power and the contrary vision in which layers of socialist transformations have to be accomplished *before* the state can be loosed from the imperatives of capital. First:

> I have no doubt that the short revolution, to use that phrase, also has to occur. I wouldn't at all dissent from the traditional notions of the violent capture of state power.

And then:

> So I am always uneasy about talk of short revolution when the problems of the run-up to it have not been fully appreciated. I have found that most of the images of the inherited tradition do not bear very much on this complicated process of preparation and learning.[29]

The contradiction is glaring. The "images of the inherited tradition" and the "traditional notions of the violent capture of state power" are, after all, the exact same thing.

Despite the power and insight of the essay "Tragedy and Revolution," it is haunted by an unsolved problem. Resonant with Hegel's idea of the "causality of fate," Williams postulates that the unjust society is a torn whole. And, like Marx, he seems to imply that those most oppressed or excluded by the disordered order of society are driven to overthrow it. But it is just that Marxian assumption that Williams in fact does not make. Nowhere in his work does he project the proletariat as the historically necessary agent of revolutionary change. The moral imperative to change society is not objectivated in any group. His temptation to this view, or, at least, his failure to set it aside—"I see revolution as the *inevitable* working through of a deep and tragic disorder"[30]—is what led him in the decade that followed this essay to idealize the General Strike of 1926 and mythologize the Chinese Cultural Revolution.

The insights and the difficulties in Williams's idea of tragedy and of revolution stem from the difficulty he had in interpreting the direction of the workers movement in light of the Labour Party's integration into capitalism. The crisis form of that question burst upon him in 1966. Social change revealed its tragic face. Henceforth the socialist movement would have to encounter the Labour Party itself as an antagonist. Long-standing solidarities would have to be broken in any process of radical social change. This sharpened Williams's sense of the disorder in contemporary society and the suffering exacted by political struggle.

The revolutionary myth became tempting because it gave symbolic shape to the sense of potential upheaval. And it returned the events of 1926 into the present not only as a source of radical commitment but also as an emblem of revolutionary social transformation. Williams's fidelity to the General Strike also, and at the same time, intensified his commitment to the democratization of culture and sharpened his sense that the resources of social transformation reside in people's everyday practices, relationships, and obligations. The long rather than the short revolution, the deep transformations of the "run-up" rather than the violent seizure of power, pointed up a process at once socialist and democratic.

Williams never squared the two views. The ambivalences persisted. In my view, his most significant contributions are those that illuminated the democratization of culture. *The Long Revolution* (1961) is, finally, the starting point of his best insight into the links between socialism and democracy. The concept of long revolution itself was meant to address modern Western capitalist societies. The term signals that the transformation of capitalism into socialism would require a deep, pervasive change in institutions and in the very character of social relationships, from the impersonal relationships through which the society's wealth is created and distributed down to the personal relationships in which moral attitudes and mutual obligations are enacted. In this respect, there can be no socialism without revolution.

For the same reasons, however, it is a long revolution. The imperatives and values of capitalism organize layer upon layer of social life. As a process of democratization, the long revolution has to transform distributions of wealth, power, and decision through these many layers, extending participation and inventing new forms of participation. Williams believed, on the one hand, that this struggle has been going on for decades in capitalist society through various social reforms and in the structural changes in the public sphere and education. On the other hand, capitalism vigorously defends itself, and its antidemocratic tendencies are never merely dormant. Gains are not always permanent; reforms do not always combine to create enduring social changes; innovations that might anchor socialist institutions can be reabsorbed into capitalist ones.

Williams consistently refuses to denigrate such *incorporated* gains, reforms, or innovations. They have not merely been "co-opted." Incorporations cannot be judged wholesale, only in their particular contexts and effects. *Incorporation* is a descriptive rather than an evaluative term in Williams's vocabulary. Because capitalist society absorbs so many pressures for change, its institutions have to be continually reassessed and diagnosed anew. They at once embody instruments for the survival of capitalism and fragments of potential socialist institutions. Capitalist tool or revolutionary latency? The evaluation of particular reforms and institutions cannot be furnished through a theory; it always has to come from the open-ended process of social criticism and political decision taking.

Williams was, to borrow Pier Paolo Pasoloni's phrase, a "heretical empiricist." Reform-or-revolution has to be decided in struggles over moral-political questions steeped in people's actual social relationships, not from within the matrix of revolutionary theory. So, too, cultural and literary interpretations belong to the moral and political domain.

Where a deconstructive critic might relish discovering in a text those nuances that seem to gather themselves into a dark yet playful aporia; where an Althusserian might home in on those structures of meaning that can at once be associated with a dominant ideology and yet seem to crack the more tightly they cohere; or where a critic inspired by Benjamin or Adorno might delight in the emergence of a text's inner form at just the point where the resulting sense of aesthetic inevitability suddenly acquires the meaning of social prophecy or negation—Williams's mind by contrast seems to have thrilled to those moments in reading where it flashes upon you that this text could only have been written, could only have come into being at all, because of the forms of learning that had consolidated at that point in history; because of some coordinated effort or shared purpose on the part of a class, a movement, a class fraction or a formation; because of perceptions, feelings, values that belong to the everyday life of some social group.

The capacity for such responses to literature was Williams's gift as a critic, and it is his intellectual legacy to us. It is worth imagining how to keep faith with it.

Yet like all paternal legacies, especially symbolic ones, the one Williams bequeathed is burdened. He often shortchanged the liberal traditions of individual right and failed to think through the importance of plurality in modern societies. His failure to grasp the relevance of feminism or to really examine how racism and imperialism have shaped British culture mars a project that was expressly designed to open culture to a "free, contributive and common *process* of participation."

The distorting contours of the public sphere are not carved out along merely class lines. The whole history of women's writing unfolds in the tortured development of the public sphere and education that excluded women, channeled their learning, devalued their forms of communication, and defined the very ideas and institutions of "public" and "private" in gender terms. Colonialism is in-scribed in our literature just as indelibly as feudal and capitalist ex-ploitation is inscribed on the English landscape; moreover, Britain's centuries of destroying and controlling the literacy and learning of Asians and Africans has unwittingly created the social conditions for writing that has completely altered the meaning of "English" litera-ture.

That these other histories and struggles are so central to the project Williams defined and yet so absent from his work serves doubly to criticize him and reaffirm the project itself. In the decade or more of crisis that followed his break with the Labour Party in 1966, a time in which the women's movement and immigration certainly brought home the changing face of political struggle, Williams was not ready to accept that the working class could no longer be the ground or ref-erence point of socialist politics.

The working class, and not just the Labour Party, had become in-corporated into the institutions of capitalism in unprecedented ways. Williams could never have bombastically announced, as André Gorz did, *Farewell to the Working Class*! But Gorz's insights would have sharpened his sense that the task of the democratiza-tion of culture and the struggle for socialist institutions was pro-ceeding through new social movements that certainly traversed but could never unite the working class.

So much in Williams's work potentially speaks to just these new hopes and needs for social transformation. Unlike Kureishi's disillu-sioned journalist, Williams never gave the working class a mission. He did not demand that they fulfill *his* dreams for society. He did not limit the agency of the working class to their supposed revolu-tionary agency. Indeed, it is not the unique fate of any social group to be the agent of revolution. The long revolution does not have a historically necessary subject. Unlike Lukács, Williams did not await this subject's (inevitable) awakening. And unlike Adorno, he did not lament its (inevitable) passing. And unlike Althusser, he did not be-lieve history is a process without a subject, the (inevitable) crisis of a system. It is a process with subjects, a process of uncertain outcome that will succeed in suffering the birth of a new society only if these empirical, complex, contradictory "subjects"—a.k.a. people—reinvent our governing forms of wealth, power, and sociality. It is, Williams understood, a painfully (and inevitably) human task.

NOTES

I am extremely grateful to Carla Kaplan for her comments and suggestions.

1. See Margaret Morris, *The General Strike* (Harmondsworth: Penguin, 1976), and Patrick Renshaw, *The General Strike* (London: Eyre Methuen, 1975).

2. Raymond Williams, *Politics and Letters: Interviews with New Left Review* (London: New Left Books, 1979), p. 27.

3. Raymond Williams, *Border Country* (London: Chatto and Windus, 1962), p. 87. All the quotations from the novel come from chapter four, pp. 85–137.

4. Williams discouraged readers from equating Harry Price with his own father: "Many people have assumed that Harry Price, the signalman with his gardens, was a portrait of my father; but this is not really so. I found that to get the real movement I had to divide and contrast what I had seen in my father as conflicting impulses and modes. I had to imagine another character, Morgan Rosser, the politician and dealer, who in his relation to Harry Price could express and work through what I believed I had seen as an internal conflict" (*The Country and the City* [New York: Oxford University Press, 1973], p. 299). In reading the novel autobiographically, it is not really a question of assuming that Harry Price is an accurate "portrait" of Williams's father. What counts is Harry's relation to his son Matthew; the autobiographical tenor of the novel comes from the identification of Williams with Matthew. It is therefore the writer's relation to that father-son relation itself that needs to be illuminated. Terry Eagleton, in what is a generally injudicious commentary on Williams, raises a pertinent criticism of this splitting of the father figure on the grounds that it syphons off from Harry Price the troubling or ambivalent values of the rural community and thus idealizes that community by letting him stand as the "almost wholly admirable representative of [its] best values"; see *Criticism and Ideology: A Study in Marxist Literary Theory* (London: New Left Books, 1976), pp. 30–31.

5. Raymond Williams, "The Social Significance of 1926" (1977), in *Resources of Hope: Culture, Democracy, Socialism*, ed. Robin Gable (London: Verso, 1989), p. 108.

6. Raymond Williams, "The Importance of Community" (1977), ibid., p. 119.

7. Williams, *Politics and Letters*, p. 426.

8. Ibid., p. 373.

9. Ibid., p. 375. Italics added.

10. Ibid., p. 415.

11. Raymond Williams, *Keywords: A Vocabulary of Culture and Society*, rev. ed. (New York: Oxford University Press, 1983), p. 96.

12. Ibid., p. 94.

13. Ibid., pp. 97–98.

14. Williams, *Politics and Letters*, p. 404.

15. Ibid., p. 403.

16. Raymond Williams, *Marxism and Literature* (New York: Oxford University Press, 1977), pp. 75–107. I have commented on the relevance of Williams's critique and related it to a submerged and abandoned tendency within Marx's thought in my *Culture and Domination* (Ithaca, N.Y.: Cornell University Press, 1987), pp. 72–76.

17. Raymond Williams, *The Long Revolution* (New York: Columbia University Press, 1961), pp. 125–55.

18. Raymond Williams, "Writing," in *Writing in Society* (London: Verso, 1984), p. 3.

19. Pierre Bourdieu, *Distinction: A Social Critique of the Judgement of Taste*, trans. Richard Nice (Cambridge, Mass.: Harvard University Press, 1984).

20. Pierre Bourdieu, "Reading, Readers, the Literate, Literature," in *In Other Words: Essays Towards a Reflexive Sociology*, trans. Matthew Adamson (Stanford, Calif.: Stanford University Press, 1990), p. 95.

21. Raymond Williams, "The Idea of a Common Culture" (1968), in Gable, ed., *Resources of Hope*, p. 38.

22. Williams, *Marxism and Literature*, p. 167.

23. Raymond Williams, "Notes on English Prose: 1780-1950," in *Writing in Society*, p. 72.

24. Ibid.

25. Williams, *Country and the City*, pp. 105-6. On this passage, see also Jonathan Arac, *Critical Genealogies: Historical Situations for Postmodern Literary Studies* (New York: Columbia University Press, 1987), p. 278.

26. Williams, *Politics and Letters*, pp. 308-9.

27. Ibid., pp. 211-12.

28. Raymond Williams, *Modern Tragedy* (1966; rev. ed., London: Verso, 1979), pp. 76, 80-81, 83.

29. Williams, *Politics and Letters*, pp. 420, 422.

30. Williams, *Modern Tragedy*, p. 75.

Culture and Society or "Culture and the State"
David Lloyd and Paul Thomas

> *The higher and middling orders are the natural representatives of the human race. Their interest may be opposed, in some things, to that of their poorer contemporaries, but it is identical to that of the innumerable generations which are to follow.*
>
> —Macaulay

> *The idea of representation is a modern one. It comes to us from feudal government, from that iniquitous and absurd system under which the human race is degraded and which dishonors the name of man. In the republics and even in the monarchies of the ancient world, the people never had representatives: the very word was unknown.*
>
> —Rousseau

Few would dispute the assertion that Raymond Williams's *Culture and Society 1780-1950* has had and even continues to have a definitive influence on what appears to be the dominant British tradition of thinking on culture in its relation to social and political theory. As Williams himself indicated in *Politics and Letters*, the work more or less archaeologically reconstructed an occulted tradition.[1] More importantly, it countered "the appropriation of a long line of thinking about culture to what were by now decisively reactionary positions."[2] At the present moment, in the context of a resurgent, militant cultural conservativism, such a venture might well seem not only relevant but to require an even more radical repetition. *Culture and Society* defined the canon of cultural thinking as being in opposition to the detrimental effects of industrialization and democratization.

For Williams, of course, the emphasis fell on the former process; for contemporary conservatives the emphasis falls, more often than not, on the latter. Both appeal, neither without reason, to the tradition that, as Williams taught us, runs from Burke through Arnold to Orwell. The possibility of this dual appeal lies in the fact that this very tradition defines the terms by which culture is differentiated from the political, social, or economic spheres of society as a corrective supplement. The values to which the discourse of culture appeals and that it seeks to preserve are those by which it is defined: wholeness, disinterest, humanity, cultivation, reconciliation.

The second part of our title, "Culture and the State," signals both our debt to and our differences from Williams. We wish to address the tradition of culture that he first sketched but propose to do so in connection not with the concept of society that, for reasons we will analyze later, remains somewhat nebulous in *Culture and Society*, but rather with that of the state. We will argue that the undertheorization of the state in Williams's early work prevents him from adequately addressing either the striking parallels between state and cultural theory or the reasons for the gradual subordination of the institutions of culture to the work of the state that occurs in the period he analyzes. In addition, we will show that his emphasis on an "intellectual history" or "history of ideas" concerning culture, rather than on debates around industry, politics, and culture, prevents Williams from grasping more radical possibilities—missed opportunities, perhaps, but nonetheless fertile and suggestive ones—that existed outside his chosen terrain. We hope to show that the discourse on representation always implicit in the theory of culture has to be understood in connection with debates concerning representation within the radical press and the emergent socialist or protosocialist movements of the period. Since our emphasis will fall precisely on the fact that what concerns us here are debates rather than *positions prises*, we will want to consider Williams's account of the critical values of culture in relation to other recent accounts and criticisms of emergent English socialism. We hope to show that in all these accounts a certain uncritical acceptance of a division of spheres—whose features were indeed crystallizing in the 1830s and 1840s, but which were by no means set in stone—leads to a foreclosure of the very open and still critical terms of debate about education, representation, and exploitation in radical circles. Divisions such as culture and society, politics and economics, even theory and practice are taken for granted in a manner that assumes the self-evidence of distinctions that only subsequently became canonical, within the period of their emergence. For us, on the contrary, what is pointedly of interest in these moments is the fluidity, perhaps even the contra-dictoriness, of debates over representation, education, and class at the moment (that of the first Reform Bill and its immediate after-math) when representative democracy was an idea profoundly con-tested on both left and right. Beyond this lies a broad question, or agenda, that cannot be settled—though it can, in a preliminary sense, be raised—here: that of the early-nineteenth-century conjuring trick by which democracy (which in its original signification had nothing to do with representation, as Rousseau reminds us) became rede-fined as, and unthinkable apart from, representative democracy.[3]

What is more immediately at issue for us, in relation to the tradi-tion isolated by Williams, is the place of culture in the formation of citizens and the legitimation of the state. For the debates around is-sues of representation and education that we discuss concern pre-cisely the question of the legitimacy of representation and of the kind of subject to be formed for or against the emergent state and the economic relations that subtended it. In the tradition from Burke through Coleridge to Mill and Arnold that is ultimately most impor-tant to Williams, culture occupies the space between the individual and the state, forming the citizen as ethical "best self." But it is pre-cisely that process that was under contestation in working-class rad-ical circles. Contrary to the concerns that Williams is able to draw from the "high" tradition of culture (concern with the fragmentation of the human by the divison of labor, concern with mechanization, deracination, and the cultural impoverishment as well as the ex-ploitation of the mass of the population), our interest is in reading in that same tradition an account of the function of "culture" in its in-tersection with the state and in the foundation of what Althusser was to term "ideological state apparatuses." If our account differs from Williams's, the difference is in large part due to the different historical juncture at which we write. Our interest in reading back into the relatively occulted tradition of working-class discourse on education and representation is connected with a timely suspicion of the grand narrative of culture in which Williams's generosity was able to read a humane and still viable potential.

A full analysis of relations between culture and the state demands a more extensive project than is possible here.[4] But in order to clarify our differences from Williams, it is worth outlining our sense of his project, of its strengths and, from our perspective, its omissions. To do so demands also a sketch of two different institutional moments as a means of articulating the exigencies of Williams's project and our own. The title of a largely forgotten English journal, *Universities and Left Review*, mentioned in Williams's foreword, offers an illuminating epiphany of a cultural moment—*Culture and Society* was first published, by Chatto and Windus, in 1958—and its perceived possibilities. Easily overlooked at the opening of *Culture and Society*, the title of this journal gains an effect of strangeness when one considers entitling a journal in this fashion at the present time. The title speaks to a moment of British intellectual socialism at which educational and other institutions seemed an available territory for hegemonic struggle and of which Williams's own trajectory is not untypical. It seemed possible that the institutions of education and communication at long last might be genuinely open to the reception and dissemination not only of working-class students and teachers but also to left-wing thought. Accordingly, *Universities and Left Review* was not the oxymoron it might now seem. At the same time, the possibility for such optimism rested in a relative confidence in the efficacy and value of state intervention when it is directed by more or less socialist policies. The long revolution of representative democracy could be seen to be leading gradually to the occupation of the institutions of the state by at least representatives of the people and in the name of a left agenda.[5] Accordingly, it is necessary to read in *Culture and Society* a covert and revisionist institutional history. Although Williams is never very explicit about this, the canon of cultural thinkers that he effectively establishes is a canon of those thinkers who furnish the theoretical bases for educational institutions generally and for cultural education (especially literature) in particular. Williams is retrieving for the socialist tradition the cultural concepts that had by and large been appropriated by conservatives; in so doing he is regrounding the institutions themselves as a means of establishing them as sites with an increased potential for socialist inflection. Understood in this sense, *Culture and Society* is a counterhegemonic work of enormous strategic value. At the same time, the desire to reoccupy cultural positions appropriated all too monolithically by reactionary elements necessarily involves Williams in what now seems a rather problematic overidentification with the positions themselves. For it is not simply that Williams performs a work of rearticulating the historical logic of the discourse on culture so that it points toward a socialist community. There is also an attempt on his part to insert himself into that tradition as a means of reappropriating its ethos as well as its institutions. It is for this reason that, throughout, it is exactly the concept of tradition, rather than, for example, theology or discourse, that recurs.

Williams's attempt leads him to incontestably significant transformations of the discourse on culture, but these transformations remain deeply problematic by virtue of what they cause him to overlook. We can isolate two distinct but related transformations in the discourse on culture that Williams undertakes. First, there is the reclamation of the idea of "wholeness" for the socialist tradition, a tradition from which, in a line of attack running back at least to Burke's assaults on Paine and on sundry heartless rationalizers, conservatism has sought to divorce socialism. Small wonder that his interlocutor in *Politics and Letters* is quick to note that Williams's sympathy often seems to be on the side of conservative "structures of feeling" as opposed to radical demystifications.[6] The tone is set early on and significantly through Arnold's praise of Burke:

> Arnold is himself one of the political heirs of Burke, but again this is less important than the kind of thinking which Arnold indicates by the verb "saturates." It is not "thought," in the common opposition to "feeling"; it is, rather, a special immediacy of experience, which works itself out, in depth, to a particular embodiment of ideas that become, in themselves, the whole man.[7]

Given the recurrence of such terms throughout *Culture and Society* and Williams's work as a whole, it is not enough to characterize it as a mere vestige of F. R. Leavis's—here very evident—stylistic and intellectual influence. Williams's understanding of socialism's utopian moment is always inseparable from a desire to overcome division and contradictions in the self (a desire doubtless accentuated by his own biographical displacements). Accordingly, it is the explicitly extrapolitical category of the "whole man" that determines Williams's selection of the canonical figures of the cultural tradition.

We will skirt here such problematic issues as the adequacy of a notion of wholeness to, for instance, the complex of repression and development that separates the "best" from the "ordinary" self in Arnold or in the similar narratives of many nineteenth-century novels. Our particular interest here is rather in how and why Williams's implicit values cause *Culture and Society* to reproduce the theoretical structure of representation that the discourse on culture has consistently been deployed to produce. What is at stake in Williams's invocation of a concept of wholeness, a concept instantiated for him in Burke, is the adequacy of certain figures to humanity itself. The divisions that are seen to characterize bourgeois society, either those between feeling and thought or those between politics and culture, are divisions within a prior concept of the human. Whether or not one accepts the notion of an organic wholeness of the human, what is crucial here is the manner in which the prepolitical concept of "the whole man" posits an undivided concept of humanity to which particular individuals are more or less adequate. In this concept Williams reproduces the regulative idea of the discourse of culture for which the representative human is he (principally he) who most adequately, though never entirely, approximates to wholeness. The concept is prepolitical precisely insofar as the political stands for a division of the human into partialities. The same, by analogy, applies to every other conceivable division by which the human is alienated from itself: the "whole man" of culture is by the same token above economics and above class, strictly indifferent. Williams thus well represents the tradition of culture but at the same time continually risks merely ventriloquizing that culture. *Culture and Society* establishes not only a canon of cultural texts by virtue of the importance of their individual propositions; it also establishes a canon in the stronger and proper sense of a body of texts that represent or embody their own ideal and accordingly stand for humanity as a whole. Williams's selected texts on culture thus come to have the status and all the self-evidence of Arnoldian touchstones, being exemplary in their form as in their content. Let us simply stress at this juncture a point to which we shall shortly return: what governs the canonicity of culture's texts is their approximation not so much to reality as to a regulative idea.

The argument of *Culture and Society* indisputably seeks to pass beyond the purely formal definition of representativeness articulated in Coleridge, Mill, and Arnold, a definition that is devoted to determining and restricting the terms by which the capacity for either self-representation or consensual representation by others seems possible. Williams's argument proceeds, however, not by critiquing the manner in which "culture" is established as a distinct domain, devoted to the cultivation of the "whole man" against the divisions of labor and politics. It proceeds by collapsing these distinctions. As *Culture and Society* progresses, it becomes increasingly difficult to differentiate Culture in the specialized sense that Coleridge and Arnold gave to it from "culture" in the anthropological sense of functionally integrated life worlds. Clearly, this apparent confusion on Williams's part belongs with his large strategy, which is to establish, in the face of reactionary distinctions, the vitality of working-class or popular culture. Accordingly, his conception of culture is increasingly articulated as tied to "an effective community of experience"[8] rather than to a canon of works to be absorbed. A "common culture" is recast not as the legacy of the best that has been known and thought and directed at the production of best selves, but as only possible "in a context of material community and by the full democratic process."[9]

With Williams's call for "material community" and "the full democratic process" we can only agree unreservedly. At the same time, however, the full context of that citation will serve to indicate the extent to which we must dissent from the terms by which the relation of culture to those conditions is presented:

> The emphasis that we wish to place here is that this first difficulty—the compatibility of increasing specialization with a genuinely common culture—is only soluble in a context of material community and by the full democratic process. A skill is only an aspect of a man, and yet, at times, it can seem to comprehend that man's whole being. This is one kind of crisis, and it can only be overcome as a man becomes conscious that the value he places on his skill, the differentiation he finds in it, can only ultimately be confirmed by his constant effort not only to confirm and respect the skills of others, but also to confirm and deepen the community which is even larger than the skills. The mediation of this lies deep in personal feeling, but enough is known to indicate that it is possible.[10]

Consistent with Williams's general argument, the distinction maintained in the traditional discourse of culture between Culture and other domains of practice tends to erode here. What remains of that discourse, and remains as a powerful presence, is a vestigial conception of culture as representing the possibility of "the whole man" against the division of labor. What is valued in Burke at the outset as a representative individual is transposed here onto a collective, but the form of the opposition remains. And though it would be difficult to specify from here the contents of culture as opposed to any "specialization," it is precisely our principal contention that this form of thinking is of crucial importance to understanding the historical role of culture in relation to the state.

Indeed, the strength of Williams's desire to save the discourse of culture by giving it a socialist terminus prevents him from subjecting its formal properties to sustained critical analysis. Yet it is exactly from the distinction between the wholeness sought in culture and the division of labor characteristic of society in general that Arnold and others derive the notion that "culture suggests the idea of the State." If we replace the slightly nebulous term *society* with the more technical *civil society* the point may become clearer. Culture is to a civil society conceived as the site of the war of all against all a domain of reconciliation precisely as is the state. But while the function of the state is to mediate conflicts among interest groups, it is the function of culture to interpellate individuals into the disposition to disinterested reflection that makes the state's mediations possible. Culture produces the consensual ground for the state form of representative democracy by drawing the formal or representative disposition in every individual out of each person's concrete particularity. The ethical moment in each individual that Arnold terms the "best self" suggests the state, and the state is in turn the collective representation of the ethical disposition. The importance of the discourse on culture lies in its theorization of an extrapolitical, extraeconomic space in which "freedom" and "the harmonious development of the whole person" can be pursued as the very ground on which representational politics can be practiced. Culture mediates the shift from self-representation to being represented by developing in each that "indifferent" disposition of the Subject in which material differences are annulled. While allowing representational politics to take place by formalizing political subjects, it simultaneously allows that politics to take place as if material conditions were a matter of indifference.

Williams's fastidious and deprecatory comment on Arnold, that "the State which for Burke was an actuality has become for Arnold an idea,"[11] is not only misplaced with regard to the theoretical and institutional importance of Arnold's work. It expresses a critical position that logically prevents Williams from undertaking the critique of cultural discourse that will be a necessary prelude to making the transition from representative democracy to "material community and the full democratic process," to, that is, radical democracy. The differential position of culture with regard not to "industrialization" and "democracy," as Williams has it, but to the political and the economic is so deeply imbricated in the structure of bourgeois society that even the so-called aestheticization of daily life in the postmodern era has not fundamentally altered its significance. The structure of "recreat?onary space," whether it is defined as Arnoldian culture or the mass media, is, in relation to the specialization of the workplace or the interests of politics, fundamentally little changed and continues to provide the mechanisms by which the formal subject of the state is produced as in this domain undivided. Without a radical critique not only of the terms but also of the conditions of possibility of such differentiation of spheres, the function of culture in the reproduction of the state and material social relations cannot adequately be addressed.[12]

In view of the fact that it was written, as Williams points out, in the same moment as E. P. Thompson's *Making of the English Working Class* and Richard Hoggart's *The Uses of Literacy*, it is perhaps surprising at first sight that *Culture and Society* turns so little to working-class writings on education, politics, society, or culture. Williams's comments on "working class culture" make clear why this is so. Pointing out that often enough what gets termed working-class culture is generally not produced by working-class people, he goes on to a more substantial point:

> To this negative definition we must add another: that 'working class culture', in our society, is not to be understood as the small amount of 'proletarian' writing and art which exists. The appearance of such work has been useful, not only in the more self-conscious forms, but also in such material as the post-Industrial ballads, which were worth collecting. We need to be aware of this work, but it is to be seen as a valuable dissident element rather than as a culture. The traditional popular culture of England was, if not annihilated, at least fragmented

and weakened by the dislocations of the Industrial Revolution. What is left, with what in the new conditions has been newly made, is small in quantity and narrow in range. It exacts respect, but it is in no sense an alternative culture.[13]

We have no quarrel with the proposition that popular and working-class cultural forms have suffered damage, even fragmentation and annihilation, in the history of capitalism and exploitation that defines them as "working class." Indeed, not to recognize this would be to remove a principal rationale from class struggle and would reduce—in a way now not hard to conceive—working-class culture to one more equivalent variation among the many cultures of a jagged pluralist postmodernity. But it is critical to note how a judgment of working-class culture from the perspective of a culture devoted to supplying an alternative space to "industrialism" and "democracy" relegates that culture to the status of a mere "dissident element" rather than reading in it the outline of terms for self-representation that refuse the differentiation of spheres imposed by the rationale of capitalist social forms. An alternative reading of radical and working-class discourse might show that, while recognizing its own damaged status as a consequence of exploitation, such a discourse does not do so by confessing inadequacy to an imposed model of cultural fulfilment.[14]

Dissident Elements or Contested Terrain? The Pauper Press

Our own researches have in this respect been profoundly instructive at a personal as well as an archival or interpretive level. Attempting to locate a counterhegemonic discourse on culture critical of the bourgeois tradition outlined in *Culture and Society*, we turned to radical and working-class publications of the late 1820s and early 1830s, the historical moment, that is, of the first Reform Bill and of Coleridge's seminal work on culture and the state, *On the Constitution of Church and State*. Expecting to find some critical acknowledgment of and engagement with the concept of culture and education developed in this and other contemporary bourgeois writings, we were at first considerably disappointed to find scarcely a mention of such concepts. Reading further into the material, mostly in penny papers and other ephemeral publications, it rapidly became apparent that this ignoring of what has seemed since *Culture and Society* the dominant tradition was by no means simple ignorance but a systematic refusal on the part of working-class and some petty bourgeois radical writers to accept the division of education, politics, and economics into separate if interinfluential spheres. What is critical here is that the terms by which, between Coleridge and Arnold or Mill, the notion emerges that education must precede franchise and that that education should be disinterested, or cultural, simply do not have the self-evidence that they do in the dominant discourse.

Furthermore, the very concept of representation, which in the dominant discourse is narrativized into a developmental schema running from savages and the working class, who are said to be too self-interested and narrow to represent themselves, to the intellectuals, ethical apexes of civilization and representative humans, is remarkably fluid and shifting. There is, for example, none of the self-evidence by which, in Mill and Arnold, representation at the local level of classroom or parish, in the minimal example of the "representative" touchstone, folds over into representation at the level of state and parliament. To the contrary, concepts of representation that would seem quite contradictory according to that narrative are held at one and the same time within the same periodicals and about different institutions. Writers able to accept representation at the state level reject it vehemently within working-class institutions like trade unions while other writers who argue against political representation by others may be found supporting a representative structure within those same unions. What is being discussed, immediately before and after the first bill that promised but did not deliver a massive extension of the franchise, is the very nature and value of representative structures themselves. Within these debates, despite the occasionally "avant-gardiste" positions on enlightening the laborers taken by some petty bourgeois radicals, there is little call for a discourse on culture in which "whole men" become representative archetypes of fulfilled humanity. There is, to the contrary, remarkably little interest in the supposedly destructive effects of the division of labor, but plenty of attention to the fact that lack of political power or even representation was closely bound up with the inability of laborers to put an end to their exploitation. For this reason in turn, education is to be directed not toward cultivation and harmonization of the inner man but toward political knowledge. As John Henry Baden Lorymer put it in *The Republican* of April 1832:

> If a Nation be almost unanimous in its demand for REPRESENTATION, what should prevent those citizens who are desirous of being represented, from actually having representatives? Nothing can prevent them but a most beastly ignorance of their RIGHTS, and a most pig-like apathy with regard to the mode of acquiring them.

Or, as one "C. H." put it somewhat later in "Plain Reason.-Useful Knowledge" in Richard Carlile's *The Gauntlet*, December 15, 1833:

> In a country where every thing relating to the science of Government has grown radically corrupt—where both precept and practice are inimical to, or destructive of, true liberty, and where the oppression of the administration, is the most grievous burden borne by the state, political knowledge is necessarily the most "useful knowledge."

There is here no claim that what is to be "cultivated" by this education is disinterest: it is an explicitly political education but by no means an education directed at politics for its own sake. Education is rather directed at producing political understanding that will ultimately enable the transformations in the material conditions of the working classes that will free them from exploitation.

It is possible to trace among the more centrist of the radical papers, such as James Morison's *Pioneer* or George Pilgrim's *Cosmopolite*, the outline of the notions that education must precede the attainment of the franchise or that education is a good in itself in calming the passions of the people, notions that later become the staple of liberal discourse on education and franchise. But the more radical writers argue uncompromisingly against the hegemonic use of education to defer the franchise, whether by the state or by individual reformers. "Senex," in one of a series of remarkably uncompromising articles entitled "On Associated Labour" for *The Pioneer*, makes the following comments ("On the Pretended Ignorance of the Labouring Classes"):

> Under this pretence [lower-class ignorance], they rob us, and almost work us to death; and yet there are persons who really mean well to us, crying out, Ah, this is but too true! the majority of the people are not sufficiently instructed to be entrusted with power: we must illumi-

nate their minds before we can venture to advocate their elevation in the scale of society!

Brethren, there is an immensity of benefit in what is called education; but do not suffer yourselves to be tricked and bamboozled out of your rights under the notion that you must have education before you are fit to have justice. Education is a very good thing; but men and children must live as well as learn; besides there is such a thing as education without knowledge, and there is also such a thing as knowledge without education, and of these two things the last is much better than the first. . . . All useful knowledge consists in the acquirement of ideas concerning our condition in life; and there are few men of common observation who do not get into their minds, whether they can read and write or not, the ideas that are most serviceable to them. The position of a man in society, with its obligations and interests, forces ideas upon him which all the theory of education would not have impressed upon him as long as he was not called upon practically to make use of them.

At stake in this and other such writings, which remarkably prefigure later theorists like Gramsci, is in effect the mediating function of educational institutions, in at least two senses. The first thing criticized here is the assumption that knowledge is valid only when it is mediated through institutions defined by their distance from the conditions of labor. Such distantiation permits the "representative" claims of educational institutions by asserting their emancipation from interests or class positions while at the same time disenfranchising knowledge that derives from what become the merely "local" conditions of oppression. Senex, to the contrary, radically affirms the value of such knowledge, not because of any essential class basis for it, but because of its relation to the specific "obligations and interests" and the practical uses that constitute and further it. Connected to this is the second mediating function of education, which is Senex's most explicit target, its invocation as the necessary but, of course, infinitely extensible condition for the exercise of the political franchise. The two kinds of mediation are closely related within the general concept of representation, for the differentiated space of the educational institution is a spatial correlative of the temporal deferral demanded as the precondition for participation in representative democracy.

Though much of the discussion of representation in the radical papers of the moment circulates around the Reform Bill and strictly political concepts of representation, there is a constant awareness that what is at issue in both the radical appeals for reform and conservative opposition is the relation of the state to production. Putting an end to exploitation is the rationale for political reform, and the processes are not distinct precisely because the formal equality offered by bourgeois notions of representation is never accepted. But the debate on representation and the need for a working-class legislature constantly opens onto the question of representation within other organizations and institutions. Two instances of debate will serve to indicate the range of the discussions and the variety of positions taken in the realm of education and trade unionism as well as in politics.

Henry Hetherington, "the Poor Man's Guardian," was editor of one of the most radical of working-class periodicals, *Penny Papers for the People*, from 1830 to 1831. A printer and proprietor of his own press, he militated weekly against the Reform Bill's splitting of the middle classes from the working classes through the £10 franchise, against the property qualification and against deferral of the franchise on grounds of laboring-class ignorance. At the same time, as his nom de plume suggests, he espoused a kind of intellectual avant-gardism, believing—unlike Senex but to the same end—that the poor do not know what they want:

> The working classes are, by the blessing of our blessed constitution, generally speaking, too ignorant to form a correct opinion for themselves; they only call for a change, because their animal feelings tell them that a change is necessary, without knowing or imagining what change it is that they require: they want an adviser—they want a Guardian; we, for want of a better, have elected ourselves into that situation; and we, in their name, assert our unqualified disapprobation of the proposed measure.[15]

At the same time as he claims the right to represent the poor, given their ignorance, Hetherington does not proceed to extend this judgment to deferral of franchise. To the contrary, here he agrees with Senex:

> Anarchy and confusion of any sort, though it might for a short time exist, would very soon give place to "order," which would every day improve, while ignorance would every day diminish; and why? because the ignorant and disorderly would have their interests repre-

sented by persons capable of sympathizing with them—by persons, in fact, who would themselves be interested in removing the disabilities and misfortunes under which they labour, instead of by persons interested in keeping them as they are, in order that their ignorance and their wretchedness may be excuses for not rendering them their rights.[16]

Representation can take place on grounds of sympathy but is always a prelude to the removal of disabilities that hinder self-government. In the sphere of trade unionism, however, Hetherington's probably complex rather than contradictory position runs him into trouble. The *Penny Papers* for April 23, 1831, carries a report of a meeting concerning an "Important Union of the Working Classes" held to discuss the constitution of that union. Among the resolutions proposed for it is the following: "That as this Union is intended to raise the working classes from their present degraded condition, it is necessary that it should be done by themselves, therefore no person shall be eligible to act on the Commitee [*sic*] unless he be a wealth producer; that is, one who gets his living by his labour."

The report recounts that Hetherington, among others including Benjamin Warden, a saddler, opposed this resolution on the grounds of its exclusive spirit, its restriction of choice of officials, and its infringement on the liberty of the union's members. The resolution was accordingly amended to permit all members to participate on committees. This organizational dispute was immediately grasped by more radical unionists to be an instance of appropriation of working-class institutions and to have far-reaching implications. A letter from "A Friend to the Poor" in the following week's issue connects a general statement of principles on representation to the events that had just transpired at the union. The letter is worth quoting at length since it articulates very clearly a position radically opposed to representative democracy in any sphere that belongs in a long-standing tradition of British radical thinking running back at least to Thomas Spence's writings in the 1790s:

People who live by plunder will always tell you to be submissive to thieves. To talk of representation, in any shape, being of any use to the people is sheer nonsense; unless the people have a house of working people, and represent themselves. . . . Representation, therefore, by a different body of people to those who are represented, or who live by an opposite source, is a mockery, and those who persuade the people to the contrary, are either idiots, or cheats. . . . The people should drop all contention, therefore, about electing a legislature in its present shape, and contend night and day, every moment of their lives for a legislature of their own, or one made up of themselves. . . . .

This resolution spoke a volume, by showing the people's desire to take the lead in favour of themselves. This resolution you and Mr. Warden destroyed (not from bad, though from mistaken motives) by insinuating, like the present lawmakers, that the people were not intelligent nor honest enough to conduct their own concerns. I shall only observe on this matter that if the wealth-producers be intelligent and honest enough to raise every thing in the world, from a pin to a first-rate ship of war, they are certainly intelligent enough and honest enough to regulate the affairs of a union among themselves. You and Mr. Warden, then, will do well in withdrawing yourselves from their committee, and every one else who is not absolutely a man who works for a master, or working man. Attend their meetings, hear what they have to say, report their proceedings, and encourage them to go on; but at the same time give them the lead, learn them to go alone, and encourage them to be no longer slaves but men. There must be a house of the people. . . . The people, therefore, to be well represented must represent themselves. This is the way in which representation began, and this is the way it must end.

Passages like these from Senex and A Friend to the Poor do more than recall Marx's characterization in *The Eighteenth Brumaire of Louis Bonaparte* of the French peasantry of a later year. (The peasants, says Marx, "cannot represent themselves. They must be represented.") Senex and A Friend to the Poor indicate the degree of critical consciousness among English working-class circles as to the stakes involved in the discussion of representation and of the close relationship between being represented, being educated, and being appropriated. They do not constitute a culture, by any means, if we mean by culture a distinct recreational domain of disinterested reflection, but rather criticize the very terms that require and maintain that separate domain. Culture is not invoked here precisely because what is being envisaged allows for no separation between economic, political, and educational self-management.

This brief encounter within English radicalism has a counterpart in one between a radical position on education and liberal/utilitarian patronage some six or seven years before. This second episode is part of a longer story involving the emergence of what is now Birkbeck College out of the London Mechanics Institute. The *Mechanic's Mag-*

azine, founded in 1823 and edited by James Robertson, was a poly-technic encyclopedia designed to promote self-instruction among working-class mechanics. Its principal aim was to make better mechanics of its readers, yet, though it is a very different kind of periodical from the penny magazines or unstamped press of the next decade, it contains frequent editorials connecting the process of self-education to the political process and to the self-management of working-class institutions. A long article by the editor on October 11, 1823, "Institutions for the Instruction of Mechanics," brings these issues together in calling for the foundation of a London Mechanics Institute on the model of those already established in Edinburgh and Glasgow. Robertson is quite explicit on the necessity for self-education:

> The education of a free people, like their property, will always be directed most beneficially for them when it is in their own hands. When government interferes, it directs its efforts more to make people obedient and docile, than wise and happy. It desires to control the thoughts, and fashion even the minds of its subjects; and to give into its hands the power of educating the people, is the worst possible extension of that most pernicious practice which has so long desolated society, of allowing one or a few men to direct the actions and control the conduct of millions. . . . The people only want to have the means of educating themselves left in their pockets untouched by the tax-gatherer, and there is no doubt but they will employ those means more for their own advantage than they can possibly be employed by men who, for the very reason they belong to the upper classes, can know little or nothing of what the lower classes need, nor what is fitting for them. They know, indeed too well what is proper to them as subjects, as tax-paying machines, as slaves, but not what is suitable to them as labourers and as men.[17]

Robertson's proposal was successful, and a Mechanics Institute that included among its institutional laws that two-thirds of the thirty-member committee "must be taken from the working classes" was founded. William Cobbett concurred with Robertson, apparently, remarking at the public meeting for its establishment that "the thing should be managed by the mechanics themselves. . . . If they allowed other management to interfere, men would soon be found who would put the mechanics on one side, and make use of them only as tools."[18]

Robertson's and Cobbett's fears were rapidly realized, as Henry Brougham, Whig member of Parliament and promoter of "Useful Knowledge" publications, and John Birkbeck, a philanthropist who had been closely involved in the founding of the Edinburgh and Glasgow Institutes, indeed began to set aside the mechanics. Birkbeck's interventions, not unlike Hetherington's, were "from mistaken motives" rather than bad ones; they radically undermined the autonomy of the Mechanics Institute all the same. He donated money for a lecture theater and for courses of lectures which, as Robertson put it in a lengthy and frustrated editorial in July 1825, should have been erected "with their own savings, and with their own hands." The upshot, he argues, is that "Instead of the men being encouraged to depend entirely on their own contributions, they have been taught to place their chief hope on the benevolent assistance of the great and wealthy, and to applaud, to the very echo, every announcement of a new subscription from Lord this and Sir that."[19]

Robertson's protestations, and those of a number of other correspondents who discuss especially the principle of paying for lectures as a crucial element in self-governed education, were evidently of little avail. They indicate, nonetheless, the widespread and articulate nature of English working-class awareness of the stakes involved in the intricate connections between self-representation, education, and economic self-management. Rather than accepting passage through the intermediary institutions of a disinterested education, they insist on self-determination in that as in other spheres. *Mechanic's Magazine*, like the penny magazines, has little to say on the question of culture, precisely because its definition of knowledge is devoted to making mechanics better mechanics rather than to assimilating them to bourgeois notions of wholeness and harmony. In both kinds of publication, what is emerging is a highly articulate conception of what is meant by, in Gramsci's later words, the "organic intellectual." It is, however, our contention that in order fully to comprehend Gramsci's important distinction between "organic" and "traditional" intellectuals, we must extend and even subvert the meaning he gave these terms, which are not necessarily polar opposites or even alternatives.[20] "Traditional" intellectuals can prove to be "organic" to bourgeois social formations. Culture—in Raymond Williams's understanding of the term—requires intellectuals who are every bit as "organic" to the cultural sphere as engineers are to the industrial sphere. Conversely, our nineteenth-century mechanics in effect remind us that non-"traditional" intellectuals of the kind envisaged by radicals are essential to a different understanding of the social formation. Even though the concentration on political and practical/mechanical information may scandalize those who see the remedy to the damage inflicted on working-class culture as lying in more cultural freedom and development, a shrewd if ultimately unsuccessful political intelligence clearly determined these options. If what follows is the increasing hegemony of the view that "universal education must precede universal franchise" (to cite Mill's *Representative Government*), we should not foreclose the multifaceted debates current among English radicals of the 1820s and 1830s. Nor should we assume that their recalcitrance to the "culture and society" tradition has nothing to teach us at this juncture about the value of a political and material critique that emerges from self-consciously positioned knowledge.

Dissident Elements or Contested Terrain?: The Chartists Reconsidered

> *Hurrah for the Masses,*
> *The lawyers are asses,*
> *Their gammon and spinach are stale!*
> *The law is illegal,*
> *The Commons are regal,*
> *The Judges are going to gaol.*
> —Chartist broadside[21]

At first glance, E. P. Thompson's characterization of working-class constitutionalism as "the illusion of the epoch"—he means the epoch that culminated in 1832—appears to be complemented by Gareth Stedman Jones's insistence that Chartism too suffered from a cognate "illusion." Chartism, a response to the setbacks the workers movement suffered in 1832 and 1834, was in Stedman Jones's view stymied by what was "first and foremost a vocabulary of political exclusion"[22]—exclusion, that is, from the franchise. The Chartists on this view were misled by their commitment to a shopworn legacy of natural rights and of traditional forms of protest. They signally failed to see that by the 1830s these resources were no longer appropriate, having been overtaken by that convenient alibi of the historian (and of the political economist), the "logic of events."

Stedman Jones's criticism points forward as well as back, to the way in which (in Dorothy Thompson's words) "the political impulse of Chartism [was to become] constricted into the narrow confines of popular liberalism in the second half of the [nineteenth] century."[23] Even later than this, Stedman Jones reminds us, working-class aspirations in Britain were to find political expression only through a Parliamentary Labour Party that was self-consciously constituted as the "political" (read "parliamentary") arm, or tail, of an otherwise relentlessly and defensively economistic trade union movement. The argument is that working-class politicians were to bite the fruit of parliamentarism because this fruit had so long been forbidden them; and that they were to do so even though parliamentarism deflected the socialist impulse and made possible successive betrayals of socialism at the hands of successive political stalwarts, not all of whom even called themselves socialist.[24]

That such betrayals were to take place is not at issue. What is at issue is Stedman Jones's casting of the Chartists as having been fixated on the franchise in such a way as to have made them possible. His argument, like so many prospective arguments, is armed with hindsight—hindsight about later developments about which the Chartists could have known nothing. Stedman Jones's thesis is in any case not immune from what E. P. Thompson memorably termed "the enormous condescention of posterity";[25] it judges and condemns Chartism in the light of the very distinction between "the political" and "the social" that during the Chartist decades had yet to take shape. To the contrary, what Ellen Meiksins Wood, in her critique of Stedman Jones, terms "the unity between political and appropriative powers"[26] was made possible by the 1832 Reform Bill and made manifest in the New Poor Law of 1834. It was to the Chartists themselves neither a concept, nor a threat, nor yet a distant prospect. It was lived reality.

It was in response to this looming reality that the working-class movement was constitutionalism's heart, after 1832 as before.[27] In 1832 the working-class reform movement needed middle-class representatives, *Vertreter* like Francis Place, who used the threat of working-class insurrection, and the reality of revolution in France, alongside that of the Swing Riots, melodramatically ringing London with flames,[28] to negotiate a line of retreat acceptable to all but the most diehard defenders of "Old Corruption." By admitting to the franchise only the unambiguously, solidly middle class, by drawing the line between them and the lower orders with scrupulous care, and by superimposing the parliamentary representation of the newly enfranchised onto an established system of "virtual representation," without seriously dislodging this system,[29] middle-class reformers proffered to a reluctant Parliament the very compromise that would strengthen all parties concerned—except, of course, the workers movement, which was left high and dry. "They had united all property against all poverty," said James Bronterre O'Brien.[30] Only such an accommodation on favorable terms of the manufacturers with the landed elite would enable yet another line to be drawn, in short order, in 1834: the Less Eligibility Principle as enshrined in the Poor Law Amendment Act, the New Poor Law.

The workers movement's fervent opposition to this Draconian measure suggests that workers understood full well what later historians proved able to ignore: that the 1832 Reform Bill could be considered an advance in democracy (as opposed to liberalism) only in the light of subsequent developments that 1832 was designed not to encourage or promote but expressly to forestall.[31] The newly augmented ruling-class coalition, however divided on issues of principle (most dramatically, the Corn Laws) it may have been, could at a pinch always close ranks against the (rarely insurrectionary) threat of universal suffrage from below. This is why there was no solid phalanx of aristocratic opposition to the rise of industry and of political economy, its intellectual counterpart. The landed classes duly survived the repeal of the Corn Laws in 1846. The landed gentry continued to populate the cabinet, to monopolize the representation of rural areas in Parliament, and often to represent urban areas too. It never needed to fight a rearguard action against capitalism. The manufacturers, for their part, gained virtually unlimited freedom of maneuver from the 1832 settlement. George Loveless described the Whig governments of the 1830s as a "tyrant faction," and there is no reason to regard this view of them as exaggerated. We need only look to the measures it enacted. The Tithe Commutation Act of 1836 and repeal of the Corn Laws in 1846 were hits at the aristocracy, to be sure, but the hits at the workers were much more serious, concerted, and bitterly contested. There was the Irish Coercion Act (1833), the Poor Law Amendment Act (1834), the Tolpuddle Martyrs episode of the same year, the Municipal Reform Act (1835); the Newspaper Act (1836), and, to cap this legislative barrage, the proposal to set up constabulary forces in rural districts in the late 1830s—forces that, it was feared, would busy themselves both with regulating the leisure and educational activities of the working class in the unincorporated towns that were to be important centers of Chartist support, and with enforcing the New Poor Law and employers' interests during trade disputes.[32]

Feargus O'Connor was under no illusions about the shift in the class composition of the magistracy that the much-trumpeted municipal reform would entail, a shift that would influence the very definition of law and justice.[33] The transition from "Old Corruption" (Cobbett's "Thing") to the new "tyrant faction" bid fair to reproduce itself anew at the local level; the pelf and place that had characterized municipal as well as parliamentary politics would give way to the reproduction of the values of a new, more covetous gentry. Their interest was all too frequently in the interpretation of newly enacted industrial legislation: the Master and Servant Act of 1823, the passing of which in some respects overshadowed the more paradoxical, more dogmatic repeal of the Combination Acts the following year; the Truck Act of 1831; the Mines Regulation Act of 1841; the "Gagging Bill" of 1848, which for the first time made seditious speech a felony and significantly increased penalties for it. Masters-as-magistrates looked likely to sit in judgment over court cases where they (or their cohorts) were interested parties. These cases often involved industrial practices that were being redefined as crimes. Traditional perks such as the garnering of waste material, wood and coal, as well as "fents" of cloth, were being refigured as theft, and the perpetrators prosecuted accordingly.

Reaction against such measures can seem backward-looking, since it was directed against the newfound "freedom" of a newly hegemonic class to destroy customary rights. The customs in question were, however, not believed to have existed since time immemorial but to be those of an already-formed market society. The point needs making (against Stedman Jones and others who argue that workers movements were simply shackled by their respect for tradition) that reaction was directed against a barrage of recent interventions, the sheer volume of which is enough to give us pause. It was against the patterns of an already-established market society that new machinery was freely introduced, the factory system freely extended, unlimited competition freely espoused, wages freely beaten down, standards of craftsmanship and community life freely undermined.[34] In the words of James Leach's *Stubborn Facts from the Factories* (1844): "The working class will ever look upon this as a brigand system that allows employers to assume a power over the law and by a nefarious plotting first create what they are pleased to call offences and then punish them. They are lawmakers, judges and jurors."[35] The Chartist desideratum could not be more succinctly put: "to assume a power over the law," as both the manufacturers and the workers movement were aware, meant to establish new legal precedents. By focusing on issues involving fines or imprisonment, working-class radicals (including those who wrote for the unstamped press) were at the same time moving into new territory, removing the debate about "free labor" from the confines of "political economy," which was quick to redefine labor as "free" to circulate among alternatives (which included the workhouse) to the moral realm. Here, labor, however mobile in principle it was supposed to be—and we should recall that the penny post was advocated before 1840 (when it was introduced) on the grounds that it would assist the Poor Law in freeing the labor market[36]—was fundamentally unfree because it was palpably oppressed and penalized.

In advancing these arguments the workers movement was advancing itself onto the terrain, which was moral as well as economic, already staked out by political economy. The uneasy coalition that had pushed the 1832 Reform Bill through Parliament had fallen apart. Henceforward, liberalism was to mean laissez-faire, constitutional reform of a piecemeal kind, and the existing franchise; radicalism, the extension of the franchise without necessarily maintaining (let alone extending) laissez-faire. What declined, but not until the 1850s and 1860s, was "the presence of a working-class 'alternative' form of political economy in which progress within the existing economic system was deemed impossible and where the interests of the working class and the middle class were held to be always and everywhere diametrically opposed."[37]

Earlier, however, this "working-class 'alternative'" had enjoyed a real existence, one that overlapped both with Chartism and with Owenism, and that found its characteristic means of expression in the unstamped press. It would be unwarranted to characterize this alternative either in terms of the working-class economism and constitutionalism that succeeded it, or in terms of the eighteenth-century radicalism from which it emerged. In particular, there was and could have been no apolitical trade unionism at this time; the repression of the 1790s alone, by penalizing conspiracies among workmen and movements for parliamentary reform simultaneously and by means of the same statutes, had effectively coupled together economic and political radicalism: "The aristocracy were interested in repressing Jacobin 'conspiracies' of the people, the manufacturors were interested in defeating 'conspiracies' to increase wages: the Combination Acts served both purposes."[38] The "working-class 'alternative'" in any case denoted a shift within this coupling—a shift, in Claeys's words, "from moral economy to socialism," which helps give the Chartist decades their specificity.

Radicalism at the end of the eighteenth century, prior to the systematic repression of British Jacobinism, primarily entailed a drive to reform a visibly corrupt Parliament and extend the franchise. It envisaged no specific economic program.[39] The point of no return to this political universe was reached when early "socialism discarded the notion that there should be any connection between the right of the franchise and the ownership of property"; rejecting such a connection became practically obligatory among those who were so painstakingly denied the franchise in 1832. Ownership of property was now "perceived as itself a fateful source of social and political corruption, blinding the possessors to the suffering of the dispossessed, and with the increasing inequality of wealth gradually threatening the entire society with cataclysm."[40]

The year 1832 signified a new and glaring contrast, between "the political" (the narrow caste in power, which had proved itself capable of controlling access to its ranks) and "the social" (the rising demands of the unenfranchised majority, and the notion of popular participation in general). "The political" came to coincide with individualism and competition, "the social" to connote the problem of poverty, working-class movements of all kinds, and the condition of labor in general. The working class came to see itself, and to be seen by some others, as the most "social" or even "sociable" (in the sense of moral) of classes, and at the same time as "the democracy," the largest class or the numerical majority of the population.

These distinctions help us countenance Chartism, the most characteristic mass movement of "the democracy":

> What they wanted was a voice in making the laws they were called upon to obey; they believed that taxation without representation was tyranny, and ought to be resisted; they took a leading part in agitating in favour of the Ten Hours question, the repeal of the taxes on knowledge, education, co-operation, civil and religious liberty and the land question, for they were the true pioneers in all the great movements of the time."[41]

Chartism, we should remember, was a movement, not just a doctrine; as such, like the Owenism with which it frequently intersected at the local level, it "provided cultural facilities, ways of life, and modes of identity linked to what was largely understood as a common ideal, a world in which all were accorded dignity, a decent standard of living and a full range of civil, religious and political liberties, privileges which far too many were denied under the existing system."[42] Chartists, far from being fixated on the franchise as a nostrum or a panacea (as, for instance, Stedman Jones would have it), constantly stressed that economic and social reforms were expected to follow from the inception of popular government. "What else has the [People's] Charter ever been regarded as but as the means to social ends?" asked the O'Connorite Chartist Thomas Clark in the 1850s. In the words of Joan Wallach Scott, "Stedman Jones does not entertain the possibility that economic grievances are about power and politics, that Chartists might have sought economic change by political means, that their visions of power intertwined economics and politics."[43] Eileen Yeo has put the point well:

> The six points of the Charter, however revolutionary for their time, were not all that the Chartists meant by self-government. . . . The very way in which the Chartists tried to govern their movement disclosed a blueprint for collective control which involved much more than periodic voting for parliament. . . . It is interesting to speculate on how parliamentary democracy might have been different if won by the Chartists and erected on a foundation of vigorous local self-activity.[44]

As "a Christian Socialist" (probably F. D. Maurice) put it in 1850:

> The Democratic Politician looks now upon political reform, but as a
> means to an end—that end being socialism. The watchwords of Char-
> tism in 1839 were 'a full day's wages for a full day's work'. That cry
> long since gave way to the more defined idea of the 'organization of
> labour'. This latter opinion is, I am quite aware, far too little compre-
> hended by many of those who are loudest in their demands for the
> Franchise, but it should also be borne in mind that the leaders of the
> Popular Party in this country are not so ill-informed thereon.[45]

Our "Christian Socialist" is by no means alone either in pointing up
debates, contested terrain, among the Chartists or in noting the shift
that was taking place among them "from moral economy to socialism." Older slogans were commonly seen among the Chartists themselves as invoking the habits and assumptions of a bygone, but by
no means necessarily premarket, age when master and man were
more intimately acquainted and where competition had not yet
erupted into universal viciousness, before the great extremes of
wealth and poverty had made the two nations so sure of their mutual antagonism. In Asa Briggs's words:

> During the last years of the agitation there was an unmistakeable shift
> in emphasis from the demand for political reform within the frame-
> work of a parliamentary ideal, a demand which grew naturally out of
> eighteenth century radicalism, to the search for social democracy, a
> search that led some Chartists—notably [Ernest] Jones and [George Ju-
> lian] Harney—into socialism."[46]

Not all Chartists, then, were constitutionalist and hidebound in
Stedman Jones's required sense. How else could we account for the
fact—largely unexamined in historians' accounts—that

> [Chartism's] female membership appears to have been very large and,
> as in earlier radical-democratic agitations, very militant: throughout the
> peak years of Chartism tens of thousands of women campaigned for
> the Six Points, leading mass demonstrations, organizing "exclusive deal-
> ing" campaigns, teaching in Chartist Sunday schools, praying in Chartist
> churches, and sometimes acting as violent shock troops in struggles
> with the military and the police.[47]

Or that "at least eighty female Political Unions and Chartist Associations were established between 1837 and 1844"?[48] Women did not

stand to get the vote; we have reason to suspect that once historians finally get around to examining what women Chartists had to say—as opposed to what male Chartists had to say about them (which is all that Dorothy Thompson, for instance, gives us)—they will uncover traces of an alternative and wider discourse on representation than Stedman Jones and others have been able to identify.[49] That Chartist conceptions of legality and of political action shifted "from moral economy to socialism" is in any event scarcely to be wondered at: there could be more than one interpretation of the law, and everybody knew this. Middle-class interpretations were at once innovatory—they commonly used the (capitalized) word *Radical* about themselves—and hegemonic. Chartist memories of other, competing interpretations were above all else frighteningly recent. During the early 1840s every worker in a manufacturing town like Blackburn, Lancashire, could recall its preindustrial character from personal experience; what to later generations, and to later historians, was to appear as "progress," the wave of the future, was to its victims at the time at best an uncertain experiment, a leap in the dark, whose ultimate effects no one could foresee but whose immediate effects—on them—were all too evidently, and all too disastrously, apparent.[50]

Yet its political counterpart, the Whig hegemony, we should remember, had more than one face to present. The abrupt triumph of liberalism-without-democracy had depended upon the stirring up of a democratic sentiment that had little enough of the traditional about it. Dorothy Thompson quite rightly points to a "political awakening" that (however uneasily) attended the Reform agitation and that survived in its wake, outliving its own betrayal:

> A combination of mass pressure and threats of violence as well as reasoned argument and constitutional petition had [after all] apparently achieved the impossible. Faced with popular pressure, a corrupt parliament, based on patronage and interest, had voluntarily extended its privileges to a section of the hitherto unenfranchised."[51]

That this concession, once wrung out of Old Corruption, should have left in its wake a degree of what Michael Loewy (sounding rather like Ernst Bloch) in another connection terms "utopian surplus" is not very surprising. Society, after all, had changed radically, and the changes in question had duly received their political ratification in the form of the Whig ascendancy. Why then should not further, more fundamental change be on the radical agenda?

Dorothy Thompson misprises the openness of this agenda by insisting, against the evidence, that Chartism contained "no proposal for the complete replacement of existing property relations," and by asserting that, in the eyes of the Chartists, labor as the property of the laborer was "*as much* in need of protection by the law as any other form of property."[52] This is a misleading way of making the valid point that Chartists were not, by and large, opposed to property per se, since it overlooks the central fact that there was one form of property to which they were unalterably opposed: the property whose untrammeled movement the laws of political economy were bent upon establishing, defending, and extending. While this position may fall short of a wholesale theorizing of expropriation, the point remains that there is no warrant for unduly liberalizing it, as, in effect, Dorothy Thompson does. As far as the Chartists were concerned, political liberalism and economic liberalization were assailable by virtue of their intrinsic connection with one another. Conversely, democracy, understood expansively, and socialism were cognate concepts that involved each other for the good and simple reason that each aimed to promote people's control over the conditions of their own existence. Democracy and capitalism were by contrast antithetical principles; liberalism and capitalism stood and fell together. This perception helps explain Chartism and by so doing points beyond it. It helps us confront the question of whether political and economic liberalization have ever been more than contingently related—a question that is, as we write, being raised all over again in the very different context of Central and Eastern European societies in the 1990s. Had there been democracy of the kind the Chartists espoused in early-nineteenth-century Britain, would there, could there have been capitalism too? The question strikes us as an open one, since genuine democratization would have enabled the populace to have resisted capitalism, and there is much evidence that they would have seized the chance of doing so.[53]

This is of course to speculate, but not groundlessly. It is not hard to uncover a strain in Bronterre O'Brien's speeches—let alone Fergus O'Connor's—that disparages on principle any notion of balancing out the claims or "rights" of capital vis-à-vis labor. Capitalism in this frequently expressed view quite simply has no rights. Capital is the wrongs done to labor given tangible form; we should recall that Chartist stalwarts were often familiar with the writings of the so-called Ricardian socialists (Thompson, Hodgkin, Bray, et al.), where the notion of a labor theory of value was given its first socialist form. For all these reasons, there is discernible within Chartist writings and speeches a line of argument specifying that democracy and "wage slavery" exclude and contradict each other, and that any attempt to graft one upon the other would be incoherent and contradictory.

This line of argument, of course, had no claim to monopoly and in fact jostled rather uncomfortably with others. Chartism was in the first instance a multifarious movement within which desire for the franchise—for "universal suffering and animal parliaments," as one contemporary wag put the matter—was more of a least common denominator that helped keep the movement together than anything else. It is important to keep this multiplicity of beliefs in mind, in view of the danger of selecting some of them arbitrarily, wresting them out of their context, and then deciding that the chosen few are the important ones because later developments appear to echo them. Chartist actors and beliefs that seem to prefigure liberalism are cases in point. It has often been pointed out that Ernest Jones made the fateful transition to liberalism in his own lifetime, and with little apparent difficulty; and Bronterre O'Brien, for his part, is on record as having favored, in 1848, a middle-class alliance—even if this proposal did provoke the withering and scornful opposition of Feargus O'Connor. There again, William Lovett can readily enough be seen (as he is seen by Dorothy Thompson, for instance) as having prefigured later working-class liberalism. Lovett, indeed, is particularly important for our present purposes not only because he was the foremost Chartist theoretician of education, but also because in this capacity he shifted from the quintessential early Chartist view that political participation was a form of education that alone could make possible other forms of education to the quintessentially Victorian-liberal view that prior education was needed in order to prepare the lower orders for the exercise of political rights (understood now as the suffrage).

It was of course the latter view that won out—to the extent, indeed, of having been trotted out all over again in our own century and applied first to women and then to colonized peoples in their struggles for political independence. More to the point with respect to Lovett, however, is the fact that only when he convinced himself and others of the (temporal and logical) priority of education over the suffrage did he gain significant support from the middle class. We should not wonder at such support, for reasons that will become clear shortly; we should, however, take note of the fact that this support was not of the Chartists at large in any direct sense, since many of them disputed Lovett's conclusions—as did, to give the most prominent example, Feargus O'Connor, whose *Conservative Chartism, Christian Chartism and Temperance Chartism* (1841) was a broadside directed at Lovett. Middle-class support as it was extended to Lovett is best regarded, perhaps, as one of a series of attempts to sever "respectable" Chartism from the disreputable remainder. That such severance appears to have succeeded in the long run should not, however, be allowed to obscure the resistance to it during the Chartist period itself. For it was resisted vigorously, and it matters greatly how we are to assess this resistance.

To see this we need only ask ourselves, in the first instance, what it was that needed to be resisted, since this issue went beyond Lovett himself. Educating the poor was not just a Victorian obsession. It merits being read as an ideology, since it served at once as one (and often the) means of shelving dangerous political reforms, and at the same time operated as an important mechanism of social control. Time and again, crudely deterrent legal and penal mechanisms of control were supplemented by officially sanctioned attempts at educational rehabilitation, which were themselves an expression of the same imperative. Chadwick's New Poor Law was duly supplemented by Dr. Kay's workhouse and district schools; factory inspectors' reports were similarly supplemented by riders in their concluding paragraphs about the pressing need for tightly regulated and closely supervised education. As Richard Johnson succinctly puts it, "the condition of the poor came almost to mean the condition of their education."[54] Dr. J. P. Kay, who gave his name to the influential document known as Kay's Minutes[55] represented education as being, for the employer of labor, analogous to the use of profit to ensure against capital loss.

The "legitimate educator" was, in the idiom of Kay's Minutes, there (or supposed to be there) in order to preempt the "socialist."

His task was to be aided by the fact that the "appalling concatenation of evils that would reduce the working population to utter debasement, destroying the very structure of society by the explosive violence of volcanic elements" had a "remote or accidental origin" and was in no way implicit in capitalist society as such. By "judicious management" this concatenation might be "entirely removed." After all, continued Kay, with no discernible irony, "a system which promotes the advance of civilization and diffuses it over the world cannot be inconsistent with the happiness of the great mass of the people." Utopian as it was, Kay's optimism was tempered by two conditions, "environmental" and "moral." The former involved public health, sanitation, adequate policing, and—needless to add—the repeal of the Corn Laws; the latter entailed "teaching the poor man his political position in society, and the moral and religious duties attendant upon it." In insisting that "environmental" could not do its work unaided by "moral" reform, Kay was, in Johnson's words, "attempting to express the connection between environment, consciousness and culture in the language of moral censure [and] of providential causation." This language should not obscure the fact that Kay's moralistic and paternalistic admonitions were superimposed upon arguments that were, at root, economic. He was attempting to denounce working-class decadence—his emphasis on "disorganizing doctrines" was designed to link irreligion, sedition, and moral iniquity—moralistically and "scientifically" at the same time. His words of 1838 are not disarming: "The attention the [Poor Law] Commissioners have given this subject [education] is likely to prove a means for vindicating their opinions and designs from the imputation of being under the influence of cold-blooded economic speculations, without the infusion of a more generous sympathy for the happiness of the poorer classes."

Since working-class parents were by definition disqualified, incapacitated from fulfilling their "natural" role as educators, "a little artificial world of virtuous exertion"—Kay means the school, not the workhouse, though his language (here as elsewhere) betrays him—is to be substituted for parents' baneful influence on their young. By substitution is meant not addition but replacement: "We cannot let farmers or labourers, miners or mechanics be judges of our educational work. It is part of that work to educate them all into a sense of what true education is." Salvation, in other words, must come from outside if the vicious circle of iniquity is to be broken. The teacher, a social "emissary," is himself to be tightly controlled lest he "go native" among his charges. Small wonder, then, that Richard Johnson characterizes Kay's Minutes as "an enormously ambitious attempt to determine, through the capture of educational means, the patterns of thought, sentiment and behaviour of the working class" and concludes that as "a system of control . . . the Minutes rival any Parliamentary statute dealing with a social matter in the first half of the nineteenth century."[56]

Orthodox nineteenth-century educational theory, with its well-known emphasis on "character" building for the poor as a prerequisite for the franchise, attempted to redistribute guilt away from those responsible for the condition of the poor onto the poor themselves. But it also, rather less obviously but no less insidiously, reduced social relations to individual characteristics, thus replaying at a different level the decisive shift already effected by political economy. Political economy had given particular interests, or some particular interests, the aspect of universal beneficence, via Smith's "hidden hand." This interpellated the individual economic actor in a new way by validating in advance the outcome of his self-interested actions. Educational theory interpellated the working-class subject in a cognate manner: as he who had to prove himself worthy of admission to the franchise on the basis of educational attainment. In this way the notion of the individual as the agent of causality gets reintroduced and reinforced, and social problems at the same time get redefined as problems that admit of (re)solution without any need for reconstruction of the social order, since it is individual changes in aptitude or attitude that can solve or resolve them. Orthodox educational theory even managed to reintroduce political economy and Malthusianism by the back door, thus closing the ideological loop once and for all. Dorothy Thompson quotes the following revealing passage, advocating "such education as would correct their [the workers'] prejudices, increase their self-respect, elevate their minds, and more especially impart the degree of moral and religious principle which would more effectively deter them from the habit of marrying without the means of rearing families in comfort."[57] Opposition to "education," so defined—as subjugation—is not to be wondered at. Neither is the fact that against these views, the Chartists "were continually trying to keep control of essential aspects of their lives, including education and the workshop, against the influence of the state or of profit-seeking speculators."[58] *Chartism, a New Organization for the People*, written by Lovett and John Collins in gaol, proposed, accordingly, a national system of education under democratic control, to be financed by a levy of a penny a week on all signatories of the Chartist petition. This was to finance education at all levels, from kindergarten to training college. The idea was stillborn. In Dorothy Thompson's words:

> The post-Chartist years were characterized by a series of Factory Acts with educational provisions, paralleled by the growth of a network of "provided" schools, provided [that is] by rival religious bodies and supported by government grants which culminated in the 1870 [Education] Act, after which school attendance was gradually made compulsory. . . . The life of the School Board as an institution was short, and it did not live to flourish in the era of universal suffrage. . . . Though the volume of provided schools expanded, the control which working people exercised over their children's education lessened considerably.[59]

We may of course never fully know what, or how much, was lost with this lessening of control—a lessening that was, correspondingly, a triumph for culture (as Raymond Williams characterized it, at least in 1958) and for the state (which Williams, we have argued, failed adequately to characterize). It was a triumph for each alike, much (we have reason to suspect) as Matthew Arnold would have wished. It is a point of considerable importance that the differentiation of culture from the political, economic, social, and class spheres of people's existence—a differentiation that, by making of culture both a supplement and a standard, provided Williams with both an opportunity and a predicament—was no mere intellectual desideratum. It became a fait accompli, with consequences we can only guess at (as we still wrestle with them). What can be established with some certainty, however, is that the linkage beween culture and the state—even, or especially, at the level of potentially ever recessive educational qualifications for the suffrage—was in no way an innocuous coupling. Nor indeed was it regarded as innocuous by those who contested it at the time of its juncture. To the contrary, the discourse on representation, which was always implicit in the idea of culture as Williams and others characterize it, and which Williams effectively reproduces in *Culture and Society*, was disputed and contested in different ways and at a variety of different levels at the moment of its historical emergence.

We have argued that the division of spheres that resulted from, and was an intrinsic part of, the liberal-representative settlement that was to become hegemonic for British politics in the nineteenth century and beyond was an outcome, not a demiurge; and that to read back its features uncritically into earlier debates is seriously to misrepresent what was at stake in these debates. Within this circle, the idea of culture produces the consensual grounds for representative democracy and the liberal settlement by annulling individual differences while drawing the formal or "representative" disposition in every person out of the real, particular conditions of that person's life. Only thus can the state become the collective representative of an abstract ethical quality, and culture must be seen accordingly as not merely the preserve of Gramsci's "traditional" intellectual, but the agency and site of the formation of citizens for the state. Culture is an *organ* of the state that, as Arnold put it, it suggests. Williams is of course the spirit as much as the object of our critique; his own intellectual and personal itinerary can be taken as a commentary on the distinction Gramsci delineated between the "traditional" and the "organic" intellectual. For contradiction inheres not simply, as Williams seems first to have thought, between a "tradition" of culture and the dehumanizing effects of industrialism, but also *within* the intellectual whose "organic" function for the state is to represent and produce the universality that is in other spheres denied. The functional position of the left cultural intellectual is in contradiction with the traditional critique she or he performs. Yet this contradiction, so deeply implicit in *Culture and Society*, helps us stake out what we take to be a corresponding difference, between purely political emancipation and real human emancipation, that was first proffered in Marx's prescient essay "On 'The Jewish Question'" in 1843. What our inquiry suggests is that the position occupied by what Gramsci designates as the "traditional" intellectual is in fact organic to the bourgeois social formation, understood as the articulation of differentiated social spheres (economic, political, cultural). What is at stake, then, is not merely the resistance of the left intellectual from within a structurally traditional location, but a remobilization of an entirely different conception of the social formation, a conception for which Gramsci's distinction between traditional and organic would make little sense. This alternative conception involves grasping simultaneously the ideological effectivity of the sphere of culture itself and the necessity for its dissolution in the name of human emancipation.

NOTES

The authors' thanks are due to Greg Foster, Michel Chaouli, Françoise Vergès, and our students.

1. Raymond Williams, *Politics and Letters: Interviews with New Left Review* (London: Verso, 1981), pp. 99-100.

2. Ibid., p. 97.

3. It is fair to point out that Williams, reflecting later on *Culture and Society* in *Politics and Letters*, recognizes the lack of any sustained discussion of the state in the earlier volume. See *Politics and Letters*, pp.119-20. In general, we should stress here that our critique of *Culture and Society* in this essay does not constitute a critique of Williams's later revisions and intellectual developments. What we have sought to isolate is a critical moment in cultural materialism that continues to exert considerable influence quite apart from Williams's later revisions. (As he puts it in *Politics and Letters*, p. 100, "It is the very success of the book that has created the conditions for its critique.") We are not convinced, however, that even these later self-criticisms and transformations constitute a rethinking of the fundamental commitment to culture as defined in *Culture and Society*, a rethinking that, we argue here, would require a rearticulation of the social spaces differentiated historically as well as conceptually as the economic, the political, the cultural, etc. In the terms of "A Hundred Years of Culture and Anarchy," (*Problems in Materialism and Culture* [London: Verso, 1980], pp. 3-10), the concepts invoked are still the "known" rather than the "knowable" of much cultural theory, the separate sphere of culture continuing to provide a self-evident basis for even radical cultural critique.

4. For some work toward this project, see Paul Thomas, "Alien Politics," in *After Marx*, ed. Terence Ball and James Farr (Cambridge: Cambridge University Press, 1984), pp. 124-40; David Lloyd, "Analogies of the Aesthetic: the Politics of Culture and the Limits of Materialist Aesthetics," *New Formations* 10 (Spring 1990): 109-26.

5. For some background to this intellectual moment, see Williams's own discussion in *Politics and Letters*, pp. 61-63, and Alan Sinfield, *Literature, Politics and Culture in Postwar Britain* (Berkeley and Los Angeles: University of California Press, 1989), pp. 6-22.

6. "Structures of feeling" is, of course, a later theoretical concept introduced by Williams to deal in many respects with precisely the kind of problem we are indicating here in the earlier work. It has the advantage of addressing the social construction of emotion while allowing the importance of "feeling" as a crucial site for hegemonic and counterhegemonic struggles. With regard to the recurrent opposition between socialist enlightenment and feeling, Williams reveals his continuing sensitivity to this debate in defending *Culture and Society* in the introduction to the Morningside Edition, where he remarks that along with Hoggart's and Thomson's works of the same period, *Culture and Society* had been "assigned to a kind of cultural radicalism which had since been outdistanced by a clearer, harder and indeed more traditional kind of socialism" (*Culture and Society 1780-1950* [New York: Columbia University Press, 1983], p. xi).

7. Williams, *Culture and Society*, pp. 4-5.

8. Ibid., p. 316

9. Ibid., p. 333.

10. Ibid., p. 333.

11. Ibid., p. 123.

12. For a discussion of this relation between the state and culture, see David Lloyd, "Arnold, Ferguson, Schiller: Aesthetic Culture and the Politics of Aesthetics," *Cultural Critique* 2 (Winter 1986): 137-69.

13. Williams, *Culture and Society*, p. 320.

14. The relationship between our critique of Williams here and current critiques of American pluralism from the perspective of "minority discourse" could be elaborated. The political force of minority (as distinct from particular ethnic) cultures derives from their historically damaged position, which obliges a critical take on dominant cultural formations. See Abdul JanMohamed and David Lloyd, introduction to *The Nature and Context of Minority Discourse* (Oxford: Oxford University Press, 1990), pp. 4-11. Lisa Lowe has given a very cogent critique of current cultural pluralisms in "Imagining Los Angeles in the Production of Multiculturalism," forthcoming in *Multiculturalism?* ed. Avery Gordon and Chris Newfield (Minneapolis: University of Minnesota Press, 1995).

15. *Penny Papers for the People*, March 18, 1831.

16. *Penny Papers*, March 26, 1831.

17. *Mechanic's Magazine*, no. 7 (October 11, 1823): 99-100.

18. *Mechanic's Magazine*, no. 12 (November 15, 1823): 190-91.

19. *Mechanic's Magazine*, no. 99 (July 16, 1825): 238-40.

20. Antonio Gramsci, *Selections from the Prison Notebooks*, ed. and trans. by Quintin Hoare and Geoffrey Nowell-Smith (New York: International Publishers, 1971), pp. 7-9.

21. Quoted by Martha Vicinus, *The Industrial Muse: A Study of Nineteenth Century British Working Class Literature* (London: Croom Helm, 1975).

22. Gareth Stedman Jones, *Languages of Class: Studies in Working Class History 1832-1982* (Cambridge: Cambridge University Press, 1983), passim.

23. Dorothy Thompson, *The Chartists, Popular Politics in the Industrial Revolution* (New York: Pantheon, 1984), p. 301.

24. See Ralph Miliband, *Parliamentary Socialism* (London: Merlin, 1972), passim.

25. E. P. Thompson, *The Making of the English Working Class* (New York: Vintage, 1966), p. 12.

26. Ellen Meiksins Wood, *The Retreat from Class* (London: Verso, 1986), p. 111.

27. E. P. Thompson, *Making of the English Working Class*, p. 807.

28. See Eric Hobsbawm and Georges Rudé, *Captain Swing: A Social History of the Great English Agricultural Uprising of 1830* (New York: Pantheon, 1968), passim.

29. See S. H. Beer, *British Politics in the Collectivist Age* (New York: Vintage, 1969), pp. 15-20; E. P. Thompson, *Making of the English Working Class*, p. 823.

30. Asa Briggs, ed., *Chartist Studies* (London: Macmillan, 1960), p. 295.

31. E. P. Thompson, *Making of the English Working Class*, p. 812.

32. D. Thompson, *Chartists*, pp. 243-44.

33. Ibid., p. 256.

34. E. P. Thompson, *Making of the English Working Class*, p. 549.

35. Quoted in C. Aspin, *Lancashire, the First Industrial Society* (Lancashire: Helmshore, 1969), p. 73.

36. David Vincent, *Literacy and Popular Culture: England 1750-1914* (Cambridge: Cambridge University Press, 1989), p. 37.

37. Gregory Claeys, "Radicalism and Socialism in Nineteenth Century Britain: An Intro-

duction," in *Radikalismus in Literatur und Gesellschaft des 19. Jahrhunderts*, ed. Gregory Claeys and Liselotte Glage (Frankfurt: Peter Lang, 1987), p. 25.

38. E. P. Thompson, *Making of the English Working Class*, p. 198; cf. p. 181.

39. For a good summary, see Eric Foner, *Tom Paine and Revolutionary America* (Oxford: Oxford University Press, 1976), pp. 7–8.

40. Gregory Claeys, *Citizens and Saints: Politics and Anti-Politics in Early British Socialism* (Cambridge: Cambridge University Press, 1989), p. 4; cf. D. Thompson, *Chartists*, pp. 276–77.

41. Benjamin Wilson, "The Struggles of an Old Chartist," in *Testaments of Radicalism*, ed. David Vincent (Frankfurt: Europa, 1977), p. 210; Claeys, *Citizens*, pp. 216–17.

42. Claeys, *Citizens*, p. 224.

43. Joan Wallach Scott, *Gender and the Politics of History* (New York: Columbia University Press, 1988), p. 58.

44. Eileen Yeo, "Practices and Problems of Chartist Democracy," in *The Chartist Experience*, ed. J. Epstein and D. Thompson (London: Macmillan, 1982).

45. Claeys, *Citizens*, p. 283.

46. Briggs, *Chartist Studies*, p. 250.

47. Barbara Taylor, *Eve and the New Jerusalem: Socialism and Feminism in the Nineteenth Century* (New York: Pantheon, 1983), p. 265.

48. David Jones, *Chartism and the Chartists* (London: Allen Lane, 1975), p. 24. David Jones's "Women and Chartism," *History* 8, no. 222: 1-21, is far and away the best short study—and a pioneering one—of this subject.

49. A fascinating line of inquiry is suggested in Kathleen B. Jones and Françoise Vergès, "'Aux Citoyennes!': Democratic Politics, Women's Politics and the Paris Commune of 1871," in *History of European Ideas* (Oxford: Pergamon, 1991).

50. See Karl Polyani, *The Great Transformation* (Boston: Beacon, 1949), passim.

51. D. Thompson, *Chartists*, pp. 16–17.

52. Ibid.; emphases added.

53. See also Paul Thomas, *Alien Politics: Marxist State Theory Retrieved* (London and New York: Routledge, 1994), passim.

54. Richard Johnson, "Educational Policy and Social Control in Early Victorian England," *Past and Present*, no. 49 (November 1970): 97.

55. Form of Report for Her Majesty's Inspectors of Schools, Minutes of the Committee on Education, 1840–41.

56. Johnson, "Educational Policy," p. 119.

57. D. Thompson, *Chartists*, p. 241.

58. Ibid., p. 259.

59. Ibid., pp. 335–36.

Part III

Cultural Studies

Raymond Williams and Cultural Studies
Catherine Gallagher

There was something decidedly asymmetrical about interdisciplinary literary studies prior to the 1980s. The title of the Modern Language Association division devoted to the study of literature and society, Sociological Approaches to Literature, says a great deal about
our recent past. Critics "approached" literature via "sociological" ideas
—concepts developed in a discipline that took "society" as its object
of inquiry. Obviously, the relationship between literature and society must have been conceived of as intimate for the methods of one
discipline to seem applicable to the objects of another: literature was
embedded in social practices, was itself a social practice, yielding
representations of other social phenomena, and could be analyzed
as the worldview of a class, an ethnic group, a nation, or a gender at
a particular historical moment. Most of these "approaches" assumed
that in the related dyad literature/society, "literature" was the representational, symbolic, or signifying entity, while "society" was the set
of human relationships and conditions informing the lived experience of the readers and writers.

No matter how intertwined literature and society were imagined
to be, however, the relationship between literary and social studies
in those days in America was essentially nonreciprocal. The American Sociological Association may have had a division on the sociology of literature, but it did not have one called "literary-critical approaches to society." I do not mean by this that researchers into the
nature of particular societies never used literary evidence. I mean
instead that they did not use the methods of literary analysis. No lit-

erary critics or social scientists that I know of suggested that *The Seven Types of Ambiguity* could yield a useful "approach" to the problem of social stratification. But today, in the wake of the application of ordinary language philosophy to social theory, the linguistic turn in French social thought, and the general spread of hermeneutic self-consciousness, one is not surprised to find Ernesto Laclau and Chantal Mouffe, for example, writing about the hegemonic class's metonymic displacements, Hayden White defining the tropes of historical analysis, John S. Nelson detailing the complex "plots" of political science or enumerating the rhetorical parts of public affairs, Benedict Anderson elucidating nationalism with the help of Erich Auerbach, or Charles Lemmert using linguistic models to analyze social theorists.

I do not want to claim too much for this reciprocity. Methods developed in linguistic and literary studies are hardly dominating American social and historical inquiry, but they have gained some limited acceptance among a generation of social thinkers who see all social phenomena, not just literary ones, as linguistically mediated and "signifying." The reciprocity has encouraged us, in turn, to extend our range of objects, so that we are now likely to "approach" almost anything. We no longer confine ourselves to a separate realm of representation peculiarly saturated with symbolic value because we do not believe there is one.

The new reciprocity in which social and literary-critical thinkers exchange both methods and objects of inquiry seems to me to be the essence of what is now being called "cultural studies." "Cultural studies" specifies neither a well-defined object nor a method of analysis, unlike "sociological approaches to literature," which rather clumsily insisted on both. Not that a great deal has not been written recently about the putative object of study, "culture," and the appropriate modes of understanding it. The puzzling thing about these writings, however, is their almost programmatic refusal to tell us what culture is not. "Nature" was once its most widely agreed-upon opposite, but since the category of nature is now itself often perceived as culturally created, even that broad distinction has been weakened. In literary studies, the word *culture* generally has no stable diacritical term at all, no antonym against which it might be contrasted. Perhaps this terminological looseness is a reaction against Matthew Arnold's idea of Culture with a capital *C*; for Arnold and his followers, Culture had nothing but antonyms. The content of the term—"the best that has been thought and said"—managed to be both ludicrously narrow and utterly unspecific, but the catalog of things that *were not* Culture was long and detailed: nature, society, progressive civilization, the economy, technology, industry, mass education, mass communications, daily life, most forms of politics, and, of course, anarchy. Since today's cultural studies adherents have consistently opposed the Arnoldian concept of culture precisely because of its restrictiveness, they have tried, following the lead of anthropologists, to include in the term the very things the Arnoldians defined it against: that is, almost everything in social existence.

The inflation of the word, however, has made its contemporary users vulnerable to many of the same charges that were brought against Matthew Arnold. Contemporary critics accused Arnold of tossing the word *culture* around because it sounded rather profound but at the same time specified very little. But surely today's cultural critic is guilty of a similar rhetorical maneuver. We tend to use the adjective *cultural* when we want to indicate that the phenomenon we are describing is both externally and internally generated (i.e., social and psychological, in old-fashioned terms), material and symbolic, class- and gender-specific, specific also as to ethnicity, race, religion, language group, region, profession, nationality, historical period, and so on. *Cultural* is a world-conjuring adjective; you cannot go wrong when you call something cultural, for it is the one term that, without necessarily specifying anything, carries the full weight of all possible forms of specificity.

It is this absence of specifics conjoined with a heavy investment in the *idea* of specifics that gives the word *culture* as used by cultural critics an uncanny resemblance to its much-maligned Arnoldian twin, high Culture with a capital *C*. We may have rejected the restriction of Culture to a privileged realm of "art" and the belief that its value derives from transcendent human universals rather than from concrete historical circumstances; nevertheless, our use of *culture* and Arnold's have more in common than is generally recognized.

As Arnold described it, the work of art is that which always escapes its determinations through an excessive particularism, that is, uniqueness. It is for this reason that the products of Culture, the great works of literature, for example, have no definitive qualities in common. That is, one cannot recognize great works of art by looking for certain properties because that would indicate that greatness was somehow outside the works, separable from them as an abstraction of which the works are merely examples. For Arnold great works of art are utterly irreducible; they are so dense with specifics that they defy every attempt to specify them. Arnoldian Culture, therefore, is in a constant crisis of signification because what it stands for—the principle of particularity—is violated by any general definition one could give of it.

Our new understanding of culture resonates with the older insistence on the art work's irreducibility, despite our attacks on the idea of autonomy. Precisely because we take an inexhaustible field of relationships to determine the significance of cultural phenomena, and all other entities inside the field must also be "read" as culturally significant, the objects we study often take on the same dense resistance to analysis that Arnold claimed was the special characteristic of the artwork. This tendency is most marked when we signal the partialness of our analyses, our inability to give a "full" account of any cultural phenomenon. We are apt to use "culture" in such circumstances, as Arnold used "Culture"—that is, as a god-term denoting the inexhaustibility, utter repleteness, and total presence (or at least presence somewhere at some time) of the object that at once calls forth and exceeds our analyses. When we use the word *cultural* this way, to conjure the object's particularity as a peculiar thickness or fullness, or to indicate that it is so crisscrossed with lines of determination as to be ineffable through excess, we may be succumbing to a new mystique of culture.

The following is a discussion of how Raymond Williams's works encouraged such a mystique. For students of modern Britain, Williams's books are more than merely illustrative of cultural studies; they are formative of it. Williams can be credited with having invented the field, and no one had a more nuanced understanding of its complexities and perils. Williams, moreover, was fully aware of the conflicting meanings of the term and resolutely refused simply to choose one definition of culture over another. In book after book, he tried to play the meanings off against each other in an attempt to avoid what he might, at one stage in his career, have called reification. His early books were, to be sure, specifically aimed against the exclusionary tendencies in the Arnoldian use of the word, but he argued that critics could hardly avoid *Culture* when referring to the arts. Williams attempted to investigate the relationships between Culture (the arts) and culture in the anthropological sense of "a whole way of life." He purposely chose the ambiguity in the term in order to avoid both the false polarity and the one-way determinism that might result from choosing some other term, such as *society*, to designate the social totality. In *The Long Revolution*, for example, he protests:

> It was certainly an error to suppose that values or art-works could be adequately studied without reference to the particular society within which they were expressed, but it is equally an error to suppose that the social explanation is determining, or that the values and works are mere by-products. We have got into the habit, since we realized how deeply works or values could be determined by the whole situation in which they are expressed, of asking about these relationships in a standard form: "what is the relationship of this art to this society?" But "society," in this question, is a specious whole. If the art is part of the society, there is no solid whole, outside it, to which, by the form of our question, we concede priority.[1]

We cannot possibly fall into such specious and reductive categorizing, Williams implies, if, instead of asking, "What is the relationship of this art to its society? we ask, "What is the relationship of this Culture to its culture? Categorical rigidity, binarism, and determinism will certainly not survive such a question. But then one is faced with the opposite problem: How am I to separate these things I am trying to bring into relationship? Williams never fully succeeded in answering this question.

He did, however, succeed in replacing the idea of artistic autonomy with that of specificity, and as a result those of us who learned from him tend, almost automatically, to privilege particularity and eschew analytical abstraction. Williams taught us to substitute the word *culture* for *society* wherever possible and to believe that in so doing we were referring to a "complex of lived relationships," a "vital whole" that was more comprehensive, more continuous, and more deeply constitutive of subjectivity than the word *society* could suggest. He seems to have been quite conscious of the effects of this choice of words. When asked by interviewers from the *New Left Review* to explain his substitution of *culture* for *society* in 1977, he responded:

> Historically, culture was cultivation of something—it was an activity; whereas society can seem very static. I often liked the term for this reason. Its modern derivation is actually from Vico, who used it with precisely this emphasis on process. The term "the long revolution" was meant to convey a similar sense of a movement through a very long period.[2]

"Culture," in short, was vital and enduring, yet evolving; "society," by contrast, seemed at once static, inert, and inorganic. The vitalism at the heart of this substitution was certainly not the least of its attractions. Historical cultural criticism promised (much in the tradition of romantic historians—think of Carlyle) to resuscitate the past, to restore it to life.

Precisely because *culture* connoted presence, particularity, irreducibility, and fullness, though, it also doomed him to a necessary analytical shortfall, a shortfall one often experienced in reading Williams's work as an asymmetry between the programmatic buildup and the often rather modest yield of the readings themselves. But how could any readings, no matter how skillful or insightful, possibly give an adequate sense of that living, particular, unique, common, communicative, active, interacting, creative, ordinary, daily, exceptional thing Williams called culture? All the adjectives in the previous sentence are taken from one page of *The Long Revolution*. Our very sense that Williams's analyses are somewhat deficient or truncated, therefore, is ultimately in the service of the mystique of culture that privileges an excessive particularity.

In a late work, Williams explicitly addressed the issues I have been discussing here. He reconsidered his early stress on lived experience and made a conscious attempt to distinguish cultural from other aspects of what he then called the "social process," the "social order," or "social life"—still, notice, generally avoiding that word *society.* The title of the book devoted to this effort, however, was simply *Culture* when it came out in England in 1981, but (perhaps significantly) it appeared under the title *The Sociology of Culture* when it came out in the United States a year later. In this book, Williams also uses semiotic terms more frequently than he had before, defining culture as "the *signifying system* through which necessarily (though among other means) a social order is communicated, reproduced, experienced and explored." The idea of "the signifying system," he goes on to explain, allows a "convergence between (i) the anthropological and sociological sense of culture as a distinct 'whole way of life'" and "(ii) the more specialized if also more common sense of culture as 'artistic and intellectual activities.'" Defining culture as "the signifying system" restricts it to a single albeit essential function within "all forms of social activity," while simultaneously expanding the specialized sense of the word "to include not only the traditional arts and forms of intellectual production but also all the 'signifying practices'—from language through the arts and philosophy to journalism, fashion and advertising."[3] In short, Williams argues, in this sometimes torturously convoluted book, that all social activities, products, and so forth are cultural insofar as they signify, or contain an element of signification, but some are more manifestly cultural than others because their overt function is signification.

But how, we might still ask, can we tell the difference between signifying systems that announce signification as their primary function and those that "dissolve" signification in what Williams calls "other" processes? Williams's answer to this question is, it seems to me, complicated, odd, and worthy of detailed attention. In those "other" (not manifestly cultural) activities, he claims, "quite different [nonsignifying] human needs and actions are substantially and irreducibly present: the necessary signification, as it were, more or less completely dissolved into other needs and actions."[4] Food, for example, has "signifying" moments; one can make semiotic analyses of food, demonstrating the various social meanings of how and what people prepare and consume. But the signifying function of food, Williams claims, is submerged in its primary function of sustaining life. He suggests that we can delineate the cultural by analyzing the degree to which the nonsignifying is covered by the signifying or vice versa. Money is another case in point:

> While a coinage can be studied as a specific sign-system, and moreover, as in many examples, also analyzed aesthetically, there is no real doubt that in any genuine currency the needs and actions of trade and payment are dominant, and the signifying factor, though intrinsic, is in this sense dissolved.[5]

Food and money, therefore, are not manifestly cultural because, as signifying systems, they are too much "in solution."

This distinction between solid or visible and dissolved or invisible signification blinds Williams to the fundamental difference between these two examples. In the case of food, a material, physiological function takes precedence over an ideational meaning. The more food obtrudes itself as a material necessity, the more its social "language" is effaced. Williams fails to see that the situation is exactly the opposite in the case of money. Money, Williams claims, does its job best the more it makes itself transparent and unobtrusive as a signifier; that is, the better it works as a transparent sign of something else, the less it seems like "cultural" signification to Williams. On the other hand, the more the signifier money thickens into a material thing-in-itself (say, in the case of an extremely rare and beautiful coin), the more Williams is willing to grant it the status of signification—culture. Williams thus stumbled into an unconscious paradox in the course of *Culture*.

Phenomena disappear from "culture" for two opposite reasons: such "other" phenomena are either too material, as in the case of food, or not material enough, as in the case of money. Despite Williams's overt thesis, then, the criterion for inclusion in the "cultural" is not the degree to which the phenomenon signifies, for in the case of money it is clear that when the signifying system works efficiently, it tends to disappear, to dissolve; when it is inefficient, though, clogged with the resistant materiality of the signifier, it is "culture." If we concentrate our attention on what Williams calls cultural in his brief discussion of money we are not observing simple signification but are instead observing the moments of its breakdown due either to the introduction of additional meanings and values foreign to money's primary signifying function or just to the burden of excessive materiality.

What are the implications of these contradictions for cultural studies? Williams's confusion here is potentially very valuable because it opens a field of investigation that lies beyond the metaphysics of presence, the view of the object as replete and fully (although indescribably) meaningful. The idea of a signifying system implies, at least to some extent, a certain abstract interchangeability of objects, their ability to stand for things other than themselves, to circulate as carriers of meaning, and to undergo modifications of meaning in the process of circulation. The particularity of cultural phenomena, the very thing that allows us to specify them as objects of analysis, is always going to act as a moment of negativity, of obstruction and resistance to the unproblematic extraction of meaning.

In other words, Williams, in his analysis of food and money, comes rather late on an insight that is by now a cliché: the more one concentrates on the immanence of a signifier, for example, the materiality of the coin, the more opaque it seems, the less transparent, translatable, and smoothly functional it becomes qua signifier. When we say, then, that culture is made up of all the things that are integrated into signifying systems, we should realize that the thingness of the things exists in tension as well as in cooperation with their function as moments in a system.

The problematic materiality of the signifier, then, is one issue raised by Williams's remarks on money. Its problematic immateriality is a second. As we have remarked, the coin becomes decisively "cultural" for Williams only when it ceases to function as a normal coin, only when it calls so much attention to itself that it is no longer useful as currency. Williams is once again unconsciously echoing Arnold, for whom signification did not distinguish culture, for signification implies substitution; culture, rather, consisted in unreplaceability produced by the layering of different and perhaps incompatible kinds of significance. This hostility to the fungible makes Williams's use of the word *signifying* puzzling, but it makes his use of the word *system* practically incomprehensible. For, according to Williams, it is precisely the fact that a "genuine currency" allows systematic substitutions that somehow makes it ineligible for the status of "cultural process." He *contrasts* the operations of "trade and payment" to money's "signifying factor," as if one receded while the other came into focus, whereas, in the instance of money, the two things are almost identical. It is only because money ideally would be *nothing but* a signifying system, because it strives historically to erase its very materiality and obliterate its supplementarity, that it accomplishes "trade and payment," which themselves aspire to be *nothing but* substitution.

Money's attempted disappearing act might be said to be typical of signifying systems, which have a general tendency to minimize the problematic materiality of the signifier. Signification itself depends on this minimalization. The history of money, moreover, should be particularly interesting to the cultural critic because it is comparatively modern and therefore traceable. Even a brief look at this history reveals the logic of immateriality in a sign system.[6] Bank money, from which the currency we now simply call "money" derived, was originally a form of credit designed to keep gold money out of circulation and thus avoid its debasement. For whenever a precious metal is used as a currency, the coins themselves wear away, their materiality gradually diminishes, and a gap thus develops between the actual amount of metal in the coin and the value it is authorized to represent. As Brian Rotman has explained:

> This reliance on its own materiality, whereby gold money operates through signifiers whose weight is supposed to guarantee the sign values in question, contains an inherent instability. . . . A gap arises between "good" money (the pure unsullied issue of the state) and "bad" money (the worn and fraudulently diminished coins in circulation). This gap in signified value between the ideal, nominal signifier corresponding to the face value and the materially debased signifier which reduces the sign to a function of its actual, that is contingent, weight became known as the *agio*.[7]

This *agio*, an assumed average debasement of coins that Adam Smith defines as "the supposed difference between the good standard money of the state, and the clipt, worn, and diminished currency,"[8] led state banks to create "imaginary" money, coins with little metallic worth or paper vouchers, that would stand for the gold, which lay in pristine heaps, supposedly invulnerable to material disintegration. If the intrinsic worth of gold was what allowed it to circulate freely, across national boundaries, in and out of local economies, circulation was also the very process that opened the gap between what was believed to be its immanent, intrinsic worth and its signifying function. Hence, when the banking system developed sufficient reliability, coin symbols began replacing the gold coins in circulation. The essence of these symbols was that their material qualities would be conventionally specified, that they would have no intrinsic worth that could interfere with their signifying function. Of course, the materiality of the coins mattered because they had to bear the marks of having been coined by a legitimate agency in order to foil counterfeiters, but such symbolic features were carefully differentiated from intrinsic ones. The amount of nickel, tin, copper, and so on, in a coin should ideally, according to the theory of bank money, be "immaterial," insignificant as a determinant of the coin's value.

The history of money has been the history of such *de*materializations of the signifier: from coins to paper to blips on computer screens. Ironically, whereas these changes have often come about under pressure to create a more transparent signifying system, one "dominated," to use Williams's words, by the "needs and actions of trade and payment," each stage of dematerialization has actually been anxiously experienced as an increase in money's autonomy. To be sure, the long debate about money's referent, the growing awareness that it may be unspecifiable, accounts for some of this anxiety, but the very shrinking of the signifier, the decrease in its bulk alone, has frequently made it seem dangerously potent, a signifying system magically capable of rearranging reality. Thus, for example, Alexander Pope, in his 1732 "Epistle to Bathurst" depicts paper credit not as a false representation of gold but as a frightfully efficient one, whose minimal materiality can make transactions invisible. In the following passage, Pope contrasts the clumsiness of bribing officials with gold with the ease of doing so with paper:

> Once, we confess, beneath the patriot's cloak,
> From the crack'd bag the dropping guinea spoke,
> And, jingling down the back-stairs, told the crew,
> "Old Cato is as great a rogue as you."
> Blest paper-credit! last and best supply!
> That lends corruption lighter wings to fly!
> Gold imp'd by thee, can compass hardest things,
> Can pocket states, can fetch or carry kings.[9]

The contrast between "Old Cato's" clanking, self-accusing golden bribe (from William III, according to the footnote) and the "imp'd," or enchanted, gold of paper credit stresses that the "lighter" currency is necessarily more powerful because it is more insubstantial, more secretive. Indeed, its magical disappearing act steals the substance of the very things it represents: "can pocket states, can fetch or carry kings." Disembodied signification is imagined to work so well here that it threatens to become a species of antimatter that can translate everything into a different ontological dimension. And in this sense, Pope's anxiety about paper credit is part of a larger anxiety about the minimal materiality inherent in "signifying systems."[10]

Williams's unwillingness to consider money as a cultural "signifying system" might well have been determined by the conjunction of two quite separate "materialist" considerations. First, although he had

repeatedly questioned the old-fashioned Marxist difference between base and superstructure in his earlier books, in both *Politics
and Letters* and *Culture* he is more willing than he formerly was to
let the distinction stand. Hence money's ineligibility for culture
might stem partly from its dissolution into the economic, which
Williams seems to have decided was out of bounds. The other consideration, though, seems to have been money's own problematic
lack of defining matter; the cultural materialism that Williams frequently advocated privileges, as its name implies, matter. Hence the
rare and beautiful coin that no longer circulates as a coin at all seems
more "cultural" to Williams than any piece of currency that actually
functions in a signifying system. It is this cultural materialism, I have
been arguing, that avoids confronting the conditions under which
signification actually occurs and is hence in danger of relapsing into
an Arnoldian belief that matter and signification are harmoniously
integrated.

Cultural critics should instead, I am suggesting, be interested in the
tension between immanence and signification, not because it gives
us a timeless truth about meaning, but because the tension takes so
many different forms and has so many different functions. The way
things refuse integration into signifying systems is historically specific. For example, the dynamic I have been describing by which
money is dematerialized to accomplish its function of circulation
and is then, because of its lack of material substance, regarded as
dangerously autonomous, is crucial to an understanding of other
cultural developments in modern Europe. It is just such instances of
immanent opacity and nonsignifying emptiness that often prove
most resonant. To be sure, in the course of any analysis the resistance to meaning will necessarily be reclaimed as itself meaningful,
and, therefore, the levels of immanence and signification will once
again be collapsed. It should not be our intention, however, to erect
a barrier between these two aspects of "culture." I am arguing, rather,
that we cannot understand the historical function of the object until
we understand its peculiar ways of emptying itself of immediate
comprehensibility.

Indeed, Williams, at the very time that he was redefining culture
as "the signifying system" admitted that it was the word's refusal to
signify anything coherent that led him on: "I've only become more
aware of its difficulties, not less, as I have gone on," he confessed to

his interviewers. "You know the number of times I've wished that I had never heard of the damned word."[11]

NOTES

1. Raymond Williams, *The Long Revolution*, rev. ed. (New York: Harper & Row, 1966), p. 45.

2. Raymond Williams, *Politics and Letters: Interviews with New Left Review* (London: NLB, 1979), p. 154.

3. Raymond Williams, *The Sociology of Culture* (New York: Schocken, 1982), p. 13.

4. Ibid., p. 209.

5. Ibid., p. 210.

6. The following paragraphs rely on several sources: Adam Smith, *An Inquiry into the Nature and Causes of the Wealth of Nations* (New York: Dutton, 1970), especially vol. 1, pp. 250-94; Georg Simmel, *The Philosophy of Money*, trans. Tom Bottomore and David Frisby (Boston: Routledge, 1982), pp. 146-60; W. Graham, *The One Pound Note in the History of Banking in Great Britain* (Edinburgh: J. Thin, 1911). They are, however, most heavily indebted to Brian Rotman's excellent study *Signifying Nothing: The Semiotics of Zero* (New York: St. Martin's, 1987).

7. Rotman, *Signifying Nothing*, p. 24.

8. Smith, *Inquiry*, p. 423.

9. Alexander Pope, "Epistle to Bathurst," *Alexander Pope: Collected Poems*, ed. Bonamy Dobree (London: Dent, 1983), pp. 235-36.

10. "Blest paper credit," to be sure, is traceable in theory; it bears numerous tokens of its origin and history. Indeed, one might point out that the "intrinsically valuable" gold can support anonymity whereas paper money not only must have but also simply is nothing more than its own record. The historical record, with all of its identifying signs, one might continue, is generated by the very dematerialization Pope laments. Such objections to Pope's complaint, however, remind us not that paper money should not have caused anxiety, but that the anxiety it caused is inscribed in its form.

11. Williams, *Politics and Letters*, p. 154.

Between Criticism and Ethnography: Raymond Williams and the Intervention of Cultural Studies

Stanley Aronowitz

According to conventional institutional history, the three founding spiritual parents of the intellectual movement known as cultural studies are E. P. Thompson, whose revival of historiography "from below" changed the face of history writing for several generations;[1] Richard Hoggart, who insisted on the continuing salience of a popular, working-class culture in the wake of the pervasive influence of the media and founded the Centre for Contemporary Cultural Studies (CCCS) to document this culture and directed the center for its first five years;[2] and Raymond Williams, who, despite his lack of institutional connections to CCCS and its progeny in some twelve British colleges and universities, was perhaps the most important influence on the movement.

At first glance, Williams may be viewed as an unlikely candidate to inspire a movement that, in the end, veered substantially from his own intellectual orientation and specific political vision. For example, Williams never swerved from his conviction that the labor movement was a fundamental cultural institution of the working class, contrary to 1960s radical cant according to which it has become bureaucratically and even oligarchically addled.[3] Moreover, even as many practitioners of cultural studies were beginning in the late 1970s to challenge historical materialism's faith in the redemptive character of the working class and discovering new agents—particularly women and working-class youth subcultures—for Williams, the workers always remained the key to any possible emancipatory social transformation. And, even as many intellectuals embraced the two major "posts" of contemporary social and cultural thought—postmodernism and post-Marxism—after publishing almost exclusively in cultural history and popular culture, Williams wrote extensively in his later years in Marxist theory.[4] In fact, Williams first seriously engaged Marxist theory only in the 1970s, precisely the decade when it came under fire from, among others, many proponents of a version of cultural studies that tacitly identified with dethroning Marxism.

But, as we will see, it is neither his version of Marxist cultural theory nor his specific ideological perspective that continues to commend Williams to cultural studies. His early contributions, still controversial in literary studies, consisted of two crucial moves: he adopted and elaborated F. R. Leavis's position that took literature as a sign of *culture* rather than Matthew Arnold's repository of the "best that has been thought or said" in aesthetic or formal terms;[5] and he extended the purview of critical studies to television and other communications media.[6]

As important as these innovations might have been, especially in the 1950s and 1960s, I want to argue that Williams is less a critic than an ethnographer. He reads poetry and novels in a way that is profoundly at variance with any accepted critical methodology, even that ascribed to conventional Marxism, which is, intentions to the contrary notwithstanding, honed in a disciplinary mode. For, as I shall argue, he is less interested in the intrinsic merit of the work in terms of criteria of aesthetic value such as felicitous writing style, formal innovation, or narrative elegance than in the extent to which it is a *signifying practice* of a concrete historical conjuncture. His object is whether the novel or poem provides *knowledge* of what he calls the "structure of feeling" of a specific historical moment, and even more concretely of a given *class*, not whether it is a source of pleasure.[7] Few among literary critics, even the historians, have followed him into these precincts; while some may teach courses in various genres of mass or popular culture, the object of "reading" is to plumb the formal character of the artwork. Alternatively, some critics choose to elucidate the ways in which film or other popular media may be taken as "art." Their point is to argue that aesthetic value inheres in these forms. And, especially from the 1930s through the 1950s, Williams's Marxist precursors, notably Christopher Caudwell and Ralph Fox, subjected English literature to historical materialism's ideology critique.[8] Of these critiques, Caudwell's was clearly the most interesting because, while he was pitilessly critical of the class standpoint of most works of the canon, he was able to acknowledge their greatness by situating them in their historicity.

In contrast, Williams's readings are pieces in a puzzle: how to construct the space between economic and political structures to forms of "thought"; how to get at the "structure of feeling." For in the contexts he variously calls "feeling" or "experience" lies what may be called the "life world," a sphere that theory-saturated abstractions such as "ideology" invariably miss. From his writings on drama and criticism in the 1950s to his magnificent *The Country and the City*, narrative fiction and poetry are the raw materials from which one can construct the ways in which vast historical changes are interpretively configured and the ambiguous sphere of the life world is revealed. Williams pieces this world together from the fragments of experience of which literature is a register rather than performing the conventional "connection" between pristine literary representations and the world to which, putatively, it refers. Just as Bakhtin reads Rabelais's *Gargantua* as a chronicle of the underside of sixteenth-century French peasant life, so Williams grasps the meaning of the transition from agrarian to urban society as a multifaceted process of which contemporary reflections are coded experiences.[9]

Williams's excursions in Marxist cultural theory are marked by a certain woolliness. Readers come away from his essays in this genre unsure of what they have read. We know that Williams is earnestly trying to enter the discourse of theory free of deterministic economism and its antinomy, voluntarism, which had tainted Marxism between the wars and carried over to the early postwar period. In a large measure he succeeds, but, in the wake of his rejection of the linguistically infused "French turn" in Marxist theory—which was heavily influential in cultural studies during the late 1970s—and the fact that only in the last decade before his death in early 1988 was he aware of the work of the Bakhtin circle, his major theoretical interventions, particularly *Marxism and Literature* (1977) are, compared to, say, the magisterial and evocative *The Country and the City* (1973), labored.

For example, between his many explorations of literature and social context and his theoretical work there is a distinct problem in the lucidity of the writing itself. Although Williams is never the graceful stylist, his voice was, before the adventures in theory, clear and forceful. As an ethnographer, he is thoroughly in charge of his material; he knows what he thinks about it, and his utterances are crisp and almost invariably to the point. In contrast, the theoretical formulations are riddled with qualifiers; the sentences bulge with digression; the circularity of the prose is all too evident. Williams struggles to get a handle on elusive concepts by adopting a strategy of evolving category-definitions. But, like Thomas Kuhn's famous keyword, *paradigm*, which he uses in no less than twenty different ways, Williams's unique idea, "culture," suffers from nearly as many usages. Here is a not atypical instance:

> At the very centre of a major area of modern thought and practice, which is habitually used to describe, is a concept 'culture', which in itself, through variation and complication, embodies not only the issues but the contradictions through which it has developed. The concept at once fuses and confuses the radically different experiences and tendencies of its formation. It is then impossible to carry through any serious cultural analysis without reaching towards a consciousness of the concept itself: a consciousness that must be, as we shall see, historical. This hesitation, before what seems the richness of developed theory and the fullness of achieved practice, has the awkwardness, even the gaucherie, of any radical doubt.[10]

From this issues a disquisition that fails to clarify; it sinks into multiple locutions, all of which are suggestive and none is fully satisfying.

So begins the chapter "Culture" of *Marxism and Literature*. Williams never succeeds in getting out of awkwardness either of thought or expression, which, as it turns out, is characteristic of the entire book. Williams is plainly uncomfortable in the theoretical twists and turns of contemporary Marxism, and where there is no concrete literary or visual text he is at sea. What commends Williams to us is not his theoretical perspicacity but his powerful ethnography. His great innovation, before the Bakhtin circle enjoyed wide celebrity, is to have transformed the study of literature and other art forms from Arnold's conservatory of the "best that has been thought and said" into a form of social and cultural knowledge.[11] His tacit assumption, expressed in the concept of "cultural materialism," is that these signifying practices are immanent in the material world; that thought and its object constitute not an un-bridgeable gulf or even logically separate spheres, but together con-stitute a single substance. Here, the silent figure of Spinoza comes into play as it does more openly in the work of Louis Althusser and Gilles Deleuze.[12]

Since Williams is no philosopher but, instead, works de facto less in criticism than in historical ethnography, he is less interested in weighing the aesthetic value of poetry and novels than in assessing the ways in which they constitute and are constitutive of historical *experience*. Of course, what he means by experience may not be confused with the ruminations of the classic English empiricist philosophers; Williams employs experience most saliently in terms of his "structure of feeling" category. Among the clearest expositions of what he means by the notions of cultural materialism, structure of feeling, and, perhaps most importantly, his celebrated distinction of emergent, dominant, and residual cultures is found in his well-known but otherwise failed essay "Base and Superstructure in Marx-ist Theory":

> Now if we go back to the cultural question in its most usual form—what are the relations between art and society?, or literature and soci-ety?—in the light of the preceding discussion [in which Williams devel-ops his proposition that the "dominant mode of production, therefore dominant society, therefore dominant culture exhausts the full range of human practice"], we have to say first that there are no relations be-tween literature and society in that abstracted way. The literature is there from the beginning as a practice in the society. Indeed, until it and other practices are present, the society cannot be said to have fully formed. . . . We cannot separate literature and art from other kinds of social practice.[13]

Williams goes on to say that literature, including theories, goes on in "all areas of culture."

To be sure, literature does not correspond to an independent real-ity of which it is a (mediated) reflection. Instead, Williams's texts and those he examines—the poetry of Goldsmith and Wordsworth no less than the novels of Jane Austen and George Eliot—are inter-pretive recodings that are themselves part of the historical conjunc-tion within which they occur. Williams consistently argues, by de-scription more than anything else, that the object of knowledge is history, of which beliefs, values, and especially "feelings" are an ineluctable component and must be studied, in conjunction with economic and political institutions, as a "whole." The awkwardness of Williams's theoretical discourse may be ascribed to his own ambivalence about "theory" as opposed to his own ethnographic criticism and historical method. Since he lacks the categories of explication for a concept of totality in which experience is not a representation, Williams gropes for a vocabulary of immanence as he treats works of art as constitutive material signs, and this is the reason, despite the tortured expression surrounding his theoretical interventions, that he continues to exert so much influence on his own and succeeding generations.

Williams is reading social and historical context through the text, an orientation to criticism he learned from Leavis. Compare Williams's insistence that literature is valid social knowledge to the following passage from Leavis's *Great Tradition*, perhaps his most influential work. Discussing *Middlemarch*, which he sees as the "only book [that] can be said to represent [Eliot's] mature genius," Leavis remarks:

> The necessary part of great intellectual powers in such a success as *Middlemarch* is obvious. The sub-title of the book, *A Study of Provincial Life*, is no idle pretension. The sheer informedness about society, its mechanism, the ways in which people of different classes live (if they have to) earn their livelihoods, impresses us with its range, and it is real knowledge; that is to say, it is knowledge alive with understanding.[14]

In a corroborating footnote on the same page, he cites Beatrice Webb's *My Apprenticeship*: "'For a detailed description of the complexity of human nature . . . I had to turn to novelists and poets.'"

Unlike many of his erstwhile acolytes, Williams was a populist even less than he was an orthodox or "Western" Marxist. Rather, as a cultural historian, he plumbs the canonical works of English literature to reveal the ways in which, in Leavis's terms, they may provide "real knowledge" not only of the complexity of human nature but also of the density of everyday life, with which economic and political structures invariably intersect. We see no better example of this work than in *The Country and the City*, which, from a methodological perspective, is exemplary. Indeed, in *Politics and Letters*

(1979), his long autobiographical interview with the editors of the *New Left Review*, Williams readily acknowledges the powerful influence Leavis had on his own early thinking about culture:

> The immense attraction of Leavis lay in his cultural radicalism, quite clearly. This may seem a problematic description today, but not at the time [1939–40]. It was the range of Leavis's attacks on academicism, on Bloomsbury, on metropolitan literary culture, on the commercial press, on advertising, that first took me.[15]

But it was Leavis's stress on the importance of education that became, for Williams, a most enduring mandate. Before becoming a Cambridge don, Williams was inspired to seek a teaching position in Oxford's Workers' Education Association, an adult education night school—a vocation that also attracted other left intellectuals, notably E. P. Thompson. And it was from these worker education experiences that one of the founding concepts of cultural studies emerged: that cultural education, as much as trade union and political education, in the strict sense, was an important task of the labor movement and to confine the study of culture to the academy was to risk deradicalizing it. Although Thompson and, especially, Richard Hoggart shared some of these ideas, Williams, ever the pedagogue in writing as much as in teaching, became the most important figure in "English" cultural studies precisely because he made the explicit connection between cultural study and educational policy. But for Williams "education" was not identical with formal schooling. Instead, his was a broad, political notion of education that led him to what might be termed cultural "policy," the most important aspect of which, in the postwar era, was the study of communications media in virtually all of its crucial manifestations.

An example of the degree to which these pedagogical and educational policy experiences informed early ventures into cultural study may be found in the 1968 preface to his textbook *Communications*, first published in 1962. Williams's study of communications media—not only television and films but also books, advertising, and theater—is framed in terms of the idea of *permanent education*:

> What I have said about growth can be related to the idea of permanent education, which is now so important in French cultural thought, and with which I have had valuable recent contacts. This idea seems to me to repeat, in new and important idiom, the concepts of learning

and of popular democratic culture which underlie the present book. What it valuably stresses is the educational force (education as distinct from *enseignement*) of our whole social and cultural experience. It is therefore concerned, not only with continuing education, of a formal or informal kind, but with what the whole environment, its institutions and relationships actively and profoundly teaches. To consider the problems of families, or town planning, is then an educational enterprise, for these, also, are where teaching occurs. And then the field of this book, of the cultural communications which, under an old shadow, are still called mass communications, can be integrated as I always intended with a whole social policy. For who can doubt, looking at television or newspapers, or reading the women's magazines that here, centrally, is teaching and teaching financed and distributed in a much larger way than a formal education?[16]

While many—Williams himself but especially Thompson and Christopher Hill—uncovered the treasures of popular tradition in order to contest, intellectually, ruling-class hegemony over the national past, few were prepared to enter the muddy waters of institutional controversy, to perform the often mundane sociological research as a necessary concomitant to making a more direct intervention. In *Communications* we find Williams using that staple of mass communications research, content analysis, to "measure" (his term) the growth of advertising in the respective print media in Britain, followed by a detailed examination of news coverage—both the type and the standpoint—to determine the degree to which newspapers become increasingly beholden to those who provide substantial advertising income. Of course, Williams's discovery is fairly well known: he who pays the piper calls the tune. But what is remarkable about his study is not its assertions but the degree to which he is prepared to engage in statistical research to serve his pedagogic ends, to, in Audre Lord's terms, "use the master's tools to dismantle the master's house." This exercise describes as well as any other Williams's rhetorical strategy. A Cambridge don, he explored English poetry, drama, and prose, not to celebrate them as signifiers of the greatness of English civilization, but to disrupt the powerful pastoral images that, since Blake's own deconstruction, remained a characteristic feature of ideological hegemony. But he was not willing to rest comfortably within disciplinary boundaries. His bold adventure into empirical social science reveals how seriously Williams took his role as a teacher. His methodological catholicity was a function of the essentially political context within which he placed problems of culture.

In *Communications* Williams is not content to stop where direct intervention begins. After an extensive analysis of the ambiguity of the high/low debate in which he finds himself straddling the line between advocacy of the Great Tradition of English culture and a more complex critique of its relation to both the popular and the "mass" culture, Williams directly enters the dangerous waters of policy, where, at the outset, he reiterates the principle that, with a few detours, guided his entire career as a public intellectual: "that men should grow in capacity and power to direct their own lives—by creating democratic institutions, by bringing new sources of energy into human work, and by extending the expression and exchange of experience on which understanding depends."[17] From this declaration issue suggestions for improving teaching of writing and the sociology of institutions; for extending "criticism" to include newspapers, women's magazines, and advertisements; for "comparative visual studies" not only of television but also of modern architecture; and for "a comparative study of 'social images' of particular kinds of profession" the object of which is "to bring all cultural work within the same world of discourse: to see the connexions between Elia and the manufactured television personality as well as the difference in value between *Lord Jim* and *Captain Condor*."[18] At this juncture, Williams declares that "academic criticism does nothing to help" generate "confidence in our own real opinions," still a controversial pedagogic aim, especially among those who fear that an open pedagogical environment might work to the detriment of the great tradition's standing—and their own.

Despite his distance, both institutionally and—after 1970, when Stuart Hall boldly moved CCCS in the direction of the structuralist Marxism of Louis Althusser—ideologically, Williams more than anyone else theorized the incipient movement that came to be known as cultural studies. His earlier work, particularly *Modern Drama from Ibsen to Eliot* (1952) and *Culture and Society* (1956), remained basically within the Leavisite and even Arnoldian mode of moral literary criticism, despite the strong political concerns of the latter. But with *The Long Revolution* (1961) he began a twenty-year effort to provide a solid conceptual basis for a new approach that would embrace historical, anthropological, and social conceptions of culture. Perhaps the most important move in this work was to "define culture as a whole way of life," thereby obliterating the conjunction *and* between culture and society.[19] This strategic intervention introduced into social as well as literary theory the significance of culture in the anthropological sense, that is, the ways in which everyday rituals and institutions were, alongside art, constitutive of cultural formation (perhaps his most startling and original conception). Williams was, at the end of the day, a somewhat murky theoretical thinker whose thought manifests itself in a characteristically British disdain for abstraction and complex theoretical formulations. But, more than any writer of his generation, he inspired the groups that elaborated cultural studies after 1965 through his insistence on the persistence of practices, such as those of trade unionism, that were ordinarily viewed by critics as outside culture. For the crucial shift between the regime of cultural studies in Hoggart's era to that of Hall's stewardship at the CCCS consists precisely in the latter's privileging ethnography over criticism. Field studies such as those Paul Willis and Dick Hebdige did in the early 1970s marked a new direction for cultural studies that had been signaled by Williams's implicit repudiation of the premises of high literary criticism in *The Long Revolution* and his studies of television and communications.[20]

In what sense is Williams straddling the boundary between addressing representations such as literary texts and the "pressing of the flesh" that forms the core of ethnographic study? Surely, he did no traditional "field" work. Rather, it is his epistemological stance that marks him off from traditional criticism. Like Bakhtin, Williams takes fiction not as "representation," if by this term we signify the problematic of correspondence between text and context that is independent of it. Rather, the text embodies its unique space and time; the characters of a novel or the poet's evocations are as constitutive of the life world as a conversation between two bikers or school dropouts in Hebdige's and Willis's texts. In fact, like most good ethnographies, much of Willis's "Hammertown" case study of twelve nonacademic working-class kids is written as dialogue; although the narrative employs a quasi-theoretical discourse, his account of the speech of the "lads" reveals a writerly ear:

> Bill: It's just hopeless round here, there's nothing to do. When you've got money, you know, you can get to a pub and have a drink, but, you know, when you ain't got money, you've either got to stop in and just walk round the streets and none of them are any good really. So you walk around and have a laff.
>
> Joey: It ain't only that it's enjoyable, it's that it's there and you think you can get away with it . . . you never think of the risks. You just do it. If there's an opportunity and the door's open to the warehouse, you're in there, seeing what you can thieve and then, when you come out like, if you don't get caught immediately, when you come out you're really happy like.
>
> Bill: 'Cos you've shown others you can do it, that's one reason.
>
> Joey: 'Cos you're defying the law again. The law's a big tough authority like and we're just little individuals yet we're getting away with it like.[21]

Of course Richard Hoggart's early work, especially his extremely influential *The Uses of Literacy* (1957), had been suffused with this dimension, but only implicitly. And, unlike Williams, Hoggart never considered the *institutions* of the labor movement, especially unions, as signifiers or even sites of working-class culture. Nor did Hoggart's understanding extend explicitly to the category of *practices* rather than representations as the core upon which cultural formation is constructed, although the best parts of *Uses* concern what, in contemporary terms, would be "discursive" practices that might be considered distinctly working class. On the other hand, Williams significantly broadened the concept of culture to embrace its materializations.

The notion of language as material practice had, by the late 1960s, been introduced by critics and linguists who wished to break from the Cartesian premises of the discipline. At one moment, Williams appropriates this shift in his definition of culture as "signifying practices," thus preserving, not unwittingly, the distinction between the production of meaning and the objects to which they refer. Similarly, in the wake of Althusser's frontal assault on Marxist orthodoxy's separation of base and superstructure by acknowledging the determination of the economic, but only in the "last instance" (which, according to Althusser, never comes),[22] Williams struggled to retain a class perspective despite his fairly tangled effort to show that determination was not a one-way street (the superstructure determined aspects of the infrastructure as well as being determined by it). Of course, in his essays on the subject, especially the chapter in *Marxism and Literature* (1977) resuming his earlier discussion of base-superstructure, Williams acknowledges complexity.[23] Yet, in the end, he remains reluctant to throw out the power of the Marxist formulation of the primacy of the economic lest the political significance of class relationships be diluted. It is as if, presciently, Williams grasps the fundamental tendency of Althusserianism and its Spinozan roots: when you effectively give up the determination by the economic, and retain the formula, but only as an incantation, it is a short distance to giving up the maxim "all history is the history of class struggles." From this issues Althusser's own assertion of the priority of the mode of production, taken by his "school" as a structured totality of which class relationships are derivative, only one sphere (the others, virtually equal in weight, are political and ideological relations). In short, while Williams came in the late 1970s to appreciate some elements of structuralism, he resisted its crucial entailment: turning a back on the Hegelian social dialectic whose core is the master-slave relation.[24] For the son of a railroad worker and a former communist whose break with the party was quite "soft," such a move was tantamount to discarding the centrality of the working class as historical agent.

Of course, this obstinacy was Williams's strength as well as his weakness. It was a strength because it was precisely his lifelong connection with the workers movement that contributed, even determined, his capacity to take the emanations of high culture as "data" rather than as cultural ideals to which the working class should aspire, and to insist on the cultural significance of working-class communities. Beyond the questioning of canonicity, which runs like a thread throughout his work after 1960, is his attempt to leave open all questions of artistic value and, more controversially, to remove the argument from the exclusive purview of academic experts. It was a weakness because, smitten with what Wright Mills once termed the "labor metaphysic," his theoretical range remained limited.[25] It was as if hanging on to the primacy of class was a shield against the dissolution of his socialist faith. As events after his death have unfolded, one can only admire this "weakness," for many who were theoretically lighter on their feet than Williams, including some of his students and erstwhile admirers, have drifted away from socialism, let alone Marxism. It may be said that they have confused the concept of "crisis," which, indeed, suffuses the contemporary socialist and workers movements, with the obsolescence of these movements.

What is at stake here is more than the collapse of the Berlin Wall, the Soviet Union, and the Eastern European communist states. It is important to recall that by the 1960s, in such documents as the May Day Manifesto (1967), written as a prelude to a stillborn New Left political initiative, Williams had from a democratic perspective already called attention to the insufficiency of parliamentary institutions and argued, alternatively, for a *participatory democracy*—but not, in his view, strongly enough. In fact, Williams moved leftward in the last decade of his life: "The distinction between representation and popular power has to be now sharply put. I have tried to do that recently in *Keywords*. But I still find that when I criticize representative democracy, even to quite radical audiences, they react with suprise."[26] By the 1960s Williams had joined with a group of former communists of his generation and younger intellectuals who attached themselves to a long-suppressed tradition of antibureaucratic, antistatist popular power that had been associated with traditions that were hostile not only to Leninism (if not always to Lenin) and Stalinism but also to modern social democracy. What for many of them was a short-lived left-libertarianism (many others drifted into the neo-Leninist-Trotskyist movements or became left-wing laborites) was to become Williams's political creed for the remainder of his life. And during the last twenty years, he openly espoused a radical democratic politics within a militant socialist framework. There is no evidence that either Williams or the British New Left recognized the anarchist and left-communist roots of this critique. But there is no doubt that, despite his frequent excursions into educational reform, a tacit acceptance of the statist framework for broadening democratic participation, Williams's radicalism was unmistakable.

In tandem with this orientation, the burden of Williams's later work marches steadily in the direction of sundering the older Marxist categories. Williams spent nearly a quarter of a century trying to resolve the dilemma of spanning representation and material practices, to cobble a conception of culture that avoids the land mines of epistemological realism, which, it is fairly clear to see, is merely the expression of a politics of representation. That he did not succeed is not suprising. The problem of all efforts to overcome correspondence theories, which posit the distinction between the knowing subject and its object, resides in the political as well as philosophical question of *agency*. If there can be knowledge without a knowing subject and objects are always constituted discursively, how are human agents constituted? Together with his colleagues, especially those at CCCS for whom he was a constant referent and inspiration, by the late 1970s Williams determined that culture is not entirely encompassed by art, artifact, or those representations that have been hegemonically valorized as "civilization." At the same time, unsatisfied with the persistence of the base-superstructure gulf, he worked with a play of alternative formulations that could satisfactorily overcome, if not entirely overturn, the scientific worldview and its categories of determination and mechanical causality. That his work remained relentlessly discursive and bore the telltale traces of his moral training remained an object of pity and even scorn for the next generation of Marxist theorists, notably his pupil Terry Eagleton and *New Left Review* editor Perry Anderson, who wished to produce a sophisticated but ultimately orthodox Marxist theory of culture on the basis of analytic categories from which what Williams understood as *experience* could be properly interpreted.

Marxism and Literature and *The Sociology of Culture* (1980) failed to shed the elements of empiricism and especially historicism that marked his earlier writings. Williams was trying to figure out how to articulate the two meanings of culture: "It became a noun of 'inner' process specialized to its presumed agencies in 'intellectual life' and the 'arts.' It became also a noun of general process specialized to its presumed configurations in a 'whole way of life.'" In the latter instance, culture is seen as "constitutive social process."[27] Thus, it cannot be understood as a category of the superstructure within the framework of determination by the economic infrastructure. This conclusion permeates all of Williams's work in the last fifteen years of his life and, in consequence, it is not difficult to discern his skepticism about the effectivity of base-superstructure distinction as well as its premises, the reflection theory of knowledge and the correspondence theory of truth, themselves grounded in epistemological realism. At the same time, and not unexpectedly, he was unable to generate a satisfactory alternative, in part because of his deep-seated ethical belief in the class basis of socialist politics and the suspicion, shared by many of his generation, that the many varieties of post-Marxism that began to surface in the late 1970s threatened the emancipatory project to which he had devoted his life.

Still, Williams, like Stuart Hall, Richard Johnson, and many others in cultural studies, was plainly influenced, as Thompson and Hoggart were not, by many of the tenets of structural linguistics and the epistemological claims for language and discourse that informed it. Meanings were not embedded in history or in the Mind underlying the utterances of essential subjects, but were produced locally, within specific contexts; language has no fixed referent, but instead is constituted as practices whose "meanings" are spatiotemporally contingent. Williams never went as far as, say, Ernesto Laclau and Chantal Mouffe, for whom the social itself is impossible precisely because, following Michel Foucault, the concepts of society and of social relations connote an essential ontology of social being.[28] Rather, they maintained that human subjects, as much as their relations, are interpellated by discourse. Moreover, if the idea of a subject is problematic, so is the notion of human or social relations, for "relations" imply subjects who interact, a claim that is logically inconsistent if, indeed, the constitution of "subjects" is context-dependent. In place of the conscious subject, Foucault and Laclau and Mouffe substitute a "subject position" whose rules constitute the space of the discourse.[29]

In contrast, Williams never adopted the position that language or discourse displaces human agency. He remained wedded to what might be termed the "ontology of consciousness" according to which intentional human practice is an effective counterweight to both mechanistic materialism (associated with some versions of Marxist orthodoxy that emphasized the determination of cultural, ideological, and political practices by the already given economic infrastructure) and idealism, which, while insisting on the active side of cultural practices, lost sight of all but the signifying subject. We might express this formula by inverting Marx's famous dictum: specific social circumstances condition how history is made, but history is made by humans.

In what is perhaps the most powerful statement of his position, Williams displays the most "dialectical" of all his cultural writings, showing the degree to which he wants to separate himself from the passivity associated with structural linguistics while, at the same time, declaring that "language is material" and the sign active. Here Williams makes plain his adherence to a concept in which relations between various aspects of the social totality are indeterminate *in advance.*

In *Politics and Letters* Williams seems on the one hand to agree on the conventional distinction between economic and cultural re- lations, even if he inferentially refuses a one-way determination of culture by production relations. Nevertheless, in context, he was also drawn ineluctably to a position that "cultural production was mater- ial," a perspective that leads to this:

> Because once cultural production is itself social and material, then this indissolubility of the whole social process has different theoretical ground [than classical Marxism]. It is no longer based on experience, but on the common character of the respective processes of produc- tion.[30]

Here Williams adopts a productivist conception of culture within a broad theory in which material production loses its exclusive con- nection to what might be described as "physical" need. Thus, pro- duction of various kinds *together* constitute the whole social process whose relations of determination are contingent not on a priori metaphysical categories but on concrete circumstances. The course of British cultural studies is fundamentally altered since the mid- 1970s by these shifts. Following Williams, and despite the profound influence of what has been termed poststructuralism, much of British cultural studies refuses to abandon the emancipatory telos of Marxism even as the shift occurs away from the "always already" privileging of the working class to a more contextualized position, where the subcultures of, say, race, gender, and generation may con- stitute the primary identity of social groups.[31]

However, cultural studies, in the interest of maintaining a political as well as a theoretical standpoint, is required to retain categories such as production and agency without imputing finality to the ways in which they are employed and to retain the concept of to- tality, albeit altered from its Hegelian connotations.[32]

Armed with some elements of the democratic ethos Williams helped to generate, cultural studies enters its greatest period of growth as it opens itself to the critique of scientificity, to feminism, and to other subaltern discourses that arise on the ruins of a withered ideology of class. From the methodological standpoint, Williams bears considerable responsibility for the crucial movement within cultural studies away from criticism and toward ethnography, although not always in the way Williams would have wanted. For after an initial decade during which cultural studies embedded its work within the humanities, especially literary history and criticism, with the departure of Hoggart in 1969 CCCS turned away from representations and engaged almost exclusively in subcultural ethnographies—except Stuart Hall, who, as its leading theorist, directed his efforts toward textual analyses of, among other things, television.

What distinguishes Williams from critics and theorists, Hall among them, who followed Althusser in the mid-1970s is his implicit refusal of the distinction between the representations found in literary and other (high) artistic texts and other forms of cultural practice such as culture in the anthropological sense—the interactions of small groups whose practices and rituals, rules, and rewards and punishments were the privileged objects of study for the social scientifically oriented Centre for Contemporary Cultural Studies at Birmingham. In fact, CCCS and its friends turned from Williams out of a misunderstanding. With the exception of the persistence of Stuart Hall's largely textual criticism of the media and its products, works of so-called high art were abjured.

But if the object of cultural studies is a "whole way of life," then one may not take this path. "High" is part of this way of life no less than bikers' banter, the response of women to daytime "telly," or shop-floor culture in a car assembly plant. For if fiction is a form of social knowledge, one may treat literary texts ethnographically, and this is the culmination of Williams's methodological legacy. To understand the subtlety of Williams's approach—which reveals the degree to which his democratic passion is upheld, even as he insists on the importance of retaining elements of the great tradition—we may consult his comments on the pedagogical significance of addressing the high-low controversy.

Williams reminds us that many of the works included in the canon were themselves considered "'low' in terms of the 'high' standards of the day." Williams argues that film, jazz, and the theatrical musical, for example, have been regarded by guardians of high culture as a threat to "standards." But, he remarks, the "distinction between art and entertainment may be much more difficult to maintain than it looks." Although he acknowledges that we are "in danger" of losing the great tradition, for which Williams never lost affection, he also points out that it may not be a problem of the works, whatever their conventional categorization, but the standardization of all culture, the flattening of difference that appears to be endemic to social life. Williams insists that if the power of the great tradition is to challenge us to change our routine ways of thinking, this property may be experienced in the reception of journalism or popular genres as well as the so-called minority culture.

In the end, Williams calls into question the conventional high-low distinction without making the postmodern turn away from the great tradition; he does not insist that considerations of "value" are merely ways to preserve elitist art. Rather, he wants to democratize the scope of those works that may be included in a canon, but he refuses the aestheticist criteria for determining its formation. Williams's democratic move is to shift the terms from categories of beauty to categories of pedagogy and the social knowledges to which both the art and the teaching refers.

Finally, when we are relieved of the pointless questions associated with evaluating Williams's work in literary theoretical terms and can come to terms with his position as a teacher and public intellectual, the contemporary relevance of his work for cultural studies is crystal clear. What we learn from his vast corpus is that the point of cultural studies is to empower ordinary people to take control over their own lives by, among other means, fully appropriating cultural things, whatever their status in the hierarchy. That he remained, despite this perspective, close to literary studies is more a function of the intellectual division of labor than of intention. Nonetheless, more than any theorist of his or the subsequent generation of British intellectuals, he points the way out of the antinomies that continue to plague us.

In this moment when cultural studies is rapidly being absorbed by universities and, in the process, losing its political edge—in Meagan Morris's word, it is overcome with "banality"—Williams's example may be taken as a "tradition" worthy of emulation.

NOTES

1. E. P. Thompson, *The Making of the English Working Class* (New York: Knopf, 1963).
2. Richard Hoggart, *The Uses of Literacy* (Boston: Beacon, 1961).

3. Raymond Williams, *Politics and Letters* (London: New Left Books, 1979), pp. 419 passim.

4. Raymond Williams, *Marxism and Literature* (Oxford and New York: Oxford University Press, 1977); *Problems of Materialism and Culture* (London: New Left Books, 1980), especially "Base and Superstructure in Marxist Theory."

5. Matthew Arnold, *Culture and Anarchy* (New York: Bobbs Merrill, 1971).

6. Williams, *Politics and Letters*, p. 66. Here Williams acknowledges Leavis's influence on his early literary criticism, but especially the influence of "Leavis's great stress on education . . . the emphasis seemed completely right."

7. Williams, *Politics and Letters*, pp. 156-58. "The way in which I have tended to apply the term in analysis is to the generation that is doing the new cultural work, which normally means a group which would have a median age of around thirty, when it is beginning to articulate its structure of feeling. It follows that one would then identify the structure of feeling of the middle-aged and the elderly with earlier decades." (p. 157). On the next page a modification of this formulation: "I would now want to use the concept much more differentially between classes. But it is important to note that this diversity is itself historically variable" (p. 158). Williams tells us he first developed the concept in his book *A Preface to Film* (1954) and then employed it more methodologically in *The Long Revolution* (1961); (reprint, London: Pelican, 1975). In the earlier work, Williams notes that the "structure of feeling" of a given generation may be discerned only in the work of art itself because "there is no external counterpart," a formulation that infers that the work of art is *constitutive* of what may be termed the "social" rather than a reflection of it.

8. Christopher Caudwell, *Studies and Further Studies in a Dying Culture* (New York: Dodd, Mead, 1938, 1949, 1958); Ralph Fox, *The Novel and the People* (New York: International Publishers, 1945).

9. Mikhail Bakhtin, *Rabelais and His World* (Bloomington: Indiana University Press, 1984).

10. Williams, *Marxism and Literature*. p. 11.

11. As we shall see, Williams was not so much attached to the canon as he was to the idea that its constituents' works could be grasped as forms of social and cultural knowledge alongside the artifacts of popular culture in genre fiction, film, radio, television, and popular music, the forms that have preoccupied cultural studies in the United States as much as in Britain since the 1960s.

12. Baruch Spinoza, *Ethics* (New York: Dover, 1951); Gilles Deleuze, *Expressionism in Philosophy: Spinoza* (New York: Zone, 1990). See also Louis Althusser, *For Marx*, trans. Ben Brewster (New York: Vintage, 1969). Althusser's Marxism owes a great deal to Spinoza: "If we want a historical predecessor to Marx in this respect we must appeal to Spinoza rather than Hegel. Spinoza established a relation between the first and the second kind of knowledge . . . which presupposed precisely a *radical discontinuity* [between truth and its antecedent error]." Where Hegel regards the later "supercession" of earlier "error" as the truth of this earlier approximation, Althusser argues that Marx assumes a *rupture* between science and ideology. Since the theory of ideology is among Althusser's crucial contributions to Marxism, his ascribing "predecessor" status to Spinoza is highly significant.

13. Raymond Williams, *Problems of Materialism and Culture* (London: New Left Books, 1980), pp. 43-44.

14. F. R. Leavis, *The Great Tradition* (New York: New York University Press, 1963), p. 138.

15. Williams, *Politics and Letters*, p. 66.

16. Raymond Williams, *Communications* (London: Penguin, 1969), p. 4.

17. Williams, *Politics and Letters*, pp. 125–26.

18. Ibid., p. 133.

19. Ibid., p. 135.

20. Paul Willis, *Learning to Labor* (New York: Columbia University Press, 1981); Dick Hebdidge, *Subculture: The Meaning of Style* (London: Methuen, 1979).

21. Willis, *Learning to Labor*, p. 41.

22. Althusser, *For Marx*.

23. See also Raymond Williams, "Base and Superstructure in Marxist Theory," in *Problems of Materialism and Culture*.

24. Georg Wilhelm Friedrich Hegel, *Phenomenology of the Spirit*, trans. A. V. Miller (Oxford: Oxford University Press, 1976).

25. C. Wright Mills, "Letter to the New Left," in *Power Politics and People*, ed. Irving Louis Horowitz (New York: Oxford University Press, 1963).

26. Williams, *Politics and Letters*, p. 415.

27. Williams, *Marxism and Literature*, pp. 18–19.

28. Ernesto Laclau and Chantal Mouffe, *Hegemony and Socialist Strategy* (London: Verso, 1982).

29. Critics of Marxism have criticized the orthodox notion that the proletariat is the identical subject/object of history in the capitalist epoch on theoretical grounds rather than on empirical and historical criteria. Drawing from Althusser's concept of the "epistemological break" between the early, humanistic Marx and the later, scientific Marx, they have turned on Marx himself by declaring that there is no fixed, essential agent of history linked to the structural features of the system. In fact, they argue that agency itself must be understood as a local, contextually specific "position" in which discourse interpellates individuals and groups.

30. Williams, *Politics and Letters*, p. 139.

31. It may be argued that poststructuralism is a post-Marxism, if *post* signifies both identity and difference. British cultural studies is post-Marxist—or, at least, post- one hegemonic version of Marxism—by its discovery of subcultures (and, therefore, its tacit addressing of the problem of generations as well as of the significance of school as a fundamental "ideological apparatus of the state") and its skepticism concerning orthodox Marxism's valorization of high art as an ineluctable legacy of any socialist movement (Trotsky), among other innovations. At the same time, as Foucault's late interview "Critical Theory/Intellectual History" in *Politics, Philosophy Culture* (New York and London: Routledge, 1988) indicates, even as Foucault tells us he was never a Marxist, a structuralist, or a Freudian, his own assessment that a "nonfalsified" Marxism might be theoretically useful and the persistence of some of the Marxist questions in his work indicate that the reports of the death of Marxism are premature. Yet who can deny that a certain kind of dogmatic Marxism is irrevocably surpassed and Marxism as a master discourse is finished?

32. See, for example, Richard Johnson, "What Is Cultural Studies, Anyway," *Social Text*, no. 16 (1986).

Information in Formation:
Williams/Media/China
Peter Hitchcock

In 1962 Raymond Williams noted that "all the new means of communication have been abused, for political control (as in propaganda) or for commercial profit (as in advertising). We can protest against such uses, but unless we have a clear alternative version of human society, we are not likely to make our protests effective."[1] Thirty years later there are, of course, numerous reasons for protest, but the prospects of a "clear alternative" remain radically displaced by the exigencies of the moment. It is as if what appeared to be axiomatic in 1962 (i.e., that the people should own the means of communication) is the faintest concern, while a truism (the media mediate) has dominated theoretical and political approaches. By tracing the trajectory of Williams's theorization of communications and media I hope to show not only that his critique provides a symptomatic exegesis of some contemporary dilemmas, but also that in the gaps of his own thinking lie some clues to the suspension in practice of pressing theoretical agendas (later to be explored under the rubric of "How do you represent China?"). While it would not be true to say that Williams's positions on communications constitute his most significant theoretical contribution, they nevertheless hold some crucial lessons for practical analysis of our current "subjectless" global village.

To approach the problematic of what in this essay will be seen as the technological "fix" of fixing "China" (paradoxically, as the move that Barthes makes in isolating a "certain number of features" in a "system" called "Japan")[2] I want to consider first the problems of definition in Williams's *Communications*; second, the rethinking of his approach brought about by his consideration of the impact of technology in *Television*; and third, the elaboration of a structural logic in the essay "Means of Communication as Means of Production." "China" will then be brought in to underline some practical problems that, while they do not return us to the situated knowledges of Britain in the 1960s, nevertheless suggest that our paradigm shifts have hardly shifted when it comes to the mode of information formation. I will argue that only by reinserting Williams's theory of cultural formation into media critique (a move that Williams himself only began to make) will we be able to account for the "eventness" of events and the way in which we are both seduced and abandoned by media representations.

In *Communications* Williams defines society as "a form of communication through which experience is described, shared, modified, and preserved" and says that "the emphasis on communication asserts, as a matter of experience, that men and societies are not confined to relationships of power, property, and production" (*C* 10). Of course, this can be related to his notions of culture as "ordinary" and as "a whole way of life," thereby placing his theory of communication at odds with both Foucauldian conceptions of power and forms of Marxism that emphasize the mode of production. Indeed, for those interested in either French poststructuralism or Althusserian Marxism these early formulations might seem to be easy targets: subjectivist and empiricist. Williams insists on a role for "experience": "The only practical use of communication is the sharing of real experience. To set anything above this is in fact quite unpractical" (*C* 25). One would be hard pressed to find any cultural theorist of the last thirty years with the courage to defend this position. Undaunted, Williams added *experience* to his 1983 edition of *Keywords*, both noting its relation to subjectivism and clarifying its holistic "exclusion of nominated partialities."[3] Ultimately, Williams's defense rests on generalizing the principle so that the "deepest sense of experience" requires that "all kinds of evidence and its consideration should be tried." Clearly, in *Communications* Williams has erred on the side of the individual as a feeling, experiential, and discernible subject. Yet it is just as true to say that Williams was already extremely sensitized to the role of mediation in experience, however subjectivist it might appear. Ironically, this results from the long shadow cast by Leavis and the *Scrutiny* crew, whose penchant for a great tradition impresses Williams not for its elitism, but for the possibility that some kind of great tradition might draw from the "life of actual communities" (*C* 115).[4] This experiential culture is valorized against what Williams calls "synthetic culture," which "is not the culture of the 'ordinary man.' It is the culture of the disinherited." Interestingly, this allows Williams to note that, culturally, Britain is an "American colony." There are good and bad forms of mediation.

The strongest parts of the argument are not where Williams ponders the febrile tentacles of structures of feeling, but where he shows just how undemocratically mediated are the current manifestations of communications. Of the four types of communication systems he categorizes—authoritarian, paternal, commercial, and democratic—the last remains local, exploratory, and the least realized. For all the charges against Williams concerning empiricism in his work, the argument in *Communications* rests on an absent center, for there is essentially no structural experience of democratic communications in contemporary everyday life on which this system can build. In fact, Williams acknowledges precisely the abstract nature of the democratic model, and it is this abstraction, I will argue, that allows a more nuanced conception of the means of communication.

The abstraction of the democratic model is girded by a hesitancy over the question of technological developments and the role of the state, one inhibiting by virtue of its cost, the other inhibiting by its nature. In his "Restrospect and Prospect," added to *Communications* in 1975, Williams warns:

> The development of cable television can bring new kinds of community broadcasting, and new opportunities for independent production, or, equally, can bring new kinds of commercial exploitation. Satellite television transmission, now a marginal support system, can become an international system beyond the control of any democratric authority, especially if it is linked with the development of domestic satellite receivers and with advertising finance from the powerful paranational companies. (188)

Williams's knack for prophecy, like his abstractions, has been seriously undervalued. In *Television* Williams deepens our sense of both through a cogent consideration not of content but of technological forms, a methodological shift seen in his other works of the period but here certainly augmented by Williams's writing the book while he taught in the United States (whose television experience deeply affected him).[5] Significantly, Williams eschews technological determinism and any attempt to isolate technology as a cultural form. Yet this approach also entails the restoration of intentionality ("purposes and practices") to the process of research and development, which certainly entertains a dangerous determinism all its own. Williams's point, however, is to show how television technology is a response to a crisis in social communication: the new economic and political realities of the twentieth century required a "new information." Electronic media are the cultural forms of this new information. Indeed, twentieth-century history may be articulated as an account of the cultural forms of information. The advantage of Williams's approach lies in its attack on the cause/effect simplicities of technological determinism: "It is not only that the supply of broadcasting facilities preceded the demand; it is that the means of communication preceded their content" (*T* 25). A drawback, however, is that Williams keeps the argument to a level of generality that makes many of his comments "introductory" rather than polemical. For instance, few would now dispute the distinction he draws between the state and public interest in the development of corporate and governmental forms of television interference in foreign image markets. The United States Information Agency is the apotheosis of this "development." Nevertheless, while Williams does not explore the latter in detail, the relevant implications are there in his analysis of "flow" in program sequencing.

Flow would seem to be a controversial term to describe the interrupted, disarticulated dispersions of contemporary television programming. And yet Williams's point is that "interruptions" themselves are not extraneous to the telenarrative; rather, they help constitute its discourse. Flow analysis, then, proceeds on three levels: the first looks at the programming sequences used in any given time slot; the second scrutinizes the succession of items within those sequences; and the third examines the interaction of words and images within those items. Again, this discursive and "linguistic" approach to television analysis would seem to place Williams within a structuralist mode, with which he is not normally associated. What is interesting is that the intentionalist emphases in the discussion of research and development are almost entirely lacking in the account of the television narrative itself. In his breakdown of a flow on Channel 7 in San Francisco (March 12, 1973), Williams continually asserts the "lack of conscious connection," the "lack of direct relation," and the "apparent unconsciousness of contrast" in the sequence of images and words (*T* 105). The very arbitrary nature of the flow belies, for Williams, its structure of feeling. In a news sequence, for instance, Williams points out how the order of events, while predetermined, is presented in such a way as to suggest the hurried complexity of the world in sharp contrast to the crisp editing and "cool deliberation" of the commercials (*T* 116). The overall flow, therefore, articulates the meanings and values of a culture not just in the content of the items, but in the form of their juxtaposition.

If *Communications* and *Television* bear any resemblance to each other, it is in Williams's attempt to integrate recent media developments into an overall cultural critique of everyday life. Williams is not interested in suspect oppositions between "high" and "low" cultures, just as he clearly distances himself from any "massification" of society thesis. He is, however, keenly concerned with both the possibilities and the constraints of new forms of social interaction. While never a pessimist (see, for instance, his later essay, "Culture and Technology"),[6] Williams remains apprehensive about the question of ownership of the means of communication. This is underscored in his essay "Means of Communication and Means of Production," where he attempts to schematize his previous work in terms of Marxian categories.[7] The shift here is that Williams extends his critique of the forms of communication to show that they are also fundamentally means of production, and now, instead of an experiential model, he accounts for these means in terms of ideology, although he does not specify how mediation is structured ideologically.[8] Nevertheless, this is a crucial theoretical move because it allows Williams not only to counter models based on abstract individualism but also to rethink the base-superstructure thesis to reflect the "qualitative change" in communicative production. This will obviously have implications for the media event I discuss.

The change can be summarized under what Williams calls the "alternative modes of communication," basically those of electronic media. He notes that, although they are a recent historical development, alternative modes "appear" to provide direct forms of communication not available in previous durable or amplifying means of communication. And yet, as Williams shows, the labor of communication is effaced from the means of communication so that the editing, reorganizing, and deleting of voices or images are suppressed from the communication itself. Just in case this is taken as ideology, as ideological state apparatuses, Williams stresses: "It is not only a matter of excision and selection. New positive relations of a signifying kind can be made by the processes of arrangements and juxtaposition, and this can be true even in those unusual cases in which the original primary units are left in their original state" (*PMC* 60). I would say this is true not only of television, but also of certain forms of print technology, although the innovations of the former are gradually eclipsing the impact of the latter. Yet "what is being made to be seen" is, for Williams, evidence of a radical potential within the modes of communication. Part of the challenge is a "critical demystification," but Williams warns:

> Reification will have to be distinguished from the open, conscious composition of works, or the only results will be negative, as in some contemporary semiotic tendencies, which demystify the practice by calling all such practice into question, and then predictably fall back on ideas of universal (inherent and unsurpassable) alienation, within the terms of a pessimistic and universalist psychology. (*PMC* 62)

Williams concludes by reiterating a point central to his other works: "We shall already have entered a new social world when we have brought the means and systems of the most direct communications under our own direct and general control" (*PMC* 62). This, of course, puts a heady faith in the means of communication functioning in the same way as the modes of production theories of classical Marxism, a belief that, if we accept Baudrillard's theorization of the "hyperreal," is no longer plausible: the commodity system and the sign system do not coincide. My consideration of "China" is an intervention into this schism of theory, one in which Williams may have more than the merely conventional to offer.

Perhaps this is most evident in Williams's essay "Distance," which is ostensibly about the 1982 war of the Malvinas.[9] Distance here means both the geographical distances foregrounded in television broadcasts and "the distance between the technology of television, as professionally understood, managed and interpreted, and the political and cultural space within which it actually operates" (*W* 36-37).

Williams's point is that the contingencies of the latter produce some frightening alienation effects in the former, particularly, in the Falklands example, with its slow methodical buildup framing the inevitability of war. In the structural absence of a subject (i.e., the war was yet to be), Williams is horrified by television's obsession with simulacra—using training footage and studio models to make up for the bloodshed that (for security reasons) will not be shown. The distance, then, is paradoxically a complicity, for the news analysis exploits the "safe distance" in keeping with the ideological purview of the state, which, at this point, must seek consent by any means necessary. Williams notes that it is the structural logic of the culture of distance that requires our urgent attention, for this concerns "the latent culture of alienation, within which men and women are reduced to models, figures and the quick cry in the throat" (W 43). It is from that "quick cry in the throat" that "China" must begin to intercede.

The "China" at issue is at once a historically specific sign, the China of spring 1989, and a displaced signifier that floats, somewhat eerily, in the political unconscious of the Western media. If the notes I have offered so far about Williams's thoughts on the cultural constellation of information and information technologies settle, more or less, on the question of production and ownership of the means of communication, then "China" would seem to present an immediate and pressing problematic, for it appears within the language of a systemic logic and is not simply the product of the putative ownership of particular technologies (satellite transmission capabilities, for example). The sliding signification of "China" suggests a complex logic of objectification and assimilation (the hallmark of the "informatian" society?). If the West prides itself on certain characteristic "flows" of information, it is not because it has necessarily "mastered" the logic of information production, however much, ideologically, it believes this to be the case. If the repressed moment of mediation in my introduction returns here, it is to emphasize that the facticity of facts, or the way that it is "factored" into information, is very much open to the contradictory logics of mediation. As in Williams's work, the latter is not necessarily invoked as a negative term, but as an arena for understanding over which struggles must inevitably take place. There is nothing in this inevitability, however, that suggests that media representation is the only arena of struggle, or that technological superiority in representation is a guarantee of the veracity of the information represented.

From April to June of 1989, Western reporters in Beijing gleefully announced that the revolution *would* be televised and that information itself constitutes the political vanguard in the success of the "democratic" movement in China.[10] In light of the Beijing massacre of June 4 the West has been a little more modest in its assessment of the information question. While it is true that foreign reports quite clearly stimulated and assisted the Chinese students in spreading their words, the way that information was disseminated was *not* under the control of the students. The selection of reports and quotes from students blatantly reflects the West's projection of itself onto the movement and has made it much easier for the Chinese rulers subsequently to discredit the otherwise sincere demands of the students in the eyes of the Chinese public. The projection that by dint of satellite transmission enables one to manipulate or even transform the complexities of Chinese society is hopelessly idealist and a dangerous precedent in international cultural relations. To believe, for instance, that broadcasts by the Voice of America, a U.S. government interest, are enlightening the Chinese with the democratic elixir of "pure" facts is naive in the extreme. This is not to condone the ideological productions of the Chinese government, but to rethink the question of ownership when information is at stake, so that we may account for the wily ways of information, facts by fax, as more than just a source of low-intensity interference by exterior forces in the internal workings of this or that government. Clearly, the "freedom" of information represented by major European and American transnational conglomerates does not necessarily represent the freedom to which the Chinese people may aspire. In fact, the struggle has not been won at either end of the fax machine or satellite dish, not because communists are ultimately repressive and bourgeois democracies are not, but because the fact that people do not control the means of representation fails to account for the cultural logics involved. If the information society has, in this sense, yet to be born it is because the cultural formations at issue are "emergent" (in Williams's sense), and there is as yet no political or theoretical homology between ownership per se and the means of communication. How does "China" subvert this founding principle of Williams's approach?

In the Beijing Spring of 1989 it would appear that two forms of Williams's communication schema were fighting for dominance: the authoritarian and the commercial. It is not just that the rallying cries of the students for "democracy" underlined the patent authoritarianism of the Chinese Communist Party and its news agency Xinhua, but that the more the Western news agencies focused on those specially written English banners touting democracy ("Give me liberty or give me death"), the more the unreality of their own democratic bases became apparent. For instance, when a CBS reporter stood at a crowded intersection in downtown Beijing in May and said, beaming, "It's the first time that I've been in the middle of a popular uprising," his presence is sanctioned precisely by a corresponding absence of this event from American political life. In other words, there is no question that the same cameras will be absent from the middle of a popular uprising or large-scale protest that might threaten their own legitimacy or "objectivity." It is inconceivable that the same reporter would have said this a couple of years later in the middle of Camp Solidarity during the Pittston strike or Solidarity Day in Washington, D.C. In this regard, "China" of 1989 represents a massive displacement of the undemocratic implications of Western coverage.

Yet it would be wrong to say that it is simply the ownership of those means of communication that ineluctably signified the "China" that flashed across the Western networks in 1989. The specular function of "China" also is a measure of the processes of objectification endemic to Western discourse. This, of course, recalls the orientalist desire that Edward Said, among others, has investigated as a structural logic of colonial and postcolonial representation of the other. But the Manichaean processes of orientalism are, in "China," marked by profound contradictions. On the one hand, they must celebrate the imperial exoticism of a "China" long since departed; but on the other, they must invest this image with all the trappings of China's entry into modern statehood. The former tendency is emphasized in a United Airlines ad: the doors open onto the Forbidden City while a "Last Emperor" look-alike clashes cymbals to the strains of Gershwin (this ad was temporarily dropped in the aftermath of the massacre not far beyond those gates). The latter effect is more complex since the media must simultaneously grant the student movement modernity while distancing its very possibility from communist achievements since 1949. Several strategies appeared in 1989 to dis-place the nuisances of history. One was to simply root the "democ-racy movement" back to the May Fourth Movement of 1919. (This is a tricky exercise since the protests of 1919 were not only in favor of Chinese democracy and science but against the machinations of for-eign imperialism, which was particularly heavy-handed with China in the Versailles Treaty signed that year. Furthermore, the clarion calls of the May Fourth Movement were themselves an inspiration to the fledgling communist movement in China at that time.)[11] Two other narrative twists seem closely connected. The first makes the Chinese Communist Party simply an extension of imperial China (both Deng Xiaoping and Li Peng were, on occasion, referred to as emperors and, we were told, they have lost the "mandate of heaven," which of course was said to grant imperial power). The second asserts that the Chinese will to democracy is primarily an American phenomenon (Chinese students referring to the Founding Fathers, quoting from the Constitution and the Bill of Rights, etc.). These are, we might say, the conscious levels of narrative technique that are partly in keeping with Williams's flow analysis, yet there is also an unconscious structural logic to these sequences of represen-tation.

This is evident in Ted Koppel's remark (I will mention his televi-sion special on China in a moment) that "we are in the business of facts, initially. The truth sometimes takes a little longer to come out." The split between the representative truths of media coverage and the categorical truths of historical narrative is crucial to the media "event" (just as it is endemic to populist versions of sinology). On the one hand it allows columnists like Anthony Lewis to declare that "we in the West can see things a lot more clearly" when it comes to Chinese politics (he had just opined that the "Communist Party of China does not really exist"!); on the other hand, it encourages a self-sustaining knowledge production (since no evidence has been pre-sented, none need be denied). If, as Williams maintains, techno-logical developments have facilitated a "mobile privatization" of communications within the decoding context of the media con-sumer, then there is also a concomitant mobile privatization of meaning within the means of communications themselves. The for-mal components of encoding and decoding may well be the same (as Stuart Hall has pointed out, these may be frameworks of knowledge, relations of production, and technical infrastructure),[12] but that does not mean they are symmetrical. Indeed, the representation of "China" is precisely dependent on the inequality of communicative relations, both within the producer-consumer logic of Western discourses and within the rhetoric of othering that structures West-East "dialogue."

Here the "culture of distance," the sheer abstraction of "China," allows it to be enunciated in the name of benevolent media modernization (or as one newsweekly put it: "Karl Marx, meet Marshall McLuhan"). But more importantly, distance exacerbates the narratological imperatives of Western news services. Just as Williams notes that the Malvinas war was almost inevitable, given the buildup of the military and the press coverage, so the Beijing Spring demanded airtime and columns only when the crisis clearly suggested a narrative closure in keeping with the attention span that news specials and weekly magazines can sustain.

Initially, coverage of the democracy movement was subdued. Yet as the students gave the protests more momentum, it became clear that their tactics were often designed specifically with the foreign press in mind. Indeed, although the news services originally intended to stick around only as long as Gorbachev was in town (a Sino-Soviet rapprochement being in the cards), they soon discovered the students to be much more accessible and potentially more of a human interest story. For their part, the students garnered Western attention in innovative ways. They drew banners in English and framed their demands in terms of Western democracy (although their vagueness about the latter often led to derision); they organized a hunger strike that in only three days got more attention than the much longer, fatal hunger strikes of the IRA ever did (I mention this only as a political contrast); they demanded and got a live television spot in which the student leaders met with Premier Li Peng; and, when the demonstrations had more or less stopped (classes had resumed, and Tiananmen Square was almost empty save for out-of-town students who had not yet received tickets to return home), the protest leaders hit on the idea of building a "Goddess of Democracy," which they planted in the middle of China's most hallowed square. Even Western commentators who had been quick to read the Beijing Spring in terms of their own democratic models were uneasy about the obvious resemblance of the "goddess" to "Lady Liberty." Suddenly, the distance that allowed technology to appropriate ideologically a movement using a set of culturally specific objectives also allowed a parody of it. The copper and stone that give to Liberty its aura of permanence now found its counterpart in Tiananmen Square in plaster and polystyrene. True, there was still sufficient margin for self-righteousness, but the "goddess" marked a moment where naïveté came very close to satirical masquerade: "China" had become a white woman.[13]

If this was hardly the narrative closure the networks desired, the massacre that followed shortly afterward was a godsend of epic proportions. Since one can already read at least a dozen books that focus on the horror of this event, I will provide only a footnote. The fact that the bulk of the killing occurred on Changan Avenue (which the Western spectator did not know) and not in Tiananmen Square (which, after seven weeks of coverage, everybody did) did not prevent the networks and newspapers from relocating it and reporting hearsay as fact (in the first few weeks after June 4, I collected dozens of articles that variously reported the number of dead from zero to seventy thousand). *Time*, which obviously lacked the time to get genuine photos of the massacre, printed a cover that featured a Chinese man with his brains splattered across the road under the title "Beijing Massacre." The photo is actually of a man who was knocked down by an army truck (some say an army personnel carrier) miles from Tiananmen the day before the massacre (in the background you will see an armed soldier standing with the crowd of onlookers, an impossibility on June 4). Far from the embarrassment of the "goddess," all narratives could now be rewritten and illustrated to include the bloody finale to which all previous events had obviously pointed. Western reporters then retreated to the safety of luxury hotels and, from the rush to report a civil war, foreigners were seen scurrying for every available exit. The show was over.

"China" would here seem to unravel certain aspects of Williams's approaches. Is it not the case, for instance, that the success of the packaging of this event depends precisely on an emptying out of experience from the plane of vision? True, the networks attempted to humanize the story by focusing occasionally on individuals like the student leader Wuer Kaixi and to a lesser extent Wang Dan and

Chai Ling. But the main emphasis, particularly before the massacre, was on how the processes of communication themselves were beyond even the strategic maneuvering of the students. While such a view might seem to place the burden of intentionality back in the editorial rooms of CNN or CBS, I am suggesting that it is the logic of the mode of information that structures the decision-making process, a logic that can be reduced neither to the role of experience nor necessarily to the "alienation" of ideology.[14] To account adequately for the metonymic profusions of "China" in the Beijing Spring, we should not reject Williams's theoretical framework but shift its emphasis from the intentionalist machinations of cultural *forms* to the systemic processes of encoding in cultural *formations.* This is a kind of analysis that Williams himself had called for but only began to pursue, analysis that tries "to understand right inside the productive process how these difficult modes of address and forms are actually constructed."[15]

Williams has defined cultural formations in several ways, including in terms of cultural producers whose sphere of production is tangential to or not initially dependent upon institutional affiliation: "those effective movements and tendencies, in intellectual and artistic life, which have significant and sometimes decisive influence on the active development of a culture, and which have a variable and often oblique relation to formal institutions."[16] Such formations are characterized by their internal organization through "formal membership," "collective public manifestation," or "conscious association or group identification." While this might seem adequate in explaining media cultural formations, in general the model cannot account for the fraught relations of producers to media institutions (the networks, etc.) or indeed the lack of conscious identification or intention in historically specific examples of media production. I have elsewhere argued for a fourth category of cultural formation that allows for an understanding of cultural production that may seem beyond the intention or identification of the producers concerned. As such, the "cultural event" is formed primarily through forces external to those involved in it, even if at times these principles seem to coincide.[17] The ineluctable rush of the media to "stage" an alternative cultural component of life calls into question their own norms of cultural and political orthodoxy. It is the very desire to "cover"

"China" that calls into question the logic of appropriation within the cultural event.

Two examples may clarify this specific sense of cultural formation. Since Paper Tiger (the alternative TV/video production collective) has devoted a video to the analysis of Ted Koppel's television special on the Beijing Spring, "The Tragedy of Tiananmen: The Untold Story," I will make my comments brief here. Flushed with the idealistic view that stories are there only to be unearthed (and not constructed), Koppel tells an untold one. What is stunning is that his version, a "tragedy," sounds remarkably like the Chinese government's. In the absence of juicy footage of the Chinese army's butchery, Koppel opts to show video sequences taken by a team of experts (experts because they are Westerners who speak Chinese, although the program never directly benefits from this ability). Because of the positioning of these experts on the night of June 4, the violence depicted is primarily *by the demonstrators.* One "expert" recounts in detail the demise of an army personnel carrier driver who was "literally torn limb from limb." Another remarks on the fact that several personnel carriers were burned and that, on one occasion, the occupants were still inside. This is in keeping with other reporters' fascination with the "instant justice" of the mob, which produced accounts of soldiers being castrated, some burned alive, some hung garishly from highway overpasses, and a photograph that the weeklies ran of the charred remains of a naked soldier dangling from the side of a bus (the notion of "instant justice" is an important one, not only in describing the violence of the demonstrators in the Beijing Spring, but also in the "instant books" that flowed within weeks of the massacre and give to violence another connotation).

The inference to be drawn from all of this violence is frightening, not just because of the voyeuristic delight in recording someone else's butchery, but because suddenly we are confronted with the idea that the soldiers *and* the rebels had it coming to them. Indeed, by splitting off the students involved from the "mob" (as Koppel affectionately calls them), we are presented with a situation in which the state had the right to use violence against public "aggression." This, of course, is not just the "tragedy" of Tiananmen, but also that of Kent State. Put another way, as long as the students were seen to challenge the dictates of the Communist Party, the event could be celebrated as a popular uprising; but if the uprising appears to threaten the very idea of the state, then "order" must be restored. The logic of media coverage is here caught between fetishizing the students' idealism and decrying its consequences. The overlooked factor is the role of the peasants and workers, the omnipresent id of the Chinese Communist Party. In fact, one could prove that it was their dissatisfaction that ultimately led to the massacre by the army, a point underlined by the breakdown of recorded deaths and executions (very few students were killed; none, to my knowledge, were executed). In suppressing the role of the general populace, Koppel's "version" of the Beijing Spring ironically presents the case as the Communist Party would want it to be presented. This is not to say that the cultural event is simply an expression of the state, but that the media representation of popular power must not challenge their own power and status as the narrators of the world. Interestingly, Paper Tiger points out that Merrill Lynch paid $720,000 for advertising during Koppel's show in slots that emphasized that a global capitalist network can sidestep the instabilities of local markets. A flow analysis would underline that the contradictory logic of this cultural formation unravels in the space between these two narrations.

To this end, I want to provide a second example that both stresses the value of Williams's flow formulation and supports this sense of the cultural event as a cultural formation of contemporary news networks. A West Coast television station interviewed an American air hostess as part of its postmassacre coverage of the Beijing Spring. She was asked whether she believed the rumor that the Chinese soldiers were drugged. She did, and proceeded to recount how she had heard soldiers behind some doors shouting "kill, kill, kill," comparing their enthusiasm to spectators "at a football game." As noted, the representation of rumor as fact was a dominant topos of "China" 1989, more or less allowing for the vagaries of distance. Here, however, the glaring loophole in this information formation is countered by two extraordinary moments in the sequence of presentation. First, the reporter concludes that "Amelia [the air hostess] is urging the VOA [Voice of America] to keep broadcasting in Mandarin to tell the Chinese people what is happening in their country." This rumor-mongering, like the civil war thesis, hurt some Chinese more than if they had had no information at all.[18] But in case the veracity of our American television station is in doubt, or indeed that of the VOA, the sequence juxtapositions suggest a second utterance context. Each break in the news program is punctuated by a graphic titled "China: History in the Streets" (history, rumor, what's the difference?). One break is immediately followed by an incredible sequence. The viewer sees a television within the television. A general in uniform and dark glasses is being asked voiced-over questions like "Your excellency, what's your favorite color?" A reverse shot reveals a young couple in pajamas on their couch intently watching this "news" while they're having breakfast. One says, "Oh, don't ask him that, ask him why his national bird is a jet bomber." As the general replies (in an obviously Hispanic accent), our couple suggests more informed questions: "Ask him whether he thinks that banning newspapers is the best way to preserve trees." A male voice-over then proclaims, "If you question what's going on in the world, you should be a member of the World Affairs Council." A quick succession of photos (Corazon Aquino, Henry Kissinger, Andrew Young) follows, with an explanation that these are the kinds of people you can meet and talk to about what is really happening in the world.

I do not want to labor this point, but again the fragility of this cultural logic is revealed even as it attempts to suture its patent contradictions. Whose coverage is being challenged here: The television station's? The reporter's? The informant's? Who can our couple depend on? Is the World Affairs Council an independent information resource outside the machinations of the cultural event (Kissinger, for instance, was of the opinion in June 1989 that "the occupation of the main square of a country's capital is not fully described as a peaceful demonstration")? Far from confirming the integrity of information in the cultural formation, this flow of self-correction draws attention to its mediated objectivity. Again, there is no intention to fault in this because the logic of the sequence maintains that no intent is privileged. Thus, while Williams's flow analysis allows a textual critique of the processes of information, it also underlines that experiential and intentionalist categories of mediation fail to account for the decentered and contradictory logics imbricated in the information of global communications, where truth is deferred or, as Koppel reminds us, conveniently takes longer to come out.

"China," however, is not here being invoked to displace Williams's contribution to media theory, but to suggest some avenues where his theories might be taken further. Some of these paths are clearly provided by Williams himself. For instance, in his essay "The Uses of Cultural Theory," Williams notes that "what then emerges as the most central and practical element in cultural analysis is what also marks the most significant cultural theory: the exploration and specification of distinguishable cultural formations."[19] My comments on the cultural event are a step in this direction. Nor do I wish to imply that Williams's appeal to experience in communications analysis is simply irrelevant to the cultural logic of late capitalism. Far from it. "China" shows that without an adequate grounding in cultural knowledge of the world (and not just the world as "other"), paranational media conglomerates can reproduce a dichotomy in which the unfathomable or the fabricated or both become the only alternative. To reinsert the role of experience into the communication process implies that, as Williams has made patently clear, for a network to be the eyes of world, it must be owned and run by the world. The communal self is predicated not just on access to information technology but also on communal responsibility for its uses. The problem is, of course, that we are so removed from this situation that intervention is reduced to local and sporadic acts of reinterpretation, which are as unlikely to shake commercial communication systems as they are to allow the Chinese people to overcome communication's authoritarian manifestation. Williams was always more sanguine about the possibilities of social transformation than contemporary poststructuralism would seem to allow. Yet I hope that these few notes might contribute to an interrogation of this gap by rethinking Williams's theories in terms of current contingencies. Thus, by simply contrasting Williams's emphasis on "lived experience" within the processes of communication with those of the prophets of postmodern media, with their penchant for the incommensurability of living *with* experience, one would not adequately register the ways in which both methodologies may mutually imply each other. In that regard, "China" does not self-righteously announce "Karl Marx, meet Marshall McLuhan" but looks to a more pressing theoretical project: "Raymond Williams, meet Jean Baudrillard." As Williams once asked about the state of theory, "Are we now informed enough, hard enough, to look for our own double edges?"

NOTES

1. Raymond Williams, *Communications*, 3d ed. (London: Penguin, 1976), pp. 10-11. Subsequent references to this edition will be given in the text with the abbreviation *C* and page number(s).

2. See Roland Barthes, *Empire of Signs*, trans. Richard Howard (New York: Hill and Wang, 1982). Of course, this system is a "mythology" rather than a reality but, using Williams, I will also be wondering aloud about whether "mythologizing" itself is complicit with what Barthes sees as the delay of knowledge about Asia. Early in his argument Barthes writes that "someday we must write the history of our own obscurity." Williams, at least, always wanted to bring that day a little closer.

3. Raymond Williams, *Keywords*, 2d ed. (London: Fontana, 1983), pp. 126-29.

4. This is a topos of Williams's work, although it is clearest in *Culture and Society.*

5. Raymond Williams, *Television* (New York: Schocken, 1975). Williams draws heavily on this experience in his analysis of "flow," although it would be interesting to explore whether the structural logic he discusses works primarily, or specifically, for U.S. television. Subsequent references to this work will be given in the text with the abbreviation *T* and page number(s).

6. Raymond Williams, "Culture and Technology," in *The Politics of Modernism*, ed. Tony Pinkney (London: Verso, 1989).

7. Raymond Williams, "Means of Communication and Means of Production," in *Problems in Materialism and Culture* (London: Verso, 1980). Subsequent references to this work will be given in the text with the abbreviation *PMC* and page number(s).

8. Certainly, from Williams's discussion of ideology and mediation in *Marxism and Literature* (London: Oxford University Press, 1976) we can see some ground rules for such analysis as in, for instance, "language and signification as indissoluble elements of the material social process itself, involved all the time both in production and reproduction." Ideology, like mediation, is therefore not intermediary, but is constituitive of social processes themselves. Neither ideology nor mediation is necessarily "false" or "distortive" according to this interpretation.

9. Originally published as "Distance" in *London Review of Books*, June 17-30, 1982, pp. 19-20. Reprinted in Raymond Williams, *What I Came to Say* (London: Hutchinson, 1989), pp. 36-43. Subsequent references to *What I Came to Say* will be given in the text with the abbreviation *W* and page number(s).

10. Interested readers might want to look over the weeklies' obsession with China in May and June 1989. I have supplemented my readings with both Western and Chinese newspaper reports of the Beijing Spring and television coverage. These sources were juxtaposed in a multimedia "event" (video/slides/music) called "How Do You Represent China?" that I gave at the City University of New York Graduate Center in May 1990. "China" is here based on that critique. Useful collections of documents include the special issue of *China Information* 4, no. 1 (Summer 1989) and Han Hinzhu, ed., *Cries for Democracy* (Princeton, N.J.: Princeton University Press, 1990).

11. Three relevant analyses of the May Fourth Movement are Merle Golman, ed., *Modern Chinese Literature in the May Fourth Era* (Cambridge, Mass.: Harvard University Press, 1977); Lin Yu-sheng, *The Crisis of Chinese Consciousness* (Madison: University of Wisconsin Press, 1979); and Arif Dirlik, *The Origins of Chinese Communism* (London: Oxford University Press, 1989). Dirlik is particularly provocative.

12. See Stuart Hall, "Encoding/Decoding," in *Culture, Media, Language*, ed. Stuart Hall, D. Hobson, A. Lowe, and P. Willis (London: Hutchinson, 1980).

13. For a perceptive critique of this aspect of "China watching," see Rey Chow, "Violence in the Other Country," *Radical America* 22, no. 4 (July/August 1989): 23-34. Chow's essay is the first to link the "othering" of China to Gayatri Chakravorty Spivak's dictum that "the discourse of man is in the metaphor of woman." See also Paper Tiger's video "Ted Koppel's Long March from Woodstock to Tiananmen Square," which, among other things, looks at the "absent presence" of Chai Ling, the woman student leader, from the bulk of Western coverage. My video "How Do You Represent China?" also considers the ramifications of this discursive "violence."

14. Mark Poster has developed a theory around this question using a notion of the configuration of information as electronically "wrapped" language. While I find his "mode of information" argument as compelling as Williams's "means of communication" schema, it is noticeable that the former is based almost exclusively on French poststructuralism (Williams merits only a footnote). The present argument is wondering aloud about a possible hybridization of these approaches to the problem at hand. See Mark Poster, *The Mode of Information* (Chicago: University of Chicago Press, 1990).

15. See Stephen Heath and Gillian Skirrow, "Interview with Raymond Williams," chapter 15 in this volume.

16. Raymond Williams, *Marxism and Literature* (London: Oxford University Press, 1976), p. 118. See also *Culture* (Glasgow: Fontana, 1981).

17. See Peter Hitchcock, "The Cultural Event," in *Working-Class Fiction in Theory and Practice: A Reading of Alan Sillitoe* (Ann Arbor: UMI Research Press, 1989).

18. For instance, the Chinese government intercepted a foreign report, subsequently aired by ABC, of a Beijing resident who heard on Voice of America that 20,000 people had been massacred in Tiananmen Square. The Chinese used the video to prosecute the resident for rumor-mongering. In a bizarre twist of events, the networks then began rebroadcasting footage of the Beijing Spring with Chinese faces electronically disguised (perhaps in the hope that the Chinese government did not see the broadcasts the first time around!). Even some of the instant books employed this tactic. See, for instance, Scott Simmie and Bob Nixon, *Tiananmen Square* (Seattle: University of Washington Press, 1989). Both the networks and books such as this continued to rely on second-, third-, and fourth-hand information ("[unnamed] witnesses said that . . . ," "an Australian reporter was told that . . . ," etc.), all the while contradicting each other and themselves.

19. Raymond Williams, "The Uses of Cultural Theory," *New Left Review*, no. 158 (July/August 1986): 29.

Interview with Raymond Williams
Stephen Heath and Gillian Skirrow

Transcript of an interview videotaped in Cambridge, England, March 1984.

HEATH: Raymond Williams's work over the last twenty years has been very influential for the way in which people have thought about culture and politics. In the course of that work he has had occasion many times to look critically at mass culture and he has written specifically about the media, notably television, in his book *Television: Technology and Cultural Form*. Gillian Skirrow and I talked to Raymond Williams about issues relating to mass culture. It seemed particularly important to do this as the book of interviews, *Politics and Letters*, in which he went back over his work, reassessing it from the perspective of the current situation, more or less omitted any reference to those issues—the book on television itself, for example, received only one mention. So what we wanted to do was to remedy something of that omission, to try to explore with him questions involved in "mass culture, criticism, and analysis."

Raymond, perhaps what we need first of all is actually to look at the term *mass culture* and gain some understanding of that, what we mean by it, its historical and political implications.

WILLIAMS: Yes, actually I've always opposed the term *mass culture*. This may seem presumptuous since use of the term is so widespread, but the unnoticed associations it brings with it are what I wanted at least to draw attention to. *Mass* and *masses* are modern words ranging in meaning from "multitude" to "crowd" to "mob." And if you look at the development of various phrases derived from that, you will find that, in politics, for example, the term *mass* is very ambivalent. The right use it to talk about mass democracy, which is rather vulgar and unpredictable and volatile; and the left talk about mass action as showing solidarity, people coming together to change their condition. Now that's an important and real historical ambivalence. But when you apply it to culture, and specifically to modern media, what it obscures is this: that the real institutions of mass culture in any central sense predate the modern media. I mean, the mass cultural institutions are the mass meeting and the mass demonstration, where people are physically assembled in large crowds and where certain modes of communication—the display of banners, certain shouts, and so on—are wholly appropriate to that kind of physical assembly. Now it's almost too obvious that in television, where typically there may be a very large audience—mass in the sense of multitude—but where people are distributed over their millions in very small groups or alone or in a family relationship, many of the actual techniques seem to have been developed for a more personal kind of speaking. Therefore, if we are to understand, as we must, the modes of communication characteristic of these media, possible in them, we have to distance ourselves from what is otherwise only the imposition on the media of a notion of the mass market. Mass as against quality market: this is a medium which because of its expense and so on has to reach a very large number of people. The term *mass* confuses too many questions. If it's just a label, OK, but I think it's more than a label, and a lot of assumptions come with it, particularly from antidemocratic prejudices about anything that reaches or is addressed to a large number of people.

SKIRROW: But there's another term in this debate, isn't there, which is *popular culture?*

WILLIAMS: Yes.

SKIRROW: How do you make a distinction between "mass culture," in any of the senses you've mentioned, and "popular culture?"

WILLIAMS: Well, *popular* follows the same history, of course, but with some interesting differences. When it is applied to culture it usually implies a certain difference from what has come to be called high culture or learned culture or liberal culture. On the other hand, it took on at least three meanings as it came through to the twentieth century. First, it got mixed up with folk culture: although the German term *volk* could have been translated "popular," it was translated "folk." And this had the effect of backdating popular culture. Popular culture was everything before the Industrial Revolution—so that was quite inappropriate. Then there was "popular" in the simple sense of something that was addressed to a large number of people, and the term coming into the nineteenth century meant "well-liked by a large number of people." But there are two other senses of "popular" which I think are important: one, this persistent use of "the people" to mean a body of people politically as opposed to a power, a government. Popular culture now sometimes means to some of its practitioners that which represents a certain kind of interest or experience, as against the modes of an established culture or as against a power. But that can very easily be isolated because it's almost inevitably self-consciously oppositional. People often then say, "Well, that kind of popular culture may be real and a part of the history of people's conditions and so on, but that is just a political culture"—something like that.

But the other meaning, in which I've been particularly interested lately, takes up that whole range which never got recognized as culture at all within an old dispensation: that of a very active world of everyday conversation and exchange; jokes, idioms, characteristic forms not just of everyday dress but occasional dress, people consciously having a party, making a do, marking an occasion. I think this area has been very seriously undervalued, and it isn't only that it is undervalued in itself. We're not yet clear about the relation of those things to certain widely successful television forms. There is a sense in which everyday gossip passes straight into a certain kind of serial. And there's an obvious relation between the whole joke world and certain kinds of comedy, and the question then would be whether such television forms are articulating those areas, or whether they're simply latching onto them and in fact displacing, manipulating, redirecting them. But *popular* means all those things, I think.

HEATH: So the relations between mass culture and popular culture are actually quite intricate today, the two in no way simply separate. This brings us on to something you emphasized in your last book, *Towards 2000*, which is important here inasmuch as it represents your view on future developments and possibilities, on political opportunities with regard to the media, mass culture, popular

culture. You've just been talking about the popular culture of everyday life, which is clearly, I think, not just redirected but also informed by mass cultural productions. In the book, as I understand it, you identify two areas of popular culture which are in some sense surviving and resisting and developing today. One area is bound up with memory and the establishment of forms of historical memory which you say have been able to come through in certain kinds of television drama in Britain, for example. It would be helpful to have some instances of exactly what you had in mind. The other area is that of what I just called the popular culture of everyday life, which feeds through things like gossip and jokes and so on and which you say is clearly there in domestic drama, presumably in forms of domestic television drama, in forms of soap opera. Or is this wrong, a misleading extrapolation?
WILLIAMS: No, no, it's an absolutely correct extrapolation although it leaves a lot of questions unasked. I mean, take the first area: there's been a very conscious attempt to revive, as it were, a popular history, and it is true that there has been a kind of cancellation of the lives of the majority of people, even where the evidence was recoverable, in favor of quite other versions of the past. Now I think there are difficulties inherent in that. If you think of the usual examples, *Days of Hope* and such, or if you think (which often presents fewer difficulties) of certain documentary memories, retrospective interviews of people who were in the International Brigade in Spain or people who were in the General Strike or something of this kind, there are all sorts of problems about the representation of those memories, and they raise very complex questions in the end. One of the difficulties is that the resulting piece gets that inevitably retrospective air. I mean, one has to go only a short distance from such works to *Upstairs, Downstairs,* which presents, as I think, a totally false version of those relationships because they are tidied up and glossed over and sentimentalized. But that same retrospective air—people listen to it not in order to say that this is a past which connects with our present but, almost inevitably given the manner of some of the presentations, that this is a past which *doesn't* connect with our present—"Oh, gosh, what clothes we wore then!" and that sort of thing.

The other area concerning the popular culture of everyday life raises even more difficult questions because one can at least see the dangers in this popular memory thing and work at avoiding them. With the other, one is moving into one of the most manipulative areas in all the media: domestic serials, soap opera, comedy, comedians, conscious comedy. Most intellectuals have said that this area is simply reproductive pap. I then ask why, in relation to what other kinds of culture, it has such a particular engagement. I ask the question about *Coronation Street*, which nobody would look at to understand northern working-class culture now or then. But nevertheless there is an engagement with, among other things, the sense of the continuity of human lives. Much of the more serious contemporary art, characteristically for its own good reasons, has dropped the generational succession of the nineteenth-century novel, has often focused on some crisis in a situation or a relationship. It's worked through intensively. The end. I think there are human interests in what happens next to people which are often low-order gossip interests, but some are rather high-order interests, I think, rather central interests about people—what happened next, what took place a year later, whether it worked out in this way or that. Of course you can see that a lot of it is gossip and you can see that a lot of it is manipulated, just as you can see that a lot of the everyday idioms are mimed in commercials by people who don't share them; they are just put on and attached to an ice cream or whatever. But I think there's something important there which is also saying something about what has happened in the most consciously serious art.

SKIRROW: Just to stay with *Coronation Street* for a moment, I think it is no accident that this interest in continuity of life manifests itself on television in the form of soap opera, which is mostly watched by women and in which many of the main characters are women.

WILLIAMS: Yes.

SKIRROW: Women have of course been associated with the idea of continuity since the earliest times, when they represented earth and other basic elements, and even now they often stand for a certain relationship to time and everyday life which contrasts with that of men, and against which men can appear to be moving fast and changing things. While it might be progressive if women were making these programs about a different engagement with everyday life, the fact is that women are largely excluded from television production, and programs such as *Coronation Street* seem to me only to be reinforcing a reactionary segregation of interest within popular culture in terms of gender.

WILLIAMS: Well, I think what you say is very important because the analysis is right, and it is related to the fact that everyday work outside the home is nearly always excluded. And the meeting places are characteristically the pub and so on. There's a whole problem about the representation of men's work, because even in the radical popular culture it tends to be much more often the strike than the everyday experience of work that is represented. And while that is so, the segregation is going to be complete. And the way in which the men come back into that culture, if we're seeing the continuity through the women, back into the family which is obviously a very fraught matter in a changing social structure like this, is only half said if the work the men have come from has not been represented and if the women increasingly working outside the home are not seen in those work relationships. And it wasn't that I wanted to defend that; I was saying that there is a simple, almost unargued interest in what happens next, an interest which in fact is widely shared, and that is precisely the way it then gets inflected-deflected in these forms, which can be so easily parodied as a result.

HEATH: One of the things in talking about television and popular culture, about *Coronation Street* and so on, is that what one is then talking about is reception, not production. Reception is clearly an area in which the popular culture might determine meanings, a particular engagement. But that is then in relation to mass cultural production, to keep to those terms for the moment. What are the problems in talking about the possibility of popular culture in connection with something which is, of course, in no way popularly produced? We're talking apparently about reception rather than production. What are the difficulties in that?

WILLIAMS: I think that when the newspapers started gaining a wider audience, a lot of people had to learn demotic style and popular idioms. As a result, professionals who shared nothing of the lives that they were reproducing learned to produce an extraordinary idiomatic facsimile of those lives. People learn this sort of trade; it's learned as much in copywriting as in television serials and in certain kinds of tabloid journalism—the ironic thing then often being that the professionals are speaking more like the people than the people. There is even a two-way process in which certain idioms that perform well or that some very popular performer takes up actually pass back into the everyday idiom. So we must not make the error of supposing that what is being represented is that. Rather, one is saying, the link is that there is that unsatisfied interest and all sorts of problems about why it's unsatisfied. And it then gets these forms which offer to speak to it.

HEATH: This is a little like—and it may be interesting to think about this in relation to the book *Towards 2000* today—what Enzensberger says in the famous essay at the end of the '60s on "Constituents of a Theory of the Media." Basically what he said was that the left was too quick to reject forms of, as it were, popular mass culture, forms which were clearly latching onto not false needs but real needs, latching onto them exploitatively and appropriating them in ways which had to be resisted, yes, but real needs nevertheless. What the left had then to do, the argument ran, was effectively to explore the whole area of mass culture and find ways of productively moving from it in regard to the real needs that it clearly engaged, even though in some sense, in every real sense perhaps, it falsified and alienated them.

Now surely one of the difficulties with what you're saying is that we're continually brought back to this problem of the relation between mass culture and popular culture. There's a very pessimistic account of this which isn't simply the automatic rejection of mass culture as false needs but which also leaves little hope for the popular in the mass. I'll try to give a version of it in order to provoke you. Let's go back first, though, to popular memory. In the '70s in France, for example, there was a great deal of investment in the notion of popular memory, and as an indication of cultural-political action, it gave you an idea of what to do. There was something of a feeling that provided one could only go out and locate an area that had been shut out from the existing terms of representation and represent it, then that was a good in itself. But the problem of the medium by which it was represented, indeed the problems of the assumption that it was simply a *medium* which was representing it, were never faced. To put it crudely, what you could quickly end up with was a kind of left-wing ethnological investigation of things outside the existing terms of representation that were then brought into those exclusive terms in a kind of specular, almost voyeuristic way. The problems of the medium weren't posed just because it was taken as a medium and the trap then was the imagination of an identity of a popular culture which could suddenly be revealed through it, in what were still the same mass terms.

That's the problem of the popular into the mass culture but there's crucially too that of the mass culture definition of, determination of the popular. You've talked of domestic serials and the ways in which they give onto basic interests, real human experiences and concerns, but then precisely one of the aspects of the development of mass culture, in the sense of the production by a minority who control the means of production, the effective possibilities of social representation, with financial interests so determining, is that part of the development has included a continual containing of positions, of readings: mass images that allow for all sorts of different readings and appeal within the overall limits of this mass culture. Thus, for example, television producers, writers, and so on are well aware that there's a lot of activity around women in our societies, new relations of women amongst themselves, new definitions by them of their identity as women; they're aware of women as a "problem" or a "concern" which is then built into programs. The programs respond, they recognize and produce possible new readings, new identifications, but all held together in what is fundamentally a continually repeated spectacle, the terms of which, beyond and through the alternative readings—the appeal to something popular, coming from people in the society—will always be run back into what is basically the construction of the mass, a confined version of the popular. This is opposed to real versions of the popular bound up with forms of community and group activity and so on and so forth. At one stage you include all sorts of things; at another what is endlessly reproduced is always a spectacle, the production of an inclusive mass, just because these other possibilities are coming in—indeed, they are its material. I've tried crudely to put the pessimistic view. What would you say to that?

WILLIAMS: I don't think it's pessimistic at all. That does define the problem because what I'm not saying or certainly not intending to say is that there can be, as it were, radical and popular versions, radical and popular in the positive senses, of existing popular forms. My argument was more that there were elements in those popular forms which explained things in terms other than the irredeemable vulgarity or triviality or lack of sustained attention of the masses. I've never believed that you can have radical or popular or left versions of other kinds of cultural forms. In the same way you can't say—although there are some problematic cases—"well, let's have a really good radical soap opera." Take simply the level of attention. You can't attend to human development or human crises on those finely calculated schedules of duration of attention, length of sequence, and diversity of groups. Look at it in one of its most polished forms in *Dallas*. You can time the duration of shots and you can see the diversity of groups, so that if you hate him, don't worry because in two minutes you'll be looking at her or you'll be looking at yet another him. Although such programs latch onto people's interests in what others are doing, they have radically reduced the possibilities of attention of the kind people know when they're dealing with their own lives. You can't say "let us put some new content into this form"—this is radically the truth about form—so then whether it's pessimistic depends on whether one thinks it's pessimistic to face the kind of transformation that would be involved almost anywhere in this social order, and it is a much larger job than is generally supposed.

What strikes me, what I want to emphasize most, without hostility to the people but with frankness, is that this retrospective mode was not an accident. This endless nostalgic reconstitution, which exists partly because the left for reasons of its own believed that somewhere if it could be tapped there was an essence of the people, an essence of the popular world which had somehow been lost but could be reconstituted by reconnecting it with its past. Whereas in reality—and this is certainly where the cultural analysis connects with the political one—this essence has been changed so much by actual history that the only significant connection would be strictly contemporary, not only in material but in manner, in the way it is done, whatever period is being dealt with. The greatest danger is to have fantasies about a past consciousness which, if it could only be revived and given a few contemporary trimmings, would transform the present. It precisely would not. I mean, this belief is an example of one of the insufficient kinds of opposition that led to where we are now.

HEATH: We're moving towards issues relating to audiences and the construction of audiences. Indeed, we have to ask whether *audience* is a very good term when we talk about popular culture. We can see the kind of things it means with regard to mass culture, the construction of audiences there, or at least we think we can. What is the reality of audiences today in popular culture? In mass culture? How do they come together? What do we say about audiences today given the possibilities of the whole series of new technologies that are being rapidly developed? I know you resist very strongly ideas of technological determinism. You might want to say a few words about that and about how we can work through mass culture into alternative forms of audience.

WILLIAMS: I'm against that version of technological development and its future which supposes that inherent elements of any technology determine its use. I think this is plainly not true of any of the technologies you take. This should not, however, be understood to mean that a given medium does not have specific properties crucial to understanding how it works. But very often this is not what is meant by people who say a technology like cable television, to take the crudest contemporary case, necessarily implies home banking and video shopping, because I could at once list twenty alternative uses of precisely the same technology. Those are political and economic choices; they're not carried by the technology. It's quite hard when a technology has been developed in a certain way for people to say it could have gone a different route. But when a new technology is coming through, it's crucial to be aware of its possible alternative uses.

In thinking about audiences, I keep coming back to this notion of the constitution of a false nation. There's almost now a false transatlantic community within the English-speaking world. People say, "Isn't it wonderful that seventeen and a half million of us were watching this ice skating last night?"—it's a shared national experience. It doesn't matter in that sort of case. It matters very much, however, when the program shows retired admirals and generals playing with models of war ships and airplanes over a map of the South Atlantic. Because they can't get any film of the war and this is the whole nation planning its collective military enterprise with these puppets. Now I would welcome anything which would break up this quite false sense, because this idea of the nation, of the area of relevant concern, of people whom we "recognize," excludes the majority of people of the world whom we don't recognize and watch on television.

Indeed I think these false images have only been developed because of certain specific problems in this society, problems of people knowing where they belong and how they relate. And so I am against the notion of public service broadcasting claiming to represent such ideas as the national interest or the public interest, all of which, I think, are false constructions. But I wouldn't want to rule out the possibility of actual alternatives to these ideas in terms of more real communities, which needn't only be physical communities but communities of interest, physically spread out from each other. And certainly I think then a different mode of address would happen because, to come back to your earlier point, if the broadcaster believes that he is addressing the nation he starts talking in certain ways which are bad for him, bad for us. Even if people get used to it. Because they're false ways in that all he's really looking at is a camera and people in a studio and all he's otherwise learned is a convention, usually a false one, in its most developed form. Here's an example that I first noticed in popular newspapers. "You write" was printed above the readers' letters. *I* hadn't written, *you* hadn't written, but "you write" was printed because you're all "you." And they say on television programs now, "And next week you will have a chance to take part." We won't conceivably, if there are millions of us. But it means this and this one we'll select: all you. This is a way of thinking. We are so much more diverse, much more specific.

HEATH: That's the creation of the instantaneous mass in relation to which television clearly works at the moment. One of the interesting things about what you've said, the reference to the nation, is that, of course, the examples you've cited are those of "great historical moments": the Falklands War, the royal wedding, and so on which are presented as great images of the nation and unity. But actually most television doesn't seem to be concerned with that. In fact, it doesn't seem to be so much bound up with the nation as with the "internation." It isn't clear to me that mass culture is necessarily bound up with images of nationalism; indeed, versions of television in relation to nation would appear to be found (talking about industrially developed countries) precisely in countries which have resisted as much as they can the extension to television. France is an obvious example of a country which has tried very powerfully to keep its television under direct state control as an instrument of the national ideology (the control is weakening now to some extent under the socialist government, though there's also an irony in that the terms of the weakening are those of a privatization and commercialization of television). There you get a very powerful notion of trying to protect television from mass culture where mass culture means an international version of things, to protect it against that in the name of the nation.

WILLIAMS: I think that's right and I think that the medium requires us to make political judgments and avoid adopting more abstracted models of the people being addressed. Because they substitute for that the nation, which is this notional community with all this falsehood in it but which has certain connections to otherwise observable political reality.

SKIRROW: Earlier in this discussion you made a distinction between elements of the technology which might be supposed to determine certain kinds of use, and political and economic choices which determine the uses of the technology. But in thinking about the construction of notions of community in relation to the development of satellite television, one might argue that this distinction becomes insignificant because the expense of the technology is what will determine certain political choices, and so certain kinds of use.

WILLIAMS: I suspect that with the development of a cable system, satellites should really be looked at as the technical backup to the areas that it is not possible to cable.

SKIRROW: Satellites will carry channels of mass entertainment which are sold to cable, and cable will then probably have one local access channel which will become a ghetto among, say, sixty other channels. And it won't be on a press button so you'll have to tune it in, making access in fact inaccessible.

WILLIAMS: That's not the technology telling us that but the people in power, the people making these decisions, the people giving the licenses. I mean, it's been decided who will dig up our streets to lay what cables. And our civic sense that there are streets to dig up and that we should have some say about what they're dug up to do is what is overborne now, and the opposition clusters far too much around maintaining the residual forms. So people are defending the BBC against cable. The real thing they've got to do is to think of other uses for which it could be developed. I'm not saying it would be anything but a really hard fight which in many places would be lost. But I think the other cause is much more substantially lost because then you're left forever with this declining asset and you can see cable developing in that way and BBC becoming what would soon be called the quality channel as the rest will have gone tabloid. This isn't bad in the sense that it's diminishing what's generally available. It is bad, as I've watched it over the years, for what's called the quality channel, precisely because that space is so massively occupied.

SKIRROW: Well, do you think the fight then is for regulation? We have to use this term because it seems to oppose the fashionable concept of "deregulation" although it is not at all clear how communications technology could be deregulated. Obviously it is going to be regulated in some way; the question is whether such regulation will promote commercial or social interests.

HEATH: I don't see deregulation as an issue. What in effect deregulation does is let the financial interests triumph.

SKIRROW: Which means it's regulated for profit.

WILLIAMS: I find I think increasingly about the level at which you can have regulation without it becoming one of these grand advisory bodies or government-appointed things attempting to define in advance the limits of the decent or the truthful or the possible. I find myself thinking more and more, particularly in Europe, of a civic tradition, because I think that this is one area where I could just conceive regulation to be possible. I don't think it would be possible for a nation the size of Britain to arrive through discussion at some grand rules and conventions governing cable use. But I can imagine a city doing it and, interestingly, there are signs now in Europe that the importance of the city is increasingly being recognized, although it's still very problematic. After all, throughout the history of European culture, civic responsibility has often been more important than national responsibility. And since this would affect the use of these technologies, I think it's something that should be very closely looked at and it's already happening. This would carry the possibility that you would have different stuff in one city from another and that would be a good thing because it's depressing to think of going from one city to another and finding the same stuff.

HEATH: Well yes, in the United States you could have different stuff from city to city but what you get mostly is exactly the same stuff, and we come back once again to ownership, to who is actually determining the possibilities and the limitations of our choice. But I suppose the question to you at this point is that of resistance. In one sense what you're saying is that we should resist mass culture, all along the line: the assumptions built into it, the terms of its production . . . though recognizing that mass culture now carries elements of a popular culture, that it also produces representations that do make connections, that can be read in other ways, subcultural developments and appropriations, for instance. But nevertheless, would it be right to say that we should resist mass culture? And then, a further question from the perspective of work as a critic or analyst: what kinds of things should we be doing; how should we be looking at mass culture?

WILLIAMS: Well, the resistance of course I agree with. As for analysis, I think there needs to be developed many different kinds of analysis which are in touch with each other. I think that the least developed—although it happens that in our particular conversation it wouldn't be the least developed—is that which tries to understand precisely the production of certain conventions and modes of communication right inside the form. I would put this at the top of the list not because it could answer all the questions on the table, but because it's the least likely thing to happen. People study audiences; they study the history of the institutions; and they study the technologies—something that ought to be done by more than technologists, because it isn't terribly difficult to understand enough about technology to see the diverse possibilities, rather than just taking the publicity handout. People have always studied effects, though I've never been a great fan of this approach because I know of no social or cultural norm against which supposedly divergent effects might be measured. Concentrating on deviant effects conceals the effects of the norm. So my priority, simply because it's the least developed, would be critical analysis of particular presentations and analysis of new presentations and political discourses. Hopefully such analysis would influence production. We have to understand right inside the productive process how these difficult modes of address and forms are actually constructed. It's been twenty-six years since I first did anything with television in Britain and the second thing I was asked to do, which I refused to do in the way suggested, was to discuss an education report, tear it up, and say, "This is rubbish." I said I won't do it, and the answer came (and who has not heard it since in studios across the world): "That's television." It's not any more television than anything else is television.

HEATH: One of the things that comes out of what you've just said in relation to criticism and analysis and the work we might do is the matter of quantity. What you said bears more especially on the analysis and criticism of particular aspects of television, particular modes, particular programs. But then one of the central issues is the sheer quantity of television, the volume of what we're talking about in any consideration of mass culture. Now when you did the television book, it is evident that you looked analytically and critically at quantity, which was brought into the argument qualitatively as what you called the experience of flow in television. Are there any ways in which you'd want to change that analysis now or suggest other possibilities for dealing with quantity?

WILLIAMS: You raise an important question. I think that the whole tradition of analysis has been of the discrete single work, and while something can be done with that approach, it would be rather missing the point of the normal television experience. I first realized this when I thought what a very curious word we use for some unit of television: *program*, which is defined as a whole sequence of events that kind of follow. And there is a sense in which from the planning stage now television is constructed in terms of the sequence, and there are, as people properly say, "slots." And really the professional reviewer or the professional analyst who examines this sequence is able to get at some important questions but there are others which wouldn't be discussed at all. Yet there's great difficulty I think; I was rereading the analysis of flow I gave as an example. I think it needs to be much more developed. Where the analysis seemed to me to work very clearly was in the flow of miscellaneous news items, or miscellaneous news items with commercials—which I have always argued don't interrupt the programs [but] help constitute them. And I think that we should resist the habits that have been learned from analysis of particular literary works, particular paintings, and so on, and confront this notion of flow because it really does belong to the medium in the sense that you don't know the transmitter is there unless there's some sort of signal. So there's a continuity of the signal, that is to say, the first constitution of flow.

HEATH: It's like a telephone answering machine. You dial and it always answers.

WILLIAMS: That's right. And then you qualify, heavily qualify it by this notion that you mustn't leave the screen blank for a moment or somebody will switch channels, go over to your rivals. Producers plan programs to capture the audience at certain times of the evening. This doesn't follow from the notion of medium, but the continuity of the signal does. And then the continuity of the signal becomes the flow. I think that this allows us to analyze news differently to ask more than about biased reporting. Questions about the nature of the news and the relevant area of information can only be answered in terms of flow. There's a lot of development in that, I would hope.

SKIRROW: I think your own work has been and continues to be a model of how intellectuals can work on popular culture and mass culture without being above it or outside it, or defeatist or pessimistic about it. But does it not worry you that—perhaps particularly in relation to *Towards 2000*—your optimism can be incorporated into the discourses that are around at the moment—and coming from a conservative government—about communications being the sunrise industry, cable providing instant community, and the new technologies representing progress for "the people"—discourses which are all part of the gee-whiz syndrome?

WILLIAMS: Yes, it worries me. I've talked a lot about incorporation and I suppose it's because I watched this process operating on me as well as operating on others. I don't think I've been in any situation since I could think in which I haven't been aware of the positive attempts at incorporation, many of which I have to say have succeeded. Of course I see the danger. But there's no risk of my not saying what needs to be said against the really quite specious optimism you describe. Those people are playing with fire in so many ways that it's not difficult to distance oneself from them. Of course it's a risk. On the other hand, I wouldn't want to get into the position of many of my long-standing friends in this argument who are belatedly saying how good the BBC is and so on.

We have a conception of programming which I really do want to break up, to come back to the previous answer. Talking to some graduate students in Cambridge in a seminar, people who didn't normally work much on the media, I asked them to imagine a situation in which they went to the library each week, and a very nice librarian, a charming person, the most intelligent person in the back office, said, "We've got a very interesting selection of books for you to read this week. We've got a historical novel, a history, a do-it-yourself thing, a thriller, and a gardening book," and all they had to do was to take away the books. It's preposterous to anyone who values books but this is precisely the convention which has become so naturalized in television. Good, nice people prepare a selection in a package for you . . . and then you can compare their package with other packages. And I certainly don't want to go along with those of my friends who are defending the old style packaging for fear of something worse. I think that position will be overborne in any case. It's like every other political situation: a merely defensive battle is going to lose.

SKIRROW: One voice has been consistently against the technological euphoria and also against the joy of destruction which seems to have invaded all kinds of technology, including video games—and which I think you alluded to in *Towards 2000* as an almost self-destructive force arising from the expectation that the whole world is going to be destroyed soon anyway—and that voice which has been consistently against all this has been the women's movement. There are also other voices such as the ecology movement, but these voices have not generally been taken into account in academic debates about popular or mass culture. Do you see that there are some signs of optimism in that kind of opposition which can point us toward developing new communication systems and, if so, how is it that work on that has been lacking? For example, in descriptions of popular culture there's very little on its relation to gender. Do you think that's because women have not engaged with it? Should it be left for women to engage with it, or is there something that people like you, for example, could do to engage with this argument?

WILLIAMS: I think this is the right question. It is a difficult business to learn to think and speak in new ways, and the best evidence of this reeducation process is coming from one of the tendencies inside the women's movement. There is one voice within the movement which is of an ecological kind and which can connect with the more general ecological case. The technologies can take us beyond certain social blockages we now have—absurdities of aggregated cities and dense impossible traffic systems and so on—if they connect with the new thinking about settlements and relationships that is occurring in the women's movement, in the ecology movement, and in a few associated groups. Such thinking is not happening in any orthodox political parties which are reproducing the present form and with it the present means of communication and their content.

HEATH: I suppose that's at least an area for possible development to end on. I hope we've touched on some issues in your work, Raymond, that perhaps haven't been brought out quite as directly before. Thank you.

WILLIAMS: Thank you.

Contributors

Stanley Aronowitz is professor of sociology at the Graduate Center of City University of New York. He is the author of eleven books, including *False Promises* and *Working Class Hero*, on the U.S. working class and unions as well as two books on education, *Postmodern Education: Politics, Culture, and Social Criticism*, with Henry Giroux (Minnesota, 1990) and *Science as Power: Discourse and Ideology in Modern Society* (Minnesota, 1988). His most recent book, with William DiFazio, is entitled *The Jobless Future* (Minnesota, 1994).

John Brenkman is professor of English at Baruch College and the Graduate Center, City University of New York. He is the author of *Culture and Domination* and *Straight Male Modern: A Cultural Critique of Psychoanalysis.*

Peter de Bolla teaches at King's College, Cambridge, and is the author of *The Discourse of the Sublime* (1989).

Catherine Gallagher is professor of English at the University of California, Berkeley. She is the author of *The Industrial Reformation of English Fiction* and coeditor of *The Making of the Modern Body.* Her latest book is entitled *Nobody's Story: Vanishing Acts of Women Writers in the Marketplace, 1670-1820.*

Stephen Heath is reader in cultural studies at the University of Cambridge and professor of the history of consciousness at the University of California, Santa Cruz. His books include *Questions of Cinema* and *The Sexual Fix*.

John Higgins is lecturer in English at the University of Cape Town. He has just completed a study of Raymond Williams and is editing a collection of T. B. Davie Memorial Lectures on Academic Freedom. He is founding editor of *Pretexts: Studies in Writing and Culture*.

Peter Hitchcock is associate professor of literary and cultural studies at Baruch College of the City University of New York. He is the author of *Working-Class Fiction in Theory and Practice* and *Dialogic of the Oppressed* (Minnesota, 1993). He has also published essays on cultural studies, multiculturalism, film, and feminism.

Cora Kaplan is professor of English and director of the Institute for Research on Women at Rutgers University. A feminist critic who lived and taught in England between 1966 and 1988, she has a particular interest in nineteenth-century Britain. Her publications include *Salt and Bitter and Good: Three Centuries of English and American Women Poets* (1975), and she has edited and introduced Elizabeth Barrett Browning's *Aurora Leigh* (1977). Her most recent book is *Sea Changes: Essays on Culture and Feminism* (1986); she is currently at work on a study of gender and the rise of racial thinking in Victorian England.

David Lloyd is professor of English at the University of California, Berkeley. He is the author of *Nationalism and Minor Literature: James Clarence Mangan and the Emergence of Irish Cultural Nationalism* (1987). His other works include *The Nature and Context of Minority Discourse* (1990), edited with Abdul JanMohamed, and numerous essays on Irish literature and on aesthetics and cultural politics. His most recent book is *Anomalous States: Irish Writing in the Postcolonial Moment* (1993).

Robert Miklitsch is assistant professor of English (critical theory) at Ohio University. His work has appeared in reviews and journals such as *Boundary 2, College Literature, Diacritics, Genders, Textual Studies,* and *Yale Review*. He recently completed work on a collection of essays titled *From Marx to Madonna: Culture Criticism in the Postmodern Age*. Current projects include a collection on film and theory and another on the new, post-Althusserian articulation between Marxism and psychoanalysis.

Michael Moriarty is lecturer in French at Cambridge University and a fellow of Gonville and Caius College. His publications include *Taste and Ideology in Seventeenth-Century France* (1988) and *Roland Barthes* (1991).

Christopher Prendergast is reader in modern French literature at Cambridge University and fellow of King's College. His books include *The Order of Mimesis* (1986) and *Paris and the Nineteenth Century* (1992). He is coeditor of *HarperCollins World Reader* (1994). With Margaret Cohen he is coeditor of *Spectacles of Realism: Gender, Body, Genre* (Minnesota forthcoming).

Morag Shiach teaches English at Queen Mary and Westfield College, University of London. Her publications include *Discourse on Popular Culture* (1989) and *Hélène Cixous: A Politics of Writing* (1991).

David Simpson is professor of English at the University of Colorado, Boulder. His most recent book is *Romanticism, Nationalism and the Revolt Against Theory* (1993).

Gillian Skirrow, who died in 1987, worked for Thames Television in London before becoming a producer at the Centre for Educational Practice of the University of Strathclyde, where she also developed courses in media studies. She published a number of articles on film and television, notably in the journal *Screen*.

Kenneth Surin is professor of literature at Duke University. In his previous career he was a philosopher of religion.

Paul Thomas is associate professor of political science at the University of California, Berkeley, specializing in political theory and Marxism. He is the author of *Karl Marx and the Anarchists* (1985) and *Alien Politics: Marxist State Theory Retrieved* (forthcoming). "*Culture and Society* or Culture and the State" is part of a book, *Culture and the State*, to be written with David Lloyd.

Gauri Viswanathan is associate professor of English and comparative literature at Columbia University. She is the author of *Masks of*

Conquest: Literary Study and British Rule in India (1989). She is completing a book on religious identity and colonial culture.

Cornel West teaches in the Department of Afro-American Studies at Harvard University. He is the author of many books, most recently, *Race Matters* (1993).

Index

Compiled by Robin Jackson

Absolute: as term, 13
Adorno, Theodor, 120, 264-65; and mass culture, 61-62
Advertising: in print media, 327
Aesthetics: of nature, 181
Affluence: managed, 145
After the Great Divide (Huyssen), 60
Agency: category of, 333-35
Althusser, Louis, x, 24, 35, 71, 120, 257, 324; and experience, 84-85, 129; followers of, 336; Marxism of, 127; and psychoanalysis, 124; and reflection theory, 109; and Spinoza, 338 n. 12; and structural Marxism, 11; and subject, 265; theory of ideology, 126, 264
Anderson, Benedict, 308
Anderson, Perry, 333
Arnold, Matthew, 7, 19-20, 272-76, 300; and education, 278; and idea of culture, 308-10, 321
Audience: notion of, 368-70
Auerbach, Erich, 308
Austen, Jane, 19, 66
Author: as God-father, 82

Bahro, Rudolf, 25
Bakhtin, Mikhail, 322, 329
Baldick, Chris, 44, 190
Balibar, Renée, 112
Barrell, John, 180

Barthes, Roland, 95, 126; and New Criticism, 103-12
Base/superstructure, 11-12, 78-83, 195-96, 199, 330-31, 333; and notion of culture, 253
Baudrillard, Jean, 356; and hyperrreal, 345
Bell, Andrew: system of education of, 204
Benjamin, Walter, 264
Benveniste, Emile, 95-96
Bhabha, Homi: and Williams, 118
Birkbeck, John, 285
Bloomsbury project, 64
Border Country (Williams), 6, 240-44
Bourdieu, Pierre, 254
Briggs, Asa, 293
Brontë, Charlotte, 221-22, 225-31
Brontë, Emily, 13, 66, 225-31
Brougham, Henry, 285
Brown, Capability, 181
Buci-Glucksmann, Christine, 62
Burke, Edmund, 45, 272, 275-76

Cable satellites, 370-71
Canon: formation of literary, 65-67
Capitalism: and Chartism, 295-96; and the novel, 108
Carlyle, Thomas, 37, 45
Carnoy, Martin, 198
Caudwell, Christopher, 120, 321-22; and